Sustainable Development of Rural Household Economy

Qinghua Shi · Yan Gao

Sustainable Development of Rural Household Economy

Transition of Ten Villages in Zhejiang, China, 1986–2002

上海交通大學出版社
SHANGHAI JIAO TONG UNIVERSITY PRESS

Springer

Qinghua Shi
Antai College of Economics
and Management
Shanghai Jiao Tong University
Shanghai, China

Yan Gao
School of Agriculture and Biology
Shanghai Jiao Tong University
Shanghai, China

ISBN 978-981-15-2746-3 ISBN 978-981-15-2747-0 (eBook)
https://doi.org/10.1007/978-981-15-2747-0

Jointly published with Shanghai Jiao Tong University Press
The print edition is not for sale in China Mainland. Customers from China Mainland please order the print book from: Shanghai Jiao Tong University Press.
ISBN of the Co-Publisher's edition: 978-7-313-22556-6

This Springer imprint is published by the registered company Springer Nature Singapore Pte Ltd.
The registered company address is: 152 Beach Road, #21-01/04 Gateway East, Singapore 189721, Singapore

This book is dedicated to

Mr. Runsheng Du (1913–2015)

Outstanding contributor to China's reform and opening up
Pioneer of the national rural fixed observation sites

and

All of those who have been working with the observed households and villages in the front line of the rural fixed observation sites in China

First author Dr. Qinghua Shi with Mr. Runsheng Du in 2007

The research is supported by the following funds:

National Natural Science Foundation of China

Labour mobility and village order in the era of rapid urbanisation (71773076)

China's rural poverty component identification, decomposition and change (71673186)

The research of peasants' welfare issues in the background of urbanisation (71473165)

A study on household economic development mechanism and government management behaviour in eastern and western China (70173016)

National Social Science Foundation of China

Investigation into rural tax & fee reform and rural household economic development (03BJY061)

The publication of this book has been supported by the following publishing funds:

Antai College of Economics and Management, Shanghai Jiao Tong University

The Research has Won the Following Awards

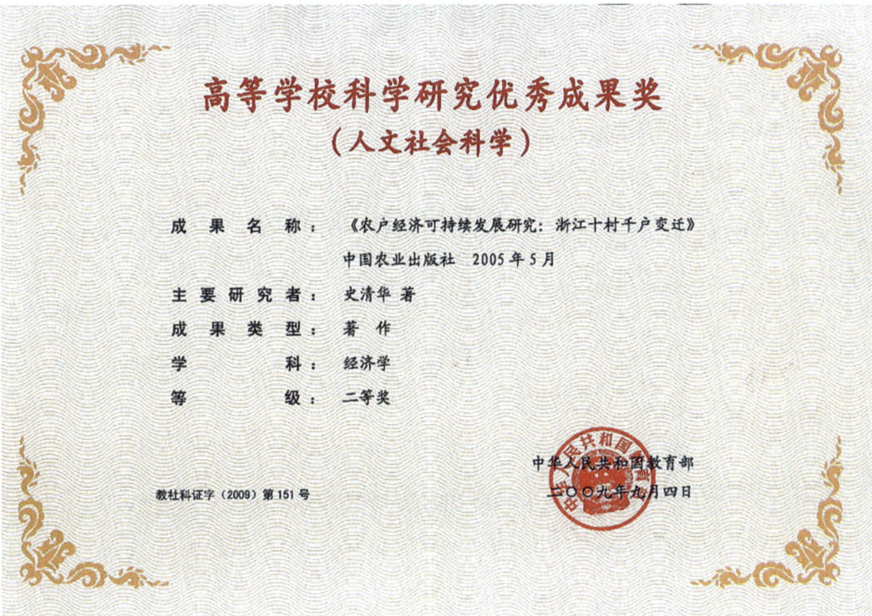
高等学校科学研究优秀成果奖

（人文社会科学）

成 果 名 称：《农户经济可持续发展研究：浙江十村千户变迁》

中国农业出版社 2005年5月

主 要 研 究 者：史清华 著

成 果 类 型：著 作

学 科：经济学

等 级：二等奖

教社科证字（2009）第151号

中华人民共和国教育部

二〇〇九年九月四日

University Science and Research Outstanding Achievement Award
(Humanities and Social Sciences)

Title: Sustainable Development of Rural Household Economy: Transition of Ten Villages in Zhejiang, China Agriculture Press, May 2005

Main researcher: Qinghua Shi
Category: Monograph
Discipline: Economics
Grade: Second

Certificate (2009) No.151

Ministry of Education
People's Republic of China
September 4, 2009

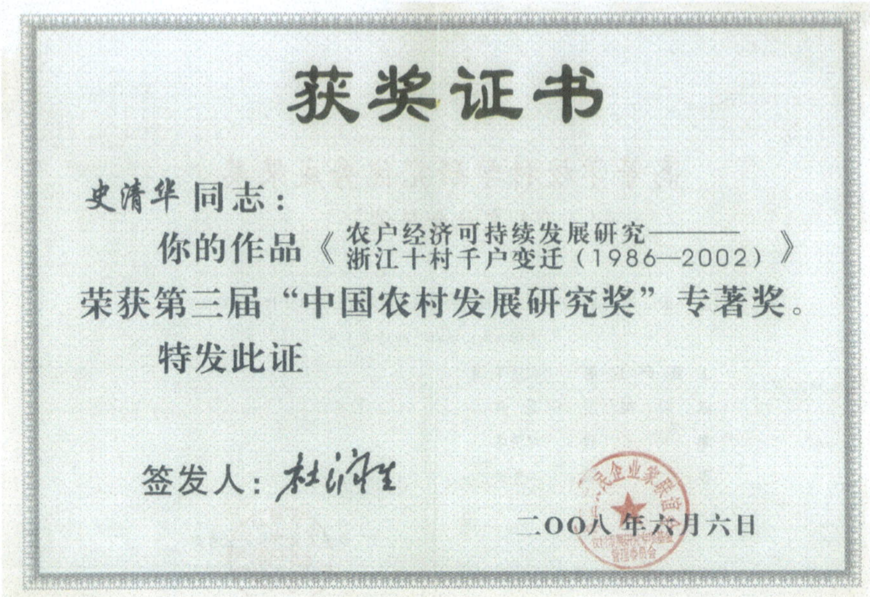
获奖证书

史清华同志：

你的作品《农户经济可持续发展研究——浙江十村千户变迁（1986—2002）》荣获第三届“中国农村发展研究奖”专著奖。

特发此证

签发人：杜润生

二OO八年六月六日

Award Certificate

Mr. Qinghua Shi,

This is to certify that your book *Sustainable Development of Rural Household Economy: Transition of Ten Villages in Zhejiang (1986-2002)* has won the 3rd China Rural Development Research Award (Monograph Award).

Issuer: Runsheng Du

Rural Development Research Fund Management Committee

June 6, 2008

English Edition Publication Statement

Sustainable Development of Rural Household Economy is the first monograph I published after I left Zhejiang University and was officially employed by Shanghai Jiao Tong University. It is also another piece of my important work concerning the 'sutra' of rural household poverty alleviation when I relocated to the southern watery region at the turn of the new century, 36 years after I left my hometown—the Loess Plateau. The book has received great attention and has been widely praised by people from all walks of life since its publication in 2005. Not only did it allow me to successfully stand on the highest podium of agricultural economics in China, with the privilege to take the 'Third China Rural Development Research Monograph Award (2008)' personally presented by Mr. Runsheng Du, who has been well-known as a 'reform pioneer', but also helped me to win the 'Second Prize of Outstanding Achievements in Humanities and Social Sciences (2009)' by the Ministry of Education, PRC. The monography is an important masterpiece of my academic career, with the essence of my thought about the 'three rural-related issues', or '*sannong* issues' (issues concerning agriculture, rural areas and farmers).

Zhejiang is mountainous. Although Zhejiang is considered as 'paradise on Earth', most rural areas in Zhejiang is not much different from other ordinary rural areas in China. Poverty was once their common synonym, and survival was also the primary goal. However, after 40 years of reform and opening up, the economy here has realised a huge growth. Zhejiang private economy is famous not only domestically but also outside the country, outstanding in the world. Zhejiang farmers not only have removed the specific label of 'poverty', but also created many of their own 'Zhejiang wonders'. Yiwu, a place with 'chicken feather for sugar' for a hungry belly, has become a world-famous 'small commodity city'. Haining, a place with nothing to do with fur, has built a well-known 'leather city' throughout the country. Wenzhou people whose language is even difficult to understand for Zhejiang natives have been doing big businesses all over the world. They would 'make a living on land', and China's 'beautiful countryside construction' originated in Anji. They would also 'make a living from the sea' in that the 'blue fishery construction' in Zhoushan of Zhejiang emerged at the forefront of the country. After the publication of the monograph, either because of the impacts of the 'Zhejiang miracle' itself, or because of the promotion of the two awards, or anything else, the limited copies were quickly sold out. Some readers would occasionally come directly and ask me for a copy, and I had no other alternative but to send them the original electronic copy.

One day, one of my fans, Ms. Yan Gao, returned from studying at the University of Cambridge and came to my office with the same idea, expecting a copy from me. Fortunately, due to the moving of the office, there was still a copy hiding in a pile of books and she became the last lucky reader.

After careful reading, Ms. Yan Gao came to my office again and proposed, 'I would like to translate this book into English and promote it abroad'.

To be honest, because of my primary English level, I never had such thoughts. Now that she had the idea, I was certainly happy to support. Even though the book was published thirteen years ago, it still has its historic meaning and practical value to help readers understand the Zhejiang case on how China has stepped out of the petty farmer pattern and thus changed from a traditional agricultural country to a modern industrial one. At the same time, this book can also serve as a window to help readers gain a better understanding of the path for China's economic development.

In traditional China, agriculture used to be an important lifeblood of the national economy. In 1952, agricultural output once accounted for half of the GDP (50.49%). After nearly 30 years of rural collectivisation and urban industrialisation, this figure fell to 27.69% in 1978, right before the reform and opening up. But in the early years of the reform and opening up (1978–1982), farmers who were liberated from collectivisation did not allow this figure to further decline, but instead helped it rise by 5%, reaching a new peak of 32.79% in 1982. After that, with the extensive deepening of China's reform and opening up, the agricultural industrialisation process restarted, and the share of agricultural output value in GDP once again fell in a difficult declining process. It had declined to the level below 30% (27.93%) by 1985, and below 20% (19.31%) by 1993, before it further fell below 10% to 9.79%, and recently to the historical low point of 7.92% in 2017. The above data have shown how difficult the process of China's industrialisation and modernisation is!

In this process, the development of Zhejiang is obviously on the top, ahead of the whole country. The long-term attention and research on its '*sannong* issues' thus provide a window for the whole country, which has important practical significance. This book describes the evolution of the industrialised process of 'the thousand rural households and ten villages' of Zhejiang in the period from 1986 to 2002. Although the book is a little dated, it is the process that most parts of China are facing today. Therefore, the experience of Zhejiang provides a good reference for other regions to study, and this is also the central reason for the publication of this book in English.

Although there are only 40 years of China's reform and opening up, its economic achievements have not only received compliments from Chinese people, but also astonished the international community. To this end, some people overseas with curiosity and the spirit of exploration would also like to carry out research and gain a more comprehensive understanding of China. However, due to the different life backgrounds or languages, there may be some biases. It is believed the publication of the book in English will present the most authentic stories of China to the readers and help to answer their confusion in some ways. This has become another important reason for the publication of this book in English.

Considering that the translation of the work itself is a process of recreation or a great part of the recreation, and in order to pay sufficient respect for Ms. Yan Gao's wisdom and efforts, I have invited the translator, Ms. Yan Gao, to serve as the co-author of the book for the publication of its English edition. I hereby clarify.

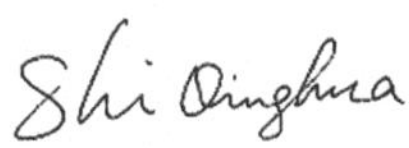

January 2019

Shanghai, China

Introduction

This book takes 'the changes of hundreds of rural households in ten villages of Zhejiang' as the core, and 'the research on rural household sustainable development' as the theme. Based on large amounts of detailed data collected from long-term and follow-up investigations of rural households at fixed observation sites, this book has examined and recorded the behaviour change of rural households in Zhejiang and its origins in the setting of ten villages in Zhejiang from 1986 to 2002 through data calculation, graphical representation and text writing.

The book has ten chapters, and it analyses the changes in rural households and rural social economy from two perspectives. From the household perspective, it investigates seven aspects, i.e. rural family organizations, economic structure, rural land transfer, saving and borrowing, imbalanced economic development, tax burden and living consumption. From the village perspective, it examines five aspects which include labour employment, village economy, village finance, community outlook and spiritual civilisation.

Chapter 1 draws on information from the investigations of rural households in five out of ten villages in Zhejiang. It first analyses the relationships concerning the ages of rural household members, their education levels and household incomes, before it moves on to elaborate on the marriage behaviour of the household members, including *hun* and *jia*, first marriage age, marriage distance and marriage gradient. It further explores the childbearing behaviour for adult females, such as first childbirth age, marriage and childbirth intervals. Then it analyses the childbearing expectations of rural households, including the number and gender expectations, as well as the influence of changes in culture and time. This chapter later analyses the decision-making patterns of rural households, emphasising on some important issues such as household operation investment, asset purchase, children's education and domestic management. It finally analyses the frequencies of major household events.

Chapters 2–7 are based on information from the investigations of rural households in ten villages in Zhejiang. It starts from the changes in rural household structure and focuses on the analysis of the results, processes, origins, as well as the environment of changes in rural household economy. It also estimates the degree of the non-agriculturalisation. Then it examines rural land, the major production factor for rural households, including land scale, distribution, transfer, development of land circulation market and the origins for land transfer. Third, it investigates rural saving and borrowing, the important economic behaviour of rural households, including saving and borrowing level, their scale, saving purpose, loan source and usage, and so on. Fourth, it analyses the imbalance of economic development, emphasising on the changes in rural household economic stratification, the degree of imbalance, its impacts and origins. Fifth, it examines the impacts of tax burden on rural household economy, including the changes in taxation level, the magnitude and its structure. Based on these previous aspects, tax burdens for different types of rural households are also compared, and the reasons for the aggravated burden at the village level are explored. Sixth, it studies the living consumption of rural households and analyses consumption level, consumption trend, as well as ownership and penetration of major durable consumption goods.

Chapters 8–10 are based on information at the village level from the ten villages in Zhejiang. It first studies the employment problem, including changes in labour scale, their education, employment structure, labour migration, estimates of labour idleness and sources of labour structural change. It then explores the village economy and financial operation, concerning land resource scale and use, asset accumulation level and structure, operation income level and composition, village fiscal revenue and expenditure, and contribution of rural households to village finance. It finally looks into the community outlook and spiritual civilisation, including population, residents, enterprises, religious beliefs, social security and relief, cultural life and village leadership construction.

Much of the content in the book has been condensed and rearranged for publishing in the past three years in various core Chinese journals, such as *Management World, Chinese Rural Economy, Issues in Agricultural Economy, China Economic Studies, Journal of Agrotechnical Economics, China Rural Survey, Chinese Journal of Population Science, Journal of Zhejiang University, Development Studies, Hebei Academic Journal*. Meanwhile, much of the content has also received a full-text reprint by Guidance of Agricultural Economics, Institutional Reform of the Newspaper and Journal Photocopying Centre in the Renmin University of China.

Foreword by Yikang Gu

China is a big developing country with a large number of farmers. Agriculture is the foundation industry of the country, with farmers as the biggest social group, and the rural areas a vast geographical community. The issues concerning agriculture, countryside and farmers are fundamentally related to the rise and fall of the nation and country. Since the Third Plenary Session of the Eleventh Central Committee, the market-oriented rural reform has brought China into an era of great reforms. After more than 20 years of reform and opening up, China has realised three major changes: from a planned economy to the socialist market economy, from being barely able to provide basic food and clothing to being moderately prosperous in general and from a traditional agricultural society to an industrial one. The Chinese economic society has undergone a tremendous transformation. Of the great changes, the most profound and far-reaching is related to the Chinese farmers. In a sense, thousands of changes have originated from the changes of farmers and their households.

Rural households are the most vital and basic units in Chinese society, and the villages are the oldest and most fundamental communities in Chinese history. At the point of the historic transition from a traditional agricultural society to a modern and industrial one, farmers are the main force not only for agricultural, rural economic and social development, but also for promoting industrialisation and urbanisation. It is the transfer of the large agricultural labour to the second and third industries, together with the transformation of farmers to urban citizens that has promoted the development of industrialisation and urbanisation. As Professor Qinghua Shi points out, rural households are very special social organisations, which integrate functions of population reproduction and economic reproduction. Anthropology, sociology, economics and politics are all deeply related to rural households and villages. The transitions of rural households and villages can reflect the changes of the rural and even the whole urban–rural society, as the Chinese idiom goes 'a falling leaf tells autumn', or 'a spot tells a leopard'. According to the theories in development economics, all the economic behaviours of rural households are rational, and farmers have the most deeply rooted concept of households. Farmers' economic behaviours are often to maximise the household interests as both the starting point and standing point. However, the household benefits according to farmers are the very complex mix of multiple interests interwoven with each other, such as economic, political and cultural interests, interests of individuals, spouses, children, families and friends, as well as short-term and long-term interests. Since Chinese farmers have long been in a vulnerable position and at the bottom of the society, their response to the outside impact and development environment has often been relatively negative and pragmatic unless on extreme cases when the harsh external conditions force them to make extraordinarily fierce reactions. Therefore, relevant research and policy-making have to be based on clearly understanding farmers' rational behaviours, for the sake of agriculture development, the countryside as well as industrialisation and urbanisation. This is why it is necessary to attach great importance to and understand the development and transitions of both rural households and villages, not only for those engaged in research concerning Chinese sociology, economics and politics, but also for the policy-makers and decision-making consultants of the government departments.

Based on the above analysis, the Central Policy Research Office and the Ministry of Agriculture selected a group of villages and rural households as fixed observation objects in the 1980s and have since then carried out long-term and systematic tracking observations, which has been of great importance. The longer such systematic and continuous quantitative observations and analysis, the more valuable they are, as more information is accumulated. Yet, the actual utility and significance of the rural observation sites depend on the systematic application and exploitation of the accumulated data. Professor Qinghua Shi is a representative figure who devotes himself to the research and development of the investigated data from the rural fixed observation sites. He is also one of the most excellent scholars away from being utilitarian and impatient and is able to commit himself to the research wholeheartedly. Early on, when Prof. Qinghua Shi was doing his postdoctoral research in Zhejiang University, he had the opportunity to get involved in the work of the rural observation sites in Zhejiang Province. He 'fell in love' with the accumulated data at first sight and was unable to part with them. He has taken the data as 'rich mineral reserves' for rural economic and social research, thus has carried out continuous development and utilisation and has achieved fruitful results. His book 'Sustainable Development of Rural Household Economy' focused on the changes of ten villages in Zhejiang Province is another piece of great work based on the research of the observed data.

It is this writing background that makes this book has a comprehensive value that cannot be found in other general writings. Based on empirical research at regular times and quantity within the framework of rural household economic sociology, this book has carried out a panoramic deep analysis on the transitions of rural economic society centred on individual households. It is rare to see such systematic, coherent and reliable data analysis, and so comprehensive, integrated and insightful content exploration as in this book. The book has ten chapters. From the viewpoint of rural households, it has conducted systematic analysis from seven aspects known as rural household organisation, economic structure, rural land transfer, rural saving and borrowing, income inequality, tax burden and living consumption. This has multiplied the value and utility of this book. It is not only a monography on rural household economy and sociology, but also a reference book with practical and historical value, worthy of reanalysis and reutilisation. Therefore, it serves a wide readership ranging from researchers in economics, sociology, politics, ethnography and demography, to those engaged in government decision-making and policy consultation. To be specific, it is a great reference for university teachers and students who are interested in economics and sociology. I hope that more readers will utilise this valuable book. In writing the foreword of this book, I would like to take the chance to show my respect to Prof. Qinghua Shi, for his pragmatic style in doing research, and express my heartfelt gratitude for his contribution towards the work in the fixed observation sites.

February 2005 Hangzhou, China

Preface—My View on Farmers

During a conversation, one of my graduate students asked me, 'What is the theory of the rural household research'? I thought twice about it and did not answer the question directly, but started with the concept of 'theory'. I asked, 'What is theory'? He gave a simple explanation and enumerated quite a few examples, such as the 'principle of supply and demand' in microeconomics, the 'scarcity theorem' in resource economics and the 'principle of comparative advantage' in international trade. When I asked whether the 'rational behaviour of farmers', the 'life cycle law of rural households' are theories, he fell into deep thought.

The Formation of a Theory

In fact, in our research and teaching, teachers usually provide the information according to textbooks, telling the students about the theories of each subject and their specific forms, but seldom give more introduction to the formation or origin of a theory.

For every student who has studied Western economics, the principle of income demand is very clear. It was seldom doubted until Giffen studied the relationship between goods sold on the market and consumers' income level. Some goods, for example potatoes, will not completely follow the principle that with the rise in income the quantity sold will increase. On the contrary, when income goes up to a certain level, the quantity sold will not increase but decline. Thus, the famous 'Giffen Paradox' was born.[1] This case not only tells us what a theory is, but also how theory is formed. A regulated or regular conclusion is a theory if it relies on practice and comes from the summary of a large number of cases or samples in practice. What if a hypothesis comes first before the empirical regulated or regular conclusion is reached? Is it a theory? Yes, of course. However, the formation of such a theory is different from the one derived directly from cases or samples in

[1]E. Mansfield, Microeconomics (Translated in Chinese), China Finance Press, 1992.

practice in an inductive way. The difference lies in the time sequencing of the theory formation, and the theory itself remains the same. However, there does exist a difference in the efficiency of theory formation in that the latter is more efficient than the former. Therefore, in academia, the theory formation with a hypothesis empirically is mostly encouraged.

In the study of rural household economic behaviour, we are facing millions of individual households, and the acquisition of a certain quantity of representative samples is both time- and energy-consuming. Accordingly, scholars will mostly carry out the empirical research with a hypothesis. Here is a well-known example, i.e. the formation of Schultz's rational farmer hypothesis where in traditional agriculture, it is rare to see the inefficient allocation of production factors.[2] In order to prove this hypothesis, the author conducted detailed investigations in two small villages in South Asia (India) and South America (Guatemala) and verified the hypothesis.

As is known to all, China is a large country with many farmers. Having experienced a period of reform and opening up, China's rural sector has transitioned from a traditional agricultural economy to a non-agricultural one, and rural household economy has been in transition as well. Is the rural household economic operation also guided by the principle of rational behaviour? How has the allocation of factors in the process of household economic structural change been carried out? Are there any behaviours of low efficiency? What is the root of the ever-growing imbalance in the process of economic development? What are the characteristics of the changing behaviours such as saving, borrowing and consumption? What are the impacts of tax burden on the economic growth for farmers? What role does village-level management play in the process of rural household economic growth? To answer these questions, we need a lot of empirical evidence. However, in order to reveal the mechanism of rural household economic operation, especially the mechanism of Chinese rural households in transition, we must grasp the track of their operation so as to find out the hidden mechanism. It is insufficient to have a hypothesis, and we also need a large number of investigation data for the basis, combined with a powerful analytical tool and solid knowledge support in economics, sociology, anthropology and behaviour management.

The Rule of Rural Household Economic Operation

We know that of all social organisations, a rural household is a very special one. It not only functions to reproduce human beings, but also plays a role in economic development. Therefore, it is a unique organisation integrating sociology, anthropology and economics. In terms of economics, like other organisations, it pursues economic profits as an important goal of its development, with little difference from

[2]Theodore W. Shultz, Transforming Traditional Agriculture (Translated in Chinese), Business Press, 1987.

the function of an ordinary manufacturer. Its investments, labour use and land allocation are all aimed at maximising benefits. In resource allocation, rural households obey the principle of efficiency optimisation,[3] according to the Schultz hypothesis. Whether we say that rural households are rational or that they are petty peasants, our analysis based on large data has revealed that the economic operation and structural transition of rural households are in accordance with the above principle. Since the reform and opening up, the non-agriculturalisation of the economic structural change of Chinese rural households has been the result based on such a principle. It has to be pointed out that there has been a behaviour divergence between individual rural households and rural households as a united group. When we talk about the evolution of the rural household economy, we are not saying that all individual households have to do so unanimously. The non-agricultural trend of rural household economic operation is like the 'zigzagging Yellow River' going to the sea, despite a lot of twists and turns, with a lot of water evaporated and used in the process, and only part of water eventually enters the sea. In the economic operation of rural households, non-agriculturalisation is one of the major features or themes for Chinese rural households in economic transition. The coexistence of such a feature and the household agricultural characteristics is the true portrait of Chinese rural household economy.

During the changing process of rural household economic structure, the allocation of resources and selection of industries have been the result of adapting to the industrial development requirement based on household capital reserves. The elasticity of capital demand between industries is an important indicator for rural households in industry selection and resource allocation. The industry with a high elasticity is usually the preferred choice for farmers in the process of leaving agriculture. This has been defined as the 'capital threshold theory in rural household non-agriculturalisation' in another book of mine, titled *Rural Household Economic Growth and Development Research*.

In the growth and development of rural households, there exists a process of capital accumulation. Households at various development stages are different in capital accumulation. Therefore, they have shown different development forms with different incomes, and the polarisation of economic development has been an objective problem for household economy. The formation and evolution of this problem are largely results of the family life cycle law of rural households. We notice that in income distribution, high-income households have occupied a larger share, and behind this is their ever-increasing capital accumulation. The 'Matthew Effect' of income distribution brought by capital accumulation is exactly the important economic origin of the imbalance of rural household economic development. In the development of imbalance in rural household economy, although there are many factors functioning at the same time, such as natural location and policy environment, in the same location and the same policy environment, the existing imbalance and its development are reflections of the inherent life cycle

[3]Qinghua Shi, Rural household economic resource utility efficiency and allocation, Chinese Rural Economy, 2000, (8): 58–61.

characteristics of a household itself. Under the influence of the rural household life cycle, there exists the imbalance of resource possession in the early stage of the household organisations' life cycles, the inconsistency of capacity in organisation and management in the middle stage, and inequality of income and utility levels in the late stage. The household life cycle law can be seen as another important principle in guiding rural household economic operation, in addition to household rational behaviour.

In terms of sociological or anthropological characteristics, a rural household organisation is different from a general economic organisation in that it performs the special function of human reproduction. Therefore, in participating in economic activities as a whole, the internal distribution of a household is different from other economic organisations. In resource allocation, its operation is not assigned, but conscious and voluntary. It is very rare for members to consider their own remuneration, as the behaviour of each member within the organisation is not based on personal utility or profit maximisation, but based on household benefit maximisation as a whole. Accordingly, throughout the economic activities, the internal distribution is seldom 'by labour', but usually according to 'needs'. Altruism is one of the most important features of rural household economic operation, which differs from other economic organisations. As A. Chayanov put it, a rural household is not a firm and cannot be analysed according to the behaviour of a firm.[4] This is because the large amount of work in the rural household economic activities is unpaid. In fact, a rural household is a special organisation with the firm behaviour embedded. This is because as a whole group of rural households, labour is paid, but inside each household, labour is unpaid due to its altruism. The firm behaviour can be said to be an external economic characteristic, and altruism to be an internal feature of rural households. Therefore, rural household organisation behaviour can be defined as the mixture of egoism and altruism. Such an organisation within an embedded framework is usually highly efficient. However, due to the serious problem in intergenerational inheritance, the proverb of 'no wealth for over three generations' has been confirmed repeatedly. This might be an important factor that restricts rural household economy to become bigger and stronger.

My View on Farmers

In the study of rural economic development, there is an unwritten rule or assumption in academia that farmers are ignorant and backward, thus needing help. From the present situation, it appears not wrong at all, but it actually does not seem quite right in that it is based on the derivation that farmers have a lot of irrational behaviours, which is rarely seen in my analysis.

Farmers are ignorant because they have limited educational resources and are less educated than other people, but it does not mean that their behaviour is

[4]The behaviour of a manufacturer is usually considered egocentric.

irrational. It is like how some water in the Yellow River is unable to reach the sea, but we cannot say that the Yellow River is not flowing towards the sea. Whether farmers' behaviour is rational should be judged from their own perspective, rather than from the observers'.

Farmers' backwardness refers to their low income and inferior consumption levels, but their intrinsic understanding of the features of Chinese culture is not worse than an average person. It is important to note that the root of Chinese traditional culture lies in the countryside and its people, rather than in the cities. Farmers are far more trustworthy than urbanites. That 'a gentleman loves wealth and takes it in a proper way' is the first creed parents of rural households would teach their children.

Their backwardness and their unwiseness are mostly from their inherent belief that 'everyone is responsible for his country', that for the development of the whole country, and the prosperity of the nation, farmers are often the models for self-sacrifice. Although peasants were also the major forces of rebellions in successive dynasties, their revolts were largely the results of oppression. As it is known to all, Chinese farmers' tolerance is the most outstanding among all people. Despite the fortified rural-urban divide, enlarged income inequality and obvious living disparity, farmers still enjoy their life in their 'paradise' and rarely cause the government any trouble. It is the mass media that will sometimes describe the farmers as 'unruly' for their righteous appeals.

Farmers need help, which is the view from an outsider. It is also an outsider's conscientious discovery from farmers' long-term contribution of no return. From the farmer's own perspective, what they need is not simply help, but respect and trust. Trust them and respect them, and they can move Mount Taishan as in the ancient Chinese fable.

In order to improve the appearance of the countryside as soon as possible, the government should treat farmers equally from the perspective of citizens, remove all the unreasonable rural–urban divide and provide farmers with trust and respect. Like in the early stage of reforms in the 1980s, we should believe that farmers are capable of improving the appearance of their hometown and their own living conditions. The formulation of rural policies should rely more on farmers' advice, and it is better not to implement policies without sufficient investigations. Here, I provide an example.

During the rural investigation in the summer vacation this year, quite a few farmers came to me that they have been over 60, each with only one child or two girls. According to the current policy, they are eligible for a lump sum compensation for family planning. However, they have neither applied for the one-child certificate nor had the sterilisation surgery eligible for another certificate, so they could provide neither of them. In the policy practice, 'no compensation should be given unless either of the certificates is provided'. So, they came to consult me if the government is right in doing so and what they should do. The case indicates that although the government has a good intention to issue the policy, which also shows the government's goodwill to respect farmers, there was a lack of investigation before the policy introduction. The rigid practice of the two certificates did not play its rightful role, but hurt some farmers who did adhere to the family planning policy. Is it true that facts are better than 'proofs'? Seeking truth from facts is the principle of the communists. However, such a principle is usually distorted due to the rigid practice of policies in real life. The policy implementation alone has been clearly against such a principle, let alone the psychological injuries of the general public due to the abuse of power and practice of favouritism.

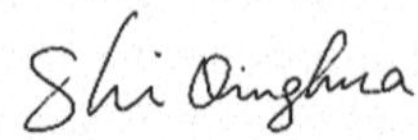

December 2004

Haodifang of Minhang
Shanghai, China

Contents

Chapter 1
Rural Households and Generational Evolution

Contents

Q. Shi and Y. Gao, *Sustainable Development of Rural Household Economy*,
https://doi.org/10.1007/978-981-15-2747-0_1

In order to understand key information of household members in the observed villages, such as their age, years of schooling, marriage behaviour, fertility pattern, and decision making over major issues, five out of ten observed villages were selected for an in-depth survey. These villages showed their interest in my research and were willing to cooperate. The survey was conducted in 2000 and the participating villages included: Longshang (LS) Village in Lin'an City, Yubei (YB) Village in Xiuzhou District of Jiaxing City, Jinhou (JH) Village in Rui'an City, Bogumen (BGM) Village in Putuo District of Zhoushan City, Hebian (HB) Village in Liandu District of Lishui City. The surveyed villagers were from households observed in my longitudinal research. The surveyed contents included their age, gender, years of schooling, marriage behaviour and fertility patterns, as well as the expectations of core household members for their children's childbearing, and their decision making over major family issues. In this chapter, I will analyse the results of my surveys.

1.1 Household Members and Their Income

1.1.1 Basic Information

The survey was conducted in late 2000, and covered five villages in Zhejiang. There were 248 households in total. Each village contained 50 households except Longshang Village with only 48 households. Survey data show that there are 908 members in the combined rural households which include 478 males and 430 females, occupying 52.64 and 47.36% respectively of the total population, equivalent to 100:89.96 in ratio. Among the members aged 25 years old and below, the male to female ratio is 100:78.16, and among those aged 60 years old and above, the ratio is 100:95.45. The age range of 93 years for females is certainly higher than that of 83 years for males. The average age of the household members in the survey is 35.97 years old, with 34.81 years old for males and 37.25 years old for females. The average years of schooling for members aged between 15 and 70 years old is 6.65 years, with 7.04 years for males and 6.22 years for females (Table 1.1). Further analysis suggests that due to differences in household labour division and labour intensity, life

Table 1.1 Basic information of rural households in 2000

	Five villages			Longshang Village			Yubei Village		
	All	M	F	All	M	F	All	M	F
Population	908	478	430	183	97	86	172	85	87
Average age	35.97	34.81	37.25	35.57	35.09	36.12	40.58	40.20	40.94
Maximal age	93	83	93	86	75	86	81	81	80
Years of schooling 15–70	6.65	7.04	6.22	6.26	6.80	5.64	5.87	5.79	5.95
Max schooling years 15–70	17	15	17	14	14	14	11	10	11
	Jinhou Village			Bogumen Village			Hebian Village		
Population	217	115	102	147	81	66	189	100	89
Average age	32.79	31.78	33.93	35.65	34.35	37.24	36.05	33.83	38.54
Maximal age	81	81	81	75	62	75	93	83	93
Years of schooling 15–70	7.12	7.60	6.60	6.27	6.79	5.67	7.15	7.41	6.88
Max schooling years 15–70	15	15	15	17	13	17	12	12	12

Note In Yubei Village, 25 households omitted the item for schooling years. Therefore, data in the table contain information of the remaining 25 households only in terms of schooling

expectancy for males is significantly lower than that of females, and the aging problem is more prominent for rural women. The rural population aged 25 years old and below has shown a serious gender imbalance, as strong preference for sons still exists in rural Zhejiang today.

1.1.2 *Age Distribution*

The age distribution of household members shows that the distribution of the villagers for different ages exhibits a typical 'M' shape (see Fig. 1.1). Among the age groups each with a five-year interval, there are two peak values for age groups of 20–24 and 45–49, representing 10.46 and 12.67% of the total population. The next high figures are for the 50–54 and 15–19 age groups, occupying 10.57 and 9.36% of the population. The age groups of 25–29, 30–34 and 35–39 only account for 6.61, 6.72 and 8.04% respectively of the total population. Why is there such an 'M' shape? There are three possible reasons: first, it is due to the family planning policy implemented in the late 1970s, second, it is related to the once growing demand for rural labour due to urban economic development and third, the institutional reform on higher education has resulted in the urbanisation of rural population. As to the gender distribution, among the younger generation with ages below 25 years old, there appear to be more males than females, especially for those less than ten years old. For the 35–49 age group, there are more females, but for those above 50 years old the male to female ratio is much more balanced. Yet, for those over 75 years old, again, there are more females. The gender distribution of rural household members is relevant not only to generational differences, but also to labour division and life expectancy.

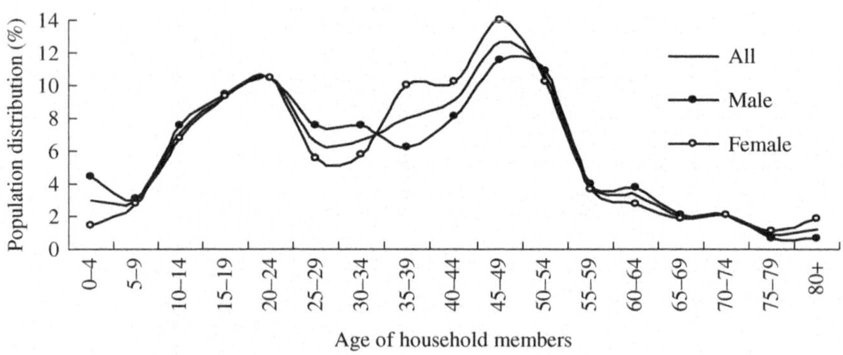

Fig. 1.1 Age distribution for rural household members in 2000

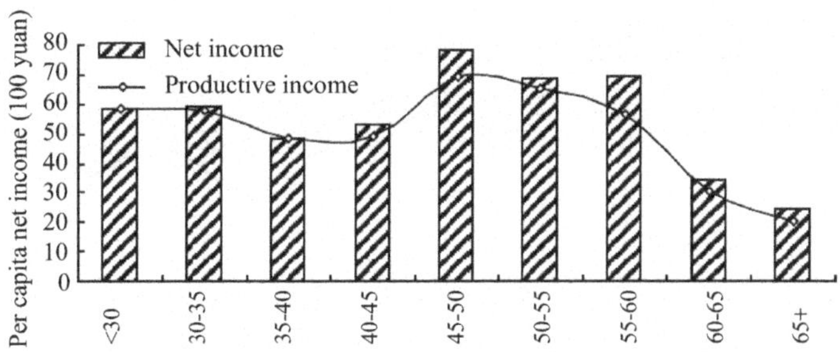

Fig. 1.2 Age of key household members and household income in 2000

1.1.3 Ages of Key Household Members and Household Income

It indicates from Fig. 1.2 that with the age difference of key household members, there are observed differences in household income. The changes in income according to age also show an 'M' shape, which is in line with the life cycle for rural households (Shi & Hou, 2001). During the early stage of a household life cycle when the dependency ratio is relatively lower, the per capita income is higher. When the financial burden for rural labour increases, the income level declines until the consuming members, or the young dependents, join the productive labour force. When household labour become consumers or dependents again, the income level for the household decreases drastically. Therefore, the income level for those aging families is the lowest among rural households. In some ways, the result suggests that the life cycle of a household is the foundational reason of the imbalanced economic development in rural Zhejiang.

1.1.4 Distribution of Schooling Years

In terms of years of schooling, Fig. 1.3 indicates that for members within the groups aged 15 to 70, the level noticeably declines as age rises. The 20–24 age group has the longest schooling time, i.e. 9.33 years. The average schooling years for the age group 30–34 is 7.48 years, almost two years less than the 20–24 age group, while the average figures for the age groups 40–44 and 50–54 decrease to 5.91 and 4.48 years. The result also shows that the education level of rural household members in Zhejiang increases over time. This suggests the increasing importance of human capital reserves for rural household economic development in Zhejiang.

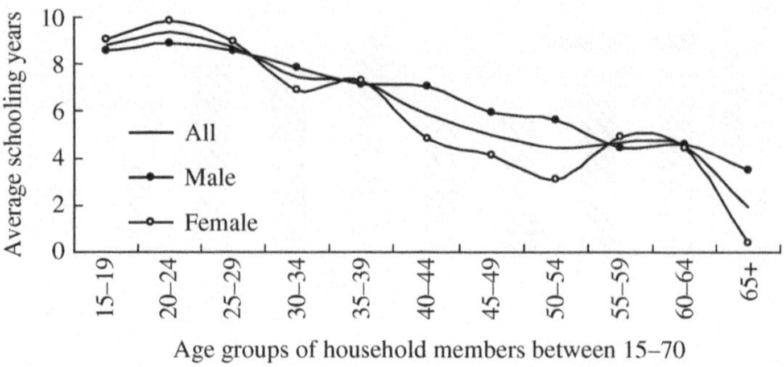

Fig. 1.3 Schooling years for household members by age group in 2000

In addition, the variation in education level for household members is also reflected in the distribution of their schooling years. As seen in Table 1.2, for villagers born before 1949, 62.35% of them received education for no more than five years, and as high as 40.74% received no more than three years of education. However, for those born in the 1950s and 1960s, most have finished primary education with 62.88% educated for over five years, and the percentage of those with less than three years of education decreases to 20.07%. For the household members born after the 1970s, their average schooling time increases to nearly nine years, with 70.09% educated for at least eight years, and 15.18% for at least 12 years, whereas the percentage of those with education of no more than three years declines to 4.91%.

1.1.5 Schooling Years and Income

According to Fig. 1.4, there seems to be a strong link between the schooling years of key household labour and rural household income. The income increases as the number of schooling years rises. Obviously, the income is the lowest if the household members only have primary education, and the income increases significantly if the members complete nine years of education to a junior high level. However, the income growth becomes less obvious for those with senior high education. There are two potential reasons. This might be relevant to the exam-oriented high school education and to the age distribution of the rural household labour (see Table 1.3). In general, the income growth of rural households is highly sensitive to the compulsory education in rural areas.[1] It follows that the improvement of education level of rural labour can be an important way to increase rural income.

[1] After calculating the income level of rural households with different schooling years by group, we have conducted a regression analysis using SPSS, and the models are: the linear function model, Y (per capita income, 100 yuan) = 39.8984 + 1.6451X (schooling years); the power function model, $Y = 29.7396X^{0.2748}$.

Table 1.2 Distribution of schooling years for different age groups in 2000 (%)

Age group	≤3 years	#0 years	4 years	5 years	6 years	7 years	8 years	9 years	10–12 years	>12 years
15–19	5.00	1.25	–	1.25	1.25	8.75	16.25	41.25	25.00	1.25
20–24	3.49	2.33	1.16	0.00	3.49	3.49	11.63	46.51	22.09	8.14
25–29	1.72	–	–	1.72	8.62	1.72	22.41	48.28	13.79	1.72
30–34	7.41	–	3.70	7.41	7.41	7.41	38.89	22.22	3.70	1.85
35–39	7.25	5.80	10.14	10.14	8.70	7.25	20.29	18.84	15.94	1.45
40–44	21.33	5.33	9.33	4.00	22.67	5.33	22.67	9.33	5.33	–
45–49	34.65	8.91	17.82	2.97	19.80	1.98	7.92	5.94	8.91	–
50–54	32.95	11.36	21.59	4.55	23.86	3.41	3.41	9.09	1.14	–
55–59	41.38	13.79	6.90	6.90	17.24	6.90	–	17.24	3.45	–
60–64	41.38	17.24	10.34	17.24	10.34	–	3.45	10.34	6.90	–
65+	81.25	56.25	0.00	0.00	6.25	6.25	–	6.25	–	–
15–70	19.56	7.01	8.61	4.38	12.55	4.67	14.60	22.77	11.24	1.61

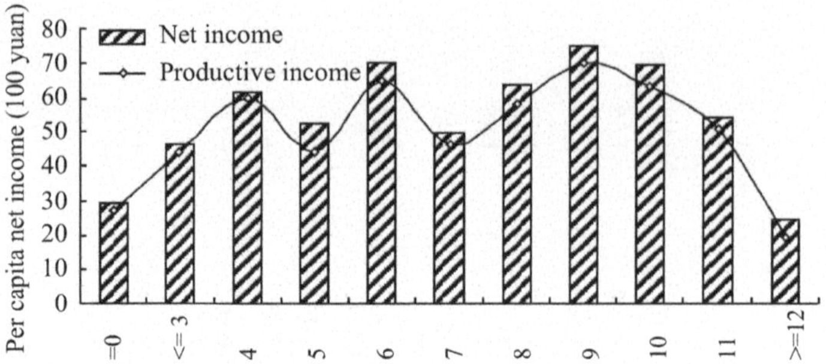

Fig. 1.4 Schooling years for key household labour

Table 1.3 Household income by age and schooling years of key labour (100 yuan/person)

		≤35	35–40	40–45	45–50	50–55	55–60	>60
Net income	≤3 years	32.13	–	38.56	63.93	62.70	100.65	20.59
	4–6 years	57.68	24.27	57.66	75.62	69.23	89.57	37.76
	7–9 years	67.36	61.97	55.11	81.03	80.58	48.64	33.63
	≥10 years	35.12	39.51	84.81	80.91	28.94	–	7.47
Net income from operation	≤3 years	32.13	–	30.33	61.02	62.31	95.95	18.88
	4–6 years	57.68	24.12	55.57	71.11	66.03	51.95	31.06
	7–9 years	65.95	61.43	49.91	67.33	74.56	47.83	28.51
	≥10 years	35.12	39.51	84.81	66.43	14.98	–	7.47

1.1.6 Household Income, Age and Schooling Years of Key Household Labour

According to Table 1.3, for the seven age groups, if those with over ten years of education are excluded,[2] there appears to be a positive correlation between household income and years of schooling for five age groups, a negative correlation for one group and an unclear relationship for another group. According to the general rule of human capital investment and economic growth, a positive correlation should exist in all age groups. However, the current study cannot provide evidence for this, and I believe this is because there are insufficient samples. For example, there is only one household where the key labour is within the age group of no more than 35 years and receives the education of no less than 10 years. Therefore, I need further study to clarify this issue.

[2]The main reason for the exclusion is that the educational objective of senior high education is different from that of junior high education and below.

1.1.7 Household Size, Type and Distribution

Table 1.4 indicates that until 2000 the most common family size in the five villages in Zhejiang was three family members, while the second most common family size was four members. These two types accounted for 56.22% of all the observed households. Households with more than five members accounted for 22.49%. As for types, most households belonged to core farm families, representing 71.08% of all samples, and the second largest type was stem family, accounting for 21.29%. These two types represented more than 90% of the total. In terms of differences in spatial distribution, rural households had relatively fewer members in Yubei Village in Jiaxing City located on the plain in north Zhejiang, and in Bogumen Village in Putuo District on the island, while households generally had more members in Longshang Village in Lin'an City located in the mountainous areas in north Zhejiang, in Jinhou Village of Rui'an City and in Hebian Village of Lishui City located in the hilly areas in west Zhejiang. In addition, Bogumen Village had the highest percentage of core families, followed by Jinhou Village, Hebian Village, Longshang Village and Yuebei Village. For the percentage of stem families, the order is reversed.

1.2 *Hun* and *Jia* Marriage of Members in Rural Households

1.2.1 Sample Information

Marriage remains an important issue in the study of internal matters of farmers' organisations. In this survey, the core focus is on the first *hun* (*jia*) marriage age of villagers and the distance between the couple's households.[3] Among the 248 households surveyed in the five villages, 482 members are involved in marriages, including 259 males and 223 females, taking 53.73 and 46.27% of the total sample. In terms of marriage types, 241 males took wives into their own families (*hun*) and 18 married themselves into brides' families (*daochamen*, or male *jia*); 209 females married into the families of their husbands (*jia*) and 14 took husbands into their own families (*zhaonüxu, or* female *hun*).

[3]In China, marriage can be divided into *hun* and *jia* according to the resident location. When a woman moves to live in a man's house with their children in the future taking the surname of the man, it is *hun* for the man and *jia* for the woman. On the contrary, when a man moves to live in a woman's house with their children taking the surname of the woman, it is *hun* for the woman and *jia* for the man, which is often termed as *zhaonüxu*, or *daochamen*.

Table 1.4 Rural households by size and type in 2000 (%)

Village	Household size (Number of members/household)						Household type			
	1	2	3	4	5	≥6	Core	Stem	Extended	Incomplete
LS	4.17	12.50	18.75	43.75	12.50	8.33	62.50	29.17	–	8.33
YB	6.00	26.00	20.00	30.00	10.00	8.00	50.00	40.00	2.00	8.00
JH	–	8.00	20.00	28.00	24.00	20.00	86.00	6.00	–	8.00
BGM	5.88	27.45	47.06	13.73	3.92	1.96	90.20	3.92	–	5.88
HB	–	16.00	38.00	22.00	16.00	8.00	66.00	28.00	2.00	4.00
Total	3.21	18.07	28.92	27.31	13.25	9.24	71.08	21.29	0.80	6.83

1.2.2 *First Marriage Age and the* Hun *or* Jia *Marriage Distance*

Table 1.5 and Fig. 1.5 show that villagers' average age of first marriage is 23.07 years, and the average distance between the couple's households is 52.98 km in these five villages. The island village Bogumen has the youngest first marriage age on average, followed by Longshang Village in the mountainous areas in north Zhejiang, and the other three villages have more or less the same number in this regard. In terms of the average marriage distance between the couple's households, these five

Table 1.5 Marriage information of adult household members in 2000 (year, km)

Current Age	5 villages in Zhejiang		Longshang Village		Yubei Village	
	FMA	FMD	FMA	FMD	FMA	FMD
<25	22.00	350.85	21.33	1000.67	22.33	14.33
25–29	23.76	105.46	22.90	342.25	25.50	256.33
30–34	23.93	93.62	24.00	34.75	25.45	273.91
35–39	23.02	6.95	24.10	15.15	22.94	3.00
40–44	23.46	8.11	23.69	19.03	24.14	2.21
45–49	23.01	26.85	22.38	42.25	24.56	69.67
50–54	21.78	39.02	21.80	54.47	22.13	91.00
55–59	21.70	31.90	21.83	54.35	22.00	67.43
60–64	23.61	67.61	22.60	86.62	20.75	44.75
65–69	26.50	143.70	–	–	27.00	102.83
70+	22.93	32.79	23.75	82.00	22.00	3.00
Total	23.07	52.98	22.87	98.51	23.71	83.27
	Jinhou Village		Bogumen Village		Hebian Village	
<25岁	22.50	2.50	23.00	3.00	21.75	377.00
25–29	23.75	4.06	23.40	2.20	23.75	14.38
30–34	24.50	2.26	22.70	24.63	23.00	123.77
35–39	23.00	1.00	22.79	2.03	22.58	13.67
40–44	24.00	1.33	22.47	1.23	23.33	12.00
45–49	25.57	2.86	20.54	3.94	24.45	5.75
50–54	22.63	3.25	20.42	4.74	22.71	30.00
55–59	22.00	4.25	20.50	3.95	22.50	5.63
60–64	–	–	23.00	2.67	25.27	85.00
65–69	–	–	–	–	25.75	205.00
70+	22.00	1.00	20.00	20.00	23.60	20.20
Total	23.79	3.02	21.65	5.38	23.57	54.45

Note FMA refers to first marriage age; FMD refers to first marriage distance

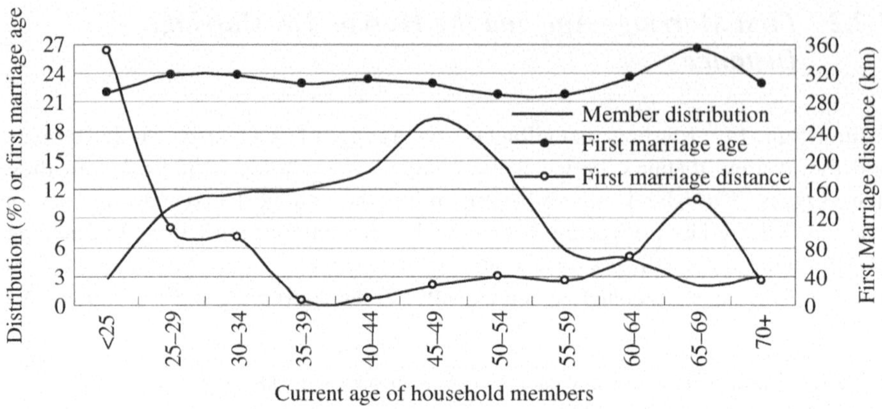

Fig. 1.5 First marriage age and the marriage distance

villages differ vastly, ranging from less than three kilometres to nearly a hundred kilometres. Longshang Village in the mountainous areas in north Zhejiang has the longest distance of 98.51 km, followed by Yubei Village on the plain in north Zhejiang with 83.27 km. Hebian Village in the hilly areas in west Zhejiang has the distance of 54.45 km, and the other two villages have similar distances, i.e. 5.38 km for Bogumen Village of Putuo District, and 3.02 km for Jinhou Village of Rui'an. For different generations, the average first marriage distance exhibits a typical 'U' shape in the age spectrum for household members in the five villages of Zhejiang. Those born before the liberation in 1949 and after the Cultural Revolution have obvious longer distances than those born in the 1950s and 1960s. Such a result should be considered as relevant to the rural economic development modes in different times. In the collective production mode, people's free time was very much restricted by their working time, which is reflected in the shortened marriage distance. With the implementation of the reform and opening-up policy, however, the family-centred production has noticeably helped to expand the networking range of rural residents, which is also reflected in their first marriage distance. This result shows that the social issues in rural areas are also economic issues. The economic development has direct impacts on the social development, and vice versa.

1.2.3 First Marriage Age and Distance for Different Age Groups

It indicates in Table 1.6 that the average age of the first *hun* marriage is 24.19 years for men, and that of the first *jia* marriage is 21.89 years for women, making a difference of 2.30 years. While the average age of the first *jia* marriage is 23.56 years for men and that of the first *hun* marriage is 20.93 years for women, with a difference of

Table 1.6 Marriage information of household members by gender in 2000 (year, km)

Age	Male *hun*		Male *jia*		Female *jia*		Female *hun*	
	FMA	FMD	FMA	FMD	FMA	FMD	FMA	FMD
<25	23.00	8.00	–	–	21.75	191.81	21.50	1501.25
25–29	24.15	9.05	25.00	3000.00	23.52	72.10	21.00	40.00
30–34	24.74	121.54	–	–	22.57	47.09	–	–
35–39	23.64	6.35	24.00	20.00	22.48	6.59	23.00	20.00
40–44	24.11	6.73	24.00	11.55	22.55	9.02	26.00	23.00
45–49	24.28	22.79	23.50	31.00	21.73	32.24	20.75	18.75
50–54	22.89	33.81	22.29	35.86	20.00	51.64	20.67	11.33
55–59	23.69	38.67	27.00	8.00	19.42	28.22	18.00	12.00
60–64	25.31	39.47	24.00	12.00	21.63	128.25	17.00	4.00
65–69	28.33	234.33	24.50	6.00	23.00	9.50	–	–
70+	26.33	56.67	24.00	1.00	19.86	16.86	–	–
Total	24.19	41.37	23.56	188.28	21.89	42.90	20.93	229.32

Note FMA refers to first marriage age; FMD refers to first marriage distance

1.63 years. By comparing these four marriage modes, I have found that the average age for men in their first marriage is older than that for women, while the average age for *daochamen* or *zhaonüxu* is generally younger than other marriage modes. In terms of first marriage age in recent years, it seems villagers tend to marry at a younger age than in the past. Comparing the group aged below 25 and that from 25 to 29, the first marriage age has dropped from 24.19 to 23.00 years for men and from 23.43 to 21.70 years for women, with the obvious trend to get married at an earlier age.

With regard to the average first marriage distance, the *jia* marriage distance is generally longer than the *hun* distance, and women have a longer distance than men do. For different age groups, generally it seems younger and older groups tend to have longer distances than those of the middle-age ones. In addition, for women of the younger age groups, the *jia* distance becomes longer, with the group of below 30 reaching as far as 97.81 km for the first marriage. On the contrary, the *hun* distance for men of the younger age groups is getting shorter, for instance, the distance is only 8.91 km for men in the age group of below 30.

1.2.4 Distribution of First Marriage Distance

According to Fig. 1.6, for most adult household members, the marriage distance is within one kilometre, as in their own or neighbouring villages. As the distance increases, distribution of married people declines. In this study, 30.71% of the surveyed villagers marry within a distance of one kilometre, including 31.66% of the

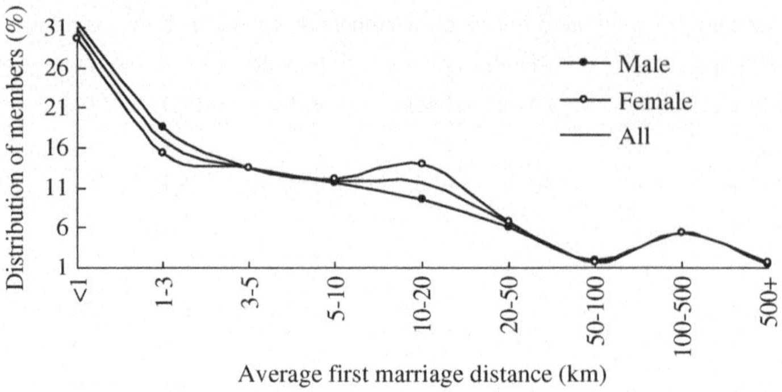

Fig. 1.6 The distance distribution of *hun* or *jia* marriage for adult household members

males and 29.16% of the females. As the radius of marriage circle expands, the percentage of married members in the sample increases rapidly (Fig. 1.7). When the radius reaches three kilometres, the percentage of married members increases to 47.72%. When the radius reaches five kilometres, the percentage rises to 61.20%. When the radius further extends to ten kilometres, the percentage increases to 73.03%, and further to 84.65% when the radius hits 20 km. Only 8.92% of the villagers surveyed have a marriage distance longer than 50 km. This indicates that the marriage circle for villagers in Zhejiang is comparatively small, so that rural young people tend to marry those within a short distance. In terms of gender differences, within a short distance of less than three kilometres, there appears to be more males than females, and within a medium-range distance between three to 50 km, there are more females. For a long distance, there is not much gender difference.

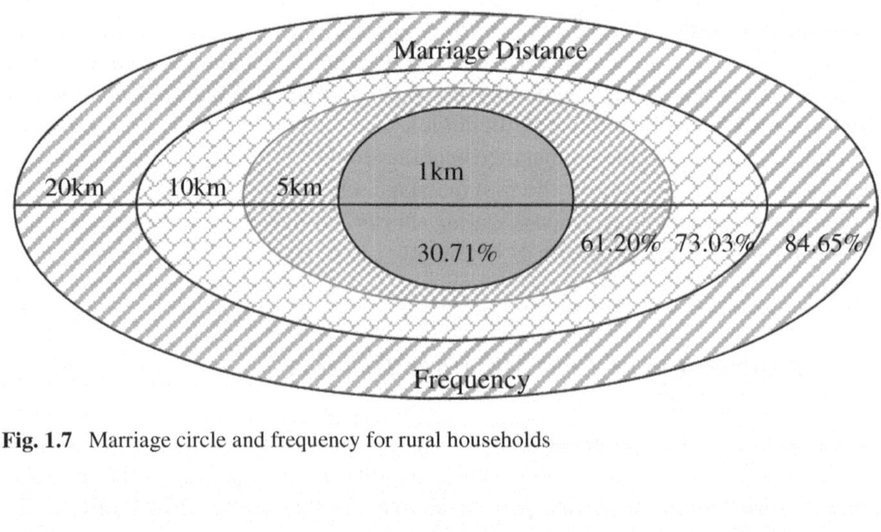

Fig. 1.7 Marriage circle and frequency for rural households

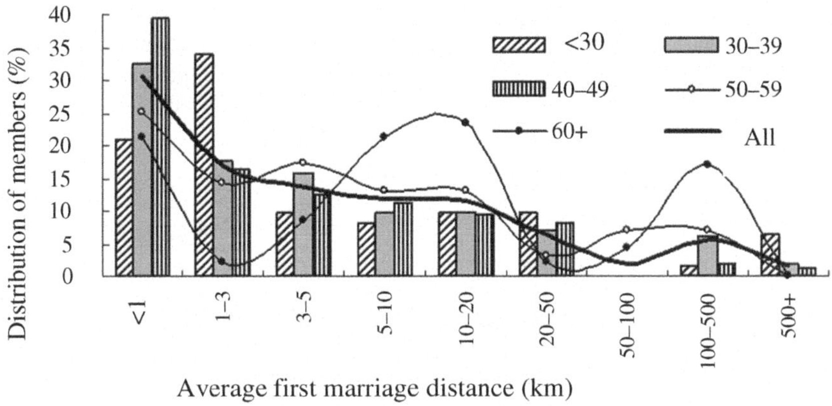

Fig. 1.8 The Distribution of first marriage distance by age group

1.2.5 Distribution of First Marriage Distance by Age Group

Figure 1.8 shows certain differences for various age groups in terms of marriage distance. In general, short-distance marriages in one's own or neighbouring villages are more common, i.e. with the frequencies of 54.84% for the age group of below 30, 50.00% for the 30–39 group, 55.63% for the 40–49 group, 39.39% for the 50–59 group, and 23.40% for the age group over 60. However, for medium-range and long marriage distances, the frequencies change to 37.10% for the age group of below 30, 42.11% for the 30–39 group, 41.25% for the 40–49 group, 46.46% for the 50–59 group, and 55.32% for the age group over 60. Such frequencies become lower for a very long marriage distance. For example, the figures are 8.06% for the age group of below 30, 7.89% for the 30–39 group, 3.13% for the 40–49 group, 14.14% for the 50–59 group and 21.28% for the age group of over 60. A question arises as to why there appear such a huge difference in terms of marriage distance for different age groups. Is it because people in different age groups are facing different choices? Unfortunately, there is limit evidence to provide a sufficient explanation for this question. Therefore, future studies are needed for further exploration.

1.2.6 Distribution of First Marriage Age

Figure 1.9 shows that in the five Zhejiang villages under observation, most household members' first marriage is at the age of 23, making up 16.60% of the sample. If we move one year away from the mode, i.e. to the age of 22 and 24, the first *hun* or *jia* marriage frequency will increase to 44.40% and further to 68.46% if we move two years away from it. Of all the villagers surveyed, 15.98% would first marry

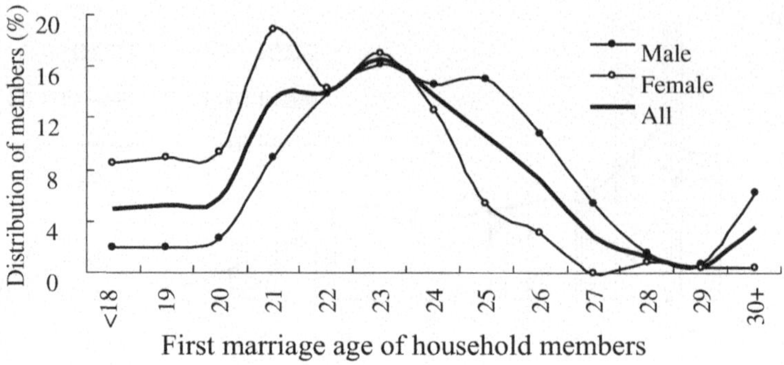

Fig. 1.9 Distribution of first marriage age for household members

before they reached 20, and 15.56% after 26. There appears to be a typical normal distribution for rural household members in terms of first marriage age.

With regards to gender, there appears to be substantial differences in that the first marriage age is much younger for women than for men. In the sample of the current study, the youngest marriage age for women is 16 (current age 52), and the oldest age is 35 (current age 37), with 21 being the mode and taking 18.83%. If we move one to two years away from the mode, we get the concentration ratios of 42.60 and 68.61%. The youngest marriage age for men is also 16 (current age 54), and the oldest age is 44 (current age 45), with 23 being the mode, standing at 16.22%. If we move one to two years away from the mode, we get the concentration ratios of 44.79 and 68.73%.

1.2.7 Distribution of First Marriage Age by Age Group

Figure 1.10 shows that people in various age groups have shown differences in terms of first marriage age. There exist normal distributions for all age groups, but the appearance times for peak values and the concentration ratios vary. For younger groups, the peak values emerge at later ages with higher concentration ratios, but the older groups are the opposite. With the increase of age, the concentration ratios are getting higher for all groups if we move one or two years away from the modes. For members currently over 50, most got married at the age of 21, and the concentration ratio for 19–23 years old is 56.16%. For the 40–50 group, the peak value appears between 23 and 24, for the 30–40 group at 23, and for the youngest group at 25. This has indicated there was an influence by the low living conditions in the countryside in the 1960s and 1970s, due to a phenomenon that rural men once postponed their marriage. For males in the 40–49 group, 39.53% married at the age over 25.

Fig. 1.10 Distribution of first marriage age by age group

1.3 Marriage Gradient

1.3.1 Sample Information

As an important indicator for studying marriage, marriage gradient is used in the current research to measure the age differences between men and women in their first marriages. In order to examine the marriage gradients of household members, I have reorganised the information gathered from the five villages and selected 217 pairs as marriage sample, including 201 pairs for male *hun* and female *jia*, and 16 pairs for male *jia* and female *hun*.

1.3.2 Marriage Gradient and Its Distribution

1.3.2.1 Marriage Gradient

Data from the 217 pairs show that the average marriage gradient of rural households in the five villages is 2.32 (the age difference between men and women in the first marriage). In comparison, residents of Bogumen, the island village, has the lowest marriage gradient of 1.17, followed by Longshang Village of 1.96 in the mountainous areas, Yubei Village of 2.66 on the Hangjiahu Plain, Jinhou Village with 2.96 in the coastal hilly areas, and Hebian Village of 3.08 in the valley along the river. From the perspective of age groups, the marriage gradients for men have shown a general downward trend for younger groups. For male members aged below 30, the marriage gradient is 1.17; for males aged 30–39, the gradient is 1.27; for males 40–49, the gradient is 1.81; for males aged 50–59, the gradient is 3.08; for males aged 60 and above, the gradient is 5.86. The marriage gradients for women exhibit a clear ‘U’ shape over age groups. For female members aged below 30, the marriage gradient is 2.60; for females aged 30–39, the gradient is down to 1.46; for females aged 40–49, the gradient is 2.29; for females aged 50–59, the marriage gradient is 3.30; and for females aged 60 and above, the gradient is 4.00. In terms of *hun* or *jia* marriage, the gradients vary. For the traditional 'male *hun* or female *jia*' marriage, the gradient is generally smaller as 2.29, whereas for the 'female *hun* or male *jia*' marriage, the gradient is higher as 2.75. This has indicated that men tend to marry women of similar age, and women tend to choose those more mature as their spouses. In extreme cases where there appears a severe shortage of males for a rural household, the marriage gradient certainly tends to become higher for *zhaonüxu*.

From the perspective of education, with the increase of schooling years, marriage gradients decrease for both males and females. With the education of less than three years, the marriage gradients for males and females are 2.94 and 2.75. When the education increases to four to six years, the gradients become 3.05 and 2.68. The gradients decrease to 1.59 and 1.88 for males and females with six to nine years of schooling, and further to 1.77 and 0.74 for those with over ten years of education.

Table 1.7 shows that, on average, the sample pairs with the marriage gradient of zero (men and women at the same age) only account for 19.35%. The sample pairs with a negative marriage gradient (women are older than men) take up 10.14%, and those with a positive gradient (men are older than women) account for 70.51%. This has indicated that rural marriages with positive gradients are the result of villagers' subjective choices. Of these marriages, most men marry at an elder age than women. The result of such marriage behaviour is that 15.67% of the sample pairs have a gradient of one year, followed by 13.82% of the pairs with a gradient of four years, 13.36% with a gradient of two years, and 11.52% with the gradient of over three years. In different villages, the conditions are also different. Marriages with no gradient mostly appear in Bogumen Village, followed by Yubei and Longshang in north Zhejiang, and Jinhou Village in southwest Zhejiang. In terms of concentration ratio, villages vary substantially. For example, in Jinhou Village, most gradients are four years, taking 25%. In Bogumen Village, the majority of the marriage gradients are zero. In Hebian Village, gradients of two years are the most popular, and in Yubei the majority of gradients are concentrated between zero to one year.

1.3.2.2 Distribution of Marriage Gradients by Gender and Age

The marriage behaviours of male and female household members vary as the time changes (Table 1.8). In terms of marriage gradient for male selection, of the marriages in which men are older than women, the distribution exhibits an overall 'U'-shape trend over time. The marriage gradients for the older and the younger generations are relatively higher than the 40–49 age group. Of the marriages in which men are younger than women, or at the same age, the distribution of marriage gradients shows an inverted 'U'-shape trend over time. For the female selection, of the marriages in which men are older, the gradient distribution also exhibits a 'U'-shape trend. Of the marriages in which men are younger or at the same age as women, the distribution

Table 1.7 Marriage gradient distribution of five villages in Zhejiang 2000 (%)

	Females older		Same age	Males older						
	>2 years	1 year		1 year	2 years	3 years	4 years	5 years	6 years	>7 years
LS	6.38	12.77	19.15	14.89	4.26	8.51	14.89	6.38	2.13	10.64
YB	4.55	4.55	18.18	18.18	6.82	15.91	9.09	6.82	4.55	11.36
JH	0.00	0.00	7.14	17.86	14.29	17.86	25.00	10.71	7.14	0.00
BGM	4.26	8.51	31.91	14.89	19.15	8.51	10.64	0.00	2.13	0.00
HB	1.96	3.92	15.69	13.73	21.57	9.80	13.73	3.92	3.92	11.76
Total	3.69	6.45	19.35	15.67	13.36	11.52	13.82	5.07	3.69	7.37

Table 1.8 Marriage gradients by gender and age in five villages of Zhejiang 2000 (%)

Marriage gradients for males										
Age	Females older		Same age	Males older						
	>2 years	1 year		1 years	2 years	3 years	4 years	5 years	6 years	>7 years
20–29	16.67	16.67	11.11	5.56	5.56	22.22	16.67	0.00	5.56	0.00
30–39	5.88	5.88	19.61	25.49	19.61	3.92	15.69	1.96	0.00	1.96
40–49	1.28	8.97	25.64	17.95	15.38	12.82	8.97	5.13	1.28	2.56
50–59	2.08	0.00	16.67	12.50	10.42	16.67	16.67	8.33	4.17	12.50
60+	0.00	4.55	9.09	0.00	4.55	4.55	18.18	9.09	18.18	31.82
	Marriage gradients for females									
20–29	6.67	6.67	13.33	6.67	6.67	26.67	20.00	0.00	6.67	6.67
30–39	7.35	7.35	14.71	20.59	17.65	7.35	17.65	5.88	0.00	1.47
40–49	1.20	8.43	24.10	16.87	14.46	10.84	7.23	4.82	3.61	8.43
50–59	2.50	0.00	20.00	12.50	7.50	17.50	15.00	7.50	5.00	12.50
60+	0.00	9.09	18.18	0.00	9.09	0.00	27.27	0.00	18.18	18.18

exhibits an inverted 'U'-shape as well. This has indicated that for both males and females, their requirement of marriage gradients has increased, which has intensified over time.

1.3.2.3 Distribution of Marriage Gradients by Gender and Education

The marriage behaviour is also related to education levels. Such correlation can be proved by the variation in the distribution of marriage gradients (see Table 1.9). As the education level of family members rises, men's requirement of marriage gradients exhibits a 'U'-shape trend, while women's requirement forms an inverted 'U'-shape distribution. For same-age marriages, as years of schooling increases, the gradient distributions for both men and women show a 'U'-shape trend, and the distribution presents an upward trend for marriages with the choice of younger spouses. The result shows the education level not only has influence on the first marriage age, but also on the marriage gradient.

1.4 Childbearing for Adult Females

1.4.1 Sample Information

Childbearing is also an important component in the study of issues within farmers' organisations. In the survey, some core concepts have already been explored such as first marriage age. In order to further define the study, the age for first or last childbirth and number of children will be analysed. Among the 248 households surveyed in the five villages, 274 couples have the experience of childbearing including females aged from 21 to 93, with an age difference of 72 years. In addition, 34 couples or 12.41% of the sample pairs are below the age of 30, 63 pairs or 22.99% belong to the 30–39 age group, 100 pairs or 36.50% are aged between 40 and 49, 55 pairs or 20.07% are aged between 50 and 59, 13 pairs or 4.74% are aged between 60 and 69, nine pairs or 3.28% of the sample are over 70. In terms of childbearing, 83 females or 30.29% of the sample pairs have experienced once (including two pairs of twins).

1.4.2 Childbearing for Females with Childbirth Experience

According to the survey (Table 1.10), the average first marriage age for adult women in the five villages of Zhejiang is 21.34, and their age at first childbirth is 22.49, with the time difference of 1.15 years. The average age at last childbirth for females with more than one child is 27.01. On average, each female has 2.11 children, with boys taking 54.06%. For different age groups, over time females have postponed their

Table 1.9 Distribution of marriage gradients by gender and education in 5 villages (%)

Marriage gradients for males										
Schooling years	Females older		Same age	Males older						
	>2 years	1 year		1 year	2 years	3 years	4 years	5 years	6 years	>7 years
0–3	0.00	5.66	20.75	11.32	15.09	9.43	15.09	5.66	5.66	11.32
4–6	1.72	3.45	22.41	15.52	12.07	10.34	12.07	3.45	5.17	13.79
7–9	7.53	9.68	16.13	18.28	9.68	13.98	13.98	6.45	2.15	2.15
10+	0.00	0.00	23.08	15.38	38.46	7.69	15.38	0.00	0.00	0.00
Marriage gradients for females										
0–3	1.30	5.19	22.08	16.88	9.09	14.29	10.39	5.19	5.19	10.39
4–6	1.59	6.35	20.63	12.70	15.87	7.94	14.29	7.94	3.17	9.52
7–9	8.62	5.17	13.79	20.69	13.79	10.34	17.24	3.45	3.45	3.45
10+	5.26	15.79	21.05	5.26	21.05	15.79	15.79	0.00	0.00	0.00

Table 1.10 Childbearing for adult females in the observed households in 2000 (years, %)

Current age	5 villages in Zhejiang					Longshang Village				
	FMA	FCA	LCA	NoC	PoB	FMA	FCA	LCA	NoC	PoB
≤25	21.29	22.00	21.00	1.14	68.75	20.00	20.00	–	1.00	100.0
26–30	22.52	23.48	27.50	1.22	71.43	22.80	23.60	–	1.00	100.0
31–35	22.43	23.21	26.60	1.21	58.82	23.00	23.50	32.00	1.25	20.00
36–40	21.69	22.52	26.76	1.76	54.05	22.40	23.40	27.20	2.20	36.36
41–45	21.87	22.96	26.08	2.09	48.94	22.23	23.46	27.25	2.00	38.46
46–50	20.79	21.98	26.67	2.39	51.49	22.00	23.00	27.22	2.22	65.00
51–55	20.42	22.09	26.10	2.61	62.79	20.00	25.00	28.00	2.80	64.29
56–60	18.93	21.00	26.79	3.07	48.84	18.20	21.80	27.00	3.00	53.33
61–70	22.20	23.80	31.30	3.40	61.76	–	–	–	–	–
71+	20.22	21.56	35.57	4.00	30.56	21.00	25.00	47.00	8.00	0.00
Total	21.34	22.49	27.01	2.11	54.06	21.60	23.33	27.95	2.19	48.57
	Yubei Village					Jinhou Village				
≤25	22.00	23.00	–	1.00	100.0	21.00	21.80	21.00	1.20	58.33
26–30	25.00	26.00	–	1.00	0.00	22.33	23.33	28.33	1.44	61.54
31–35	23.20	24.20	–	1.00	80.00	21.33	22.33	23.00	2.00	66.67
36–40	21.78	22.56	29.50	1.22	18.18	19.67	20.67	24.00	2.11	73.68
41–45	23.29	23.71	29.40	1.86	46.15	20.00	20.90	24.40	2.80	46.43
46–50	23.22	23.78	28.60	1.56	42.86	19.07	20.00	27.29	3.43	43.75
51–55	20.63	21.75	24.33	2.13	58.82	20.88	21.88	28.00	3.00	70.83
56–60	19.75	21.00	25.50	2.75	63.64	–	–	–	–	–

(continued)

Table 1.10 (continued)

	Yubei Village					Jinhou Village				
61–70	20.67	23.33	30.00	3.33	50.00	–	–	–	–	–
71+	17.50	18.50	33.00	2.50	60.00	22.00	24.00	35.00	6.00	50.00
Total	21.94	22.88	27.69	1.78	49.44	20.44	21.39	26.04	2.44	55.77
	Bogumen Village					Hebian Village				
≤25	–	–	–	–	–	23.00	23.50	–	1.00	100.0
26–30	22.75	24.00	–	1.00	75.00	20.67	21.33	25.00	1.33	100.0
31–35	21.86	22.43	–	1.00	42.86	22.56	23.44	27.50	1.22	72.73
36–40	21.67	22.67	25.00	1.56	57.14	23.10	23.60	29.33	1.90	63.16
41–45	22.13	23.25	24.40	1.75	71.43	22.14	23.86	25.17	1.86	53.85
46–50	19.67	21.33	24.08	2.17	50.00	21.17	22.83	27.33	2.17	61.54
51–55	19.75	20.63	24.63	2.88	60.87	21.00	22.50	26.00	2.00	50.00
56–60	19.00	20.00	27.50	4.00	25.00	19.00	20.33	27.67	3.00	44.44
61–70	–	–	–	–	–	22.86	24.00	31.86	3.43	66.67
71+	20.00	22.00	31.00	4.00	50.00	21.00	21.50	34.33	3.25	38.46
Total	20.94	22.08	24.82	1.96	53.00	21.90	23.02	28.43	2.11	60.47

Note FMA refers to first marriage age: FCA for first childbirth age; LCA for last childbirth age; NoC for number of children; PoB for percentage of boys

first marriage age and the age at first childbirth. In comparison of the age groups of 26–30 and 56–60, females' first marriage age has been delayed by 3.59 years, and their age at first childbirth by 2.48 years. Of the females who have almost completed the childbearing responsibility, the numbers of children have been declining, yet the child gender ratios are various for different age groups. Of the total ten groups with children, only the age groups of 41–50, 51–60 and 71 over have more girls, and the others all have more boys, especially for females below the age of 35 with boys making up 65.38% of the total number of children within the group.

In terms of differences among villages, for women who have already experienced childbearing, their first marriage age and first childbirth age are the earliest in Jinhou Village of Rui'an, followed by Bohumen Village. The average age of the two villages is 0.5–1.5 years younger than those of Longshang, Yubei and Hebian. Meanwhile, the oldest last childbirth age for the two villages is also 1–2 years younger. With regards to number of children, Jinhou Village has the most, followed by Longshang and Hebian, while Yubei and Bogumen have the least. With the implementation of the family planning policy in the late 1970s, there have appeared substantial differences among villages, and a serious gender imbalance. As for the number of children for women over 35 with birth(s), the average number is one for Yubei and Bogumen, with boys constituting 62.50 and 54.44% respectively. The next is Longshang Village with an average number of children of 1.10 and boys constituting 63.64%. This is followed by Hebian Village with a number of 1.21 and 82.35% boys. Jinhou Village has the highest number of children at 1.41, with boys making up 61.29%. Therefore, in terms of number of children, Zhejiang has been doing well in the implementation of the national family planning policy. In terms of child gender ratio, however, the situation is worrying and deserves much attention from the policy makers.

From the previous analysis, it can be said that in the five villages of Zhejiang with a high percentage of boys, the first marriage distance is short. If there is a low percentage of boys, the distance is long. There is also a link between number of children and first marriage age where areas with a younger first marriage age, there are more children. Yet, such a link has been distorted with the implementation of the current family planning policy. However, in some areas with the traditional ideology of 'more happiness with more children', there has been a high percentage of two children in each family. This will be further explored in the following chapters of the book.

1.4.3 Birth Intervals and Other Issues

For women with multiple births, the average birth interval is 1.93 years. Compared with the study in inland Shanxi, such an interval is shorter.[4] This result might be related to some factors such as the earlier biological maturity and childbearing age

[4]In 1997, I carried out a similar study in Shanxi. The birth interval there is found to be 2.47 (Shi, 1999: 23).

due to the closer distance to the equator so that offspring reproductive intervals become shorter. In comparison of the five villages of Zhejiang (Table 1.11), the inter-village differences are also evident. Hebian Village has the longest interval, followed by Yubei Village, Longshang Village and Jinhou Village. Bogumen Village has the shortest interval, and has a time difference of almost a year compared with Hebian Village. As far as the age groups are concerned, the difference is also obvious. Women over 60 years old have the longest interval of 2.49 years. This is followed by women in the 26–40 age group with an interval of 2.10 years. Women in the age group 41–60 have an interval of 1.78 years, and those in the age group of 25 and below have a shorter interval of 1.25 years. Therefore, birth intervals are closely relevant to other factors such as location and time. At the beginning of the implementation of the family planning policy, the birth intervals were once distorted as a result. However, people have improved their understanding of the policy, and the birth intervals have returned to normal levels. Such a phenomenon also exists in the data of Shanxi Province (Shi, 1999: 23).

In terms of number of children, 72.63% of the households in the five villages of Zhejiang have two or fewer children, and this has happened in more households over time. Although there appears to be some inter-village differences, the trend is generally the same that the percentage becomes higher for younger age groups. For example, for those between 31 and 40, 94.29% have one or two children, including 51.43% with one child. On the whole, the one-child percentage in the five villages is 30.29%, with the highest in Yubei Village, up to 48.00%, and the lowest in Hebian Village of 22.95%. The figures for the other three villages are ranged between these two figures.

1.4.4 Interval Distribution of Women with Multiple Births

As we can see from Table 1.12, in the five villages of Zhejiang, most birth intervals are less than one year, with 26.18% of the women with multiple births. These are followed by intervals between 1.5 and 2 years, accounting for 22.51% of the women. The intervals between 1 and 1.5 years account for 20.94%, and between 2 and 2.5 years for 13.09%. The intervals exceeding 2.5 years take up 17.28%, including 8.38% exceeding three years. For various age groups, the oldest and the youngest groups both have a peak value of 1.5–2 years for birth intervals. Yet, for the 31–50 age group the peak value for birth interval is less than one year. The birth interval distribution along the age groups changes from the shape of an inverted ‘U’ to a ‘U’, with the changing point at the interval of 2.5 years.

Table 1.11 Birth intervals for adult females in observed households in 2000

Current age		≤25	26–30	31–35	36–40	41–45	46–50	51–55	56–60	61–70	71+	All
Intervals (years)	LS	–	–	3.50	1.73	1.96	1.90	1.50	1.73	–	2.75	1.92
	YB	–	–	–	3.50	2.90	3.00	1.33	1.64	2.00	3.50	2.27
	JH	1.25	2.00	1.20	1.61	1.25	2.13	2.04	–	–	1.83	1.79
	BGM	–	–	–	1.50	0.82	1.27	1.39	1.88	–	2.25	1.38
	HB	–	2.50	2.25	2.89	1.25	2.08	1.75	2.44	2.29	3.17	2.30
	All	1.25	2.11	2.00	2.11	1.59	1.98	1.62	1.88	2.21	2.76	1.93
≤2 Children (%)	LS	100.0	100.0	100.0	80.00	92.31	77.78	40.00	20.00	0.00	–	75.00
	YB	100.0	100.0	100.0	100.0	100.0	100.0	62.50	50.00	33.33	50.00	84.00
	JH	100.0	88.89	66.67	77.78	30.00	7.14	25.00	–	–	0.00	51.56
	BGM	–	100.0	100.0	100.0	87.50	83.33	25.00	0.00	–	0.00	76.47
	HB	100.0	100.0	100.0	100.0	100.0	83.33	100.0	33.33	28.57	25.00	80.33
	All	100.0	95.65	96.43	92.86	80.00	66.07	45.45	28.57	30.00	22.22	72.63
1 Child (%)	LS	100.0	100.0	75.00	0.00	15.38	0.00	0.00	0.00	0.00	–	22.92
	YB	100.0	100.0	100.0	77.78	28.57	44.44	25.00	0.00	0.00	50.00	48.00
	JH	80.00	66.67	33.33	11.11	0.00	0.00	0.00	–	–	0.00	25.00
	BGM	–	100.0	100.0	44.44	37.50	0.00	0.00	0.00	–	0.00	35.29
	HB	100.0	66.67	77.78	10.00	14.29	0.00	0.00	0.00	0.00	25.00	22.95
	All	85.71	82.61	82.14	30.95	17.78	7.14	6.06	0.00	0.00	22.22	30.29

Table 1.12 Birth intervals for adult females in the observed households 2000

Current age	≤1 year	1–1.5 years	1.5–2 years	2–2.5 years	2.5–3 years	>3 years
≤30	16.67	–	50.00	33.33	–	–
31–40	26.47	14.71	14.71	14.71	14.71	14.71
41–50	34.44	22.22	16.67	12.22	7.78	6.67
51–60	20.45	29.55	31.82	9.09	4.55	4.55
61+	–	11.76	35.29	17.65	17.65	17.65
Total	26.18	20.94	22.51	13.09	8.90	8.38

1.4.5 Distribution of Number of Children for Adult Females

Table 1.13 and Fig. 1.11 show the distribution of number of children in the five villages of Zhejiang: one-child families account for 29.56% of the total sample, two-child families take 43.07%, three-child families account for 17.52% and lastly 9.85% families have four children or more. For different age groups, over time rural women tend to have only one or two children, and there has been an obvious decline of families with over three children. For the age groups below 40, there seldom are families with more than three children. At present, after almost twenty years since the first implementation of the family planning policy, data from Zhejiang

Table 1.13 Distribution of number of children for adult females in observed households 2000

Current age	1	2	3	4	5	6+
≤30	83.78	13.51	2.70	–	–	–
31–40	51.43	42.86	5.71	–	–	–
41–50	9.90	62.38	20.79	5.94	0.99	–
51–60	4.26	36.17	40.43	19.15	–	–
61+	10.53	15.79	15.79	36.84	5.26	15.79
Total	29.56	43.07	17.52	8.03	0.73	1.09

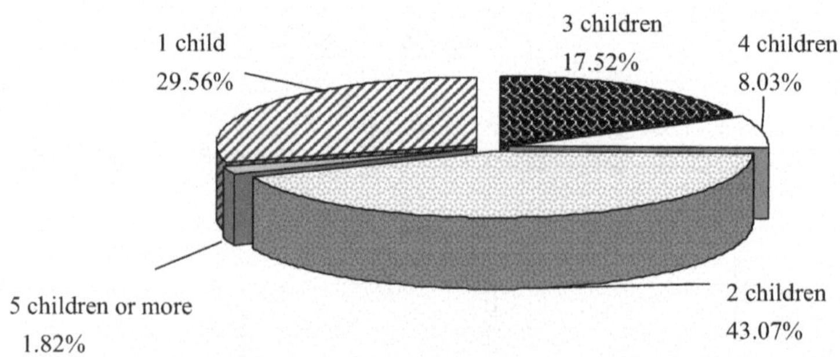

Fig. 1.11 Distribution of number of children for adult females in rural households

have provided evidence that such a policy is effective and that farmers have their understanding improved about the policy. Although the birth intervals for multi-children families seem to be rather close, families with more than two children are actually the minority.

1.5 Expectations on Childbearing

1.5.1 Sample Information

In the survey of 248 households from the five villages of Zhejiang, 371 core members answered the questions about their childbearing expectations, including 186 males and 185 females. A total of 306 members, or 82.47% of the 371 members, expressed their clear expectations including 153 males and the same number of females. In total, 64 members (32 males and 32 females) gave the answer of 'no expectation', accounting for 17.25% of the total. For the members with expectations on number of children, 82 respondents believed they had absolutely no gender expectation, consisting of 22.10% of the total sample or 26.71% of the sample with expectations on number of children. Two members expressed their 'partial expectations' on gender (to have at least one or two boys), making up 0.54% of the total sample or 0.65% of the sample with number expectations.

1.5.2 Expectations on Number of Children

In terms of number of children (Table 1.14 and Fig. 1.12), the expectations of the household core members in the five Zhejiang villages exhibit a general normal distribution. The expectations for two children account for 53.37%, followed by one-child expectations accounting for 21.83%, three-child expectations taking 6.20%, and four-child or more expectations accounting for only 1.35%. Meanwhile 17.25% of the members have no expectation for the number of children.

Table 1.14 Distribution of two-child expectations for core household members

	Sample size	Not care	>1 boy	1 boy and 1 girl	2 boys	2 girls
Male expectation	98	26.53	1.02	57.14	12.24	3.06
Female expectation	100	25.00	1.00	59.00	11.00	4.00
Total expectation	198	25.76	1.01	58.08	11.62	3.54

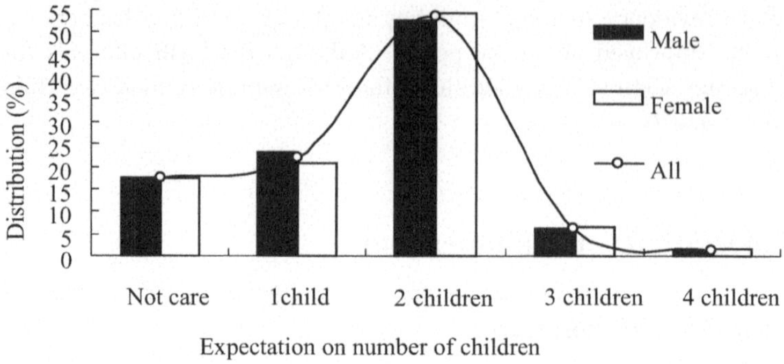

Fig. 1.12 Distribution of expectations on number of children for core family members (I)

For those expecting to have two children, the heterosexual expectations (to have one boy and one girl) account for 58.08% of the household members, whereas two-girl and two-boy expectations constitute of 3.54 and 11.62% respectively (Table 1.14). The expectation to have at least one boy accounts for 1.01% of the household members, and 25.76% of the members express the view that they have no expectation on gender.

For members with no expectation on gender (Table 1.14, Fig. 1.13), no one is from the below- 30 age group, 12.37% are from the 31–40 age group, 18.62% from the 41–50 age group, and 24.46% and 18.18% from the 51–60 and the 61-over age groups respectively. Such a result has shown that after experiencing the hardships in childrearing, older members have substantially changed their expectations on childbearing. Although there is no way to change their number of children, their attitudes have provided references for the younger generations. In terms of differences among age groups, for those with expectations on number of children, 33.33% of the members aged 30 and below expect to have one child, and 66.67% expect to have two. For the 31–40 age group, 38.82% expect to have one child, 56.47% expect to

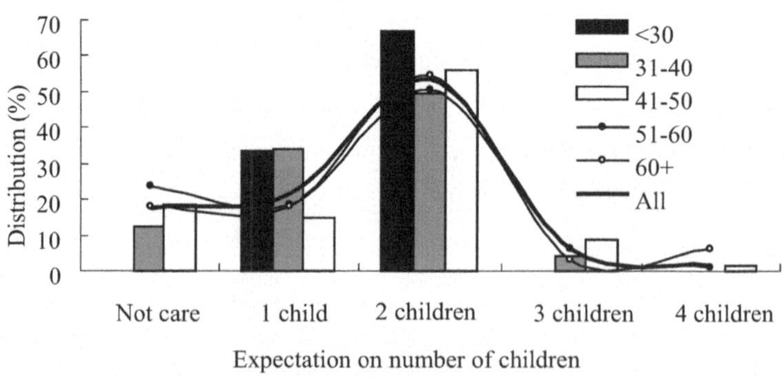

Fig. 1.13 Distribution of expectations on number of children for core family members (II)

have two, and 4.71% expect to have three. For the 41–50 age group, 18.64% expect to have one child, 68.64% expect to have two, 11.02% expect to have three, and 1.69% expect to have four. For the 51–60 age group, the percentages of expectations for one, two, three and four children are 24.19, 66.13, 8.06 and 1.61% respectively. Yet, for the group aged 61 and over, the corresponding figures are 22.22, 66.67, 3.70 and 7.41%. This has indicated that as time goes on, the role of family planning policy has been enhanced in farmers' minds, so that their expected number for children have generally declined, with a decrease in two-child expectations and an increase of one-child expectations, and there is almost no expectation to have more than three children.

In comparison of expectations from male and female core household members on the number of children (Table 1.15), men generally expect to have fewer children than women. To be more specific, men's expectations are all lower than women's, except for one-child expectation which is higher than that of women. This indicates that with regard to childbearing, the multi-child expectations mostly come from women. Therefore, the task for family planning should focus on rural women. To do well in women's ideological work means already half the success in family planning.

Table 1.15 Expectation distribution for core household members by age group

Current age		≤30	31–40	41–50	51–60	61+	Subtotal
Male	Not care	–	12.20	19.12	20.41	19.05	17.20
	1	28.57	39.02	17.65	18.37	19.05	23.12
	2	71.43	46.34	54.41	53.06	52.38	52.69
	3	–	2.44	8.82	6.12	4.76	5.91
	4	–	–	–	2.04	4.76	1.08
Female	Not care	–	12.50	18.18	28.13	16.67	17.30
	1	37.50	30.36	12.99	18.75	16.67	20.54
	2	62.50	51.79	57.14	46.88	58.33	54.05
	3	–	5.36	9.09	6.25	–	6.49
	4	–	–	2.60	–	8.33	1.62
Overall	Not care	–	12.37	18.62	23.46	18.18	17.25
	1	33.33	34.02	15.17	18.52	18.18	21.83
	2	66.67	49.48	55.86	50.62	54.55	53.37
	3	–	4.12	8.97	6.17	3.03	6.20
	4	–	–	1.38	1.23	6.06	1.35

1.5.3 Expectations on Gender and Number of Children

Among the 307 core household members with expectations on number of children in the five villages of Zhejiang (Fig. 1.14), 73.29% of them also have expectations on gender. Of the above, 64.20% of those with one-child expectations, 74.24% of those with two-child expectations, 91.30% of those with three-child expectations and 100% of those with four-child expectations also have gender expectations. Those with a certain number expectation, but no gender expectation, account for 26.71% of the total 307 members, including members with one-child, two-child, three-child and four-child expectations taking up 35.80, 25.76, 8.70, and 0.00% respectively. This has provided a good message for the family planning task. In the rural family planning, it is necessary to attach importance not only to farmers' expectations on the number of children, but also to their expectations on gender. Especially in families with relatively fewer children, gender expectation is an important issue. If the gender expectations cannot be satisfied, a possible consequence will be the increase in number expectations.

For the farmers with number expectations, the average expected number of children is 1.84 in the five villages of Zhejiang, including the expectation rate of 44.70% for boys, 30.74% for girls, and 24.56% without gender expectations. In terms of gender difference, rural males expect to have an average of 1.82 children (Table 1.16), with an expectation rate of 46.43% for boys, 28.57% for girl, and 25.00% with no gender expectations. While females' average expected number of children is 1.87 (Table 1.16), with the expectation rate of 43.01% for boy, 32.87% for girl, and 24.13% with no expectations. In general, there is a significant difference in gender expectations. For both men and women, their expectation for boys is significantly higher than that for girls. But in terms of the gender differences of the expecting persons, male members' expectation for boys is significantly higher than that of females, while females' expectation for girls is higher than that of males. For those without gender expectations, there appears to be no obvious difference between males and females. It seems that women's expectations are slightly higher.

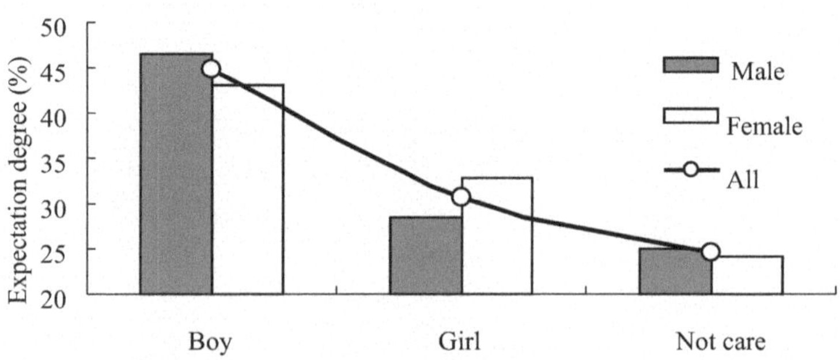

Fig. 1.14 Gender Expectations of the core household members

Table 1.16 Core members' gender expectations on children

Age group	No. expect	Male for boys (%)				Male for girls (%)			
		1	2	3	4	1	2	3	4
≤30	1.71	100.0	30.00	–	–	–	30.00	–	–
31–40	1.58	43.75	44.74	66.67	–	18.75	34.21	33.33	–
41–50	1.89	50.00	40.54	66.67	–	25.00	27.03	33.33	–
51–60	1.90	44.44	38.46	44.44	75.00	11.11	32.69	22.22	25.00
>61	1.94	50.00	50.00	100.0	100.0	25.00	40.91	–	–
Total	1.82	48.84	41.33	63.64	87.50	18.60	31.63	27.27	12.50
		Female for boys (%)				Female for girls (%)			
≤30	1.63	33.33	20.00	–	–	33.33	40.00	–	–
31–40	1.71	35.29	46.55	66.67	–	17.65	36.21	33.33	–
41–50	2.02	30.00	43.18	52.38	62.50	50.00	29.55	33.33	37.50
51–60	1.83	33.33	33.33	83.33	–	16.67	40.00	16.67	–
>61	2.00	–	35.71	–	50.00	50.00	28.57	–	50.00
Total	1.87	31.58	41.00	61.11	58.33	28.95	33.50	30.56	41.67

Note Gender expectation rate = expected number for boys/expected number for children; boy percentage + girl percentage + "not care" percentage = 100%

Among the 225 samples with both number and gender expectations for children, the expected number of children is 1.91, including 58.97% of the members expecting boys, 40.56% for girls, and 0.47% with guaranteed expectations for boys.[5] In terms of gender difference, men's expectations on the number of children is 1.87, including 61.61% expecting for boys, and 37.91% for girls. Meanwhile, women's expectations on the number of children is 1.95, including 56.42% for boys, and 43.12% for girls. With regard to different number expectations, the boy expectation rate in the one-child expectation group is 63.46%, and the girl expectation rate is 36.54%. The boy expectation rate in the two-children expectation group is 57.08%, and the girl rate is 43.88%. The boy expectation rate in the three to four-child expectation group is 68.67%, the girl rate is 31.33%. For age groups, members of different generations have different expectations on the number and gender of children. With the decline in age of the core family members, their expectations on childbearing show a downward trend and their gender expectations tend to be more balanced between boys and girls. For the core members of the households aged 30 and below, their expectations for the number of children have an average of 1.60, and the expectations for boys and girls both account for 50%. For those aged 31–40, their expectations on the number of children average at 1.76, with 59.63% members expecting boys and 40.37% for girls. For those aged 41–50, their expectations on the number of children are averaged at 1.99, with 57.14% expecting for boys and 41.67% for girls. For those over 61 years old, their number expectations on childbearing become an average of 2.05, including 60.00% expecting boys and 37.78% for girls. This result has indicated again that as society progresses, young people's expectations on the number of children are obviously lower than those of the older ones. It also provides important information for the rural family planning. It indicates that the problem of multiple childbearing in rural areas may not only come from young women themselves, but also from the expectations on them from the older generations. The implementation of the family planning should focus not only on women of childbearing age, but also other family members.

1.5.4 The Influence of Education on Childbearing Expectations

From Fig. 1.15, it can be seen that the length of education of rural family members is related to their childbearing expectations, mainly to the gender expectations, but education duration is found to be not much related to their decisions concerning whether to have children, or how many children to have. In terms of number of children, those with three years of education and below has an expectation rate of 82.22%, and the average expected number is 1.92. For those with education from four to six years, the expectation rate is 82.64%, and the expected number is 1.97.

[5]Definite expectations for number of children and for boys, with the difference between the two not being zero, and no definite expectations for girls.

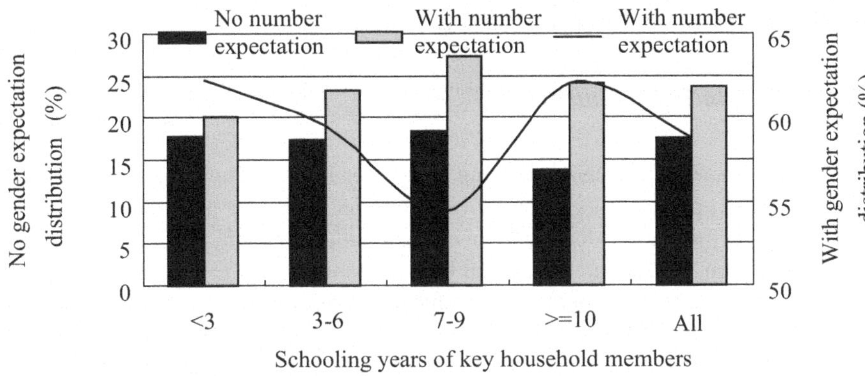

Fig. 1.15 Education level of the family core members and their childbearing expectations

For those with education for seven to nine years, the expectation rate is 81.58% and the expected number is 1.63. For those with education for more than 10 years, the expectation rate is 86.21% and the expected number is 1.88.

As far as gender expectation is concerned, with the improvement of education, the concept of boys and girls being equal is obviously on the rise. For people with no more than three years' education, the child expectation rate is 77.03%, with the boy expectation rate being 40.85%, the girl expectation rate being 37.32%, and the no gender expectation rate being 21.83%. For those with education for four to six years, the child expectation rate is 73.00%, the rate of for boys is 45.69%, the rate for girls is 29.44%, and the rate for no specific gender is 24.87%. For those with education from seven to nine years, the child expectation rate is 66.67%, the expectation rate for boys is 44.74%, the rate for girls is 23.68%, and the rate for no specific gender is 31.58%. For those with education over ten years, the corresponding figures become 72.00, 40.43, 36.17 and 23.40%. This result has provided important information for dealing with the difficulties in family planning implementation in rural areas. Strengthening rural basic education not only improves the rural household human capital reserves, enhances farmers' capabilities to increase income, but also has a good effect on the moderate growth of rural population. To make it simple, the biggest difficulty in family planning implementation in rural areas lies in gender expectation. If there are two girls in succession in a household, the villagers would be quite eager to have another child. But if the education level of rural residents is improved, the problem due to gender discrimination will be effectively alleviated.

1.6 Household Decision Making

1.6.1 Sample Information

There are six household decision making categories in the current study, i.e. domestic and external operation decisions, investment decisions for productive and non-productive asset purchases, decisions for domestic management, and education decisions for children. These categories can be re-organised into four modes, i.e. male decision, female decision, husband-wife discussion and child-engaged decision. A total of 232 out of 248 households in the five Zhejiang villages responded in the survey, taking 93.55% of the total. The participant rates for the survey were 95.83% for Longshang Village, 84.00% for Yubei Village, 88.00% for Jinhou Village, and 100% from both Bogumen Village and Hebian Village. The response rates across all villages were 91.35% for domestic operation decisions, 88.71% for household external operation decisions, 91.53% for productive fixed asset investments, 89.52% for non-production fixed asset investments, 91.53% for domestic management, and 90.32% for children's education.

1.6.2 Decision Making Modes

As it is shown in Table 1.17 and Fig. 1.16, for the rural household decision making in the five Zhejiang villages, domestic operation decisions are mostly decided by men and supplemented by husband-wife discussions. For external operations, the decision making is the opposite. However, there is not much difference between the two modes, with the difference of only 2–3%. For asset investments, regardless of productive or non-productive assets, the decision making is mainly based on husband-wife discussions, supplemented by male decision, with 5–10% difference between the two modes. In the above mentioned four categories, females seldom make decisions on their own. However, in domestic management, females dominate in decision making, supplemented by husband-wife discussions which is followed by male decisions. With regard to children's education, decisions are mostly made by husband-wife discussions, and decisions made solely by males or females are rarely seen. This shows that, for decisions relating to operation, investment and domestic management, there has been an obvious gender differentiated division of responsibilities. The concept that 'males are responsible for external affairs and females for domestic issues' still prevails in household decision making in rural Zhejiang. However, the high frequency of husband-wife discussions for decision making concerning children's education has indicated that villagers have been very cautious about education.

Decision making modes vary visibly among villages. For all six types, husband and wife discussion dominates in the mountainous area of Longshang in northern Zhejiang, while in Yubei Village on the northern plains Zhejiang, the male decision

Table 1.17 Decision making for core rural household members

		Investment		Asset purchase		Others	
		Domestic operation	External operation	Productive	Non-productive	Domestic management	Children education
5 villages	Sample	227	220	227	222	227	224
	Male decision	43.17	40.91	40.09	34.68	17.18	23.21
	Female decision	9.25	9.09	8.37	12.61	53.74	17.86
	Discussion	40.97	43.64	45.37	47.30	25.11	52.68
	Child-engaged	6.61	6.36	6.17	5.41	3.96	6.25
LS	Sample	46	43	44	44	46	44
	Male decision	30.43	37.21	38.64	27.27	19.57	25.00
	Female decision	17.39	11.63	11.36	22.73	32.61	18.18
	Discussion	47.83	46.51	45.45	45.45	43.48	47.73
	Child-engaged	4.35	4.65	4.55	4.55	4.35	9.09
YB	Sample	37	37	40	38	37	37
	Male decision	67.57	64.86	60.00	52.63	37.84	48.65
	Female decision	8.11	10.81	7.50	18.42	29.73	10.81
	Discussion	18.92	18.92	25.00	23.68	24.32	37.84
	Child-engaged	5.41	5.41	7.50	5.26	8.11	2.70
JH	Sample	44	44	44	44	44	43
	Male decision	45.45	36.36	31.82	31.82	18.18	18.60
	Female decision	6.82	6.82	4.55	6.82	70.45	6.98
	Discussion	36.36	45.45	54.55	50.00	11.36	62.79
	Child-engaged	11.36	11.36	9.09	11.36	–	11.63
BGM	Sample	50	50	50	50	50	50
	Male decision	54.00	48.00	48.00	40.00	6.00	14.00
	Female decision	8.00	10.00	12.00	10.00	84.00	38.00
	Discussion	36.00	40.00	38.00	48.00	10.00	48.00
	Child-engaged	2.00	2.00	2.00	2.00	–	–
HB	Sample	50	46	49	46	50	50
	Male decision	24.00	21.74	24.49	23.91	10.00	16.00
	Female decision	6.00	6.52	6.12	6.52	46.00	12.00
	Discussion	60.00	63.04	61.22	65.22	36.00	64.00
	Child-engaged	10.00	8.70	8.16	4.35	8.00	8.00

mode dominates. Different from the above two northern villages, in the hilly village of Jinhou and Hebian Village in south-eastern part of Zhejiang, husband and wife discussions are the majority. However, in Bogumen, the island village by the sea, decisions are mostly made by males for issues concerning operational and productive investment, and by females for issues regarding domestic management. For children's education, the husband and wife discussion mode dominates. This indicates that

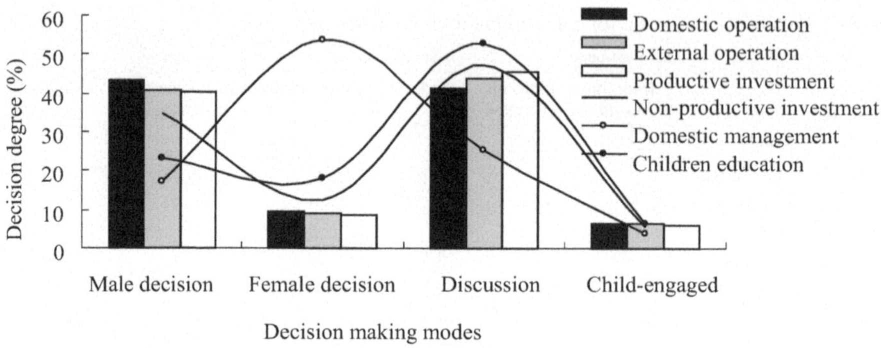

Fig. 1.16 Decision making in rural households

females in the hilly areas of Zhejiang tend to have a stronger sense in household decision making.

1.6.3 Decision Making for Different Age Groups

Table 1.18 and Fig. 1.17 indicate that decision making modes vary according to different age groups over time. In terms of domestic and external operations as well as productive and non-productive asset investments, members tend to make decisions based on husband-wife discussions. For domestic management, the female decision mode has been strengthened. Whereas the male decision mode has been gradually weakening, it has been replaced by the rising husband-wife discussion mode. For children's education, the husband-wife discussions have dominated, supplemented by the female decisions for the families of the younger generations, or by the male decisions for the families of the older generations. The result shows that there has been a 'convergence' for rural household decision making in that there appears to be a rapid increase of the husband-wife discussion mode, which has played a dominant role in rural household decision making. Therefore, the husband-wife discussions are and will continue to be an important tendency in decision making in rural Zhejiang.

1.6.4 Decision Making and Education Background

Table 1.19 and Fig. 1.18 show a link between the decision-making modes and education levels of family members. With the improvement of education level, there has been a tendency to promote 'gender equality and joint consultation' in decision making, and the concept has greatly challenged the traditional thinking that 'males are responsible for external affairs and females for domestic issues'. Although there

Table 1.18 Decision making for core rural household members by age groups (%)

		Investment		Asset purchase		Others	
		Domestic operation	External operation	Productive	Domestic operation	Domestic management	Children education
≤35	Sample	24	23	24	24	24	22
	Male decision	25.00	13.04	16.67	16.67	8.33	9.09
	Female decision	16.67	26.09	20.83	12.50	50.00	31.82
	Discussion	45.83	47.83	50.00	58.33	37.50	54.55
	Child-engaged	12.50	13.04	12.50	12.50	4.17	4.55
36–45	Sample	68	65	66	66	68	68
	Male decision	44.12	43.08	43.94	30.30	11.76	19.12
	Female decision	8.82	4.62	4.55	16.67	60.29	22.06
	Discussion	44.12	49.23	48.48	50.00	26.47	50.00
	Child-engaged	2.94	3.08	3.03	3.03	1.47	8.82
46–55	Sample	81	80	80	81	81	81
	Male decision	44.44	43.75	40.00	43.21	17.28	23.46
	Female decision	6.17	5.00	6.25	7.41	53.09	11.11
	Discussion	43.21	43.75	46.25	44.44	24.69	59.26
	Child-engaged	6.17	7.50	7.50	4.94	4.94	6.17
56–65	Sample	25	25	26	24	25	25
	Male decision	52.00	48.00	50.00	41.67	40.00	44.00
	Female decision	4.00	8.00	3.85	8.33	52.00	16.00
	Discussion	32.00	36.00	42.31	41.67	8.00	40.00
	Child-engaged	12.00	8.00	3.85	8.33	–	–
≥66	Sample	29	27	31	27	29	28
	Male decision	44.83	44.44	41.94	29.63	17.24	25.00
	Female decision	17.24	18.52	16.13	22.22	44.83	17.86
	Discussion	31.03	33.33	35.48	44.44	27.59	50.00
	Child-engaged	6.90	3.70	6.45	3.70	10.34	7.14

are still families educated at the junior high level holding such a traditional concept in decision making, for those educated at senior high level, their decision making has been mostly changed to the husband-wife discussion mode. This reveals that education has played a crucial role in changing traditional ideas. Accordingly, it can be inferred that families with higher education levels usually have higher incomes. In addition to their better human capital reserves, the change in the household decision making mode is also one of the important factors, as it helps to reduce decision risks, and improve the feasibility and possibility of success.

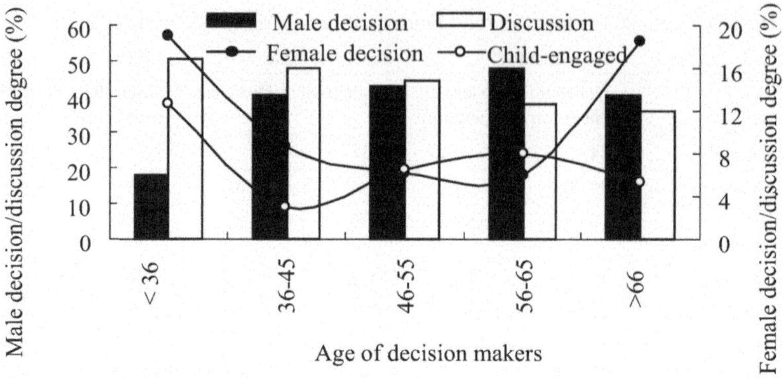

Fig. 1.17 Decision makings for operations and asset investments by age group

Table 1.19 Decision making of core household members with different education levels (%)

		Investment		Asset purchase		Others	
		External operation	Productive	Domestic operation	External operation	Productive	Domestic operation
≤3	Sample	70	69	72	68	70	69
	Male decision	48.57	52.17	51.39	44.12	17.14	30.43
	Female decision	14.29	11.59	9.72	13.24	60.00	20.29
	Discussion	32.86	33.33	37.50	39.71	20.00	46.38
	Child-engaged	4.29	2.90	1.39	2.94	2.86	2.90
4–6	Sample	75	72	73	72	75	75
	Male decision	41.33	38.89	36.99	36.11	24.00	21.33
	Female decision	5.33	5.56	8.22	8.33	49.33	14.67
	Discussion	45.33	48.61	47.95	50.00	22.67	57.33
	Child-engaged	8.00	6.94	6.85	5.56	4.00	6.67
7–9	Sample	48	45	48	48	48	47
	Male decision	33.33	22.22	22.92	20.83	2.08	10.64
	Female decision	6.25	8.89	6.25	8.33	64.58	17.02
	Discussion	52.08	57.78	58.33	62.50	33.33	61.70
	Child-engaged	8.33	11.11	12.50	8.33	–	10.64
≥10	Sample	18	18	18	18	18	17
	Male decision	33.33	27.78	27.78	16.67	11.11	11.76
	Female decision	–	–	–	16.67	33.33	23.53
	Discussion	61.11	66.67	66.67	61.11	50.00	58.82
	Child-engaged	5.56	5.56	5.56	5.56	5.56	5.88

Note In Yubei and Longshang, some villagers failed to provide the education information, thus 16 households were not involved

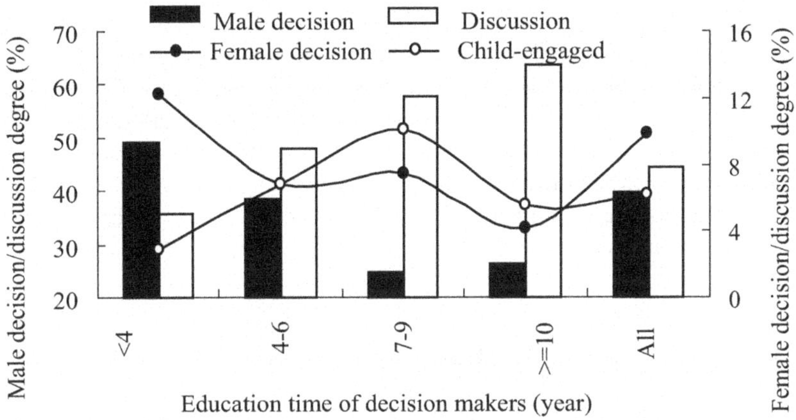

Fig. 1.18 Education and decision making for operations and asset investments

1.6.5 Choices of Decision Making Modes by Gender

Table 1.20 demonstrates that in terms of choice of decision making mode, there are gender differences as decision makers might have different perceptions and views. Despite the differences, the decision makers share one common feature in that they have been trying to increase their involvement. In decision making concerning operations, male decision makers prefer to decide on their own rather than discuss with their wives. Meanwhile,female decision makers would rather decide by discussion,and have a higher percentage than males to select the female decision mode. For asset purchase, although both men and women choose the discussion mode

Table 1.20 Decision making for core household members by gender (%)

		Investment		Asset purchase		Others	
		External operation	Productive	Domestic operation	External operation	Productive	Domestic operation
Male	Sample	120	120	125	122	124	122
	Male decision	43.33	43.33	41.60	40.16	25.81	29.51
	Female decision	5.83	5.83	4.00	9.02	50.00	12.30
	Discussion	41.67	41.67	45.60	43.44	20.16	50.00
	Child-engaged	9.17	9.17	8.80	7.38	4.03	8.20
Female	Sample	100	100	102	100	103	102
	Male decision	38.00	38.00	38.24	28.00	6.80	15.69
	Female decision	13.00	13.00	13.73	17.00	58.25	24.51
	Discussion	46.00	46.00	45.10	52.00	31.07	55.88
	Child-engaged	3.00	3.00	2.94	3.00	3.88	3.92

as their major way, there exist differences in degree of preference. In addition to trying to increase their participation for both husbands and wives, women have shown a higher preference for the discussion method. Such a phenomenon is also seen in decisions concerning domestic management and children's education. This has indicated that there has been a weakening of responsibility division in decision making over important issues, and discussions between husbands and wives have become prevalent. This has been the result of females' improved sense of participation in household decision making.

1.7 Frequency of Major Household Events

For a rural household, its income growth is usually related to such major events as the marriage and childbearing of the next generation, illness and death of the senior members, house construction and repair, and children's education. These events have direct impacts on rural income. To find out more, in designing the questionnaire survey, I added a section on 'events in your family since the observation'.

1.7.1 Major Events and Frequencies

It is shown in Table 1.21, since 1984 when the observations started, in the five Zhejiang villages, 195 out of 248 rural households have undergone major events, accounting for 78.63%, including 81.25% for Longshang Village, 60.00% for Yubei Village, 80.00% for both Jinhou Village and Bogumen Village, and 92.00% for Hebian Village. From 1984 to 2000, house construction became the most important event for rural households. In the five villages, 52.42% households have their houses renovated at least once, and the figure is 39.58% for Longshang, 52.00% for Yubei, 50.00% for Jinhou, 58.00% for Bogumen and 62.00% for Hebian. This is followed by the *hun* marriage and childbearing, consisting of 32.66 and 26.61% of all the households. The *jia* marriages make up 22.18% of the households. The occurrence rates of other events become 18.15, 17.34, 9.68 and 8.47% respectively for household separation, death, children's entrance to higher-level education and change of household head. Of the eight major events shown in Fig. 1.19, house construction has the highest rate of 27.02%, followed by the *hun* marriage, childbearing, the *jia* marriage, household separation, death, further education of children, and change of household head.

Table 1.21 Frequencies of major household events in 5 villages of Zhejiang 1984–2000

	Total	Major events							
		Hun	Jia	Birth	Death	Head change	Household separation	House construction	Children education
Number	195	81	55	66	43	21	45	130	24
As %	78.63	32.66	22.18	26.61	17.34	8.47	18.15	52.42	9.68
Number	533	96	69	81	45	21	52	144	25
As %	100.0	18.01	12.95	15.20	8.44	3.94	9.76	27.02	4.69

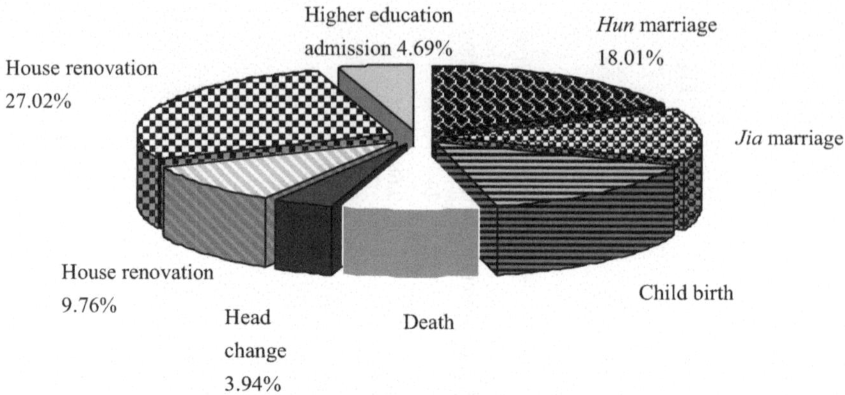

Fig. 1.19 Events for 248 Households in 5 Zhejiang Villages from 1984 to 2000

1.7.2 Frequency and Time Distribution of Events

Since the observation in 1984, due to different stages of lifecycle for households, the major events have occurred at different frequencies in different villages (Fig. 1.20). Of the 248 rural households observed in the five Zhejiang villages, the highest number of major events for a household is 10, including three *hun* marriages, one *jia* marriage, two funerals, three household separations and one childbearing. In terms of frequency, 21.37% households experienced two events, 20.16% experienced one, and 18.15% experienced three. Households with over five events account for 12.10%, and those with no event make up 21.37% (including those who have failed to answer). With regards to village differences, the households which have undergone one event account for 34.00% in Bogumen, 22.00% in Jinhou, and as low as 12.00% in Hebian. The village with the highest percentage for one to three events is Bogumen, involving

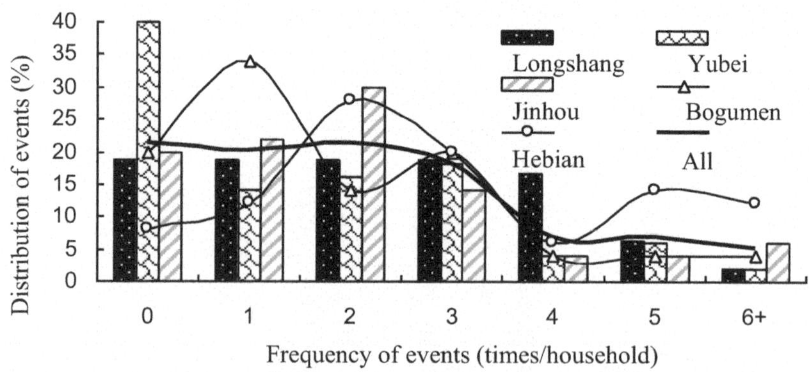

Fig. 1.20 Frequency distribution of major household events in 5 Zhejiang Villages 1984–2000

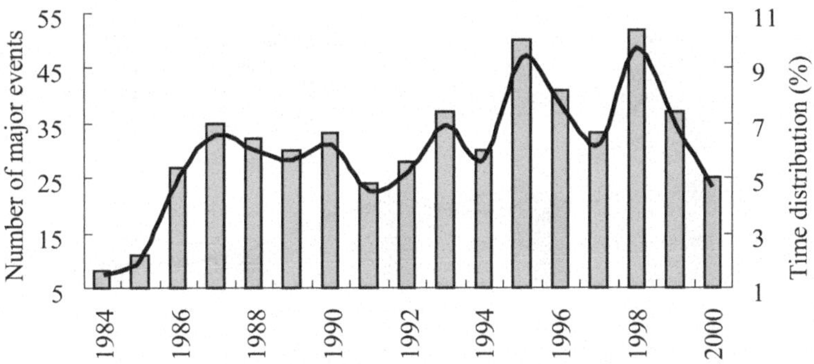

Fig. 1.21 Time distribution of major events in 5 Zhejiang Villages 1984–2000

68.00% of all its households, followed by Jinhou, Hebian and Longshang, with Longshang having the lowest figure of 48.00%. As for households which have experienced five events and above, Hebian has the highest percentage of 26.00%, followed by Hebian of 10.00%, Longshang of 8.33%, and 8.00% for both Yubei and Bogumen.

In terms of time distribution of the events (Fig. 1.21), the frequencies for major household events are generally on the rise over time in the five Zhejiang villages. To be specific, there used to be about 20 events every year in the mid-1980s and 30 events in the early 1990, while the number further increased to around 45 in the middle and late 1990s. Over the 17 observation years from 1984 to 2000, most events occurred in the middle and late 1990s. Especially in 1998 when there appeared 52 major events or a major event for every five households. Comparatively, since the 2000s, there have been less events, about 25 each year or one for every ten households.

1.7.3 Frequencies for Specific Types of Events

In terms of the distribution for marriage and childbearing (Fig. 1.22), with the increase in frequencies, the distribution shows a declining trend. The occurrence rate for one event is 19.35%, for two events 18.95%, for three events 6.05%, and for four or more events 5.24%. For different villages, Longshang has undergone the most major events from 1984 to 2000, with 58.33% households involved. Hebian has the highest occurrence rate of 24.00% for one event, while Bogumen has the lowest figure of 12.00% in this regard. Longshang has the highest rate of 27.08% for two events, while Hebian and Jinhou have the lowest of 16.00%. Meanwhile, Hebian has the highest rate of 22.00% for three and more events, and Yubei has the lowest of 4.00%. Of the 248 households in the five villages in Zhejiang, the highest frequency is seven, including two marriages, two household separations and four childbirths.

As for time distribution (Fig. 1.23), since the observation in 1984, there appeared to be a baby boom in the five villages in the mid-1980s, with the peak number of ten in 1987. Since then, the trend of childbirths became more stable until 1999 when there

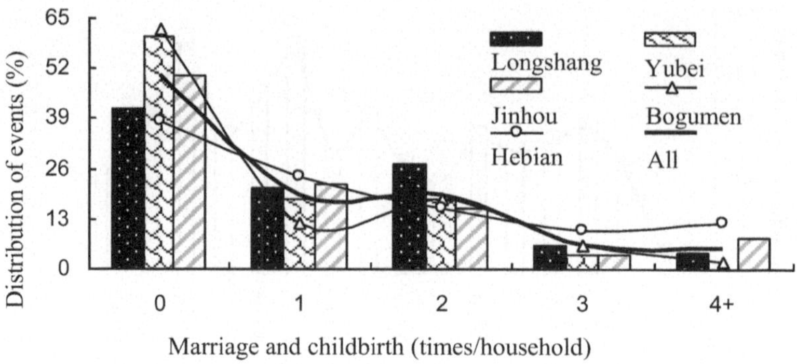

Fig. 1.22 Distribution of marriage and childbearing in 5 Zhejiang Villages 1984–2000

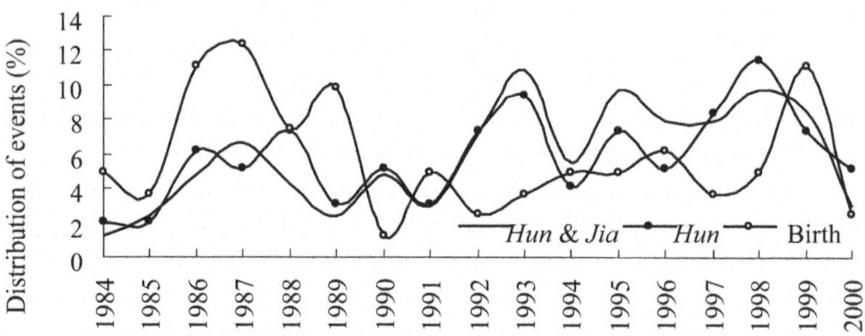

Fig. 1.23 Time distribution of marriage and childbearing in 5 villages of Zhejiang 1984–2000

appeared another high figure of nine. For rural marriages, there emerged periodical peaks at 11, 18 and 16 in 1987, 1993 and 1998 respectively, and the peak figures for marriages were seven in 1988, nine in 1993 and 11 in 1998.

House construction definitely has the greatest impact on rural household economy. Since the start of the observation, house construction has occurred in nearly half of the households. Of all the households under observation, around 116 of these have experienced house construction once, making up 46.77%, and 14 households experienced twice, accounting for 5.65%. For different villages, Hebian has the highest occurrence rate of 62.00%, including 54.00% for one construction and 8.00% for two. Bogumen has the second highest rate of 58.00%, with 50.00% for one construction and 8.00% for two. This is followed by Yubei of 52% and Jinhou of 50.00%, both with one construction only, and Longshang has the lowest rate of 39.58%, including 27.08% for one construction 12.50% for two. As for occurrence time, it is seen from Fig. 1.24 that over the 17 years of observation, there is an oscillating trend for rural house construction. In 1995, as many as 17 households had their house constructed, taking 6.85% of all major events, or 11.81% of all house constructions. The year 1998 is another year with a high occurrence rate of house

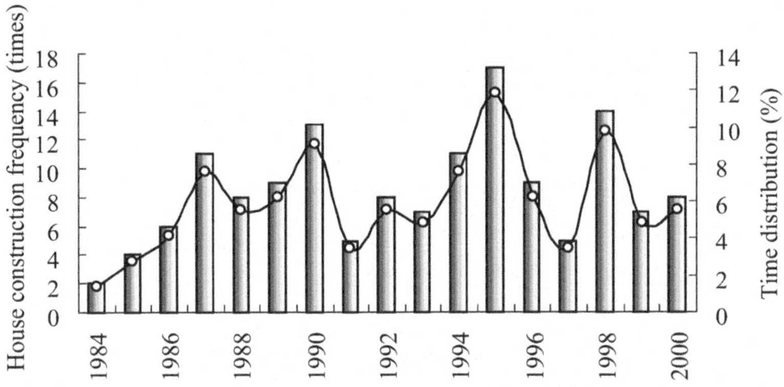

Fig. 1.24 Time distribution of house construction in Zhejiang Villages 1984–2000

construction, accounting for 5.65% of all major events and 9.72% of all constructions for the 17 years. This is followed by 1990 with the corresponding figures of 5.24 and 9.03%.

1.7.4 Impacts of Major Events on Rural Household Economy

As seen in Table 1.22, since the start of the Ninth Five-Year Plan (1996–2000), the economic growth for the observed households in Zhejiang has been related to the major events, mainly in savings and borrowing funds. The occurrence of such events will directly result in the decrease of savings and increase of borrowing funds. Due to the different natures of the events, the main indicators for impact on household economy vary (Fig. 1.25). As the biggest event in terms of funds used, house construction directly leads to sharp increase of borrowing, i.e. in 2000 household net

Table 1.22 Household income growth with major events in 5 villages 1996–2000 (%)

	Number of household residents	Impact on investment		Impact on income	Impact on savings	
		Production	Non-production		Savings	Net borrowing
1996/1995	2.92	−28.53	14.93	22.17	−3.88	23.14
1997/1996	−1.83	−52.46	12.91	17.15	−30.13	−3.90
1998/1997	−3.33	3.37	21.97	−8.29	−19.31	201.30
1999/1998	0.79	9.94	−1.02	−16.89	28.55	−23.88
2000/1999	1.30	14.46	31.69	10.51	−2.58	118.77

Note Numbers of households with seven other major events except household head change: 34 in 1996, 26 in 1997, 45 in 1998, 32 in 1999, and 22 in 2000. Savings = year-end savings + cash in hand. Net borrowing = year-end borrowing − year-end lending

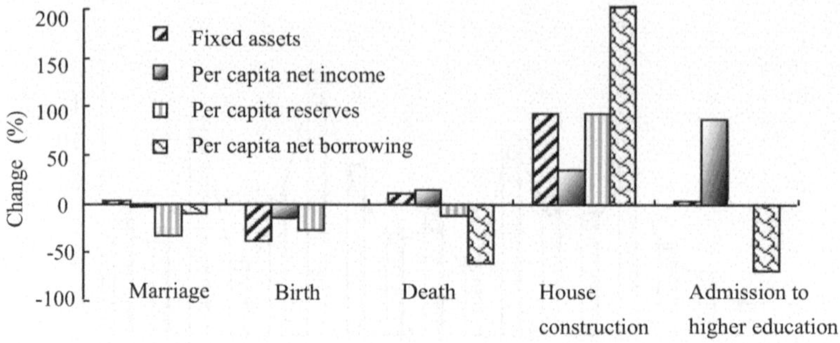

Fig. 1.25 Impacts of major events on household economy in 2000

borrowing rose to 5.68 times that of the previous year. Marriage and childbearing also have considerable impacts on per capita net income, so that both income and year-end reserves decrease as a result. However, such impacts are smaller compared with house construction. In 2000 those households that underwent marriage and childbearing had their per capita income declined by 10.60%, and their per capita reserves dropped by 27.89% compared with 1999.

Annex: Investigations on Observed Households

Since the pilot observation in 1984 and the formal one in 1986, the participating villages and households have made a great contribution to the monitoring of rural economic development in China. The observation system itself has served as a valuable information source for social economic research. Due to the very limited financial support, matching funds had to be made little by little from the central to the local authorities, and one can imagine the difficulties in carrying out the work. Therefore, we initiated a special survey among the involved households to evaluate the data acquired and the coherence of the work.

Table 1.23 shows that the participating households generally believe it is honourable to be involved. It is the sense of honour that has encouraged the villagers to persist for so many years. In terms of reliability, 65.81% of the households in the five villages believe the provided information is very reliable while 34.19% take it fairly reliable. This has proved that most households have done their best to provide the accurate information. For possible future observations, 93.59% of households agree to continue for the sake of honour, rather than for economic returns. Only 2.14% feel it a burden and would like to quit. Such results have provided a solid foundation for our future work and encouraged us to keeping pursuing our research.

Table 1.23 Views of participating households on being observed in 5 villages of Zhejiang

		Feelings of being observed			Data reliability		Future observation		
		Burden	Honour	Other	High	Fair	Continue	Withdraw	Other
All	Sample	5	179	49	154	80	219	5	10
	%	2.15	76.82	21.03	65.81	34.19	93.59	2.14	4.27
LS	Sample	2	27	18	32	15	46	–	1
	%	4.26	57.45	38.30	68.09	31.91	97.87	–	2.13
YB	Sample	3	34	3	30	10	31	4	5
	%	7.50	85.00	7.50	75.00	25.00	77.50	10.00	12.50
JH	Sample	–	38	8	41	6	47	–	–
	%	–	82.61	17.39	87.23	12.77	100.00	–	–
BGM	Sample	–	35	15	17	33	47	–	3
	%	–	70.00	30.00	34.00	66.00	94.00	–	6.00
HB	Sample	–	45	5	34	16	48	1	1
	%	–	90.00	10.00	68.00	32.00	96.00	2.00	2.00

References

Shi, Q. (1999). *Rural households economic growth and development.* Beijing: China Agriculture Press.

Shi, Q., & Hou, R. (2001). Life cycle of farmer's household and the economic operation in Shanxi Province. *Research of Agricultural Modernisation, 22*(2), 65–70.

Chapter 2
Transition in Household Economic Structure and Its Origin

Contents

Q. Shi and Y. Gao, *Sustainable Development of Rural Household Economy*,
https://doi.org/10.1007/978-981-15-2747-0_2

After China's WTO entry in the new century, there have been new challenges and opportunities for both Chinese agricultural development and farmers' income growth. The central government has made a specific deployment[1] to 'strengthen the adjustment of agricultural structure, march into the depth and breadth of agriculture, and compositely improve the quality and efficiency of agriculture' as an important measure for China's agricultural development and farmers' income increase in the new century. It can be seen that structural transformation is the most significant issue in economic income increase. Based on data from the fixed tracking observation of ten villages in Zhejiang, this chapter will focus on the empirical analysis of the changing trend for rural household economic structure and its origin for 1986–2002. The analysis gives an overview of the basic trend in rural household economic development in the developed coastal areas of China.

2.1 Consequence of Structural Adjustment: Changes in Rural Household Income Structure

2.1.1 Income Sources Dependent More on Household Operation

Since the follow-up observations in 1986, the income of farmers in the ten Zhejiang villages has shown a staged upward trend. The evolution of 17 years showed two obvious stagnated or slow periods in the growth of rural household income, i.e. in the late 1980s, and the mid-late 1990s (Fig. 2.1 and Table 2.1). The reason for these two periods is related to the overall macroeconomic environment at that time. After 2000, the general rural household economy was still in a state of fluctuation with mainly a downward trend, while on the contrary rural households in the ten observed villages of Zhejiang saw an increase in their rural household income growth. In 2002, their gross annual household income reached 74,064.50 yuan, an increase of 98.09 and 11.46% from 1995 and 2000 respectively, or an increase of 3.86 times since the beginning of the observation in 1986. Over the 17 years of observation, the annual income growth reached 18.66%, specifically 11.11% since 1995 and 6.74% since 2000. It can be seen that the rate of increase in income has declined over time. In addition to the impact from the slow increase of rural income, another important factor has been the rise in prices (Shi, 2000).

[1]It clearly points out: to continue playing the supporting role of agriculture in the national economy and social development is an important guarantee for the smooth implementation of the Tenth Five-Year Plan. It is necessary to strengthen the position of agriculture as the economic foundation, effectively solve the prominent problems facing rural areas, and ensure agricultural development, farmers' income growth and overall rural stability. In order to accomplish the above goal, the primary countermeasure is to further promote the strategic adjustment of agricultural structure, and improve the quality and efficiency of agriculture as a whole. The Opinions of the State Council on Efforts Relating to Agricultural and Rural Development in 2001, *Zhejiang Daily*, February 13, 2001.

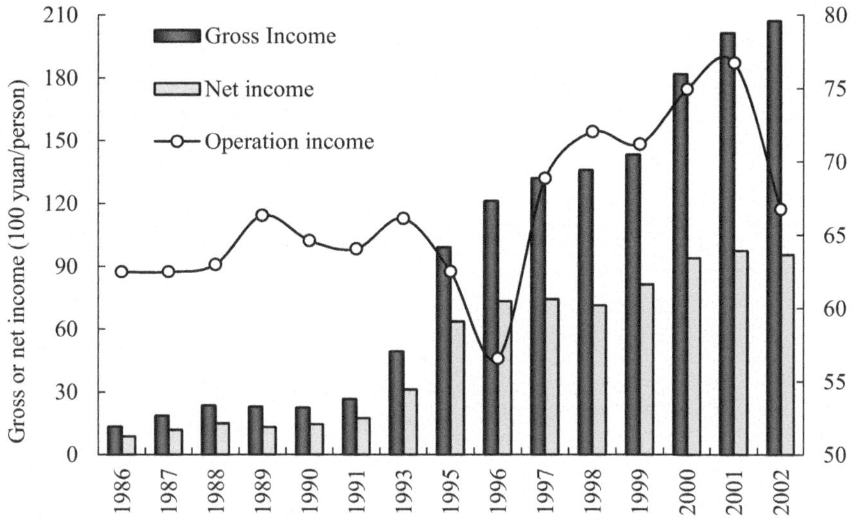

Fig. 2.1 Rural household income increase and its structural change in 10 Zhejiang villages

Meanwhile, the rural per capita income also reached a higher level. In 2002, per capita net income in the 500 observed households in the ten villages was 9540.16 yuan, an increase of 50.21 and 1.70% from the years 1995 and 2000, or an increase of 10.07 times since the beginning of the observation in 1986. Over the 17 years, the growth of rural per capita net income averages at 16.21%, 2.25% lower than that of gross income. Since 1995, the net income growth has been 5.98% and since 2000 the figure has been 0.84%, which is 5.13 and 5.90% slower than that of gross income of the same period respectively. It is clear that the era of high rural household economic growth is gradually ending, being replaced by the arrival of a constant growth. It is seen from the entire development trend that the rural household economy in Zhejiang is developing in such a way, and an important reason for this has been the rapid structural adjustment. The income increase of Zhejiang rural households is the result of the continuous strengthening of household operation. In 2002, operation income of rural households accounted for 66.92% of the total rural income. Although this figure was nearly 10% lower than the top value of 76.64% observed in Zhejiang in 2001, it was still higher than the national average of 65.65% and the average level of 59.57% in the coastal regions in eastern China.[2] In contrast, the percentage of income from collective operation was down to the historical low level of 1.40% from the level of 21.68% at the start of the observation. Meanwhile, the income percentage from agriculture in household operation also reached the lowest point of 18.20%. At the same time, income percentage from migration increased from less than 5% during the initial period of observation to 10.95% in 2002. Although it is not the highest during the entire observation period, it hits a record high in the 2000s.

[2]Source: National Rural Fixed-site Observation Office.

Table 2.1 Composition of rural household income from 10 villages in Zhejiang (%)

	Total (RMB 100/household)	Collective operation	Household operation	Including: agriculture	Migration	Non-borrowing	Others	Net income (RMB/person)
1986	53.45	21.68	62.48	32.87	4.70	5.15	5.99	861.87
1987	72.44	20.61	62.48	29.47	4.23	6.15	6.53	1181.55
1988	91.67	16.66	62.98	28.69	6.49	7.52	6.35	1489.50
1989	87.53	14.52	66.50	31.85	7.10	9.01	2.87	1307.28
1990	83.28	16.44	64.61	37.11	7.52	8.07	3.36	1444.33
1991	97.89	15.27	64.05	34.38	8.06	7.28	5.34	1730.18
1993	190.69	13.77	66.11	28.26	6.38	5.93	7.80	3110.13
1995	373.89	4.93	62.47	29.70	17.05	5.45	10.11	6351.27
1996	456.12	3.80	56.55	23.40	17.27	8.26	14.12	7323.73
1997	488.05	2.69	69.48	24.57	10.72	6.34	10.76	7425.14
1998	497.19	1.90	72.01	26.27	9.44	6.86	9.79	7121.82
1999	523.14	1.98	71.06	23.91	11.78	7.03	8.14	8113.35
2000	664.50	1.63	74.93	21.28	9.41	7.61	6.43	9381.10
2001	725.61	1.55	76.64	18.37	8.94	5.56	7.31	9730.87
2002	740.65	1.40	66.92	18.20	10.95	12.22	8.51	9540.16

Therefore, reliance on and strengthening of household operation is a major source of rural household economic growth in Zhejiang.

2.1.2 *Non-agriculturalisation of Household Operation as an Important Channel for Continuous Income Growth*

While the economic increase of rural household is more dependent on household operation, the reliance on agriculture has sharply declined (Fig. 2.2). The income from agriculture in household operation decreased from 52.61% during the initial period of observation to 27.27% in 2002 (Table 2.2). During the changing process, in the early 1990s, the household operation in Zhejiang alternated between agriculture and non-agriculture. In the late 1990s, it gradually became more dependent on non-agriculture. Since 1995, the share of non-agricultural income in household economy has been steadily rising, while income from agriculture has shown a declining trend. Compared with 1995, non-agricultural income of rural households in 2002 increased by 20.27% over seven years, with an annual increase of 2.90%. Meanwhile, agricultural income was down by 20.27%. Further analysis shows that the sharp decrease of agricultural income was primarily due to the great decline in grain farming, followed by a decline in livestock farming and tree planting, with fishery (marine fishing and aquaculture) being the only rising agricultural sector. In non-agricultural operation, the rise of tertiary industry, i.e. the commercial, catering and service sectors of rural households, became the driving force for the increasing non-agricultural income. In comparison, the income from home industry and transportation has fluctuated. Therefore, the rural household operation structure in Zhejiang has been adjusted to non-agricultural

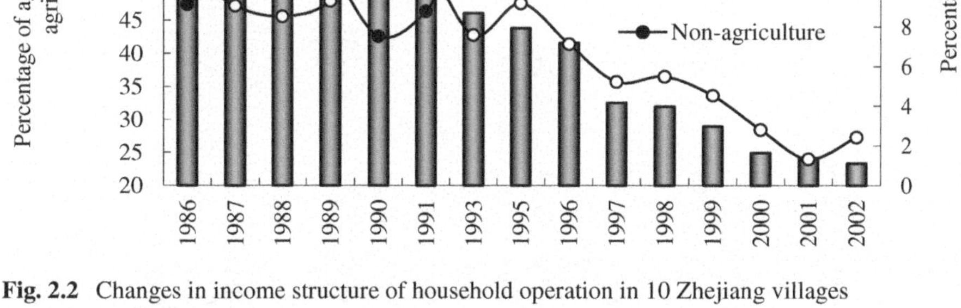

Fig. 2.2 Changes in income structure of household operation in 10 Zhejiang villages

Table 2.2 Income composition of rural households in 10 villages in Zhejiang (%)

	Agriculture	Farming	Grain farming	Orchard planting	Forestry	Animal husbandry	Fishery	Industry	Transportation	Commerce, catering and service
1986	52.61	26.66	19.15	2.74	6.90	11.32	7.73	22.15	12.80	9.24
1987	47.17	22.34	15.02	2.69	4.44	11.00	9.40	32.22	9.11	8.43
1988	45.56	18.84	12.06	2.15	2.76	15.32	8.65	29.93	10.38	9.70
1989	47.89	21.11	14.24	2.48	2.79	16.50	7.49	28.10	10.34	9.94
1990	57.44	24.15	15.67	3.06	2.48	17.58	13.23	15.52	10.30	11.39
1991	53.67	23.23	13.52	4.44	3.11	15.96	11.37	12.78	11.74	16.93
1993	42.74	14.87	8.68	2.00	3.42	14.15	10.31	27.53	7.36	18.76
1995	47.54	12.83	7.93	2.08	1.98	11.92	20.81	22.19	10.73	15.66
1996	41.38	12.05	7.20	2.36	1.36	7.98	20.00	25.53	12.59	17.42
1997	35.69	7.15	4.17	1.21	1.65	7.28	19.61	20.31	8.82	31.43
1998	36.48	7.36	3.96	1.57	1.18	6.64	21.30	13.96	7.52	39.34
1999	33.60	5.79	2.96	1.34	0.89	6.61	20.31	16.01	8.27	40.55
2000	28.40	3.76	1.64	0.92	0.79	5.02	18.83	26.20	7.78	35.98
2001	23.95	3.05	1.38	0.81	0.70	4.85	15.36	32.86	6.14	35.51
2002	27.27	3.41	1.11	1.08	1.13	4.65	18.07	25.06	7.26	38.79

operation, the third-industry operation in particular, which is followed by marine fishing and aquaculture.

2.1.3 *Migration as Important Supplement for Continuous Income Growth*

With the rural institutional reform, the operation structure of rural areas and households has been adjusted, and so has the migration employment structure of rural labour. In terms of income composition for migrants, private and joint-stock cooperative enterprises have gradually become the main sources of income for rural migrant workers. In 2002, of the income from migrant work for the household members in the ten Zhejiang villages, 38.59% came from private enterprises, 23.50% from joint-stock enterprises, and only 11.31% from state and collective enterprises (Table 2.3). Compared with 1995, there were a 23.73% increase and a 16.06% increase of income from private and joint-stock enterprises respectively, but a 2.76% decrease of income from state and collective enterprises. It can be inferred that in absorbing rural labour, private and joint-stock cooperative enterprises have been playing a major role while the role of state and collective enterprises has been weakening. Certainly, the occurrence of this process has been partially attributed to the impact brought about by the reform of some collective or state-owned enterprises.

Table 2.3 Income composition from migration labour in 10 villages in Zhejiang (%)

	Private enterprise	Collective enterprise	Joint-stock enterprise	Partnership	Private enterprise	Foreign-funded enterprise	Others
1986	23.17	23.07*	4.23**	–	–	–	49.54
1987	21.40	27.88*	4.57**	–	–	–	46.14
1988	22.36	23.75*	13.33**	–	–	–	40.56
1989	19.26	27.33*	9.57**	–	–	–	43.84
1990	24.97	17.72*	14.37**	–	–	–	42.93
1991	23.90	17.99*	12.13**	–	–	–	45.97
1993	16.26	11.54	3.09	29.64	14.34	–	39.48
1995	5.03	9.03	7.43	7.33	14.86	0.14	56.18
1996	4.04	8.42	11.55	3.71	14.34	0.06	57.88
1997	4.33	12.94	20.66	1.66	26.71	0.00	33.70
1998	7.79	14.75	24.43	2.25	33.03	1.02	16.72
1999	7.82	6.49	31.34	4.32	33.25	0.83	15.95
2000	4.54	2.73	30.19	5.65	37.61	0.80	18.48
2001	3.54	5.36	25.41	10.97	34.86	0.89	18.96
2002	7.10	4.21	23.50	5.70	38.59	0.83	20.08

*Income from enterprises in other townships; **Income from enterprises in other village groups; '–' Not listed

2.1.4 Non-borrowing Activities as Non-negligible Contents for Continuous Economic Growth

In the rural households under observation, non-borrowing activities have become a non-negligible source of continuous economic growth. In 2002, non-borrowing income reached 2529.10 yuan per person (Table 2.4). Although half of the income was from sales of household productive fixed assets, it does indicate that, in addition to income from operation and labour service, earnings from non-borrowing activities has played an important role in rural household economic growth. In fact, over the entire observation period of 17 years, it is clear that income from non-borrowing activities showed a continuous upward trend, increased from less than 100 yuan in the beginning to the current over 1000 yuan. This type of income was mainly based on gift giving and property sales among relatives and friends, accounting for about 60–80% of the income in this category. In terms of the trend, the percentage of the remittances or cash brought back by migrant members showed an obvious decline. There were also decreases in the proportion of salaries for state employees or state subsidies and in gift giving from relatives and friends. On the contrary, income from sales of household properties was on the rise. Therefore, property sales have gradually become the fundamental reason for the increasing income of rural households from non-borrowing activities. Since 1995, such income has been averaged at about 30% of the non-borrowing income, being as high as 61.29 and 69.65% in 1996 and 2002, with 32.76% in 2001 at the lowest level.

2.2 Structural Adjustment and Change of Resource Utilisation in Rural Households

In studying the structural adjustment concerning rural households, on the one hand, it is necessary to examine their income structure change, and on the other hand, it is necessary to explore the changes not only in resource utilisation, but also in conditions of household human and material capital reserves. It is seen from the previous analysis that the household income structure has been changing over the 17 years of observation. In fact, the change is to a large extent decided by the shift in both household human and material capital reserves, as well as resource utilisation. In order to illustrate this, I have carried out research on changes in household human capital reserves in rural areas and in resource utilisation.

Table 2.4 Non-borrowing income and its sources for rural households in Zhejiang (%)

	Per capita income (yuan)	Remittance or cash from migrant workers	Wage for employees	State subsidy	#Survey subsidy	Giving from relatives and friends	#Giving from relatives and friends within rural areas	Property sales	#Sales of productive fixed assets	Other income
1986	69.02	5.79	17.69	4.28	1.18	46.01	41.81	15.93	9.10	10.29
1987	113.64	4.49	13.49	5.80	4.31	32.05	29.98	29.13	21.65	15.04
1988	176.38	2.91	11.01	2.88	1.65	49.25	47.23	21.25	12.51	12.70
1989	205.88	2.92	10.25	3.02	1.83	45.90	43.70	29.98	25.92	7.93
1990	180.55	2.68	11.33	4.17	2.04	48.58	44.38	20.31	14.12	12.92
1991	193.39	2.61	10.89	4.36	1.98	45.26	44.04	26.53	20.34	10.35
1993	292.26	1.79	5.58	3.67	2.07	34.24	30.22	43.68	39.20	11.04
1995	539.41	2.26	9.15	2.68	1.68	34.49	29.63	43.34	30.99	8.09
1996	1001.21	2.94	3.23	1.62	0.87	26.28	23.26	61.29	54.26	4.64
1997	837.38	2.66	8.35	2.44	1.62	41.24	39.33	38.48	27.85	6.84
1998	931.45	3.84	11.53	1.96	1.37	32.85	31.25	40.37	38.46	9.45
1999	1006.17	2.20	9.15	2.33	1.06	40.96	38.98	34.81	15.29	10.55
2000	1381.78	1.50	7.09	1.84	1.05	27.12	25.87	42.30	38.75	20.15
2001	1118.60	2.50	10.01	2.48	1.32	28.51	24.58	32.76	30.92	23.74
2002	2529.10	1.30	4.48	2.30	0.62	15.44	14.42	69.65	54.45	6.83

Note # as part of the previous category

2.2.1 *Education Level of Rural Labour Is Essential to Household Economic Growth*

As the major driving force for household economic growth, the household human capital reserves in the ten Zhejiang villages have been on the rise annually (Table 2.5). In terms of education, household labours generally received education below the level of primary school during the early stage of observation, with an illiterate rate of 23.92%. Over the 17 years, the educational level for rural labour has been substantially improved, with a significant drop in the number of rural labours educated at primary level and below, and an obvious increase in those educated at junior high or above. Up until 2002, about 48.48% of the rural labours had been educated at junior high or above, including 9.02% at senior high and above, which had increased by 16.92 and 4.08% respectively compared to the initial observation period. On the contrary, those with primary education or below decreased to 51.52%, including a 11.13% decline in illiteracy, or decreased by 16.92 and 12.79% for primary education and illiteracy respectively compared to the early observation period. With better education quality, technical quality of rural labour force also substantially improved,

Table 2.5 Labour force scale and the education and technical level in ten villages (%)

	Labour (per household)	Education level				Technical training*		Male percentage
		Illiterate	Primary school	Junior high	Senior high+	Special skills	Trained	
1986	2.56	23.92	44.52	26.62	4.94	18.87	3.90	53.35
1987	2.53	23.11	44.29	28.04	4.55	16.76	4.66	53.95
1988	2.54	21.80	44.93	28.61	4.66	17.72	5.54	53.67
1989	2.48	21.56	43.94	29.93	4.57	18.01	6.87	53.25
1990	2.50	20.33	42.95	31.91	4.81	17.25	5.64	53.17
1991	2.48	19.94	41.91	33.07	5.08	17.89	5.67	53.46
1993	2.60	16.67	43.24	34.41	5.68	1.46	6.45	52.61
1995	2.58	14.55	42.57	36.30	6.58	6.81	9.98	52.79
1996	2.59	15.08	43.08	34.96	6.88	5.72	9.59	53.36
1997	2.50	14.55	42.45	37.01	6.00	5.92	10.15	54.12
1998	2.49	14.93	42.13	35.71	7.22	5.22	9.87	54.09
1999	2.50	13.74	40.73	37.78	7.75	5.35	10.06	53.91
2000	2.51	13.81	40.22	37.83	8.14	5.59	9.66	54.19
2001	2.46	12.19	40.94	38.42	8.45	5.36	9.34	53.21
2002	2.37	11.13	40.39	39.46	9.02	4.89	9.53	52.95

**Note* This index refers the rate of labours with technical skills before 1991; and the rate of labours with technical titles after 1993

and there has been an obvious upward trend in the percentage of household members who have received professional education or technical training, increased from 3.90% in the initial period of the observation to 9.53% in 2002, more than doubled in 17 years. However, it is also noticed that since the mid-1990s, this indicator has fluctuated and the reasons behind deserve further exploration. In terms of gender differences, there has been a majority of male labours in the ten Zhejiang villages and the percentage of males has been on a gradual rise.

2.2.2 *Non-agricultural Employment as an Important Factor for Rural Economic Growth*

In terms of the occupation changes for labour in Zhejiang (Table 2.6),[3] the percentages of agricultural labours and rural migrant workers of total labour force have declined, especially the latter, while the percentage of those engaged in enterprise operation or directly employed has increased significantly. This reflects the non-agriculturalising trend of rural employment. Further, there has been a polarising trend for famers' employment. For one thing, the proportion of rural labour directly engaged in non-agricultural operations rapidly increased before maintained a stable trend. For another, the share of rural labour directly employed has been rising sharply. Such a result is on the one hand related to rural casual workers' being changed into employees after the reform of enterprises and on the other hand related to the ever-increasing capital threshold of enterprise operation while the rural income growth has been stagnated.

2.2.3 *Non-agriculturalised Employment of Household Operation as an Important Guarantee for Promoting Household Economic Growth*

Data from the ten villages have shown that household labour employment has experienced a rise-and-fall trend over time. The average labour required for the households under observation was 313.39 in 1986 and 308.19 in 1990. Then it increased from 325.19 in 1991 to 350.94 in 1995, and 379.67 in 1999 before it declined to 372.87 in 2000 and 333.34 in 2002. In general, rural labour required has been on the rise with an increase of 19.95 in number, or by 6.37% over time. Such a trend is contrary to the change of number in the rural household labour.[4] This means that with the acceleration of non-agriculturalising of family operation, households have become

[3]The division of occupations for rural labours is based on the number of working hours in the whole year, and is further based on the amount of income earned in the same amount of time.

[4]During the entire observation period, the average labour number in a Zhejiang rural household reduced from 2.61 in 1986 to 2.48 in 2002.

Table 2.6 Employment composition of rural households in ten Zhejiang villages (%)

	1993	1995	1996	1997	1998	1999	2000	2001	2002
Rural labour	39.55	34.75	34.42	34.93	36.52	35.46	34.80	34.36	30.94
– Agriculture only	25.19	22.83	22.82	21.58	24.08	23.24	23.30	22.99	20.24
– Agriculture dominated	14.36	11.92	11.60	13.35	12.44	12.22	11.49	11.37	10.71
Rural casual workers	27.73	23.30	19.10	15.19	13.56	11.74	11.49	9.18	9.78
– Collective enterprises	15.28	11.69	9.59	7.19	5.94	4.23	4.15	3.98	2.78
– State-owned enterprises	2.30	2.32	1.62	1.44	1.44	2.00	1.52	0.97	0.93
Collective enterprise managers	0.84	0.46	0.31	0.56	0.48	0.32	0.48	0.57	0.42
Individual partnership operators	13.29	14.01	17.71	17.99	16.93	16.53	16.60	17.38	17.20
Joint-stock enterprise operators	1.92	1.63	2.40	2.24	2.01	2.08	2.00	1.79	1.85
Partnership enterprise operators	0.69	0.85	0.39	0.32	0.72	0.72	0.72	0.32	0.42
Private enterprise operators	0.46	1.16	2.55	3.12	4.17	4.63	4.23	6.26	5.40
Employed workers	6.53	11.76	11.76	13.43	13.56	16.53	18.44	18.20	21.42
Officials and those in education and science	2.00	2.01	2.01	1.76	1.69	1.44	1.76	1.54	1.60
Others	6.99	10.06	9.36	10.47	10.35	10.54	9.50	10.40	10.96

Note 1. Rural casual workers refer to the rural labours engaged in the second and third industry in rural collective enterprises, state-owned enterprises and public institutions throughout the year for most of their time

2. Employed workers refer to those employed by partnership, joint-stock, private-owned and foreign-funded enterprises, and those employed by non-state-owned or collective enterprises and public institutions, such as individual or partnership industrial and commercial units

more capable in providing employment opportunities for rural society (which will be further discussed later). Therefore, the acceleration process of non-agriculturalising of household operation is an important way to solve the current employment problem of rural labour. This also indicates the potential to solve farmers' problems by the development of farmers themselves. In order to turn potential into reality, the government shall further lower the threshold for developing non-agricultural activities in policy making.

According to Table 2.7, the employment structure of household operation in Zhejiang has shown a non-agricultural and non-farming trend (Fig. 2.3). The proportions of labour engaged in agriculture and food crop farming dropped from 72.08 and 29.66% in the beginning of observation to 45.23 and 5.41% in 2002, with a decrease of 26.85 and 24.25% over the period of 17 years. Meanwhile the proportions of labour engaged in fishery and non-agriculture have increased by 10.00 and 26.85% respectively. In non-agriculture employment, household commercial, catering and service has experienced the fastest growth in terms of labour use with the proportion of labour engaged increased from 6.42% in 1986 to 27.30% in 2002, or an increase by 20.88% in 17 years. Yet, despite the rising trend, the proportion of labour in family industry is much smaller than in the commercial, catering and service sector, with only 6.31%. Why? We have found out previously in analysis on rural non-agricultural paths that during the period when household capital reserve remains low, the commercial, catering and service is the first choice for rural household non-agriculturalisation. Only when rural household capital reserve reaches a certain level, could family industry be considered as one of the choices (Shi & Zhang, 2000). In other words, labour engaged in household operation in Zhejiang tends to be in the commercial, catering and service sector, indicating that during the process of non-agriculturalisation, rural household capital reserves, human capital in particular, have been very limited. Therefore, further capital accumulation is needed for the future development of family industry.

2.2.4 Non-agricultural Capital Investment as Another Guarantee for Driving Rural Household Economic Growth

Data from Zhejiang have shown that the amount of capital invested in household operation has increased significantly (Fig. 2.4 and Table 2.8). Over the 17 years, capital invested in household operation has increased by 18.18 times, from 1589.64 yuan in 1986 to 30,494.80 yuan in 2002. Such an increase is calculated in current price, and if inflation is taken into consideration and retail price index used for conversion, the increase is as high as six times. This trend is consistent with the changing requirement of labour in rural households. This has indicated that with the acceleration of non-agriculturalisation, rural households need a certain amount of material capital to guarantee their capability in providing employment opportunities

Table 2.7 Employment structure in household operation in ten Zhejiang Villages (%)

	Agriculture	Farming	Food crop farming	Orchard planting	Forestry	Animal husbandry	Fishery	Industry	Transportation	Commercial, catering and service
1986	72.08	42.26	29.66	3.08	2.15	19.65	8.03	8.49	6.71	6.42
1987	70.79	40.76	26.32	3.11	1.65	20.44	7.94	10.59	5.45	7.05
1988	67.57	37.56	23.64	3.17	1.49	19.84	8.68	12.83	5.27	7.56
1989	71.15	38.95	24.24	3.28	1.96	22.03	8.21	6.47	5.28	10.23
1990	69.13	37.68	22.51	3.89	1.89	20.72	8.83	7.15	4.19	11.22
1991	66.17	35.97	19.48	5.01	2.11	20.40	7.70	8.51	4.80	12.39
1993	61.99	30.35	14.35	4.20	2.14	21.63	7.86	10.16	5.34	15.04
1995	52.38	22.84	12.11	3.61	1.96	16.97	10.62	13.57	7.66	17.81
1996	56.67	24.71	13.12	3.90	2.23	15.17	14.56	8.72	7.48	20.97
1997	50.50	21.57	10.87	3.44	2.45	14.80	11.68	11.69	8.11	23.17
1998	50.87	19.82	9.76	3.20	2.17	13.29	15.59	10.90	7.36	24.77
1999	47.69	17.96	8.92	3.17	1.98	12.68	15.08	12.80	7.17	24.64
2000	44.07	15.32	6.34	2.85	1.52	11.73	15.51	13.69	7.78	26.33
2001	44.81	15.80	6.59	3.78	2.15	12.03	14.83	14.33	7.27	26.16
2002	45.23	14.29	5.41	4.13	2.32	10.60	18.03	14.80	5.72	27.30

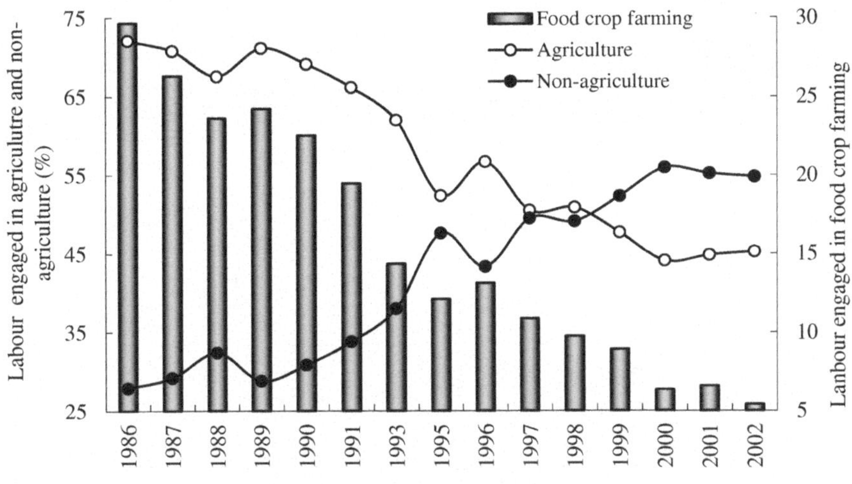

Fig. 2.3 Changes in employment structure of household operation in 10 Zhejiang villages

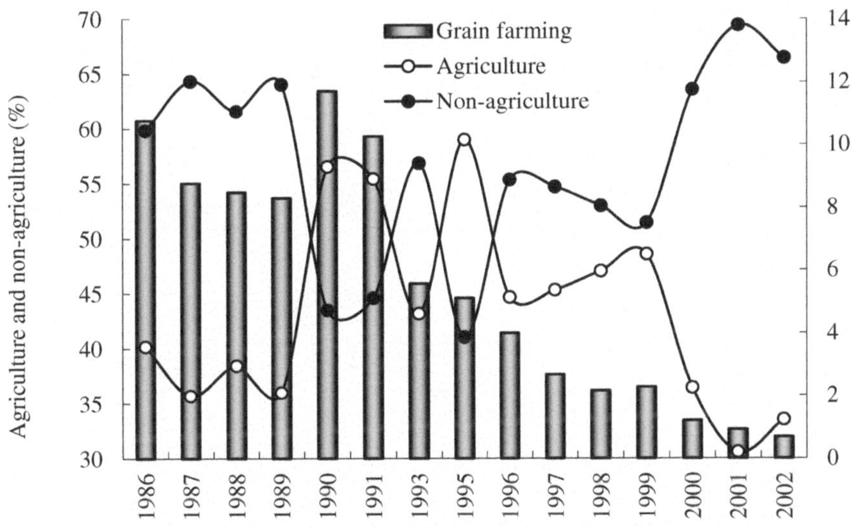

Fig. 2.4 Changes of investment structure in rural household operation

for society. This can be proved by the change of expenditure on labour use for rural households. In 1986, the average number of workers needed in rural households in the ten Zhejiang villages was 11.57 with the expenditure of 63.43 yuan. The corresponding figures were 151.72 and 3479.65 yuan in 2002, also seen as an increase by 12.11 workers and 53.86 times of expenditure over 17 years. This indicates that the cost of labour employed in rural household operation is getting higher as society develops. Labour cost has increased by 3.19 times in 17 years, from 5.48 yuan per

Table 2.8 Changes in investment structure of rural household operation in Zhejiang (%)

	Agriculture	Farming	Food crop farming	Orchard planting	Forestry	Animal husbandry	Fishery	Industry	Transportation	Commercial, catering and service
1986	40.18	14.61	10.76	1.66	1.16	15.04	9.38	36.18	13.31	9.13
1987	35.69	11.97	8.76	1.35	0.54	12.91	10.28	49.36	8.35	5.92
1988	38.43	11.70	8.47	1.39	0.32	16.26	10.16	41.92	8.55	10.29
1989	35.97	11.69	8.29	1.74	0.42	14.40	9.47	46.71	8.95	7.40
1990	56.52	16.64	11.70	2.58	0.49	21.24	18.15	23.56	11.32	6.20
1991	55.42	16.44	10.25	3.47	0.75	20.62	17.61	16.68	14.52	12.04
1993	43.16	9.11	5.56	1.71	0.79	20.59	12.66	41.83	6.89	7.63
1995	58.98	7.51	5.10	1.27	0.52	17.72	33.22	22.34	8.92	9.16
1996	44.66	5.78	3.99	0.98	0.40	9.64	28.83	32.81	11.55	10.66
1997	45.31	4.03	2.67	0.71	0.38	8.42	32.49	25.83	7.65	20.43
1998	47.02	3.38	2.15	0.54	0.45	8.42	34.77	15.21	5.57	31.84
1999	48.55	3.63	2.27	0.60	0.26	8.83	35.84	16.78	8.21	26.01
2000	36.42	2.19	1.20	0.40	0.35	5.78	28.09	35.80	6.17	20.81
2001	30.57	1.71	0.92	0.43	0.16	5.39	23.32	43.67	5.37	19.97
2002	33.53	2.01	0.68	0.51	0.39	5.36	25.77	29.22	5.54	31.10

labour day in 1986 to 22.93 yuan per labour day in 2002.[5] The rising labour cost means a higher capital threshold for rural household non-agriculturalisation. When capital reserves are relatively limited, it becomes the inevitable choice for rural households to select a non-agricultural industry with a low capital threshold.

According to Table 2.8, the investment structure in rural household operation in Zhejiang has shown a non-agricultural trend (Fig. 2.4). To be specific, it is a trend of non-farming and non-livestock herding. Compared with labour use, investment is more inclined to non-agricultural while its structure change is less obvious. This indicates that during the process of non-agriculturalisation in household operation, capital flows are at the forefront. It is under the guidance of capital investment that the non-agricultural labour use has started to accelerate. In the initial period of our observation, the investment proportions in agriculture, food crop farming, and animal husbandry started as 40.18, 10.76 and 15.04%, which shifted to 33.53, 0.68 and 5.36% respectively in 2002, translating to a decline of 6.65, 10.08 and 9.68% in 17 years. Meanwhile, investment proportions in fishery and non-agriculture were increased by 16.39 and 6.65%. In non-agriculture, most investment took place in the family industry, and investment with the highest growth rate took place in the rural household commercial, catering and service, which changed from 36.18 and 9.13% in 1986 to 29.22 and 31.10% in 2002 respectively. In terms of the structure change, investment in family industry has been going through some transformations compared with labour use. While there have been fluctuations for investment in household commercial, catering and service, investment in this sector has been generally on the rise. In fact, despite the general rising trend, there appeared an obvious drop in the late 1990 with a recovery in 2002. Compared to 1998, investment in commercial, catering and service in 2002 was actually 0.74% lower. Further explanation will be given later in the analysis of the origins of the changes. Therefore, over the 17 years, great changes have taken place in household operation investment structure with clear investment orientations in the ten Zhejiang villages. In the new century, farmers in Zhejiang are depending on fishery, family industry as well as commercial, catering and service as the important support for their income growth.

2.2.5 *Simplification of Crop Farming to Ensure Increase of Farmers' Income*

According to the data observed in the ten villages in Zhejiang, with the non-agricultural tendency towards labour employment and investment, farmland use has been simplified, and the multiple cropping index for farming has shown a downward trend. In 1986, the index was 223.75%, which was adjusted to 189.87% in 1995, then further down to 136.05% in 2000, and even further to 114.80% in 2002. Crop farming

[5]Labour cost has been increased to over 25 yuan per labour day since 1995, and hit 30.64 yuan per labour day in 2000 after continuous rise. It remained at 30.90 yuan per labour day in 2001, and dropped sharply in 2002.

has been changed from the traditional double-season to single-season. Before 1995, food grain planting stood at over 75% of all rural household crop farming (Table 2.9). Since 1995, there has been a downward trend, when the figure decreased to 67.49% in 2000, and further dropped to 65.49% in 2002, with a decrease of nearly 10% compared with the level of 75.44% in 1995. For food grain farming, paddy rice planting has been the most common form, increasing from 87.82% of total food grain farming in 1993 to 89.61% in 2002. Such a result is related on the one hand to the general good expectations for the national food grain supply, and on the other, to the rapid development of agricultural technology. Data from 17 years of observation show that the grain crop yield for rural households increased from 344.82 kg per *mu*[6] in 1986 to 373.75 kg per *mu* in 1995 and further to 429.89 kg per *mu* in 2002. Due to factors such as the increase in yields, decrease in household population and low efficiency in grain crop farming, rural households in Zhejiang have reduced grain field areas, and agricultural land use (Fig. 2.5). With the continuous implementation of 'profitable agriculture' in Zhejiang in recent years, planting structure of rural households has tended to 'increase vegetables and reduce grains'. Proportions of vegetable and rapeseed planting were increased from 7.71 and 4.41% in 1993 to 15.17 and 6.42% in 2002. This structural change would certainly improve the current situation of low efficiency in agriculture.

2.3 Origin of Structural Adjustments: Changes in Resource Use Efficiency of Rural Households

As market economy develops, rural economy in China has shifted from the conventional development with just quantity-based targets to development with both quality and quantity goals. Structural adjustments are considered as the most important strategy in China's economic development and growth in the new century. However, for rural development based on the rural household economic institution, the structural adjustments are more related to policy changes in macro-economic development. According to my previous analysis,[7] in order to realise changes in economic structure of rural households, policy making has to be in line with the rational economic behaviour of rural households.

[6]*Mu* is the measurement unit for land, 1 *mu* = 1/15 ha.

[7]According to my previous analysis, the changes in rural household economic structure are based on utilisation efficiency of household economic resources as the first priority. Namely, rural households behave according to the economic rational principles (Shi, 1999: Chap. 4).

Table 2.9 Grain farming and structural change for rural households in Zhejiang (*mu*, %)

	Planting area	Grains	Wheat	Rice	Maize	Cash crops	Cotton	Rapeseed	Other sown areas	Vegetables
1986	6.48	75.43	–	–	–	8.23	–	–	16.34	–
1987	6.18	76.16	–	–	–	8.67	–	–	15.17	–
1988	5.88	75.70	–	–	–	8.80	–	–	15.50	–
1989	5.56	75.12	–	–	–	8.34	–	–	16.55	–
1990	5.72	75.67	–	–	–	8.49	–	–	15.84	–
1991	5.32	75.90	–	–	–	10.66	–	–	13.44	–
1993	4.51	75.44	1.00	66.25	0.57	5.89	0.35	4.41	18.67	7.71
1995	4.12	75.49	0.46	70.87	0.08	7.65	0.69	6.34	16.86	6.53
1996	4.05	74.17	0.35	68.84	0.09	7.36	0.71	6.27	18.47	6.83
1997	3.64	73.32	0.34	69.07	0.08	7.21	0.67	6.37	19.46	9.14
1998	3.46	69.60	0.54	64.91	0.34	7.11	0.86	5.73	23.28	12.95
1999	3.18	74.38	0.69	69.99	0.68	7.75	0.44	6.64	17.88	12.38
2000	2.53	67.49	0.55	63.55	0.68	9.32	0.28	8.15	23.18	15.75
2001	2.12	71.76	0.00	67.79	0.95	10.19	0.55	7.65	18.05	13.43
2002	1.69	65.49	0.08	58.68	0.54	12.21	0.14	6.42	22.30	15.17

Note '–' indicates that this item was not surveyed

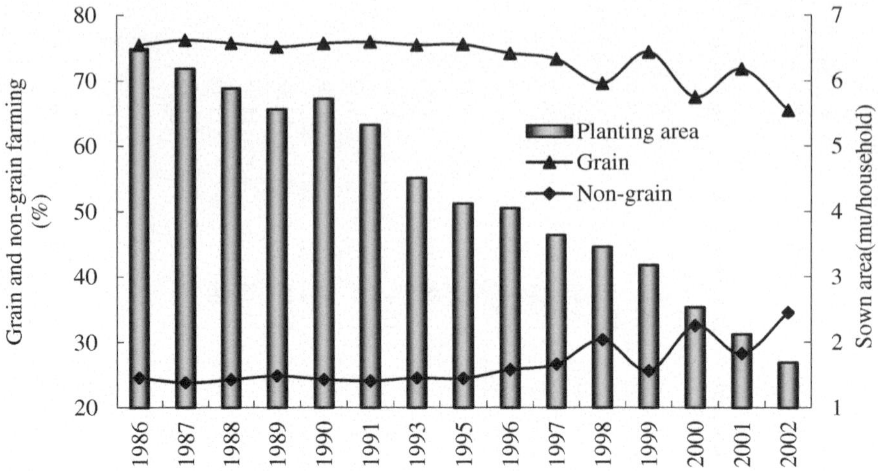

Fig. 2.5 Grain farming scale and structural change for rural households in Zhejiang

2.3.1 *Efficiency in Land Use and Its Change*

The efficiency change in rural household land use indicates that it is influenced by the allocation of limited land resources,[8] and with the rise of the labour opportunity cost the overall efficiency has deteriorated (Table 2.10 and Fig. 2.6). It suggests that it will an inevitable choice for farmers in Zhejiang to 'leave the land' if they would like to increase income. In fact, farmers in the ten Zhejiang villages are doing so. Agricultural income, farming income in particular, has played a negligible role in rural household income, which is seen clearly in Table 2.2.

2.3.2 *Labour Use Efficiency and Its Changes*

Similarly, from the perspective of labour use efficiency change (Table 2.11), the growing differences in labour use for agriculture and non-agriculture have shown that efficiency in agricultural land use is the lowest, and becoming more and more unprofitable (Fig. 2.7). There is no doubt that the non-agricultural labour use of rural households is entirely decided by the comparative labour productivity associated with different types of work. Even within the non-agricultural sector, the more labour use in commercial, catering and service stems from its much higher labour efficiency than in industry and other non-agricultural segmentations. Therefore, it can be concluded that

[8]In our previous research on behaviour studies concerning household scale operation in Zhejiang, we have found out that with the increase of operation scale, the household distribution exits a 'U' shape, while the income and efficiency in land use shows an inverted 'U', indicating the current system of land allocation is unable to encourage farmland use efficiency (Chen, Shi, & Jiang, 2000).

Table 2.10 Changes in farmland utilisation efficiency in household operation in Zhejiang (yuan/*mu*)

	Agriculture and forestry	Farming	Crops	Grains	Cash crops	Other crops	Garden farming	Woodland farming	Labour cost (yuan/person)
1986	13.17	−18.74	−12.33	−8.38	−31.56	−20.87	17.51	38.05	5.48
1987	21.67	2.60	−4.38	2.23	−18.34	−29.61	52.39	36.85	5.71
1988	0.24	−33.38	−21.31	−20.02	−24.82	−25.64	15.72	27.15	7.23
1989	15.54	2.61	−1.90	9.26	−38.63	−34.07	24.55	25.36	7.50
1990	−2.88	−28.70	−16.26	−7.08	−21.06	−57.54	0.24	17.52	8.60
1991	14.27	2.58	−6.68	6.42	−17.51	−72.08	51.02	21.18	8.48
1993	−62.51	−234.45	−142.61	−69.21	−314.58	−384.92	−134.63	43.27	19.05
1995	39.48	34.51	21.57	63.51	−226.46	−53.64	19.86	42.43	25.71
1996	67.32	144.32	62.86	102.62	−114.58	−26.11	169.79	23.82	22.89
1997	−22.65	−146.43	−102.97	−53.24	−198.24	−255.01	−55.41	46.13	28.12
1998	−1.24	−38.78	−68.14	−13.98	−369.03	−138.13	111.27	21.32	28.29
1999	−57.20	−174.72	−171.93	−131.16	−338.11	−269.55	34.90	13.40	29.17
2000	−47.33	−177.42	−198.74	−136.45	−249.46	−359.66	23.39	26.11	30.64
2001	−58.93	−210.82	−210.83	−152.54	−327.97	−376.42	−91.22	22.79	30.90
2002	33.32	−8.00	−48.94	−64.04	132.47	−103.90	58.86	53.68	22.93

Note Efficiency in agriculture and forestry = (income − expenditure − labour input × labour cost) ÷ (farmland + garden + woodland); efficiency in farming = (income − expenditure − labour input × labour cost) ÷ (farmland + garden); efficiency in crop planting = (income − expenditure − labour input × labour cost) ÷sown area; efficiency in garden and woodland use = (income − expenditure − labour input × labour cost) ÷ garden or woodland plot area

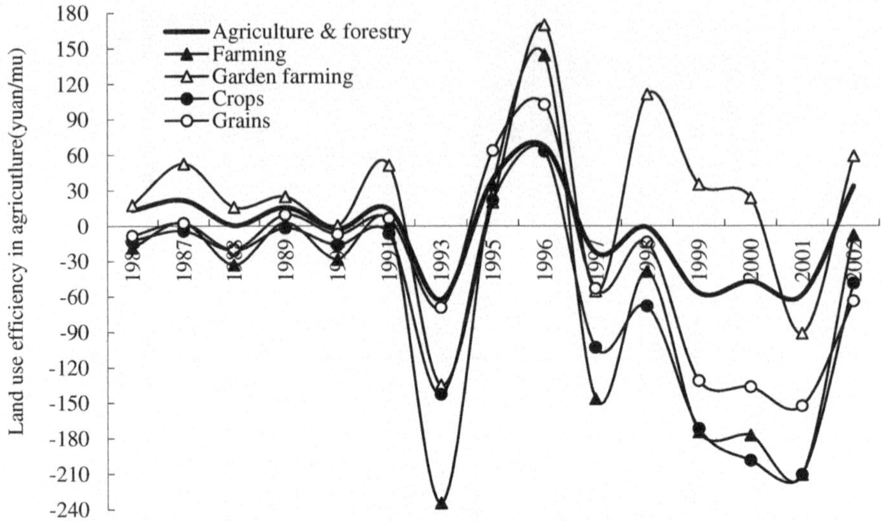

Fig. 2.6 Changes in land use efficiency in rural households of 10 villages in Zhejiang

labour use efficiency has become the theoretical foundation or principle in guiding households regarding labour input.

2.3.3 *Investment Efficiency and Its Changes*

From the investment trend of rural households (Table 2.12), the non-agriculturalised flow of household operation investment is also decided by the increasing investment difference between agriculture and non-agriculture (Fig. 2.8). Although the difference is not as obvious as that of labour use efficiency, the opposite changing directions of capital use efficiency in agriculture and non-agriculture at least indicate that in coastal Zhejiang returns from agriculture investment has been deteriorating. This is also a trend that has helped rural households make a rational investment decision—to reduce agriculture investment and increase non-agricultural input instead. In non-agricultural investment, input in commercial, catering and service is much higher than that in industry, indicating that rural households are sure to prefer commerce to industry. Thus, for rural households, in making decisions concerning investment in different industries, the investment return is an important indicator.

In summary, it is found out that in rural household operation, the structural change is a continuous process. It not only exists in coastal areas with a more developed rural economy, but also in under-developed inland areas (Shi, 1999). In addition, this type of process has existed across Chinese history, from ancient past up until present day, and as well as in foreign countries (Cao, 1996; Huang, 1986; Qin & Su, 1996). What is the origin for the continuous adjustments of rural household economic structure?

Table 2.11 Changes in labour efficiency of rural households in Zhejiang (yuan/labour)

	Household operation	Agriculture	Farming	Grains	Vegetables	Animal husbandry	Fishery	Non-agriculture	Industry	Transportation	Commercial, catering and service
1986	0.10	−0.53	−0.51	−0.44	−1.24	−3.23	−1.15	1.74	0.70	4.78	2.6
1987	1.70	0.32	0.07	0.12	−1.35	−2.36	2.30	5.03	5.88	7.60	5.54
1988	2.23	0.01	−0.92	−1.15	−1.11	−0.32	0.77	6.86	7.20	14.28	4.27
1989	1.87	0.53	0.07	0.54	−1.42	0.50	−1.44	5.16	3.51	13.56	4.18
1990	1.16	−0.39	−0.80	−0.44	−2.34	−1.69	1.70	4.62	3.88	13.49	4.89
1991	2.26	0.00	0.07	0.41	−2.68	−2.03	0.44	6.67	3.72	12.87	9.57
1993	−0.56	−6.41	−7.01	−4.45	−9.04	−11.65	0.49	8.97	8.89	7.82	15.64
1995	9.53	−0.56	1.37	4.65	−2.00	−11.66	6.78	20.64	31.57	31.14	16.67
1996	12.82	0.72	5.30	7.14	−1.07	−8.77	0.34	28.63	46.18	43.12	20.48
1997	17.16	−5.81	−5.75	−3.74	−8.98	−9.76	−8.17	40.60	26.54	28.42	57.47
1998	13.60	−9.75	−1.58	−0.94	−5.75	−14.83	−19.00	37.79	19.04	29.22	55.07
1999	19.81	−10.05	−7.49	−9.16	−8.98	−12.22	−13.75	47.03	29.17	27.74	80.38
2000	29.63	−5.13	−8.39	−9.86	−11.93	−9.57	−1.20	57.03	33.36	44.83	93.92
2001	34.10	−10.71	−10.05	−10.35	−11.03	−9.12	−16.40	70.48	43.92	34.37	115.83
2002	33.90	−1.33	−0.41	−3.94	−3.56	−4.09	−5.01	62.99	47.59	76.71	83.59

Note Labour efficiency = (income − expenditure − labour input × labour cost) ÷ labour input

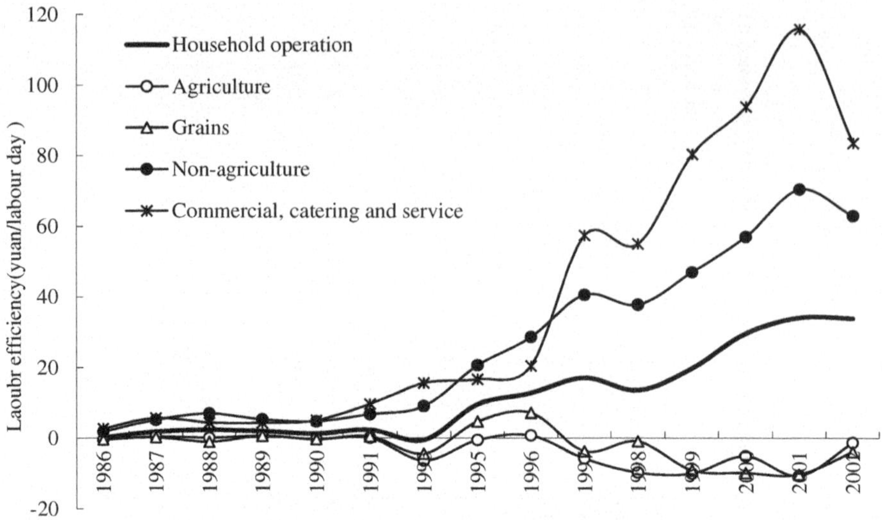

Fig. 2.7 Changes in labour efficiency of household operation Zhejiang

After observing and researching two small villages in South America and South Asia, Schultz proposed that there are rarely behaviours of low efficiency in household economic activities, and he proved his hypothesis (Schultz, 1986). In fact, such a hypothesis can also be verified in China. Under the guidance of rational economic principle, it appears that although rural households are unclear about the differences in resource use efficiency among industries, they know exactly which industry has the advantage in resource use efficiency and which does not. Accordingly, this can be proved by their priority in resource allocation. This seems to suggest to some extent that in order to develop rural economy, it is better for the government to consult farmers first, and the government insisting on structural adjustments in its own way will only lead to missing the targeted goals. An example is a story in the work by Mr. Fei Xiaotong about a person in the city and another one in the countryside. When the person in the city drives to the countryside, people there even do not know to give way, and have been looked down upon as 'country bumpkins'. In fact, this is not because countrymen are foolish, but because they have never seen it. Similarly, it is common for city men to take wheat as chives, yet how many countrymen would take this as a joke? In practice, the honesty and simplicity of rural people have been misunderstood as foolishness. The slow development of rural economy seems to have intensified the wrong impression so that in decision-making there has been a lack of attention and respect to farmers' behaviours. Even for the rural household responsibility system and the development of rural village and township enterprises which have brought about the overall reform and prosperity in China, the initial decision making was very difficult. This indicates that better understanding of farmers' rational economic behaviours and complete respect for their pioneering spirits have been the fundamental driving forces for a prosperous rural economy.

Table 2.12 Changes in investment efficiency of household operation in Zhejiang

	Household operation	Agriculture	Farming	Grains	Vegetables	Animal husbandry	Fishery	Non-agriculture	Industry	Transportation	Commercial, catering and service
1986	0.02	−0.19	−0.29	−0.24	−1.42	−0.83	−0.19	0.16	0.03	0.48	0.37
1987	0.25	0.09	0.03	0.06	−1.53	−0.55	0.26	0.34	0.19	0.73	0.98
1988	0.27	0.00	−0.36	−0.39	−0.96	−0.05	0.08	0.44	0.27	1.07	0.38
1989	0.18	0.10	0.02	0.15	−1.22	0.07	−0.12	0.23	0.05	0.77	0.56
1990	0.15	−0.06	−0.23	−0.11	−1.85	−0.21	0.11	0.42	0.15	0.65	1.15
1991	0.26	0.00	0.02	0.09	−1.72	−0.23	0.02	0.59	0.22	0.50	1.15
1993	−0.04	−0.59	−1.49	−0.73	−3.72	−0.78	0.02	0.38	0.14	0.39	1.96
1995	0.30	−0.02	0.13	0.35	−0.41	−0.36	0.07	0.77	0.61	0.85	1.04
1996	0.30	0.02	0.53	0.55	−0.28	−0.32	0.00	0.53	0.29	0.66	0.95
1997	0.34	−0.13	−0.60	−0.30	−2.25	−0.34	−0.06	0.72	0.24	0.59	1.28
1998	0.25	−0.19	−0.17	−0.08	−1.02	−0.42	−0.15	0.63	0.25	0.70	0.77
1999	0.40	−0.20	−0.76	−0.73	−1.45	−0.36	−0.12	0.97	0.45	0.49	1.55
2000	0.40	−0.08	−0.80	−0.71	−1.72	−0.27	−0.01	0.68	0.17	0.77	1.62
2001	0.35	−0.16	−0.94	−0.76	−2.31	−0.21	−0.11	0.57	0.15	0.47	1.54
2002	0.37	−0.02	−0.03	−0.34	−0.53	−0.09	−0.04	0.57	0.26	0.87	0.80

Note Investment efficiency = (income − expenditure − labour input × labour cost) ÷ investment

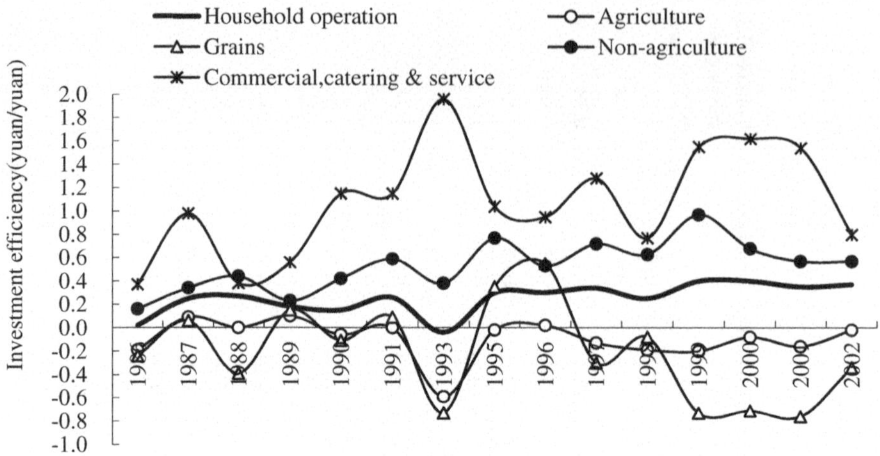

Fig. 2.8 Changes in investment efficiency of household operation in Zhejiang

2.4 Estimation of Structural Change: Non-agricultural Operation of Rural Households

2.4.1 Evaluation and Tendency of Non-agriculturalisation for Rural Household Operation

It is discovered in the above analysis that changes in economic structure in rural households in Zhejiang have enhanced household operation. In household operation, the structural change has shown a non-agricultural tendency, which dominates the economic development of rural households in Zhejiang. Traditionally, the major indicator to evaluate economic non-agriculturalisation in rural households has been the percentage of non-agricultural income of total income. In fact, this indicator tends to be overestimated. Especially when providing information for decision making, it has obvious weakness in determining resource allocation. Therefore, this indicator in the current study is modified based on the idea of input and output balance, i.e. rural household operation non-agriculturalisation degree is proposed here as a comprehensive evaluation index. It not only takes into consideration the non-agriculturalising trend of resource allocation, but also the non-agriculturalisation of income due to the allocation. The specific calculation method is: first, to work out non-agriculturalisation of labour and capital input; second, to calculate non-agriculturalisation of income source; and finally, to add up the three parts by using their weights. The method for the weights is to regard both input and output as taking 50% each, i.e. income non-agriculturalisation takes 50%, and those of labour and capital to take 50%; as for the weights of labour and capital, labour takes 20% and capital 30% based on past research experience.

According to the follow-up observation, although non-agriculturalisation for investment was high during the entire process, there was an obvious drop in the early 1990s. While despite the low starting level for labour non-agriculturalisation, it maintained a continuous rising trend. Under the influence of the above two factors, income non-agriculturalisation of rural households went up rapidly. By comparing the non-agriculturalisation levels for labour and income, there have shown growing disparities (Fig. 2.9). Since the start of the observation, the composite non-agriculturalisation for rural household operation has been rising rapidly and reached 67.26% in 2002, an increase of about 19.98% from 47.23% in 1986, while income non-agriculturalisation reached 72.73%, an increase of 25.29% compared to the start of the observation. This has indicated that during the process of non-agriculturalisation, the operation performance of Zhejiang rural households has been getting better. Meanwhile, it also suggests that in order to accelerate industrialisation in the countryside and non-agriculturalisation of rural household economy, the non-agriculturalisation of employment for rural labour is the key issue. In other words, to increase the non-agriculturalised employment of rural labour is the core of improving industrialisation in the countryside and non-agriculturalisation of rural household economy. While in order to improve non-agricultural employment for rural labour force,the development of technology and cultural education in the countryside has been the most important in decision making. Relevant issues will be analysed later in this book.

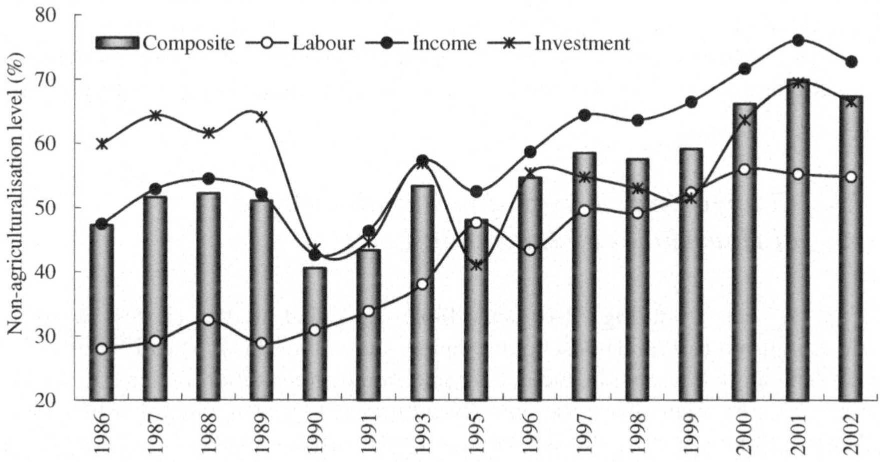

Fig. 2.9 Non-agriculturalisation and its evolution in Zhejiang

2.4.2 Distribution of Households with Different Non-agriculturalisation Degrees

As a coastal province with relatively developed rural economy, Zhejiang has a high non-agriculturalisation degree for rural households with a fast development rate (Table 2.13). As to the household distribution with different non-agriculturalisation degrees, agriculture-dominated households decreased from 73.48% in the mid-1980s to 42.60% in 2002. There were 57.40% households that had partially or entirely adopted non-agricultural operation. Agriculture has taken a smaller part in farmers' income in Zhejiang. Among the households under observation in the ten villages in Zhejiang, the percentage of rural households entirely engaged in agriculture dropped from 33.27% at the beginning of the observation to 25.40% in 2002, and that of agricultural households decreased from 61.00% in 1986 to 35.40% in 2002, with a decrease of 25.60% within 17 years. After experiencing a stagnating period, the percentage of households partially engaged in agriculture suddenly dropped at the beginning of the new century, from 21.08% in 1986 to 13.80% in 2002, with a decrease of 7.28% within 17 years. Meanwhile the percentage of non-agricultural households has consistently been on the rise, from 10.54% in 1986 to 28.40% in 2002, including the complete non-agricultural households with the percentage increased from 1.57 to 18.20%. Thus, there has been a total increase of 17.86% for the non-agricultural households, or 16.63% for the complete non-agricultural households respectively over 17 years. This indicates that when developing household economy, non-agricultural operation has become the major support for economic growth. It also suggests that in order to realise continuous household economic growth, the non-agricultural operation should be taken as the right choice as a development path.

2.4.3 Changes in Non-agriculturalisation Degrees of Households by Education Level

It can be seen from Fig. 2.10 and Table 2.14 that in the process of non-agriculturalisation of rural household economy, due to the educational differences for major labours in households, the non-agricultural degrees differ. In general, during the 17 years of observation, the non-agriculturalisation degree and that of household education in Zhejiang have been found positively correlated. Households with extremely low and high education levels have large disparities in terms of economic non-agriculturalisation degrees. In addition, households with more education have shown a steady progress in promoting non-agriculturalisation in their household economy, while households with less education have experienced large fluctuations in non-agriculturalisation. This indicates that for the steady advancement of industrialisation and household non-agriculturalisation in the countryside, the improvement of rural education has been one of the important issues, which is also necessary for rural economic structure adjustment. Especially after China's entry into the WTO,

Table 2.13 Household distribution with different non-agriculturalisation degrees (composite index) (%)

	Households entirely engaged in agriculture	Agricultural households	Agriculture-dominated households	Non-agricultural dominated households	Non-agricultural households	Complete non-agricultural households	Number of households observed
1986	33.27	61.00	12.48	8.60	10.54	1.57	1082
1987	32.87	64.08	11.42	7.67	9.76	2.09	1147
1988	30.60	60.24	14.26	7.52	10.72	3.80	1157
1989	33.31	62.32	11.94	8.92	9.42	2.19	1189
1990	32.01	61.28	12.11	10.12	9.95	2.24	1206
1991	30.71	58.56	13.67	8.39	12.11	2.68	1156
1993	38.00	55.80	13.20	9.80	13.80	5.40	500
1995	37.20	51.80	10.40	10.20	19.60	8.80	500
1996	42.40	51.00	10.40	9.80	18.20	8.80	500
1997	33.80	44.20	14.00	8.00	23.60	11.40	500
1998	32.60	46.80	9.20	7.80	25.40	13.40	500
1999	29.40	44.00	10.20	10.00	25.60	14.20	500
2000	26.45	36.27	12.22	10.42	26.45	14.83	499
2001	28.34	39.12	10.18	5.19	29.54	16.37	501
2002	25.40	35.40	7.20	6.60	28.40	18.20	500

Note Agricultural households (%) + agriculture-dominated households (%) + non-agricultural dominated households (%) + non-agricultural households (%) = 100%; households entirely engaged in agriculture as a subcategory of agricultural households; complete non-agricultural households as a subcategory of non-agricultural households

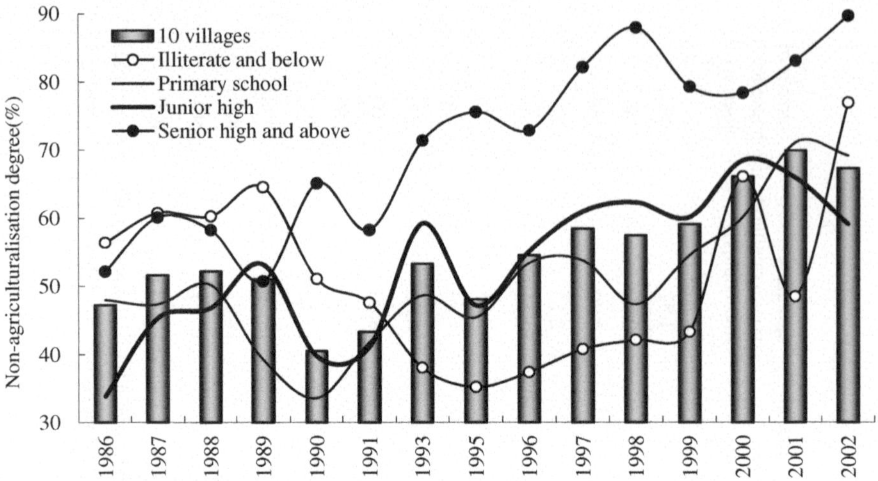

Fig. 2.10 Change of non-agriculturalisation by household education level in Zhejiang

rural education should be further enhanced rather than weakened. There was once the phenomenon in rural Zhejiang that the illiterate people could earn a lot. However, with the development of society and technology, such a phenomenon will be reduced because peoples' view on labour value tends to be more unbiased. If those who were bold and ignorant with a strong background could earn a lot in the beginning of market economic development when formal institutions were much underdeveloped, then when the market economy is developed to a certain level, one's talents definitely become more important than his boldness and background. This has been proved in western countries with more developed market economies, and has started to manifest in China. The initiative to recruit talents throughout China has been a powerful proof.

2.5 Environment Transition: Foundation of Structural Adjustments

With the further implementation of the opening-up policies, great changes have taken place in the rural economic development environment, especially for sales of agricultural products, supplies of rural production materials and rural labour employment. The sales of agricultural products have changed from a comprehensive state monopoly in the early stages of the reform to partial monopoly over purchase, allocated purchase, contract purchase before finally introducing a full cancellation of state purchase. The supplies of production materials have changed from exclusive to multiple suppliers, and labour employment changed from preventing to encouraging 'leaving the land'. The constant improvement and reform of agricultural product

Table 2.14 Change of non-agriculturalisation in 10 villages in Zhejiang

	Composite non-agriculturalisation degree (%)					Income non-agriculturalisation degree (%)				
	Illiterate and below	Primary school	Junior high	Senior high+	10 villages	Illiterate and below	Primary school	Junior high	Senior high+	10 villages
1986	56.39	47.96	33.82	52.13	47.23	56.68	48.57	33.86	55.75	47.39
1987	60.74	47.30	45.28	60.08	51.55	64.37	48.04	46.01	61.74	52.83
1988	60.27	50.17	46.82	58.24	52.18	63.74	51.95	49.57	61.30	54.44
1989	64.54	39.27	53.20	50.71	51.03	68.80	40.69	53.72	54.95	52.11
1990	51.07	33.56	39.75	65.08	40.50	52.27	35.71	43.13	67.57	42.56
1991	47.58	41.82	41.11	58.27	43.30	48.64	44.52	44.98	64.00	46.33
1993	38.07	48.63	59.21	71.33	53.28	41.96	52.32	63.83	75.17	57.26
1995	35.25	45.41	47.15	75.57	48.06	38.28	51.37	51.04	79.51	52.46
1996	37.40	53.38	55.14	72.81	54.58	40.70	58.10	58.86	76.18	58.62
1997	40.77	53.79	60.95	82.10	58.46	51.44	60.14	66.15	87.08	64.31
1998	42.13	47.31	62.29	87.90	57.48	49.08	53.19	67.54	93.41	63.52
1999	43.31	54.57	60.13	79.24	59.09	45.65	62.19	65.82	88.12	66.40
2000	66.07	60.12	68.43	78.36	66.06	64.77	67.64	73.62	82.68	71.60
2001	48.49	71.08	65.88	83.06	69.89	51.68	77.69	71.99	86.87	76.05
2002	76.92	69.11	59.10	89.61	67.26	78.37	74.78	64.59	92.86	72.73

sales, the diversification of production material supplies and the extensive reform of rural labour employment have sent a green light for accelerating the comprehensive marketisation and structural adjustments in rural economy. Such a change in agricultural and rural economic development environment has laid a solid foundation for the economic structural adjustments of rural households. I will take the sales of agricultural products and supplies of production materials as examples to illustrate, as they are closely related to agricultural production.

2.5.1 *Grain Sales and State Procurement Tasks*

First, let us have a look at grains, the special product with the largest influence on rural economic development, which is closely related to the national economy and people's livelihood. The state assignment and completion must be considered with priority for farmers' production activities. For the ten villages in Zhejiang, in the mid-1980s (1987), contract purchase took a large amount, which averaged 303.22 kg per household, equivalent to 18.81% of the household production for the whole year, while the completion rate was only 89.15%. Gradually, with the improvement of the macro environment for grain supplies, this required quota was reduced over time. Until 1990, the average quota was down to 255.52 kg per household, a decrease of 15.73%, or an equivalent of 16.69% of the total household production for the year, and the completion rate hit 100.45% for the first time. In fact, an important factor for farmers' successful completion of the grain procurement assignment from the state has been the marketisation of grain prices. As seen from Fig. 2.11, in the initial stage of the observation, the ratio of the amount of grains sold to the state to the total

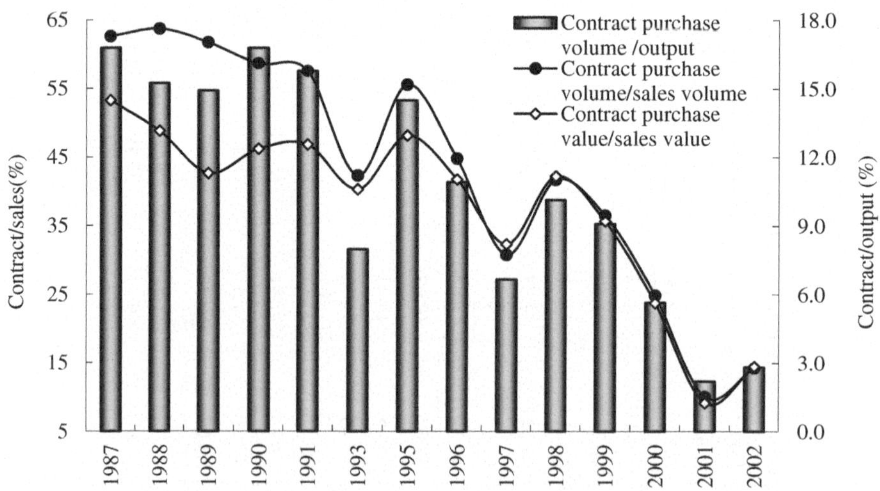

Fig. 2.11 Household grain output, sales and tasks in 10 Zhejiang villages

amount of grains sold tended to be in line with the ratio of farmers' income from state procurement to the total income from grain sales. Therefore, the state's alleviation of direct extraction from farmers through grain prices has been an important factor to ensure the completion of the procurement tasks.

During the process of the gradual alleviation of procurement tasks and the continuous marketisation of grain prices, rural households have been more and more proactive in completing their tasks. The successful accomplishment seems to be based on the reduced tasks, but in fact, it is closely related to the acceleration of grain price marketisation. To some extent, such acceleration reflects the state's more respect for farmers' agricultural production. Meanwhile, farmers' active participation in state procurement is helpful in ensuring their flexible arrangement of agricultural production, so that they are able to optimise the allocation of their own resources such as land, labour and capital. It is the change of the production environment that has given farmers the opportunity to adjust household economic structure.

2.5.2 Changes in Sales of Agricultural Products

Although rural resource allocation in Zhejiang has been obviously non-agriculturalised in the process of developing household economy, this does not have direct impact on changes in sales of agricultural products. In fact, changes in sales of agricultural products have laid an important foundation for accelerating the non-agriculturalisation of rural economic structure. Table 2.15 shows that since the 1990s, there had been an income increase from household sales of agricultural products up until 2000, when the income growth stagnated and since then the income level has levelled at around 11,000 yuan. Meanwhile, sales of agricultural products experienced rapid 'privatisation' in the 1990s and since 2000 have been in a stable period with few changes. Private purchase has been maintained as the major channel for sales of agricultural products, whereas the traditional channels for grain sales have been phased out, such as procurement by state commercial departments, purchase by state supply and marketing agencies, and village fair trade.

As for types of agricultural products sold, the households under observation in Zhejiang mainly sell two categories of products: aquatic products, and meat and egg products, and their sales have been on the rise. In terms of share of sales, aquatic products have taken the largest percentage, followed by meat and egg products, while grain sales take up a very small percentage. In 2002, with regard to sales value, aquatic products and meat and egg products made up 69.43 and 32.29% respectively, or 39.57 and 3.74% higher than in 1993 when the recording of data started. However, grain sales dropped from 4.83% in 1993 to 1.09% in 2002, with a decrease of 3.72% over ten years. Obviously, there has been a huge difference in the product structure between Zhejiang and the whole country.[9] Yet, this difference is not a cause for the

[9]According to the data from the national fixed observation sites in rural areas, income from sales of agricultural products by rural households in 2002 was 4,474.20 yuan, including grains, meat and

Table 2.15 Sales income, channels and types of agricultural products in Zhejiang (%)

	1993	1995	1996	1997	1998	1999	2000	2001	2002
Total sales amount (100 yuan)	35.77	83.09	78.90	96.49	104.31	99.42	118.01	109.43	110.71
State departments and agencies	20.54	13.62	9.11	7.04	5.06	5.42	3.52	4.44	4.44
#State purchase task	2.67	2.48	2.11	1.00	1.31	0.94	0.38	0.15	0.16
Foreign trade and commercial depts.	5.87	0.11	4.23	9.11	6.24	0.67	1.91	2.60	1.82
Collective and civil organisations	5.75	23.97	9.26	21.06	7.40	2.55	1.58	1.40	2.65
Fair trade	13.95	29.54	38.01	29.67	19.52	20.21	9.39	10.56	7.81
Private purchase	52.76	31.64	39.03	32.75	61.49	70.47	82.34	80.30	82.66
Others	1.13	1.11	0.37	0.37	0.29	0.67	1.26	0.69	0.61
Food	4.83	5.32	5.30	3.00	3.07	2.74	1.61	1.65	1.09
Fruits	4.99	2.35	3.62	2.39	4.05	1.68	1.67	2.89	5.10
Silkworm cocoons	7.12	3.55	2.47	3.14	2.26	2.14	2.47	2.47	1.26
Vegetables	3.16	3.14	2.24	2.47	2.83	2.33	1.79	1.22	1.06
Meat and eggs	28.55	20.88	16.44	15.43	15.25	15.99	11.39	13.72	32.29
Aquatic products	29.86	52.20	61.10	64.95	66.45	69.21	73.65	67.12	69.43
Forest products	6.23	1.58	1.06	1.66	1.08	1.68	0.58	1.67	0.98

Note # as part of the previous category

change in sales channels. On the contrary, it is the change of sales channels that has intensified the structural adjustments in agricultural products on sale.

2.5.3 *Changes in Purchase Channels of Agricultural Means of Production*

With the change in sales of agricultural products, purchase methods of means of agricultural production change accordingly. Such a change shows an obvious tendency towards "privatisation" as well. Apparently, during the whole observation period, the purchase of agricultural means of production has changed from the state monopoly over purchase to the breaking of the monopoly, with private dealers taking the place in distribution. Data show that in 1993, farmers purchased 59.60% of the means of production from the state organisations, while in 2002 the figure decreased to 16.12%. Meanwhile, the percentage from private dealers increased from 27.01% to 47.24% (Table 2.16). It has to be noticed that during the whole observation period, the actual amount that farmers spent on means of production has remained roughly the same at about 400 yuan.

As for types of means of production purchased by farmers, chemical fertiliser has taken the largest share of over 60%, which is followed by pesticides, accounting for 20%, and there have been few changes in the purchase structure. According to statistics and evolution data, farmers have relatively stable requirements for means of agricultural production with few changes. But changes in purchase channels are great. Such changes, at the same time, have laid an important foundation for the structural transition in rural household economy.

2.6 Conclusions and Policy Suggestions

Since 2000, after China's entry into the WTO, strategic restructuring has become an important initiative to boost the economic growth for the rural areas, agricultural industry and rural households in Zhejiang and even the whole country. However, the traditional executive orders obviously would not work during the process, and it is necessary to adhere to the laws of the market economy. For rural and agricultural economies dominated by household operation, the most effective results from

---

egg products, and aquatic products, accounting for 26.71, 30.12 and 13.90% of the total sales value, and in 1995 the corresponding figures were 30.43, 28.04 and 8.45%. Compared with 1995, grain sales dropped by 3.72%, while meat and egg products and aquatic products increased by 2.08 and 5.46%. The three main sales channels included private purchase, village fair trade, procurement by state commercial departments and agencies, accounting for 61.24, 19.64 and 9.47% of the total in 2002. Compared with the corresponding figures of 44.35, 22.52 and 22.08% in 1995, there were drops of 12.61% in procurement by state commercial departments and agencies, 2.88% by village fair trade, but an increase of 16.88% in private purchase.

Table 2.16 Purchase expenditure, channels and types for agricultural means of productions in 10 Zhejiang villages

	1993	1995	1996	1997	1998	1999	2000	2001	2002
Total expenditure (yuan)	343.75	524.59	567.24	486.94	461.09	437.15	377.46	393.47	444.20
State departments and agencies	59.60	76.07	68.63	68.23	59.07	54.46	38.73	22.45	16.12
Collective and civil organisations	12.92	11.12	10.90	12.87	17.79	17.74	29.38	17.07	35.16
Individual dealers	27.01	12.63	19.88	18.74	23.14	27.71	31.03	59.55	47.24
Others	0.47	0.18	0.59	0.16	0.00	0.09	0.86	0.93	1.49
Fine variety	8.25	5.49	6.14	5.59	6.91	7.27	8.76	7.38	6.32
Chemical fertiliser	66.02	76.97	74.32	69.51	67.32	65.49	61.58	61.55	59.89
Diesel	2.37	0.71	0.84	0.87	0.18	0.25	0.20	0.86	1.48
Plastic film	2.83	1.28	1.44	1.39	1.18	1.97	1.06	1.44	6.61
Pesticides	17.42	15.69	17.38	20.75	21.75	24.45	23.11	20.85	20.27

restructuring are achieved through respecting farmers' choices. This current study reveals that economic restructuring is an ongoing process in which farmers' choices are being aligned with the economic principles, so that such choices are economically rational. In the process of restructuring, the role of the government lies in providing guidance rather than giving orders. The rural area in Zhejiang has sustained its economic growth for over ten years and one of the key reasons for this has been the respect given to farmers' rational decisions.

References

Cao, X. (1996). *Resesarch on rural household economy in South Jiangsu of old China*. Beijing: Central Compilation & Translation Press.

Chen, X., Shi, Q., & Jiang, W. (2000). Comparison of farmland use efficiency and its change for household with different operation scales. *Issues in Agricultural Economy, 12*, 6–9.

Huang, C. (1986). *Small peasant economy and social transition in North China*. Beijing: Zhonghua Book Company.

Qin, H., & Su, W. (1996). *Idyllic and rhapsody: About the Guanzhong mode and review of the former modern society*. Beijing: Central Compilation & Translation Press.

Schultz, T. W. (1986). *Transforming traditional agriculture (Traslated in Chinese)*. Business Press.

Shi, Q. (1999). *Rural household economic development*. Beijing: China Agriculture Press.

Shi, Q. (2000). A Comparative study on the unbalanced economic development of rural households and its origin in Shanxi and Zhejiang: Evidence from follow-up observations from 1986 to 1999. *China Economic Studies, 6*, 24–31.

Shi, Q., & Zhang, H. (2000). The process of non-agriculturalisation of rural household operation. *On Economic Problems, 4*, 45–48.

Chapter 3
Farmland, Farmland Transfer and the Origins

Contents

With the development of rural economy and acceleration of urbanisation in the countryside, the flow of production factors is bound to be enhanced. In the flow of production factors, capital and labour usually attract the greatest attention. Farmland, however, although an important production factor in rural economic development, has received relatively less academic attention in previous research, mostly due to its intrinsic attribute of non-movability and its unique status in rural economic development. Farmland transfer is generally perceived to be the exchange between land owners and users. In traditional rural economy, due to higher dependence of economic development on farmland, farmers would pay relatively more attention to land, viewing the farmland as their lifeblood. Under such circumstances, farmland transfer among rural households generally becomes a compulsory behaviour required by the

Q. Shi and Y. Gao, *Sustainable Development of Rural Household Economy*,
https://doi.org/10.1007/978-981-15-2747-0_3

government. With the economic development, industrialisation in the countryside in particular and in comparatively more developed regions, farmers' reliance on land has been gradually reduced, with income from land taking a less important role in rural households, and the phenomenon of land transfer becoming more evident. The origin of the acceleration of farmland transfer, however, lies in the decline of efficiency in farmland utilisation. In order to verify such a judgement, empirical analysis in this chapter is carried out on farmland transfer among rural households based on data from the fixed observation sites of ten villages in Zhejiang.

3.1 Farmland Scale and Distribution

3.1.1 Changes in Farmland Operation Scale and Distribution

It can be seen from Table 3.1 that over time, with the development of industrialisation in the countryside and the growth of rural population, the contradiction between people and land in the countryside has become intensified. The amount of farmland contracted by rural households has declined. By 2002, the average size of farmland operated by households under observation had been reduced to 1.35 *mu*,[1] decreased by 53.44, 44.67, 36.32 and 20.59% respectively if compared with the level in 1986, 1990, 1995 and 2000. During the entire observation, the annual decrease rate for the household operation scale was 4.40%. Since 1995, the annual decline rate has been 6.24%, and since 2000 the drop rate has become 10.89% for the three most recent years. Such a result indicates that the weakening link between rural households and farmland has noticeably accelerated. In other words, farmers 'leave their land' at a faster speed. The same conclusion can be drawn from the distribution of farmland among rural households. For the households under observation, until 2002, 46.60% of the households in the ten villages had stopped farming, 5.36 times higher than the level of 8.70% in 1986, 19.20% higher than the level of 27.40% in 1995 and 6.12% higher than the level of 40.48% in 2000. Among households still engaged in farmland, the farming scale for those with an extremely small area of farmland (less than one *mu*) first increased slightly, before suddenly dropped and finally increased again, the scale for those with a small area of farmland (one to three *mu*) obviously increased, those with a medium area of farmland (three to six *mu*) dropped slightly, and that for those with a relatively large area (six to nine *mu*) and a large area of farmland (larger than nine *mu*) both dropped noticeably (Fig. 3.1). In the transition, under the influence of both the intensified contradiction of people and land in the countryside, and the accelerated industrialisation of the rural sector, land concentration has shifted

[1]Of the ten villages under observation, there is an island village mainly dependent on fishing with few households working on farmland. Especially after 1993 when the sample size was reduced, households under observation seldom have any farmland. Therefore, in calculating the average scale for rural households, the result in this study is obvious lower than that from the Zhejiang rural statistics investigation team.

Table 3.1 Evolution of rural household farmland operation scale and distribution

	Scale (*mu*/household)	Year-end farmland scale and distribution (%)								
		No land	<1 *mu*	1–2 *mu*	2–3 *mu*	3–6 *mu*	6–9 *mu*	9–12 *mu*	12–15 *mu*	15+ *mu*
1986	2.90	8.70	16.02	21.02	16.94	25.46	7.96	2.50	0.83	0.56
1987	2.75	10.64	15.95	21.45	15.78	25.46	7.76	2.18	0.52	0.26
1988	2.64	12.62	15.56	21.18	17.11	22.99	7.87	1.90	0.61	0.17
1989	2.41	11.44	18.00	21.95	17.41	23.04	6.64	1.18	0.25	0.08
1990	2.44	10.61	16.83	22.47	18.91	22.89	6.72	1.33	0.17	0.08
1991	2.39	12.20	16.96	21.89	19.12	22.66	5.62	1.30	0.17	0.09
1993	2.29	16.40	12.00	19.60	20.80	24.80	5.80	0.60	0.00	0.00
1995	2.12	27.40	6.20	18.00	21.20	22.80	3.80	0.40	0.00	0.20
1996	1.95	28.00	4.40	20.40	21.40	22.60	3.00	0.20	0.00	0.00
1997	1.90	29.40	4.80	19.80	21.60	21.00	2.80	0.40	0.20	0.00
1998	1.88	33.00	5.60	17.80	18.00	21.80	3.20	0.40	0.00	0.20
1999	1.88	32.60	4.80	19.00	18.80	21.00	3.60	0.00	0.00	0.20
2000	1.70	40.48	6.41	16.83	14.83	17.43	3.01	0.20	0.20	0.60
2001	1.55	40.92	6.39	16.77	17.56	16.57	1.40	0.20	0.00	0.20
2002	1.35	46.60	7.20	17.80	13.80	12.60	1.00	0.40	0.40	0.20

Note No routine investigation was conducted in 1992 and 1994

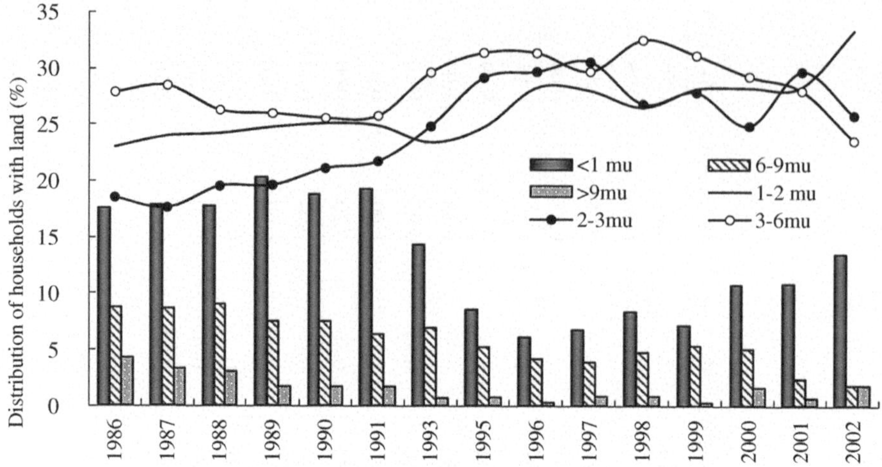

Fig. 3.1 Changes in farmland distribution of households in 10 Zhejiang villages

gradually to more expert farmers, although generally land concentration among rural households is not so obvious (Figs. 3.2 and 3.3).

It is seen from Figs. 3.2 and 3.3 that over time, distributions of both number and scale of the rural households still engaged in farming have obviously changed due to the accelerated non-agriculturalisation. Although both distributions look similar, the key difference lies in the degree of concentration, which becomes more obvious over time.

In terms of rural household land distribution (Fig. 3.2), in the beginning of the observation, the most frequently distributed scale was 1–2 *mu* including 24.37% of the rural households (the average level between 1986 and 1991). This is followed by

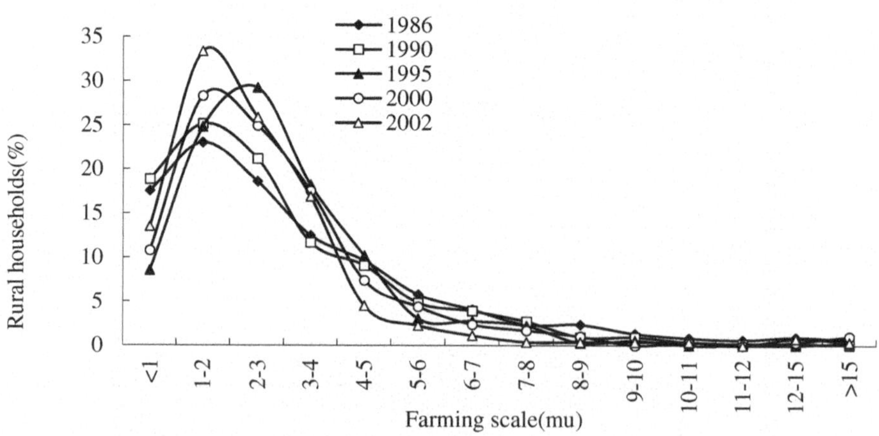

Fig. 3.2 Distribution of rural households by farming scale in 10 Zhejiang villages

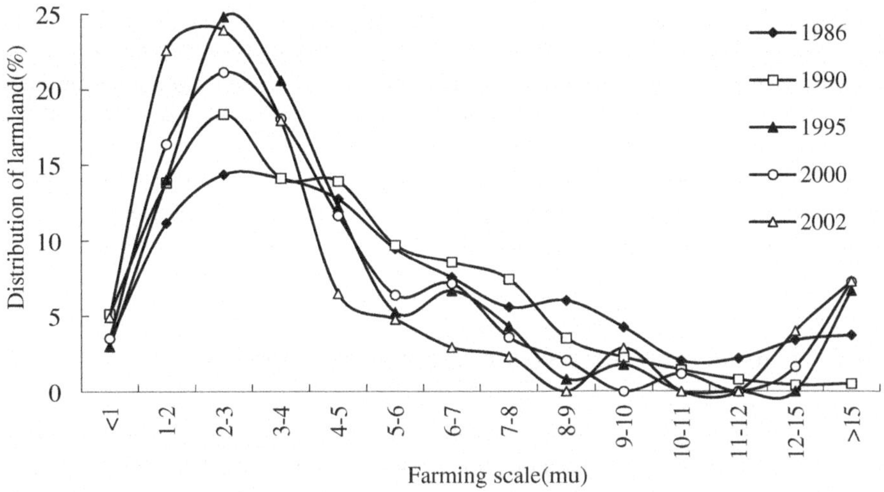

Fig. 3.3 Distribution of household farmland by scale in 10 Zhejiang villages

the scale of 2–3 *mu* with 19.75% of the households. In the middle and late 1990s, the most frequently distributed scale became 2–3 *mu* including 28.89% of the households (the average level between 1995 and 1999), followed by the scale of 1–2 *mu* with 27.17% of the households. Since the new century, great changes have taken place that the most frequently distributed scale has become 1–2 *mu* again with 29.88% of the households (the average level between 2000 and 2002), which is followed by the scale of 2–3 *mu* with 26.86% of the households. During the process, the year 2002 stands out as 33.33% of the households belonged to the 1–2 *mu* group. This indicates that although non-agricultural economy in rural areas of Zhejiang, the coastal province, is becoming more developed, there are still many households holding small pieces of farmland for operation. Therefore, farmland still plays an important role in the growth of household economy.

In terms of farmland distribution (Fig. 3.3), in all of the early, middle and late periods of observation, the 2–3 *mu* group was the largest one, but the concentration degree varied over time. In the initial stage, 16.46% of the households belonged to this group (1986–1991), and the figure increased to 24.91% in the 1990s (1995–1999). Since 2000, such distribution has been influenced by farmers' evaluation of the function of land, and there have appeared more small farmland holdings, so the size of the 2–3 *mu* group has become smaller, down to 24.19% (2000–2002), or further to 23.92% in 2002. While farmland operation has been based on small-scale farming, land transfer has shifted to farming experts. In the beginning of the observation (1986–1991), only 9.90% of the rural households had farmland of over 9 *mu*, including 1.76% with farmland of over 15 *mu*. Since the new century (2000–2002), these figures have changed to 10.42 and 6.95%, and hit 14.16 and 7.28% in 2002.

Comparing distributions of rural households and their farmland, in terms of farmland operation and in order to improve farmland operation efficiency, farmers in the coastal province Zhejiang have balanced efficiency and equality in the distribution of farmland. That is, farmers reluctant to farm will effectively transfer their land to the farming experts, while those hoping to keep their rights over land will maintain their small-scale farming. This has to some degree reflected that the industrial development in the countryside is at the same time the process of diversification of rural industries and acceleration of specialisation.

3.1.2 Fragmentation of Farmland and Its Changes

As shown in Fig. 3.4 and Table 3.2, with the promotion of rural industrialisation and non-agricultural development of household economy (Shi & Zhang, 2000), as well as household operating scale shrinking, the number of farming plots declined at a rate much faster than the rate of farmland decrease. The number of land plots per household reduced from 5.53 *mu* at the beginning of observation to 2.36 *mu* in 2002, down by 57.32%, 3.69% higher than the farmland decrease rate of 53.58%. Therefore, the change of farmland scale in Zhejiang is accompanied by the farmland fragmentation adjustment. This adjustment fluctuated during the observation before 2000, but has shown a positive trend in general. Since 2000, i.e. during the second round of land contracting and under the guidance of readjustment policies, farmland has been further fragmented, so the plot size has reduced again after a short period of increase. During the first round of land contract, the average plot area expanded by 24.45% in 15 years, from 0.52 *mu* at the beginning of the observation in 1986 to

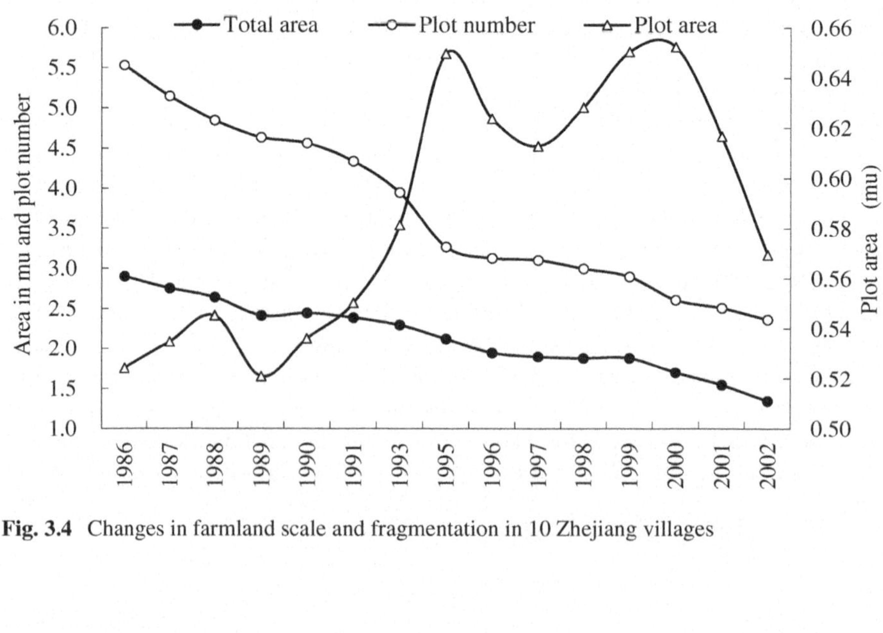

Fig. 3.4 Changes in farmland scale and fragmentation in 10 Zhejiang villages

Table 3.2 Fragmentation of farmland operation in rural households and its changes

	Plot number/household	Distribution of plots of different sizes (%)				Single plot area of households of different scales (*mu*)			
		<0.5 *mu*	0.5–1 *mu*	1–2 *mu*	>2 *mu*	<3 *mu*	3–6 *mu*	>6 *mu*	Average
1993	3.95	59.69	22.95	14.71	2.65	0.41	0.69	1.09	0.58
1995	3.27	54.26	26.33	17.27	2.14	0.51	0.67	1.18	0.65
1996	3.13	53.81	29.30	14.27	2.62	0.51	0.70	0.97	0.62
1997	3.10	52.74	30.75	14.06	2.45	0.50	0.69	0.98	0.61
1998	3.00	52.54	28.70	16.02	2.74	0.52	0.65	1.01	0.63
1999	2.90	48.90	30.94	17.33	2.83	0.57	0.69	0.82	0.65
2000	2.61	53.04	29.59	14.60	2.77	0.53	0.66	1.10	0.65
2001	2.51	53.34	30.02	14.25	2.39	0.54	0.68	0.86	0.62
2002	2.36	54.31	29.53	13.87	2.28	0.48	0.66	0.83	0.57

Note The number of sample households was 500, except 499 in 2000, and 501 in 2001

0.65 *mu* in 2000. After the second round of contract, the average size was reduced to 0.57 *mu* in 2002, equivalent to the level in the early 1990s. This has suggested that farmland fragmentation is not only related to farmers' operation ideology, but also to state policies at different stages.

Clearly, one of the fundamental reasons for the reoccurrence of farmland fragmentation has been the great influence of natural conditions, especially the intense human-land conflicts, as Zhejiang is located in the coastal area of southeast China. Of the farmland operated by rural households, there has been a high proportion of land with a single plot area of less than 0.5 μ. Although the situation improved slightly during the entire observation period, the overall structure has not been changed much, in that over 50% of the farming plots were still small in size, and plots of over 2 μ accounted for less than 3%. This has indicated that small-scale farming is a common feature of rural households in Zhejiang.

During the process of land fragmentation, it is found out that for households with large-scale operation, the improvement in land use is generally more satisfactory than others, although their farmland has also experienced fluctuations in fragmentation.

3.1.3 Farmland Source and Its Change

In accordance with the *Constitution of the People's Republic of China*, the *Law of Land Administration of the People's Republic of China*, and the *Rural Land Contract Law of the People's Republic of China*, 'land in the rural areas and suburban areas, except otherwise provided for by the State, shall be collectively owned by peasants', and rural households have the right to use the land contracted. Accordingly, there lies a question for rural households as how to acquire the right to use land. In both the first round of land contracting in the mid-1980s, and the second round in the late 1990s, the government did not give clear instructions concerning land allocation, so as a result different regions and different villages took various ways. Some allocated land based on number of household members, known as '*kouliangtian*' (food grain ration field), some based on number of labours, known as '*zerentian*' (responsibility field), and there also existed '*zhuanbaotian*' (subcontracted field), i.e. land acquired from collectives and other households. Data from the ten villages in Zhejiang indicate that the ways that households acquire the land have changed a lot for the two rounds of land contracting (Tables 3.3 and 3.4). In the first round of contracting, there was the 'three-three' allocation. Specifically, one third of the allocation was according to number of people, the '*kouliangtian*', one third was '*zerentian*' based on number of labours and the rest was transferred or acquired by other means. In the second round, this structure was greatly changed in that there was a slight increase in '*kouliangtian*', and a substantial decline of '*zerentian*'. The proportion of acquisition by other means increased greatly. Obviously, land acquisition of Zhejiang is completely different

Table 3.3 Farmland sources and the changes of rural households (%)

Village	First round of contracting (1993)				Second round of contracting (2002)			
	Ration field	Responsibility field	Subcontracted field	Other	Ration field	Responsibility field	Subcontracted field	Other
Longshang	97.09	0.00	1.59	1.32	83.49	0.00	9.77	6.74
Yongfeng	0.00	0.00	0.00	100.00	71.00	13.08	15.55	0.38
Yubei	29.15	66.96	3.88	0.00	54.25	44.12	1.63	0.00
West Shufu	61.68	32.37	1.05	4.90	83.64	0.00	16.36	0.00
Miaoyan	69.56	29.91	0.53	0.00	21.69	7.80	33.22	37.29
Xinmin	78.35	17.62	4.02	0.00	21.67	2.81	67.07	8.44
Jinhou	80.92	7.51	11.56	0.00	100.00	0.00	0.00	0.00
Bogumen	100.00	0.00	0.00	0.00	–	–	–	–
Hebian	0.00	92.13	7.17	0.70	0.00	76.57	23.43	0.00
Shibanyan	0.00	0.00	1.56	98.44	0.00	0.00	24.35	75.65
Total	33.81	32.38	2.76	31.04	38.89	14.47	25.11	21.53

Table 3.4 Rural household farmland sources and land transfer

	Farmland area (mu/household) in the beginning of the year	Farmland source (%)			Change by year end (mu/household)		Subcontracting (%)	
		Ration field	Responsibility field	Subcontracted field	Increase	Decrease	In	Out
1993	2.38	33.81	32.38	2.76	0.16	0.25	82.47	75.12
1995	2.17	30.68	35.49	2.51	0.15	0.20	100.00	58.54
1996	2.10	30.84	31.58	4.60	0.17	0.33	78.75	24.13
1997	1.92	33.67	26.57	8.58	0.13	0.15	75.83	53.58
1998	1.86	35.49	25.97	7.44	0.23	0.21	90.59	58.28
1999	1.73	39.43	25.04	7.83	0.30	0.15	73.62	75.03
2000	1.86	37.82	22.32	8.50	0.25	0.41	97.26	63.26
2001	1.51	40.51	19.67	13.45	0.24	0.20	85.39	53.87
2002	1.48	41.36	16.55	20.23	0.16	0.29	84.36	74.07

from the whole country and from the inland provinces (Shi & Jia, 2002, 2003).[2] The farmland allocation in Zhejiang was aimed at solving problems for the farmers' living, which might be related to the intense human-land conflicts. In individual villages, however, the situations vary. Among the ten villages under observation, in the first round of land contracting, six villages distributed land according to number of household members, two villages according to number of labours and two villages in other ways. In the second round, there were changes among villages in that five villages distributed land in the same way as they did in the first round, i.e. three villages based on number of members,[3] one according to number of labours and one based on other criterion. Four villages changed their ways, one changed from number of members to number of labours, two changed from number of members to other ways, one changed from other ways to number of members, while one village on the sea island was unable to be identified due to unreadable information.

From the perspective of changes in farmland acquisition during the entire observation period, with the accelerating non-agriculturalisation of rural economy in Zhejiang, more and more farmland has been acquired via subcontracting and other means rather than the form of '*zerentian*'. Farmland transfer among rural households has been accelerated (Shi & Jia, 2002, 2003). In the process of farmland circulation, land reduction activities have been more intensive than land increase activities. To be specific, both the percentage of rural houesholds with land reduction and the reduction scale have been higher than those of land increase. In 2002, 20.89% of the

[2]In general, the first round of land contracting refers to the period from 1984 to 1999, and the second round from 1999 to 2029. Some rural areas started the second round early in 1998 and some postponed to 2000. According to the data from the national fixed-observation sites, in both the first and the second rounds, rural households mainly obtained farmland according to number of labours, followed by transfer and other means, while the '*kouliangtian*' took the smallest percentage. The percentages of the three categories were 59.80, 20.65 and 13.87% for the first round of land contracting (1993) and 58.61, 30.10 and 11.29% for the second round (2002).

[3]Since 1993, there has been no farmland in operation for the households observed in Bogumen Village on the Putuo Island.

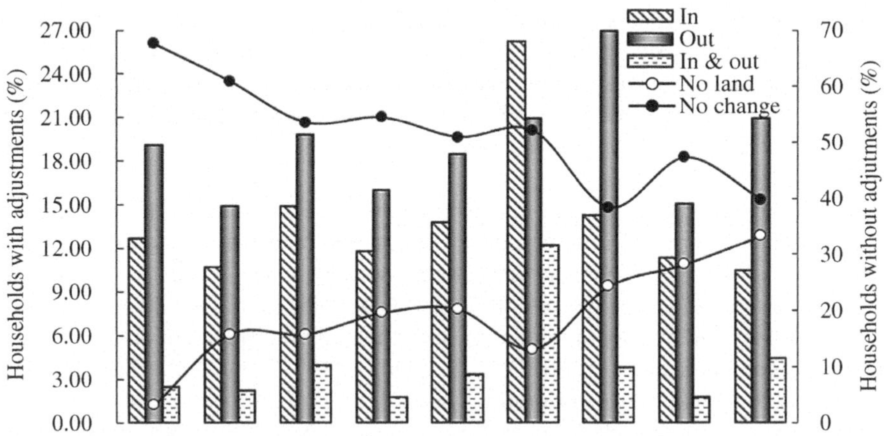

Fig. 3.5 Changes in land adjustments for rural households in 10 Zhejiang villages

total households reduced their farmland, and only 10.44% increased their farmland. Compared with 1993, the former increased by 1.78% while the latter decreased by 2.22%. This result indicates that during the process of rural economic development, it is obvious that farmers have been 'leaving the land', yet it does not mean that they would be more likely to abandon their rights entitled to them over land. In fact, in the early stage of the second round of land contracting (Fig. 3.5), there appeared a sharp farmland increase among rural households. This has indicated that despite the phenomenon of farmers' 'leaving the land' due to the reduced role of land in rural household economic growth in the process of rural non-agriculturalising development, farmers have been very much concerned with their rights over land allocation. As to how to deal with the land after the allocation, it is the business of farmers themselves. Therefore, with regards to land, the very sensible issue, the formulation and implementation of relevant policies have to be in accordance with farmers' behaviours, as respecting farmers' choices has been the foundation for government policy-making.

3.2 Farmland Circulation and Its Forms

3.2.1 Trend of Farmland Circulation

The previous analysis indicates that with the advancement of industrialisation and urbanisation of the rural sector, the idea of traditional 'peasants' associated with farmland is reduced, and has been replaced by a new generation of farmers – those with 'farmer' identities (according to household registration), but engaged in an occupation completely separate from all land use. These farmers are mostly still living in the countryside, but some have moved to towns. There has been less reliance on land for farmers (Shi, 2001). It is clear that since the Ninth Five-Year Plan, both the domestic and overseas supply markets for agricultural products have brought about great impacts on farmers' land operation. Not only investment but also labour efficiency of farmland have deteriorated (Shi, 1999, 2000, 2001), which has forced farmers to 'leave the land'.

We have mentioned previously that in farmland operation, the allocation efficiency of production factors has been declining. This, however, does not mean to encourage farmers to abandon their land and leave it idle. Instead, it is necessary to take certain countermeasures so that some rural households will abandon the land while others will take more land by way of regulating and activating farmland circulation market in order to practice scale operation (Wan & Cheng, 2001; Zhang & Shi, 2001). Due to the long-existing and ever-deteriorating contradictions of more people and less land, the household farming scale is generally small with a high degree of fragmentation.

Since the second round of contracting, the situation has been improved in Zhejiang, and farmland circulation has been greatly accelerated. Although such progress is far from the expected 'scale farming', land circulation has indeed benefited farmers, and agricultural land use efficiency has improved (which will be analysed in detail).

According to the data from the ten villages under observation, the proportion of rural households which spontaneously adjusted their contracted land has been on the rise. In 1993, 29.33% adjusted their land, while the figure decreased to 23.33% in 1995. After 1995, more land adjustments appeared and the percentage hit 30.67% in 1996 before it stagnated again. Up until 1999 when the second round of contracting started, land adjustments were once again enhanced and the proportion reached a record high of 37.42%, but declined again after 2000 dropping down to 26.89% in 2002. One of the important reasons behind such fluctuations has been the underdeveloped market for land circulation (Jia, Tian, & Shi, 2003). If household farmland circulation is subdivided into transfer in and transfer out, Fig. 3.5 and Table 3.5 show that there is a clear rise for land transfer out. In 1993, 19.11% of the households had land transferred out, which increased to 26.95% in 2000, although the percentage decreased a bit after 2000, until 2002 the percentage still remained as high as 20.89%. On the contrary, fewer households had land transferred in, accounting for 12.67% of the total households in 1993, and 14.25% in 2000, before dropped to 10.44% in 2002. Obviously, land transfer out has been the majority in the circulation.

In contrast, the proportion of rural households without land adjustments has been declining. In 1993, among the households with farmland, 67.56% had no adjustment, in comparison with 39.78% in 2002, with a drop of nearly 27% over nine years, and the trend continued. Although such a result is based on only ten villages under observation, this has been supported by another more extensive survey carried out by the Institute of Modern Agriculture and Rural Development, Zhejiang University (abbreviated as Zheda Cartel).[4] This has indicated that the spontaneous adjustments

[4]According to the survey jointly conducted by Zheda Cartel and the Agriculture Department of Zhejiang, by the end of March 2001, the villages with farmland circulation accounted for 66.4%

Table 3.5 Changes in farmland circulation of rural households

	Increase within the year (%)				Decrease within the year (%)			
	With land at the start of the year		No land at the start of the year		With land at the start of the year		No land at the start of the year	
	No increase	Increase	No increase	Increase	No decrease	Decrease	No decrease	Decrease
1993	84.22	12.44	3.11	0.22	77.56	19.11	3.33	0.00
1995	73.56	10.67	15.78	0.00	69.33	14.89	15.78	0.00
1996	69.33	13.78	15.78	1.11	63.33	19.78	16.89	0.00
1997	68.67	10.89	19.56	0.89	63.56	16.00	20.44	0.00
1998	66.00	13.78	20.22	0.00	61.33	18.44	20.22	0.00
1999	60.67	15.78	13.11	10.44	64.00	12.44	15.11	8.44*
2000	61.47	14.03	24.28	0.22	48.55	26.95	24.50	0.00
2001	60.53	9.09	28.16	2.22	54.55	15.08	30.38	0.00
2002	56.22	9.78	33.33	0.67	45.11	20.89	34.00	0.00

Note *In 1999, during the second round of contracting, although some rural households were no longer engaged in farming, they still claimed farmlands from the village committee before subcontracted the land. There were a total of 38 such rural households

of agricultural land and its fragmentation have become an important part in household economic development of Zhejiang.

Table 3.5 indicates that, for the observed households in Zhejiang, in most years there were cases when households had previously withdrawn from farmland operation, but somehow became engaged again. Although they only took a small percentage, the phenomenon did exist. The rights over land contracting have considerable practical significance for household members with the 'identity' of farmers (with rural household registration), yet their occupation and income have been completely or temporarily non-agriculturalised. The rights over land contracting, to some extent, have become the foundation for farmers' welfare acquisition in regions with relatively fast industrialisation. This has explained why during the second round of land contracting some farmers would still contract the land before subcontracted it out, even though they would not be engaged in farming anymore.

3.2.2 *Forms of Farmland Circulation*

In the process of farmland circulation, the forms are diversified, which includes free subcontracting, entrusted subcontracting, contracting back and re-rent (reversed transfer, or transfer), swap or shareholding, etc. Among them, subcontracting is the

of the total in Zhejiang (excluding four counties of Yuyao, Cixi, Xiangshan, and Beilun), and the proportion of rural households with farmland circulation was 20.8%, of which 15.9% were for land transfer out and 5.9% for land transfer in (Cartel, 2001).

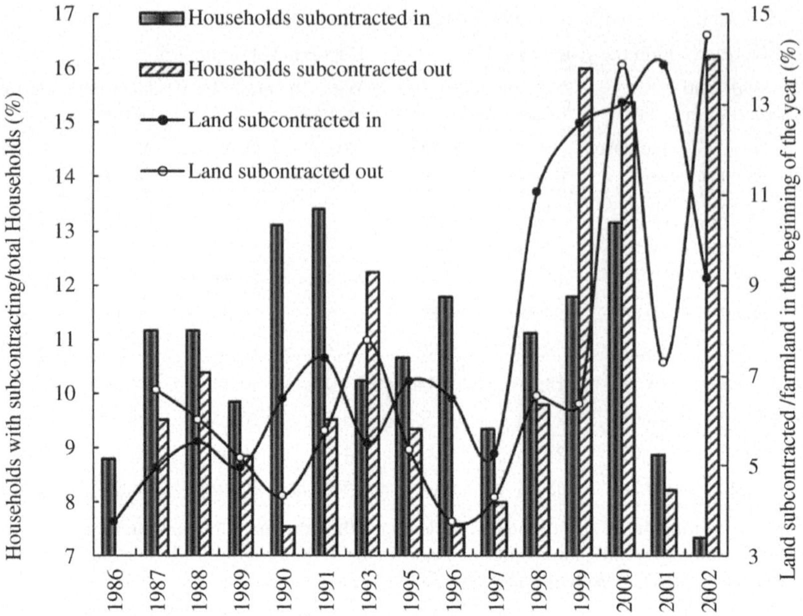

Fig. 3.6 Farmland subcontracting of households in 10 Zhejiang villages

most important form, accounting for 61.2% of the total area in circulation, followed by transfer, accounting for 20.5% (Cartel, 2001). This result is also reflected in the continuous observation of the households (Table 3.4). It can be seen from Fig. 3.6 that during the entire observation period, the subcontracting of farmland,[5] whether in terms of household frequency or proportion of farmland, has shown a fluctuating upward trend, especially after the second round of contracting in 1999. In 2000, 13.41% of the observed households increased and 15.36% decreased their farmland via subcontracting. The increased farmland accounted for 13.03%, and the reduced farmland 13.87% of the total at the beginning of the year. Two years later, in 2002, the land expansion was greatly reduced, and the land reductions became more frequent with the corresponding figures of 7.33, 16.22, 9.14 and 14.52% respectively. This result verifies the statement again that farmers 'leaving the land' has become the major feature for the rural economic development in costal Zhejiang where non-agricultural economy is quite developed in the countryside. Yet, the abnormal circulation of farmland during the second round of contracting simply shows that as long as there are existing issues concerning farmers' rights, they will be sure to protect their benefits regardless of the region. No one will easily abandon the rights over land contracting even for farmers whose economic income has been completely non-agriculturalised.

[5]The subcontracting mentioned above also includes transfer.

3.2.3 *Rent of Farmland Circulation*

In the process of farmland subcontracting, due to factors such as the non-agricultural development of the specific region, and local government policies on farmland operation and management, the subcontracting transactions among most rural households are free of charge. However, some rural households do need to pay rents for subcontracted farmland, which varies greatly in terms of payment amount, payment direction (who will pay?) and length of payment time. Generally, there are two types of payment direction: (1) land seekers should pay rents to land owners; and (2) on the contrary, land owners should pay 'rents' to the people asked to cultivate their land (the rent here is in broad sense, as it is a kind of expenditure rather than income for the land owner, i.e. negative rent). Due to limited data, in the current study, information is only provided for the households with rent payment. Other issues concerning the amount and time duration of payment will be analysed in future research.[6]

It can be seen from Fig. 3.7 that in rural areas of Zhejiang, the percentage of rural households that obtained income directly from farmland subcontracting is generally only 5–7% every year, which was not high during the first round of contracting. However, about 10% of the households needed to pay 'rents' in normal years, which increased to 14% in 1999. The situation has been changed since the second round of contracting that there has been an increasing number of households that could obtain direct income from land subcontracting, which increased from 13.36% of the households in 2000 to 20.89% in 2002, an increase of 7.53% over three years. Meanwhile, rural households with rent payment increased only slightly with a much slower growth rate from 9.35% in 2000 to 12.44% in 2002.

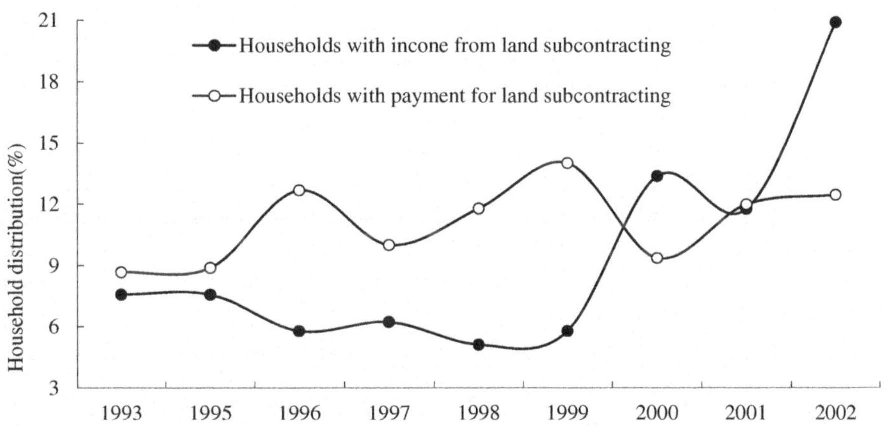

Fig. 3.7 Rent payments for farmland subcontracting

[6]According to the survey by Jiang Wenhua et al., in rural areas of Zhejiang, charging for farmland subcontracting has become more frequently, and the annual rent per *mu* of paddy rice field is generally 100–200 yuan, and even up to more than 1000 yuan (Cartel, 2001).

As for the farmland subcontracting of the observed households, since the ownership of farmlands does not belong to rural households, free subcontracting still dominates the current farmland subcontracting (Table 3.6), but this has changed since the second round of contracting, indicating that farmers' trust in national policies has changed. The most obvious changes can be seen from the two curves in Fig. 3.7, changed from a typical 'box' shape before 2000 to a pair of scissors. According to common sense, when more households are taking income from land subcontracting, there should be more other households paying the rents although not exactly the same in number. However, there exists a rising trend for both rent payers and payees. Figure 3.7 has shown the graph lines contrary to such a principle of payment. Why? I believe there might be three reasons. First, land is owned by collectives, and rural households are holding the contracting rights. Therefore, in farmland subcontracting, partial income might have been obtained by collectives, despite the fact that the rents have to be paid by households with land subcontracted in. Second, due to the efficiency deterioration of farmland operation (Shi, 2000), households mostly have taken the form of 'reversed transfer' (Zhang & Shi, 2001). Third, in rural Zhejiang, there have been quite a few 'labour migrants' (those who have left the home village but are still engaged in farming).[7] The land they have operated is mostly transferred from local villagers or collectives, but the rents would be paid directly to the collectives and rarely to the local villagers. In order to illustrate this in detail, analysis has been made concerning the relationships between rent payments and subcontracting.

It can be seen from Table 3.6 that during the observation years, the percentage of households with rental expenditure but without land subcontracting out was obviously higher than that of households with rental income. Meanwhile, the percentage of households with land subcontracting out and rental income was higher than that of households with rental expenditure. On the contrary, the percentage of households without land subcontracting in but with rental income was for most years higher than that of households with rental expenditure. At the same time, the percentage of households with land subcontracting in and rental income was obviously lower than that of households with rental expenditure. The trend has shown that in land subcontracting, the households with payments of rents and 'reversed rents' have both been on the rise. This has suggested that in rural Zhejiang, which is fairly industrialised, in order to prevent land extensive operation or non-operation due to the inefficient use of farmland, local government's policies concerning farmland management are very influential. It also indicates that as one of the main production factors, farmland has played a more active role.

[7]Labour migrants refer to the farmers who do not change their occupation after the interregional migration, and migrants that have changed their original occupation are referred to as 'vocational migrants' (Zhang, 1991: 83–94).

Table 3.6 Farmland subcontracting and rent payment (%)

	No subcontracting out within the year		With subcontracting out within the year			No subcontracting in within the year		With subcontracting in within the year		
	Rents in	Rents out	Rents in	Rents out	No rent	Rents in	Rents out	Rents in	Rents out	No rent
1993	1.80	6.00	5.00	1.80	15.20	5.40	4.40	1.40	3.40	13.60
1995	4.67	7.56	2.89	1.33	14.44	6.44	2.89	1.11	6.00	14.22
1996	3.11	11.56	2.67	1.11	11.33	4.89	5.78	0.89	6.89	15.78
1997	3.78	8.67	2.44	1.33	12.22	6.00	5.11	0.22	4.89	13.56
1998	2.89	9.56	2.22	2.22	15.11	4.44	5.33	0.67	6.44	15.11
1999	3.56	12.67	2.22	1.33	28.44	4.89	8.00	0.89	6.00	16.67
2000	5.12	8.02	8.24	1.34	21.16	12.47	4.23	0.89	5.12	20.27
2001	9.31	10.20	2.44	1.77	12.20	11.09	8.43	0.67	3.55	13.53
2002	11.56	10.00	9.33	2.44	20.67	20.22	9.33	0.67	3.11	10.89

Note In the observation between 1993 and 2000, income of rural household from farmland circulation was specifically counted, and there was no such counting before 1993

3.3 Who Is Subcontracting Farmland

In general, due to various reasons, the demand for farmland varies considerably among rural households. The farmland circulation is basically according to the principle of comparative efficiency in farmland use, that is, the farmland is transferred from the rural households with relatively low utilisation efficiencies to those with higher efficiencies (Shi & Jia, 2002). Rural households with higher efficiencies have relatively strong demands for farmland, and for those with lower efficiencies the demands are weaker. In the course of farmland circulation, which rural households may have a stronger demand for farmland? Whose demand is weaker? This is what we want to know the most. In other words, what are the attributes of households with land subcontracting in and out? What types of rural households are they? In view of this, a cross-group analysis is carried out for further investigation.

3.3.1 Economic Income Level

Table 3.7 indicates that the income level and farmland circulation of rural households are highly related. As income increases, land subcontracting in is obviously weakened, and the subcontracting out is significantly enhanced. This indicates that in the process of farmland circulation, the farmland is transferred from high-income households to low-income ones. That is to say, the households with land subcontracted out are those with relatively high incomes, while the households with land subcontracted in are those with relatively low incomes. In other words, in Zhejiang, the pattern of economic growth of rural households is represented by a typical model of 'leaving the land' or 'non-agriculturalisation'.

3.3.2 Types of Household Operation

Table 3.8 indicates that the farmland circulation is also closely related to the household operation types. With the acceleration of non-agricultural operation of rural households, land subcontracting in has been significantly weakened, whereas land subcontracting out enhanced. That is to say, the farmland is transferred from non-agricultural households to those partially or completely engaged in agriculture. Rural households with a higher degree of non-agriculturalisation are the main source of land subcontracting out, and those with a lower degree are the major recipients of land subcontracted. It is worth noting that due to the very intense human-land contradictions in Zhejiang, agricultural households only take a small percentage, and the percentage of households completely engaged in agriculture is extremely low, representing 35.40 and 25.40% of all households under observation (Fig. 3.8). Generally, farmland is not directly transferred from non-agricultural households to agricultural

Table 3.7 Farmland subcontracting and household income level (%)

	Household frequency of land subcontracting in (%)					Household frequency of land subcontracting out (%)				
	Low	Lower middle	Middle	Upper middle	High	Low	Lower middle	Middle	Upper middle	High
1986	12.96	10.65	9.26	8.33	2.78	N/A				
1987	17.83	12.66	11.79	7.86	5.65	12.17	7.86	6.11	10.48	10.87
1988	13.36	9.96	12.55	9.96	9.91	8.62	5.63	10.82	9.96	16.81
1989	10.50	14.71	10.55	6.30	7.14	10.50	8.40	9.28	5.04	10.92
1990	13.69	20.33	11.57	12.03	7.88	12.45	2.90	6.20	6.64	9.54
1991	15.58	15.58	17.24	11.26	7.36	9.96	9.52	9.05	6.93	12.12
1993	15.00	10.00	11.00	6.00	4.00	9.00	10.00	6.00	11.00	19.00
1995	13.00	16.00	9.00	3.00	7.00	7.00	10.00	5.00	9.00	11.00
1996	15.00	14.00	10.00	7.00	7.00	6.00	8.00	5.00	8.00	7.00
1997	11.00	14.00	12.00	4.00	1.00	8.00	4.00	7.00	11.00	6.00
1998	16.00	15.00	8.00	5.00	6.00	6.00	11.00	8.00	11.00	8.00
1999	16.00	15.00	11.00	8.00	3.00	5.00	15.00	17.00	20.00	15.00
2000	13.00	18.00	12.00	11.00	5.05	12.00	12.00	14.00	17.00	14.14
2001	3.00	17.00	10.00	6.00	3.96	8.00	7.00	7.00	9.00	5.94
2002	9.00	7.00	10.00	7.00	0.00	24.00	10.00	12.00	16.00	11.00

Note The abnormal changes around 2000 may be related to the second round of contracting. It may also be related to the implementation of new grain policies for complete marketisation in Zhejiang

Table 3.8 Farmland subcontracting and household operation types (%)

	Households with subcontracting in					Households with subcontracting out				
	Non-agricultural	Non-agricultural dominated	Agricultural dominated	Agricultural	Complete agricultural	Non-agricultural	Non-agricultural dominated	Agricultural dominated	Agricultural	Complete agricultural
1986	5.26	5.38	4.44	11.84	6.96	N/A				
1987	6.25	11.36	6.11	13.88	9.55	16.07	15.91	7.63	6.39	7.96
1988	8.06	5.75	9.70	14.06	13.56	25.81	6.90	4.24	6.74	7.06
1989	10.71	8.49	7.04	11.61	6.57	22.32	2.83	4.93	5.67	5.30
1990	10.83	12.30	8.22	15.97	12.44	15.83	8.20	6.16	4.33	3.89
1991	10.00	10.31	13.92	16.10	10.99	17.86	8.25	5.06	6.79	8.45
1993	2.90	14.29	15.94	9.42	8.47	20.29	10.20	7.25	10.51	12.17
1995	3.06	11.76	11.54	12.74	10.75	13.27	7.84	11.54	5.79	4.84
1996	6.59	16.33	13.46	12.55	12.26	13.19	4.08	7.69	4.31	4.72
1997	2.54	15.00	11.43	11.31	5.92	9.32	10.00	11.43	4.52	4.73
1998	0.79	7.69	21.74	15.38	10.43	10.24	5.13	15.22	7.26	6.75
1999	3.13	22.00	27.45	10.91	6.80	31.25	12.00	7.84	5.00	4.76
2000	4.55	21.15	29.51	13.26	9.85	15.91	11.54	16.39	12.71	12.12
2001	2.70	15.38	23.53	10.20	11.27	10.14	7.69	7.84	5.61	7.04
2002	2.82	9.09	19.44	10.17	5.51	13.38	15.15	22.22	15.25	14.96

Note Agricultural households refer to the households with 80% or more of their production factors and income invested in and obtained from agriculture, while agriculture-dominated households refer to those with 50–80%, non-agricultural dominated households refer to those with 20–50%, non-agricultural households are those with 20% and below, and complete agricultural households are those with 100%

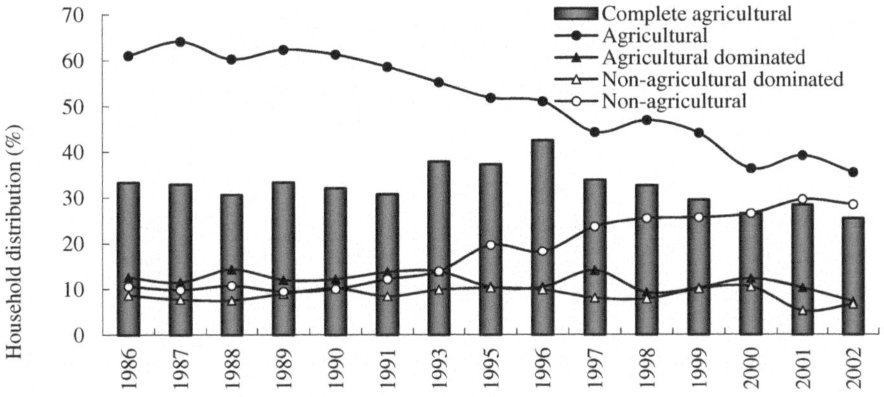

Fig. 3.8 Household operation structure

households, and households partially engaged in agriculture serve as an important bridge in the circulation process. Therefore, in the process of farmland circulation, it is difficult to achieve the one-step centralised scale operation within a short period of time.

3.3.3 Household Education

In the process of farmland circulation, in addition to household economic condition and household operation, education level of household members is also an important factor (Shi & Jia, 2002). According to Table 3.9, the percentage change of rural households with spontaneous land transfer in has shown that farmland tends to be subcontracted to those who have achieved a certain education level and adapted to the current agricultural technology. When the education level is higher or lower than this level, households tend to transfer out farmland and engage in non-agricultural activities. Such an education level is the completion of the nine-year compulsory education. It is also shown in Table 3.9 that with the improvement of education for rural households, farmland, the comparatively stable production factor, has been activated gradually. For instance, households with different education backgrounds became more active in farmland circulation in the late 1990s after they experienced a recession in the mid-1990s. Households with senior high school education have shown growing preference both for farming the land and for leaving the land. The farmland management is typically polarised, i.e. 'farmland preference' and 'farmland leaving'.

Table 3.9 Farmland subcontracting and household education level (%)

	Households with land subcontracting in (%)				Households with land subcontracting out (%)			
	Illiterate	Primary school	Junior high	Senior high+	Illiterate	Primary school	Junior high	Senior high+
1986	8.22	10.83	6.49	1.85	N/A			
1987	7.97	13.08	11.88	3.85	11.59	8.24	9.20	13.46
1988	11.06	12.52	10.03	3.51	15.04	9.43	6.92	19.30
1989	9.68	10.23	10.97	1.69	9.68	8.47	5.48	18.64
1990	14.22	13.47	13.60	3.13	8.19	6.56	6.34	20.31
1991	11.68	14.63	14.88	1.52	11.68	8.70	7.44	19.70
1993	8.47	10.53	9.03	0.00	13.56	9.40	13.19	9.68
1995	7.55	9.58	11.41	6.25	11.32	7.28	10.07	6.25
1996	9.62	10.81	11.32	6.67	3.85	6.56	8.18	6.67
1997	9.62	6.80	12.20	0.00	3.85	7.20	8.54	5.88
1998	6.00	10.98	10.49	6.06	6.00	9.02	8.64	12.12
1999	9.62	8.82	14.53	5.26	7.69	15.97	13.37	18.42
2000	6.25	11.76	13.79	10.26	20.83	12.18	13.22	17.95
2001	8.51	9.66	7.30	0.00	12.77	4.62	9.55	7.89
2002	4.44	8.12	6.01	2.63	15.56	14.10	16.39	7.89

3.3.4 Household Location

Similarly, the farmland circulation is also related to household locations. Table 3.10 indicates that in the ten villages under observation in Zhejiang, only four villages have had relatively frequent farmland circulations since the observation, including Yongfeng Village of Huzhou and Longshang Village of Lin'an in north Zhejiang, and Hebian Village of Lishui and Shibanyan Village of Jinhua in southwest of Zhejiang. Farmland circulations in the other five villages (Bogumen Village is an island fishing village) are relatively less frequent in both land subcontracting in and subcontracting out. This phenomenon has not occurred in a certain period of time, but throughout the entire observation period. It is important to note the four villages with relatively frequent farmland circulations are the ones where agriculture plays a more important role in the economic structure among all the observed villages. This indicates that, in the process of economic growth, the areas with frequent farmland circulations are not those with a high degree of non-agriculturalisation, but those with a higher reliance on agriculture. Certainly, a specific level of non-agriculturalisation in the countryside is a major premise, as this is not applicable to the underdeveloped inland areas (Shi & Jia, 2002, 2003). In villages with a higher degree of non-agriculturalisation, farmland circulation is usually a one-off transaction without obvious continuous fluctuations. For example, in Jinhou Village of Rui'an in south Zhejiang, 84% of the

Table 3.10 Farmland subcontracting and household location (%)

	Households with land subcontracted in									
	Longshang	Yongfeng	Yubei	Xishufu	Miaoyan	Xinmin	Jinhou	Bogumen	Hebian	Shibanyan
1986	2.82	8.33	13.10	2.90	4.91	4.00	7.27	1.59	24.65	13.68
1987	5.56	14.88	15.29	4.29	4.32	6.67	10.00	0.00	20.28	23.38
1988	6.58	18.90	22.09	2.86	3.68	4.46	15.60	0.78	12.50	22.70
1989	6.41	8.89	8.51	1.33	6.29	3.48	21.05	0.00	11.56	25.00
1990	10.13	22.14	8.42	5.33	5.17	7.63	23.48	0.87	16.54	24.07
1991	7.79	20.00	6.06	8.97	5.00	6.56	23.21	0.00	19.85	25.77
1993	6.00	18.00	2.00	2.00	2.00	14.00	14.00	0.00	12.00	22.00
1995	22.00	24.00	0.00	12.00	0.00	8.00	2.00	0.00	10.00	18.00
1996	14.00	32.00	0.00	10.00	2.00	14.00	4.00	0.00	6.00	24.00
1997	24.00	22.00	0.00	2.00	0.00	8.00	6.00	0.00	0.00	22.00
1998	26.00	28.00	8.00	0.00	4.00	4.00	0.00	0.00	4.00	26.00
1999	42.00	12.00	2.00	0.00	0.00	8.00	4.00	0.00	12.00	26.00
2000	37.50	18.00	0.00	4.00	0.00	10.00	6.00	0.00	24.00	20.00
2001	27.08	20.00	0.00	6.00	2.00	14.00	0.00	0.00	10.00	1.89
2002	26.00	12.00	2.00	0.00	0.00	6.00	6.00	0.00	12.00	2.00
	Households with land subcontracted out									
1986	N/A									
1987	1.39	1.65	2.35	7.14	15.43	16.19	19.09	0.00	12.59	11.69
1988	1.32	4.72	10.47	0.00	7.98	17.86	33.03	0.78	9.72	14.18
1989	0.00	0.00	7.45	2.67	9.43	9.57	25.44	0.00	11.56	16.67

(continued)

Table 3.10 (continued)

	Households with land subcontracted out									
1990	2.53	2.14	9.47	2.67	2.30	8.47	13.91	0.87	9.77	19.14
1991	2.60	2.86	17.17	6.41	6.67	11.48	12.50	0.00	8.40	21.47
1993	6.00	6.00	12.00	10.00	6.00	20.00	4.00	4.00	8.00	34.00
1995	22.00	4.00	2.00	4.00	4.00	16.00	10.00	0.00	10.00	12.00
1996	16.00	10.00	2.00	10.00	0.00	4.00	6.00	0.00	16.00	4.00
1997	26.00	12.00	0.00	6.00	0.00	8.00	2.00	0.00	12.00	6.00
1998	30.00	20.00	0.00	10.00	0.00	16.00	0.00	0.00	4.00	8.00
1999	34.00	6.00	2.00	0.00	0.00	8.00	84.00	0.00	4.00	6.00
2000	29.17	14.00	2.00	12.00	4.00	44.00	6.00	0.00	14.00	14.00
2001	25.00	16.00	2.00	6.00	2.00	10.00	2.00	0.00	8.00	3.77
2002	26.00	30.00	2.00	2.00	8.00	42.00	0.00	0.00	30.00	6.00

rural households experienced land subcontracting out 1999. The rate of land subcontracting out decreased with the rise of household income. Of the low-income and lower-middle income households, 100% had their land subcontracted out, compared with 90.91% for the middle, 88.98% for the upper middle, and 64.29% for the high income households. Meanwhile, the rate of land subcontracting out has developed according to a 'U' shape with the improvement household education. The percentage with land subcontracting out is 100% for the illiterate, semi-illiterate and above high school groups, 89.29% for the primary school group, and 68.75% for the junior high group. It has been also developing according to an inverted 'U' with the increase of household non-agriculturalisation, where the figure is 85.71% for non-agricultural households, 100% for partial agricultural households, and 66.67% for agricultural households.

As analysed previously, in rural Zhejiang, land circulation generally follows the route from high-income to middle-income then to low-income households, and from non-agricultural to partial agricultural and then to agricultural households. Farmland operation has been concentrated to the households with certain levels of education. As for land circulation, it happens more frequently in agricultural areas, while in areas with a higher level of non-agriculturalisation or economic development, land circulation tends to show a one-time or concentrated nature.

3.4 Development of Farmland Circulation Market

Although the ownership of farmland does not belong to farmers, after 15 years of the first round contracting practice, farmers' understanding of land ownership has changed significantly, which can be seen from the changes in farmers' perception of the farmland use right transfer (Cartel, 2001). In rural areas of Zhejiang, the traditional use right transfer of farmland among households used to be unpaid, and transfers with payments were rarely seen. However, significant changes have taken place over time, and paid transfers have become more frequent among rural households. This change indicates that the development of farmland circulation market has achieved a new level of development. As one of the most important production factors, farmland has been integrated into the entire market economy. The concept of land wealth has become increasingly important in people's lives.

3.4.1 Economic Income Level

In the process of farmland circulation, as mentioned previously, the farmland is transferred from high-income to low-income households. According to the general principles of market economy, in terms of rental income, it follows that the percentage of high-income households with rental income should be higher than that of the low-income households, whereas the situation for rental expenditure is the opposite.

However, existing data show that this is not the case. According to Table 3.11, in terms of rental expenditure, it is true that the percentage of low-income households is higher than that of the high-income households. However, in terms of rental income from land subcontracting, the percentage of high-income households is not significantly higher than that of other income groups, only higher than other groups in some individual years. In my opinion, this can be explained as:during the land subcontracting, low-income households did have land subcontracted in by way of rental payment. However, such land subcontracting in has not been directly from high-income households. Instead, it might come from rural collectives or other agencies. For high-income households, farmland has mostly been transferred out free of charge.

3.4.2 Types of Household Operation

Although a clear conclusion on the relationship between rural household economic development and rent payment for farmland subcontracting cannot be drawn, a relatively obvious conclusion can be obtained for the relationship between household type and rent payment (Table 3.12). In the process of farmland subcontracting, most payments out occur among agricultural dominated and agricultural households, while most payments in occur among non-agricultural and non-agricultural dominated households. This result indicates that there has been certain development of farmland circulation market in Zhejiang, especially after the second round of land contracting, in that the percentage of households directly receiving income from farmland subcontracting has increased significantly.

3.4.3 Household Education

Table 3.13 indicates that there are certain differences in rent acquisition for households with different education backgrounds, but the changing trend is not clearly defined and irregular. For example, in 2000, with the improvement of household education, the proportion of households with rent income from farmland subcontracting showed a significant downward trend, while in 2002 it was the opposite. Similarly, the proportion of rural households paying rents showed a trend of an inverted 'U' shape between 1997 and 2000, yet it was on the rise in 2001. Taking into consideration of the changes in macroeconomic environment for agricultural operation, it is roughly concluded from existing data that in years with better agricultural operation returns, more households would obtain farmland rents. In comparison, the number of households paying rents would be less than in other years. This has indicated that although farmland circulation is based on increase in efficiency of farmland unitisation, i.e. households with land subcontracted in should have more efficiency than those with land subcontracted out, rent payments have been related to the macroeconomic agricultural background (Shi & Jia, 2002, 2003). Meanwhile, they are also related to the economic status of individual households and their geographic locations.

Table 3.11 Rent payment and household economic status (%)

	Households with rental income					Households with rental expenditure				
	Low	Lower middle	Middle	Upper middle	High	Low	Lower middle	Middle	Upper middle	High
1993	31.82	27.78	26.67	11.76	45.00	22.73	27.78	33.33	11.76	25.00
1995	29.41	19.05	21.43	0.00	12.50	64.71	47.62	21.43	8.33	12.50
1996	22.22	13.64	13.33	21.43	7.14	77.78	40.91	46.67	14.29	7.14
1997	6.25	5.56	26.32	20.00	14.29	43.75	50.00	31.58	20.00	0.00
1998	19.05	17.39	7.14	6.67	7.14	57.14	39.13	42.86	33.33	7.14
1999	4.76	17.86	16.00	3.70	5.56	57.14	28.57	12.00	18.52	5.56
2000	28.00	25.00	38.46	26.92	41.18	36.00	32.14	11.54	23.08	0.00
2001	54.55	18.18	7.14	14.29	0.00	9.09	40.91	28.57	21.43	20.00
2002	38.71	37.50	36.84	45.45	72.73	35.48	31.25	10.53	13.64	9.09

Table 3.12 Rent payment and household operation type (%)

	Households with income from subcontracting					Households with expenditure on subcontracting				
	Non-agricultural	Non-agricultural dominated	Agricultural dominated	Agricultural	Complete agricultural	Non-agricultural	Non-agricultural dominated	Agricultural dominated	Agricultural	Complete agricultural
1993	31.25	36.36	20.00	31.25	35.29	12.50	9.09	26.67	29.17	26.47
1995	13.33	0.00	36.36	19.51	7.69	0.00	11.11	27.27	56.10	42.31
1996	29.41	10.00	30.00	9.76	11.76	5.88	40.00	50.00	56.10	52.94
1997	35.71	20.00	13.33	3.03	0.00	0.00	20.00	33.33	54.55	50.00
1998	14.29	20.00	14.29	10.20	4.00	14.29	20.00	50.00	46.94	32.00
1999	2.27	20.00	5.56	16.13	28.57	0.00	6.67	50.00	61.29	50.00
2000	38.46	31.25	29.63	29.55	38.46	7.69	25.00	18.52	36.36	34.62
2001	15.79	0.00	13.33	22.22	27.27	10.53	0.00	40.00	40.74	40.91
2002	40.91	12.50	15.38	45.24	60.00	4.55	25.00	30.77	35.71	44.00

Table 3.13 Rent payment and household education (%)

	Households with income from subcontracting					Households with expenditure on subcontracting				
	General	Illiterate	Primary	Junior high	Senior high+	General	Illiterate	Primary	Junior high	Senior high+
1993	29.35	8.33	22.00	44.44	100.00	23.91	8.33	24.00	33.33	0.00
1995	17.50	33.33	12.50	18.52	25.00	33.75	22.22	32.50	37.04	50.00
1996	15.66	14.29	17.07	16.13	0.00	39.76	42.86	31.71	48.39	50.00
1997	14.67	0.00	15.63	11.76	100.00	33.33	42.86	34.38	32.35	0.00
1998	12.64	33.33	13.33	10.00	0.00	37.93	50.00	33.33	46.67	16.67
1999	10.08	11.11	9.09	10.87	11.11	24.37	33.33	21.82	26.09	22.22
2000	31.15	69.23	25.00	27.66	30.00	22.13	7.69	23.08	27.66	10.00
2001	18.31	22.22	17.24	13.33	66.67	26.76	22.22	27.59	30.00	0.00
2002	43.43	44.44	39.58	47.37	50.00	22.22	0.00	31.25	18.42	0.00

3.4.4 Geographic Location

Table 3.14 indicates that, in the process of farmland subcontracting, rent payments vary significantly in the ten villages of Zhejiang. In terms of rental income, except for Bogumen village located on an island, it occurs in other nine villages, and persists in most villages. In comparison, the four villages of Longshang, Yongfeng, Hebian and Shibanyan have higher frequencies of rent payments, while in Xinmin, Maoyan, Jinhou and Yushubu where non-agricultural economy is comparatively developed, there have been only intermittent occurrences of payments. Therefore, rent payments are concentrated in the above mentioned four villages of Longshang, Yongfeng, Hebian, and Shibanyan, but rarely occur in other villages. It can be seen that there are two types of farmland circulation markets developing in rural areas of Zhejiang: one is the private farmland circulation market that is spontaneously formed (four villages), and the other is the farmland circulation market with the participation of agencies or the collectives (three villages of Xishufu, Xinmin and Jinhou). Land circulations in the former mostly occur among fellow villagers, and the latter between villagers and 'immigrants' or companies, where agencies and collectives play an intermediary role.

3.5 Origin of Farmland Circulation

In previous studies, I have discussed the transformation of rural household economic structure (Shi & Huang, 2001) and the origin of farmland circulation (Shi & Jia, 2002). It is found that all the economic behaviours of rural households are consistent with economic rational principles. This also applies to the farmland circulation of rural households in coastal Zhejiang. Table 3.15 indicates that the utilisation efficiency for economic resources of rural households has shown a declining trend over time, especially for farmland, because its efficiency deteriorating is even worse than that in inland Shanxi, and the central-western regions (Shi, 2000; Shi & Hou, 2001; Shi, Ma, & Wu, 2001). This result partially explains why more and more rural households in coastal areas are 'leaving the land'. Existing research has shown that rural household economy in Zhejiang is typically non-agricultural, and the income from farmland plays a trivial role in household economy (Shi & Huang, 2001). Although there has been constant increase of farmland transfers, it has had little impact on alleviating the land efficiency deterioration. The origin of such a result, in my opinion, has been decided by the expected benefits from farmland. Many rural households in Zhejiang with a higher degree of non-agriculturalisation do not pay much attention to agricultural operation. However, their nostalgia for farmland and the expected benefits make them unable to give up the contracting right over farmland but rather choose to transfer the right of use. Due to the differences in farmland management in different areas, subcontracting in some areas requires a certain price,[8] while in others

[8]Land subcontracting out in the Wentai area requires paying some fees to the contractor.

Table 3.14 Rent payment and household location (%)

	Households with income from subcontracting									
	Longshang	Yongfeng	Yubei	Xihufu	Miaoyan	Xinmin	Jinhou	Bogumen	Hebian	Shibanyan
1993	0	27.27	0	16.67	0	29.41	0	0	25	69.57
1995	5.88	21.43	–	–	–	0	–	–	40	54.55
1996	15.38	26.32	0	–	–	0	–	–	36.36	14.29
1997	8	14.29	–	–	–	37.5	–	–	50	7.14
1998	11.54	21.05	–	–	0	0	–	–	0	23.53
1999	14.71	37.5	–	–	–	0	–	–	25	13.33
2000	12.9	21.43	0	–	50	83.33	–	–	15.79	41.18
2001	16	38.46	100	–	0	8.33	–	–	12.5	33.33
2002	17.39	63.16	0	–	100	65.22	0	–	25	75
	Households with expenditure on subcontracting									
1993	0	81.82	0	50	0	0	22.22	0	25	26.09
1995	17.65	85.71	–	–	–	–	–	–	40	72.73
1996	30.77	78.95	–	–	–	–	–	–	18.18	85.71
1997	12	78.57	–	–	–	12.5	–	–	0	71.43
1998	23.08	68.42	–	–	–	20	–	–	0	70.59
1999	29.41	87.5	–	–	–	0	–	–	0	80
2000	9.68	28.57	–	12.5	–	–	–	–	52.63	52.94
2001	24	76.92	–	–	–	–	–	–	25	33.33
2002	13.04	73.68	–	–	–	8.7	–	–	10	25

Note '–' indicating no such event

Table 3.15 Resource utilisation efficiency for farming households

	Land use efficiency (yuan/*mu*)			Labour efficiency (yuan/*mu*)			Investment efficiency (yuan/*mu*)			Average labour cost
	Farming households	Households with land in	Households with land out	Farming households	Households with land in	Households with land out	Farming households	Households with land in	Households with land out	
1986	−12.33	−8.92	–	−0.65	−0.47	–	−0.39	−0.26	–	5.48
1987	−4.34	−8.16	11.88	−0.22	−0.40	0.79	−0.12	−0.20	0.37	5.71
1988	−21.28	−27.86	17.87	−1.11	−1.30	1.15	−0.45	−0.51	0.40	7.23
1989	−1.80	3.15	42.46	−0.09	0.17	2.76	−0.03	0.05	0.84	7.50
1990	−16.14	−21.01	9.91	−0.89	−1.14	0.53	−0.28	−0.36	0.16	8.60
1991	−6.69	−10.66	6.62	−0.35	−0.56	0.34	−0.10	−0.15	0.08	8.48
1993	−143.30	−106.69	−79.04	−6.69	−5.37	−4.12	−1.50	−1.15	−0.85	19.05
1995	21.55	−64.19	63.09	1.32	−3.57	4.11	0.13	−0.32	0.40	25.71
1996	62.87	33.00	78.77	3.71	1.82	4.33	0.38	0.19	0.42	22.89
1997	−102.97	−153.50	−271.11	−5.91	−7.84	−12.43	−0.64	−0.88	−1.47	28.12
1998	−68.17	−127.15	36.65	−3.86	−6.39	2.56	−0.41	−0.63	0.20	28.29
1999	−171.39	−307.43	−406.17	−9.73	−13.44	−13.56	−0.97	−1.33	−1.70	29.17
2000	−198.81	−278.55	−122.85	−10.82	−12.22	−8.30	−1.03	−0.85	−0.33	30.64
2001	−210.78	−163.98	−286.41	−10.93	−10.70	−14.81	−1.04	−0.55	−1.73	30.90
2002	−209.09	−156.14	−434.55	−10.45	−6.78	−15.28	−0.77	−0.34	−0.85	22.93

Note Land use (labour, investment) efficiency = (revenue − cost − labour x average labour cost)/crop planting area (labour required, cost)

subcontracting of farmland will obtain 'unearned' benefits.[9] The rapid development of non-agricultural economy among rural households has accelerated farmland circulation in this area. However, due to the higher opportunity cost of labour in this area, there is no doubt that the efficiency of households with land subcontracted out is slightly better than that of households with land subcontracted in.

By comparing farmland circulation and utilisation efficiency in coastal and inland regions(Shi & Jia, 2002), it is found out that under the premise of the national unified market for agricultural products, there exists a huge potential to develop between inland and coastal regions in terms of opportunity cost of labour engaged in crop planting. When rural households in the coastal areas are "leaving the land", there is no doubt that many gaps appear in farmland operation, and these gaps will be filled by the 'labour migrants' from the inland to the coastal areas (Zhang, 1991: 83–94). On the surface, it seems the operation efficiency of farmland in coastal regions is lower than that of inland areas. However, the result is the opposite if the average labour cost in inland Shanxi is used for calculation. Take the year of 2000 as an example, one *mu* of farmland would lose 55.52 yuan if maintained by a Zhejiang farmer, but would earn 106.93 yuan by a Shanxi farmer. Accordingly, the investment returns of one labour engaged in crop planting would change from negative 3.07 yuan to positive 5.91 yuan, and the return of one yuan change from negative 0.56 yuan to positive 0.55 yuan. Therefore, it can be seen that there does exist comparative advantages in farmland operation. Such advantages belong to inland farmers only, and not for local farmers in coastal regions. Such a result has explained why there are more rural households with land subcontracted out than those with land subcontracted in, and the situation is the opposite in inland regions.

3.6 Conclusion and Comments

In summary, farmland circulation is closely related to economic development. In economically underdeveloped areas, income growth of rural households is highly dependent on farmland. Heavily influenced by the macro agricultural economic situation, household income growth has stagnated or declined, eventually leading to the shrinkage of farmland circulation. In the economically developed regions, the situation is the opposite. By comparing the relationships between rural household farmland circulation and farmland operation in both economically developed and underdeveloped areas, it shows that household farmland circulation is economic rational. Increasing farmland utilisation efficiency is the fundamental motivation for rural households to circulate farmland. The appearance of 'labour migrants' in coastal areas is due mainly to the existing and growing disparity in labour opportunity cost in developed and developing areas. Against this background, establishing and improving the market mechanism for farmland is of practical significance.

[9] Land subcontracting out in Shaoxing will receive certain compensation.

References

Cartel, Z. (2001). Rural land transfer: New situation and new thinking—Investigation of rural land circulation in Zhejiang. *Chinese Rural Economy, 10,* 11–18.

Jia, H., Tian, C., & Shi, Q. (2003). *Development patterns of market for farmland use and policy analysis in East China.* Beijing: China Agricultural Press.

Shi, Q. (1999). *Rural household economic development.* Beijing: China Agriculture Press.

Shi, Q. (2000). Resource use efficiency and comparison of its allocation directions in rural household economy. *Chinese Rural Economy, 8,* 58–61.

Shi, Q. (2001). *Rural household economic activity and behaviour.* Beijing: China Agricultural Press.

Shi, Q., & Hou, R. (2001). Life cycle of farmer's household and the economic operation in Shanxi Province. *Research of Agricultural Modernisation, 22*(2), 65–70.

Shi, Q., & Huang, Z. (2001). Transit of rural household economic structure and its origin. *Management World, 4,* 112–119.

Shi, Q., & Jia, S. (2002). A comparison between the farmland factor trend and its origin. *Management World, 1,* 71–77.

Shi, Q., & Jia, S. (2003). Rural houeshold land transfer and its origin:Evidence from three coastal provinces of Jiangsu, Shandong and Zhejiang. *Economic Issues in China, 5,* 41–54.

Shi, Q., Ma, S., & Wu, Z. (2001). On the income increase and the transference of Chinese famers and its causes. *Hebei Academic Journal, 5,* 24–28.

Shi, Q., & Zhang, H. (2000). The process of non-agriculturalisation of rural household operation. *On Economic Problems, 4,* 45–48.

Wan, G., & Cheng, E. (2001). Effects of land fragmentation and returns to scale in the Chinese farming sector. *Applied Economics, 33*(2), 183–194.

Zhang, P. (1991). *Agriculture and industrialisation: The adjustments that take place as an agricultural country is industrialised (translated in Chinese).* Changsha: Hunan Press.

Zhang, Z., & Shi, Q. (2001). Farmland productivity change and comparision of households with different scales. *Chinese Rural Economy, 1,* 67–73.

Chapter 4
Evolution of Saving, Borrowing and Lending Behaviour

Contents

Rural household saving and lending are important aspects which reflect the development of household economy. With the deepening of China's reform process, constant change in its financial system, and continuous increase of household income, there have been various changes in household saving and lending behaviour. In order to have a clear understanding, this chapter carries out a comparative study on household saving and lending from 1986 to 2002 based on data collected from the fixed observation sites of ten villages in Zhejiang.

4.1 Saving Behaviour and Its Changes

As an economic term, saving can be interpreted from both broad and narrow perspectives. Broadly speaking, saving is surplus, i.e. the remaining amount after the income minus expenditure over a certain period. It could be in the form of cash, and could be in kind. In the narrow sense, it refers to one's monetary income surplus,

Q. Shi and Y. Gao, *Sustainable Development of Rural Household Economy*,
https://doi.org/10.1007/978-981-15-2747-0_4

which has to be deposited in a financial institution (Ma, 1993: 169). In this study, saving is analysed in the narrow sense, i.e. farmers' behaviour to deposit the cash in a financial institution such as a bank or credit cooperative.

4.1.1 Changing Trend of Savings

It can be seen from Table 4.1 and Fig. 4.1 that since the follow-up observation in 1986, the level of savings for rural households in the ten villages has increased continuously, which is obviously supported by the associated continuous increase in household income. The per capita level of savings increased from 105.00 yuan in the beginning of the observation to 11,842.09 yuan in 2002, with an annual average growth rate of 34.36% over the 17 years, more than doubled the income growth rate of 16.21%. With the increase in savings, the amount of cash in hand also grew rapidly, as seen by the per capita level increase from 246.56 yuan in 1986 to 1215.66 yuan in 2002, with an average annual growth rate of 10.49% during the 17 years. This is calculated according to the current price without consideration of factors in price change. If the retail price index in Zhejiang is used, taking the price as 100 in the year of 2000, during the 17 years of observation, the average growth rate of rural household savings is as high as 26.14%, much higher than the income growth rate of

Table 4.1 Changes of saving level and saving ratio

	Saving level per capita (yuan)				Interest/income (%)	Interest/saving (%)	Saving ratio (%)
	Bank saving	Cash in hand	Net income	Interest income			
1986	105.00	246.56	862.53	–	–	–	61.76
1987	208.98	376.98	1181.55	–	–	–	68.09
1988	236.33	531.34	1489.50	–	–	–	64.65
1989	274.01	547.95	1307.28	–	–	–	62.57
1990	346.72	693.10	1444.33	–	–	–	59.95
1991	506.75	695.70	1730.18	–	–	–	56.57
1993	878.52	667.03	3110.13	64.44	2.07	7.33	46.60
1995	1939.01	965.76	6351.27	96.18	1.51	4.96	44.60
1996	2502.95	910.36	7323.73	152.80	2.09	6.10	45.00
1997	3263.87	1189.62	7425.14	156.99	2.11	4.81	46.40
1998	4627.73	1063.95	7121.82	158.27	2.22	3.42	44.20
1999	5961.45	1887.93	8113.35	118.63	1.46	1.99	44.80
2000	7919.44	1513.23	9381.10	123.18	1.31	1.56	49.70
2001	10061.76	1202.20	9730.87	91.69	0.94	0.91	54.69
2002	11842.09	1215.66	9540.16	78.70	0.82	0.66	57.40
1995–2002	5368.63	1174.40	7524.87	115.55	1.54	2.15	48.16

Note Saving ratio = households with savings/all observed households

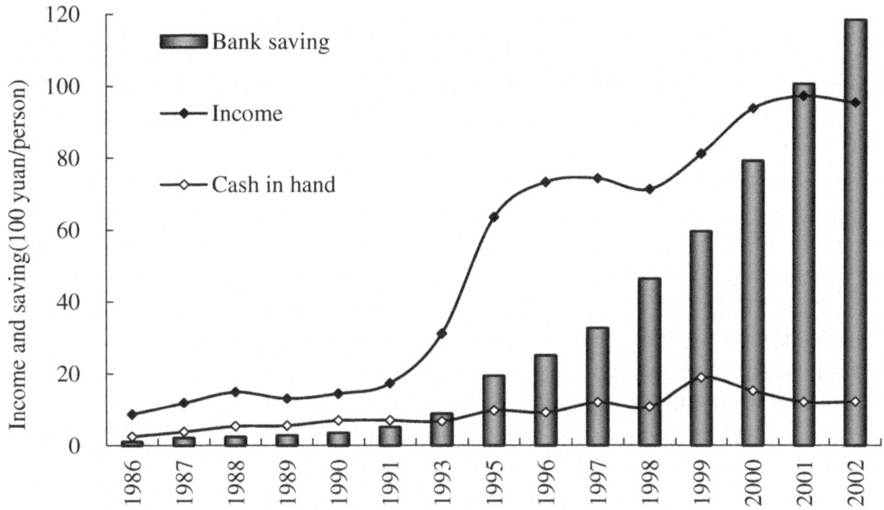

Fig. 4.1 Changing trend of income and savings of rural households

9.10%. During the entire changing process of saving levels, the growth trend can be generally divided into two stages (Fig. 4.2). The first is an accelerated growth period before 1995, when the average growth rate reached 38.26%, with the rate of 34.80% between 1986 to 1990 and 41.10% from 1990 to 1995. The second period is after 1995 when there was an obvious slowdown in the growth rate, i.e. the average growth rate dropped to 29.50% from 1995 to 2002, with the rate of 39.00% between 1995 to 2000, and 22.28% from 2000 to 2002. It is obvious that the changes in savings for rural households are closely related to the growth of income, and the accumulative

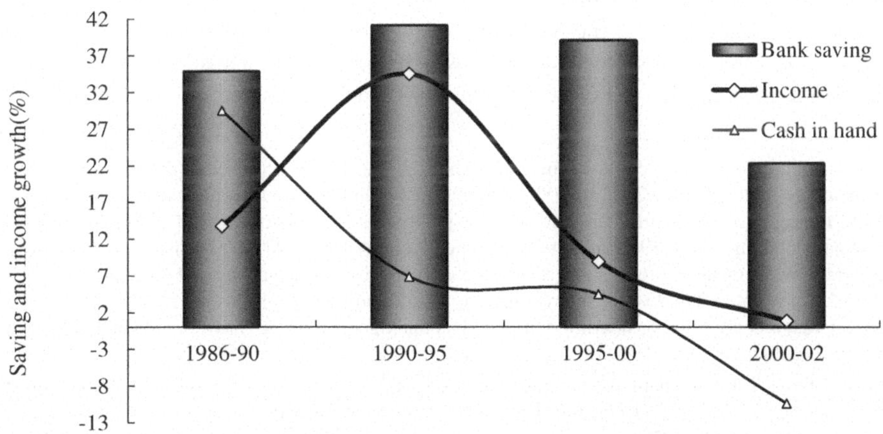

Fig. 4.2 Changes in growth rates of the income and saving levels of rural households

effect of savings has ensured that both the saving level and the saving growth rate have far exceeded those of income. Although in the late 1990s, in order to stimulate domestic demand against the background of the Asian financial crises, the Chinese government introduced quite a few financial policies and measures, such as reducing bank deposit interest rates for seven consecutive times and levying interest tax, the farmers' saving behaviour was not greatly affected and their bank deposit balance increased as usual. This is totally different from the staged and stagnated slow growth of income. Why? To answer this question, I have carried out multiple detailed studies on farmers' saving behaviour in different provinces in China (Shi & Chen, 2002; Shi & Li, 2003; Shi & Zhuo, 2003), and have found out that farmers' saving is not aimed at the bank interests but something else.[1] There are farmers who do expect to gain from the interests, but such farmers are few in number.

However, it should also be noted that along with the continuous increase of farmers' savings, the interest income indeed took a certain share of the rural household income, but the proportion decreased sharply in the ten villages of Zhejiang after the state's reducing of the saving interest rate eight times[2] and the start of the levy of interest tax. It decreased noticeably from the highest level of 2.22% in 1998 to 0.82% in 2002. Therefore, the original intention of such a policy implemented by the state was to stimulate domestic demand and enhance residents' purchasing power, so as to turn farmers' deposits into production power. Yet, farmers' saving purpose and the intention of state policy were mismatched—the foundation of the state policy was that the residents saved for earning interests, but this was not the farmers' saving purpose. Therefore, the consequence of such a policy was that the savings of farmers rose straightforward, and the proportion of farmers' interest income decreased sharply, while the goal for stimulating domestic demand could not be truly realised.

Another reason for poor performance of the policy lied in the inconsistency between saving levels and saving ratios: the saving levels of farmers were indeed increasing continuously, but the saving ratio did not rise simultaneously. Instead, it shrank. According to the situations of the observed households in the ten villages of Zhejiang (Table 4.1), at the beginning of the observation, the proportion of rural households with savings exceeded 60%, which decreased to a level below 60% after the 1990s, then further to below 50% in 1993, and maintained a level between 40

[1] I once conducted a survey involving 1968 households in 23 provinces (municipalities and autonomous regions) from 2002 to 2004. When asked whether they had interest income, 50.29% of the farmers gave a positive answer, and the positive answers concentrated in Hubei, Jiangsu and Shanxi, taking 53.02, 39.59 and 59.39% respectively. When asked the purpose of bank savings, farmers answers included: for the elderly life 24.56%, for children's marriage 19.44%, for accidents 27.63%, for nothing 29.82%, for interest income 3.36%, and for other reasons 10.96%. If we only take interest income into consideration, Shanxi has the highest ratio of 7.38%, followed by Jiangsu of 3.85% and Hubei of 1.92%.

[2] From 1996 to 2002, the bank interest rate was decreased for eight times, i.e. in April 1996, August 1996, October 1997, March 1998, July 1998, December 1998, June 1999 and February 2002. There were three times in 1998. The changes in interest rates were (taking the one-year lump-sum deposit and withdrawal as an example) 9.18, 7.47, 5.67, 5.22, 4.77, 3.78, 2.25 and 1.98% respectively. The loan rates were (taking the short-term loan of six months or less as an example) 9.72, 9.18, 7.65, 7.02, 6.57, 6.12, 5.58 and 5.04% respectively—Global Times, November 1st, 2004.

and 50% until the 21st century when it rose back to 49.70% in 2000, 54.69% in 2001, and 57.40% in 2002. According to this analysis, when the policy was introduced, farmers' saving ratio was at a low level. After the policy introduction, not only farmers' saving level but also their saving ratio was on the rise. Obviously, this was contrary to the original intention of the policy. Therefore, it serves as a reminder that a successful policy needs extensive and in-depth investigations concerning the foundation of the policy implementation. Otherwise, the policy will not be practical if it is solely based on the analysis and judgment of several theoretical experts, or according to the reference of some overseas experience.

4.1.2 Savings of Households at Different Income Levels

It can be inferred from Table 4.2 that with the increase of household income, the saving level also presents an uptrend with a typical 'horn' shape. If the average saving level of all sample households is taken as the baseline, for low-income households, their saving level was only 20.31% of the average at the beginning of the observation, then rose slightly for a short term and reached the peak in 1989, equivalent to 25.40% of the average. Since the 1990s, this figure had decreased continuously, and bottomed out in 2001, equivalent to only 7.42% of the average, before it rose again to 13.66% of the average in 2002. For middle-income households, the saving level was about 92.86% of the average level at the beginning of the observation, which was followed by a fluctuating process with an obvious downtrend, reaching 68.27% in 1990 and 58.40% in 1995, and reached a low level of 25.37% since the start of the observation before rebounding and rising to 48.10% in 2002. For high-income households, their saving level was 2.08 times of the average at the beginning of the observation, and rose continuously to 2.23 times in 1990 and 2.82 times in 1995, and reached the top level of 3.90 times in 2000 since the start of the observation. Then, it decreased to 3.49 times of the average in 2002. This result has indicated to some extent that the savings of farmers have presented a polarising trend; the continuous rise of savings was caused by a small number of households, and the saving level was not high for the majority of the rural households. This result has also been reflected in the changes in the saving ratio of the households (Fig. 4.3).

In terms of saving ratio and household income growth (Table 4.2 and Fig. 4.3), with the growth of household income, household saving ratio exhibits a typical inverted 'U'-shape uptrend during the observation period (1986–2002). The saving ratios for the bottom to top five income quintiles were 34.27, 55.42, 62.57, 65.70 and 65.56%, with the average level of 56.70%. The specific situation varied for different time periods. Before 1995, household saving ratio showed an inverted 'U' shape with the growth of income, which was changed after 1995 when the inverted 'U' was gradually replaced by the rising trend, and this has been especially obvious since the new century. From 1986 to 1990, the saving ratios for the five income quintiles from bottom to top were 36.73, 62.77, 71.95, 73.59 and 71.91% respectively, which became 34.67, 48.67, 55.00, 62.33 and 69.00% from 2000 to 2002. Over time, regardless of

Table 4.2 Saving level and ratio of rural households by income

	Saving level (yuan/person)					Saving ratio (%)				
	Low-income households	Lower middle-income households	Middle-income households	Upper middle-income households	High-income households	Low-income households	Lower middle-income households	Middle-income households	Upper middle-income households	High-income households
1986	21.33	63.15	97.50	116.43	218.28	39.81	68.06	72.69	67.59	60.65
1987	39.94	96.40	124.96	207.87	540.94	42.17	70.31	75.98	77.73	74.35
1988	56.44	102.04	155.16	246.45	587.88	37.93	65.37	74.46	74.89	70.69
1989	69.61	123.83	210.66	342.56	643.32	32.77	54.62	71.31	75.21	78.99
1990	62.04	191.76	236.72	459.44	771.91	31.54	56.43	65.70	72.20	73.86
1991	119.20	222.68	422.33	632.11	1094.56	35.50	52.81	65.09	66.67	62.77
1993	135.57	369.39	572.32	1015.73	2372.78	32.00	46.00	51.00	58.00	46.00
1995	341.53	689.12	1132.44	2076.54	5462.73	31.00	47.00	52.00	50.00	43.00
1996	374.73	984.33	1099.94	1888.98	8444.36	25.00	51.00	44.00	45.00	60.00
1997	494.07	706.75	1456.79	2929.50	10765.03	34.00	41.00	50.00	53.00	54.00
1998	355.74	775.84	1725.34	3376.90	16694.59	25.00	45.00	45.00	53.00	53.00
1999	486.35	1804.67	2023.84	3192.23	22214.94	26.00	44.00	42.00	52.00	60.00
2000	1043.18	1834.51	2009.04	4726.43	30905.67	30.00	45.00	46.00	59.00	68.69
2001	746.57	1717.10	3757.72	6940.52	36624.60	35.00	48.00	58.00	61.00	71.29
2002	1617.15	3237.92	5696.35	7006.98	41325.00	39.00	53.00	61.00	67.00	67.00
1995–2002	607.73	1336.47	2125.41	3650.39	19256.33	30.78	46.67	49.89	55.33	58.11

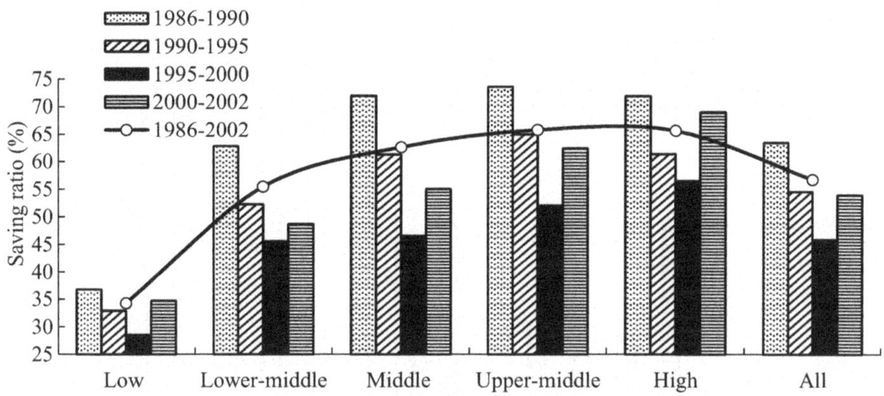

Fig. 4.3 Changes in saving ratio of rural households with different incomes

which income group the households belong to, their saving have all shown the 'U'-shape trend. Between 1986 and 1991, the average ratio was 63.38%, which was reduced to 54.52% in the Eighth Five-Year period, and further decreased to 45.78% in the Ninth Five-Year period, before back to the average level of 53.93% for the three years from 2000 to 2002. This has further proved that the increasing level of savings has been the contribution of some households, and their proportion has been shrinking over time. Although there has been a slight increase since the new century, it is nearly 10% lower than that prior to the 1990s.

In order to further illustrate the polarisation of the saving levels of rural households, I calculated the Gini coefficients of savings.[3] The calculated result was surprisingly high. Over the observed 17 years, the minimum Gini coefficient of bank savings for households in the ten villages of Zhejiang was 0.7761 in 1987, and the maximum value was 0.8839 in 1998. Even though the Gini coefficient has been decreasing since 1988, the value in 2002 still remained at 0.8528. By comparing the Gini coefficients of household income and savings (Fig. 4.4), it is evident that their trends are surprisingly similar, both presenting a rising trend over time. In other words, there exists an extreme inequality in the total amount of savings, so that a small number of rural households own much of the savings while there is little or negligible for the majority, and this situation has been reinforced over the years. Figure 4.4 shows that when the policy was implemented to decrease bank interest rates and to levy interest tax, the inequality for rural bank savings was at its extreme level which was alleviated after the policy was implemented. Therefore, the implementation of the policy mitigated the continuous worsening of the situation, and could be considered as the unexpected gain of the policy.

[3]The empirical formula for calculating Gini coefficient is: $G = \frac{2}{n}\left[\sum_{i=1}^{n}\left(i\frac{x_i}{\sum_{i=1}^{n} x_i}\right) - \frac{n+1}{n}\right]$.

G is the Gini coefficient, n is the number of the observed rural households, x_i is the year-end bank savings of each household (Zheng, 1996: 60).

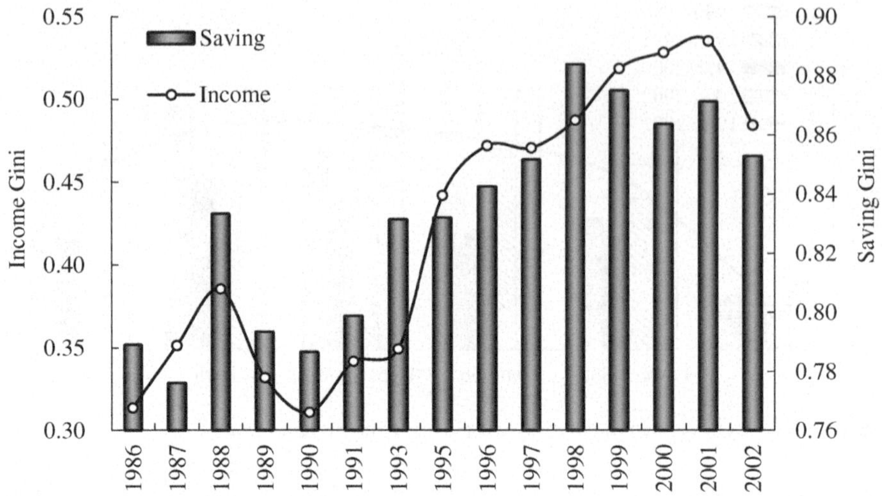

Fig. 4.4 Gini coefficients for income and savings of rural households

4.1.3 Saving Behaviour of Rural Households with Different Operation Types

From Table 4.3, it can be said that the farmer's saving level is closely related to the household operation type. To be specific, with the increase of non-agriculturalisation degree in household operation, the saving level of rural households generally presented a downtrend in the early stage of the observation, but displayed a 'U' uptrend after 1995. Here, I take two six-year periods (1986–1991 and 1997–2002) as examples. In the first six years, the per capita saving level was 286.64 yuan for agricultural households, 284.57 yuan for the agriculture-dominated households, 202.98 yuan for the non-agricultural dominated households and only 188.13 yuan for the non-agricultural households. In the more recent six years, the per capita saving level for agricultural households was 2961.76 yuan, as low as 2122.05 yuan for agriculture-dominated households, as high as 2885.70 yuan for non-agricultural dominated households, and at a higher level of 16,894.57 yuan for non-agricultural households. The changes in saving levels for rural households have indicated that in the early stage of non-agriculturalisation, farmers were precautious in non-agricultural investment, and they were risk averse. In the middle and late 1990s, the higher income brought about by non-agricultural practice has encouraged farmers to be risk takers, which can be reflected in the changes in saving ratio for rural households.

From Table 4.3 and Fig. 4.5, the saving behaviour of farmers in the ten villages of Zhejiang has experienced great changes from the traditional agricultural to the non-agricultural era. In the early stage of the observation, rural non-agricultural industry was in its infancy. During the process of changing from planting or husbandry to non-agricultural industry, farmers were cautious in capital investment.

Table 4.3 Saving level and ratio of the rural households with different operation types

	Saving level (yuan/person)					Saving ratio (%)				
	Completely agricultural	Agricultural	Agriculture-dominated	Non-agricultural dominated	Non-agricultural	Completely agricultural	Agricultural	Agriculture-dominated	Non-agricultural dominated	Non-agricultural
1986	111.20	102.09	128.45	62.86	65.74	79.11	48.15	54.84	42.98	69.35
1987	216.69	189.78	296.67	147.32	144.30	84.35	66.41	63.64	53.57	72.11
1988	231.02	223.69	225.95	109.06	327.58	84.46	55.76	48.28	58.87	69.58
1989	336.51	289.97	254.23	217.15	170.38	79.55	51.41	61.32	59.82	66.26
1990	499.04	390.34	292.08	240.41	175.00	80.05	53.42	54.10	55.83	63.06
1991	705.83	538.48	522.18	443.21	234.02	76.90	49.37	50.52	47.86	61.60
1993	655.74	631.03	1032.48	1084.36	1024.14	60.32	49.28	28.57	26.09	54.71
1995	1994.36	1586.76	1341.62	1158.06	1675.67	56.99	51.92	45.10	28.57	50.97
1996	2000.56	1738.66	934.83	3472.63	1548.59	50.94	40.38	53.06	31.87	48.63
1997	2600.00	2171.79	1144.98	1145.45	6557.82	52.07	47.14	42.50	38.98	49.32
1998	2910.76	2316.88	1519.21	1674.52	10839.03	50.92	45.65	53.85	36.22	46.58
1999	4001.36	2961.16	2375.13	1328.28	14268.38	55.10	49.02	34.00	44.53	47.27
2000	3568.14	3507.16	2544.83	2545.92	18050.97	53.79	47.54	51.92	51.52	48.07
2001	4322.81	3335.92	2652.75	5461.68	22622.89	59.15	56.86	69.23	54.05	54.08
2002	4469.37	3789.90	3076.34	7610.17	26458.89	59.06	52.78	51.52	61.97	54.80
1995–2002	2752.02	2291.19	1760.55	2504.32	13001.26	55.21	48.77	46.27	43.68	50.47

Note Non-household operation is excluded, so that 'agricultural households + agriculture-dominated households + non-agricultural dominated household + non-agricultural households" ≤ 100; the non-agriculturalisation degree of household operation = non-agricultural income/total operation income × 0.5 + non-agricultural expenses/total operation costs × 0.3 + non-agricultural labour/total operation labour × 0.2. Households with the non-agriculturalisation degree of less than 20% are agricultural households, those of 20–50% are agriculture-dominated households, those of 50–80% are non-agricultural dominated households, and those of over 80% are non-agricultural households. Those with the zero degree are the complete agricultural households

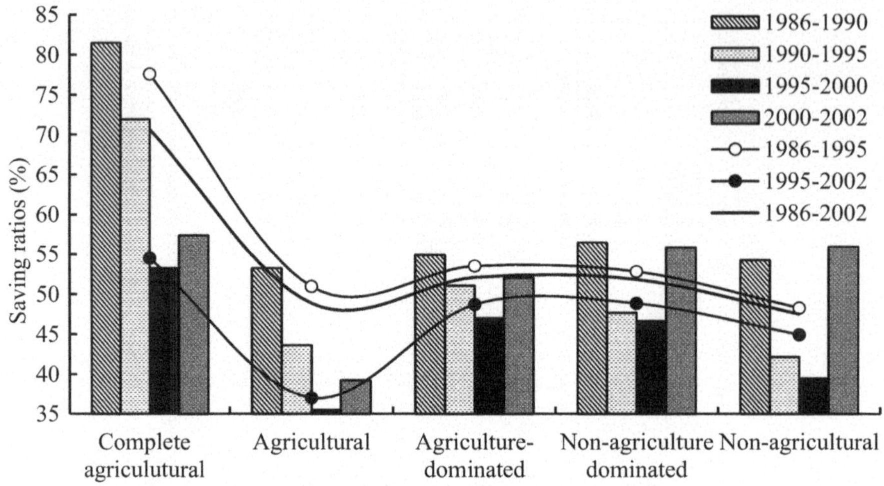

Fig. 4.5 Saving ratios for rural households with different operation types. *Note* Agricultural households in the above figure do not include complete agricultural households

Although the demand for funds was very high for developing non-agricultural industries, famers had to make sure to maintain a certain level of savings in their economic development. Over time, with the deepening of non-agriculturalisation, the demonstration effect of income growth brought about by non-agriculturalisation has been gradually increasing. As a consequence, farmers became more adventurous in non-agricultural investment. Once their investment direction is decided, the majority of the savings will be withdrawn, so an obvious drop appeared in the saving ratio during the transition from agricultural to non-agricultural economy. From 1986 to 1995, with the increase of non-agriculturalisation degree of rural households, the changes in saving ratio became 77.56% for completely agricultural households, 50.94% for agricultural households, 53.51% for agriculture-dominated households, 52.81% for non-agricultural dominated households, and 48.26% for non-agricultural households. From 1995 to 2002, the saving ratios were generally decreased to 54.46% for completely agricultural households, 36.99% for agricultural households, 48.69% for agriculture-dominated households, 48.82% for non-agricultural dominated households, and 44.92% for the non-agricultural households.

Therefore, the savings for farmers are largely temporary in order to achieve an ultimate goal. Non-agriculturalisation is likely to be one of the most important goals of farmer's saving behaviour. In comparison of the five different operation types, it is shown that agricultural and non-agricultural households generally have higher and more stable saving ratios, while the saving ratios for the other three types are less stable. Over time, the saving ratios for all categories of rural households have shown a 'U' shape or a 'U' downward trend.

4.1.4 Saving Behaviour of Rural Households with Different Education Levels

It is seen from Table 4.4, with the increase of the education level of the main labours in rural households, the saving level presents an obvious uptrend, and the difference in savings of the households with the highest and lowest education levels have been enlarged during the process. From 1986 to 1990, the per capita saving level was 139.35 yuan for illiterate and semi-literate households, 247.37 yuan for households with primary school education, 277.95 yuan for households with junior high school education, 278.53 yuan for households with senior high school education or above, and level of the lowest group was 50.03% that of the highest group. From 1999 to 2002, the corresponding saving levels were 3753.30 yuan for illiterate and semiliterate households, 8458.91 yuan for households with primary school education, 6169.94 yuan for households with junior high school education, 18,490.63 yuan for households with senior high school education or above, and the level of the lowest group was only 20.30% of that of the top group, which decreased by nearly 30% compared to the level at the beginning of the observation. Meanwhile, there were also changes in saving ratio, which exhibited a 'U' shape relationship with household education levels due to saving ratios for households with low and high education levels being higher than those with middle-level education, while the ratios for illiterate and semiliterate households were higher than those with high

Table 4.4 Saving level and ratio of rural households with different education backgrounds

	Saving level (yuan/person)				Saving ratio (%)			
	Illiterate	Primary	Junior high	Senior high+	Illiterate	Primary	Junior high	Senior high+
1986	81.31	109.91	111.55	113.71	49.77	65.14	65.65	57.41
1987	145.15	207.47	252.84	333.83	57.61	72.40	68.97	73.08
1988	94.93	244.33	286.76	437.85	56.19	67.41	64.71	70.18
1989	159.56	295.87	329.73	212.36	52.82	66.84	63.55	62.71
1990	217.94	379.50	380.44	290.85	48.28	63.56	60.12	68.75
1991	366.54	522.00	549.68	550.76	46.26	60.00	57.14	59.09
1993	767.01	827.15	884.53	1456.00	52.54	44.74	48.61	41.94
1995	1486.81	2048.49	1484.76	3965.85	49.06	45.59	38.93	59.38
1996	1513.62	2767.25	1764.85	5686.44	50.00	45.17	43.40	43.33
1997	1554.38	3153.76	2373.16	10240.74	50.00	44.40	48.17	47.06
1998	2360.39	3966.00	3906.70	15203.01	52.00	44.31	41.36	45.45
1999	3641.88	5949.54	3951.67	17226.89	55.77	49.16	36.63	39.47
2000	3176.88	8629.80	5696.81	17921.57	64.58	52.94	41.38	48.72
2001	3912.95	11179.68	7905.63	19164.63	68.09	57.14	48.31	52.63
2002	5908.82	13132.75	9103.77	22701.61	75.56	57.69	53.55	52.63
1995–2002	2553.40	5473.05	4246.20	13173.15	56.99	48.82	44.58	47.92

school education and above. During the entire 17 years of observation, the saving ratios have been 66.07% for illiterate and semi-illiterate households, 59.10% for households with primary school education, 54.64% for households with junior high school education, and 56.99% for households with senior high school education or above. The corresponding ratios for the initial observation period (1986–1990) were 53.12, 67.06, 64.35 and 66.43%. During the Eight-Five Year Plan period, the ratios became 77.06, 56.50, 54.06 and 59.59%, and changed to 53.42, 46.84, 41.63 and 47.09% for the Ninth-Five Year Plan period. From 2000 to 2002, they were 69.29, 55.92, 47.85 and 51.30% respectively. It can be seen from this result that as time goes on, except for the illiterate and semi-literate households, the changes in saving ratios of households all presented a 'U' trend. Taking the saving level into consideration, it is seen that saving for the illiterate and semiliterate households has been a highly popular but low-standard behaviour. On the contrary, saving for households with senior high school education or above is a less popular but high-standard behaviour. The significance and function of saving is entirely different for these two household groups. Saving is preventative for the former, while for the latter the saving purpose is aimed at investment and development.

4.2 General Changing Trend of Borrowing and Lending Behaviour

Research on borrowing and lending (B&L) behaviour generally includes two parts: borrowing behaviour research and lending behaviour research. These represent the behaviours of debtors and creditors respectively. As there are usually differences in time point and time period in data collection, the data consist of year-end loans and those within the year. This study is carried out according to these aspects.

4.2.1 Changing Trend of B&L Level and Its Composition

4.2.1.1 Changing Trend of Year-End B&L Level and Its Change

It can be seen from Table 4.5 that the year-end B&L level of rural households in the ten villages of Zhejiang presents a continuous uptrend over time. Compared with the initial stage of the observation, the year-end borrowing and lending balances of rural households increased by 17.87 and 13.29 times respectively, and the net borrowing balance increased by 23.36 times. The annual average increase rates for the above figures were 20.15, 18.08 and 22.08% respectively. Of course, the calculation is based on current price. When converting according to the retail price index of Zhejiang and using 100 as the value for 2000, during the 17-year observation the average growth rates of the B&L levels were as high as 12.81 and 10.86%, with the average growth

Table 4.5 Year-end B&L level for rural households (yuan/person)

	Borrowing	Borrowing source (%)		Lending	Net borrowing
		Bank and credit cooperative	Private		
1986	176.73	8.80	91.20	96.34	80.38
1987	205.32	9.56	90.44	109.29	96.03
1988	394.43	5.36	94.64	125.11	269.32
1989	542.55	2.93	97.07	147.08	395.48
1990	557.68	3.07	96.93	153.84	403.84
1991	729.93	3.70	96.30	205.43	524.50
1993	844.05	4.59	95.41	401.89	442.15
1995	1625.32	15.59	84.41	760.97	864.35
1996	2467.60	18.79	81.21	1350.68	1116.91
1997	2526.87	9.91	90.09	1492.39	1034.49
1998	2929.85	7.55	92.45	1496.40	1433.44
1999	3037.88	10.16	89.84	1452.80	1585.08
2000	2845.32	11.52	88.48	1188.77	1656.55
2001	2918.94	14.14	85.86	1240.46	1678.48
2002	3334.54	28.13	71.87	1376.89	1957.66
1995–2002	2703.23	14.61	85.39	1293.13	1410.10

rate of the net borrowing reaching 14.62%, all exceeding the annual income growth rate of 9.10%. Meanwhile, it is clearly seen from the changes in the growth rates, the B&L increase of rural households has experienced a fast-to-slow process. In terms of the changes in borrowing balance, the average growth rate was 33.28% from 1986 to 1990, which decreased to 23.85% in the Eighth Five-Year Plan period, 11.85% in the Ninth Five-Year Plan period, and 8.26% from 2000 to 2002. This result shows that in rural Zhejiang, the capital movements of rural households have been very frequent, and the development capability of such capital has become higher.

For the sources of B&L funds, private lending obviously has been the major part for rural household loans in Zhejiang, and the proportion in the early 1990s once exceeded 95%. In the mid-1990s, with the development of the bank credit system, the proportion of loans that farmers obtained from the banks once increased to 15.59% in 1995 and 18.79% in 1996. Afterwards, due to the changes in the state macro policies, rural households encountered difficulties in obtaining loans from the banks, so the proportion of bank loans decreased significantly, and until the beginning of the new century, the proportion of loans obtained from banks to the total household borrowing stayed at about 10%. Since the start of the new century, with the strengthening of the importance of farmers' income in the state's decision-making, the mainstream government ideology has paid more attention to farmers' issues, and more opportunities have appeared for farmers to obtain support from the banks. The proportion of farmers' loans from banks to their household borrowing increased substantially from 11.52% in 2000 to 28.13% in 2002, setting a record throughout the 17 years of observation.

4.2.1.2 Changing Trend of Current-Year B&L and the Structure

Similarly, it can be seen from Table 4.6 that the current-year accumulative B&L level of rural households also presents a continuous rising trend over time. The accumulative current-year borrowing increased from 129.42 yuan/person in 1986 to 2924.30 yuan/person in 2002, up by 21.60 times over the 17 years, with an annual average increase growth rate of 21.51%. To be specific, the growth rate was 18.13% from 1986 to 1990, 51.87% in the Eighth Five-Year Plan period, 1.67% in the Ninth Five-Year Plan period, and 14.98% from 2000 to 2002.

In terms of sources of borrowing, private loans are the absolute majority, accounting for 78.70% from 1995 to 2002, while bank loans only took up 18.81%. Since the middle and late 1990s, farmers' sources of borrowing were much influenced by the state macro policies. The financial austerity policy once made private loans more prevalent, but with the adjustment of government macro policies the situation has been changed since the new century with farmers' bank loans taking a higher percentage. Until 2002, the percentage was increased to 33.43%, which was 23.79% higher than the level of 9.64% in 1998, being the lowest level since 1995. This result has indicated again that in Zhejiang with developed rural economy, the borrowing behaviour of rural households is featured with private loans. Our previous studies on private loans have indicated that loans based on 'double *qing*' (known as *qinqing* and *youqing*, or family relationship and friendship) have been the majority, and that such loans would take relationships as the guarantee and do not require payment of interests (Shi & Chen, 2002; Shi & Zhuo, 2003). In observation of the ten villages in Zhejiang, however, the interest rates of private loans were very high during the ten years of observations where the lowest interest rate was 22.47% in 1995, and the highest 41.44% in 1998, with the average level of 34.53% from 1995 to 2002. This is because the loan purpose in rural areas of Zhejiang has been very different from other regions (Shi, Qinghua, Wan, & Huang, 2004). In Zhejiang, the farmers' loans are mainly used for productive operations. From 1995 to 2002, 72.40% of the household loans were used for production, and the figure for living was only 23.30%. In other regions, in the underdeveloped areas in particular, farmers' loans were used mainly for living. This has indicated that the payment of interests is reasonable as long as the loans are used for production regardless of the sources. To some extent, the interests paid are probably at a very high rate (Shi & Li, 2003), but compared with the difficulties in loan acquisition, interest rates are only considered a minor problem. In other words, with regard to farmers' loans, interest rates are certainly important, but what is more vital is whether it is possible to obtain the loans quickly. The formation and accelerated private lending has been based thereon.

Table 4.6 Current-year accumulative borrowing of rural households

	Borrowing (yuan/person)	Borrowing source (%)			Borrowing purpose (%)			
		Bank*	Private**	#Interest payment	Other	Living	Production	#Agriculture
1986	129.42	16.47	83.53	–	–	–	–	–
1987	178.75	17.79	82.21	–	–	–	–	–
1988	341.60	9.77	90.23	–	–	–	–	–
1989	329.96	6.50	93.50	–	–	–	–	–
1990	252.03	12.37	87.63	–	–	–	–	–
1991	424.10	8.64	91.36	–	–	–	–	–
1993	1037.89	6.56	91.25	38.24	2.19	24.50	75.50	12.75
1995	2036.04	18.90	77.98	22.47	3.12	16.73	82.05	40.07
1996	2268.27	21.46	76.01	36.55	2.53	25.75	73.75	51.95
1997	1651.17	17.00	81.23	40.78	1.77	35.16	61.61	33.25
1998	2119.22	9.64	88.55	41.44	1.80	31.41	66.09	40.73
1999	1970.95	15.00	79.41	35.52	5.59	22.88	72.21	35.41
2000	2211.91	16.02	82.60	39.43	1.39	21.35	73.67	37.56
2001	2679.71	19.31	79.58	31.60	1.12	17.87	76.89	31.67
2002	2924.30	33.43	63.51	27.18	3.06	19.53	69.00	30.97
1995–2002	2090.24	18.81	78.70	34.53	2.49	23.30	72.40	36.14

Note *Bank loans here refer to loans obtained from banks, credit cooperatives and rural cooperative foundations. **The private loans from 1986 to 1991 included all non-bank loans of rural households. #Items being part of the former category. "–" data not available.

4.2.2 B&L Ratio and the Changing Trend

From the above analysis, as time goes on, the B&L level of rural households in the ten villages of Zhejiang has presented a continuous rising process. However, there has been a big 'secret' influence behind this rising trend, i.e. the continuous shrinking of the B&L ratio (Table 4.7). This shrinkage is reflected not only in the sharp fall of the proportion of borrowing households, but also in that of lending households. At the beginning of the observation, the ratios of rural households with borrowing and lending at the year-end were 43.43 and 37.96%. Yet, after 17 years of transition, the ratios decreased to 26.80 and 16.60% in 2002, with declines of 16.63 and 12.90% respectively. In terms of loan sources, the shrinking of the year-end B&L ratio was mainly reflected in private loans, while those between rural households and banks did not change much. This can also be proved by the changes in current-year B&L ratio of the rural households.

In the current-year loans of rural households, as time goes on, the loan ratio has also presented a downtrend, i.e. from 33.70% at the beginning of the observation to 21.80% in 2002, down by 12.90%. In terms of the loan sources, the occurrence of loans from both banks and private sector demonstrates a downtrend, but the decreasing shown is a fast-to-low process. Since the new century, there has been the indication that bank loans have been replacing private ones, which is not very obvious, and large loans still occur mostly between rural households and banks rather than among individual households (Table 4.8). Influenced by the state's adjustments of macro polices, the loan policy for farmers has been relaxed continuously, and there has been constraints of private loans with high interest rates in rural Zhejiang. Accordingly, there has appeared a substantial decline in interest payment for private loans. The interest payment percentage decreased from the top level of 19.60% since the observation to 8.40% in 2002, showing a decline of 11.20%. With regard to the loan purposes, loans were mostly used for production rather than for living, although the occurrence of both purposes decreased over time, from 14.00 and 22.00% in 1995 to 9.00 and 13.40% in 2002, with drops of 5 and 8.60% over eight years. To be specific, the occurrence of loans for production decreased from 10% in 1995 to 6.20% in 2002.

Taking into consideration of the previous analysis, it can be seen during the entire observation that the household B&L behaviour has exhibited a polarising trend in the ten villages of Zhejiang. That is to say, with the continuous increase of B&L level, the B&L ratio shrinks constantly. On the one hand, this result reflects the satisfactory economic income growth of rural households in Zhejiang. On the other hand, it shows that the aggravation of economic development inequality of rural households is closely related to the changes in B&L behaviour of the local farmers.

Table 4.7 Household B&L ratio and its change (%)

	Year-end loan			Current-year borrowing	Borrowing source			Borrowing purpose		
	Borrowing	#Bank	Lending		Bank*	Private**	#Interest payment	Living	Production	#Agriculture
1986	43.43	9.07	37.96	33.70	13.15	28.98	–	–	–	–
1987	37.49	6.54	36.97	32.08	11.16	27.90	–	–	–	–
1988	42.96	4.67	32.07	36.56	7.00	33.45	–	–	–	–
1989	46.26	3.28	33.31	34.74	5.38	32.80	–	–	–	–
1990	43.20	3.98	30.76	29.60	8.04	26.29	–	–	–	–
1991	39.36	4.93	31.23	25.43	6.75	22.49	–	–	–	–
1993	30.60	3.80	32.00	30.80	4.60	28.80	17.60	13.40	19.60	6.40
1995	28.80	5.00	28.80	33.80	6.80	31.80	16.00	14.00	22.00	10.00
1996	32.60	6.00	32.20	32.20	6.60	30.00	19.60	16.00	17.20	8.00
1997	32.40	4.20	29.40	28.60	4.00	27.00	15.40	15.60	12.80	6.40
1998	34.40	4.20	28.20	29.60	3.60	28.60	18.60	16.00	15.00	7.20
1999	35.60	4.40	28.00	25.80	4.20	24.40	14.60	11.60	14.80	5.80
2000	34.67	5.21	25.25	27.45	5.41	25.45	13.63	13.43	15.43	7.01
2001	28.34	5.19	20.36	25.55	5.99	23.35	12.97	10.98	15.57	7.39
2002	26.80	5.00	16.60	21.80	6.00	18.60	8.40	9.00	13.40	6.20
1995–2002	28.18	4.36	23.20	24.98	4.73	23.24	13.24	11.84	14.02	6.44

Note *Bank loans refer to loans obtained from banks, credit cooperatives and rural cooperative foundations. **Private loans from 1986 to 1991 included all non-bank loans of rural households. #Items being part of the former category. "–" in the table refers to data not available.

Table 4.8 Current-year distribution of rural households with loans (%)

	Accumulative amount (1000 yuan)	1995	1996	1997	1998	1999	2000	2001	2002	1995–2002
Bank loan	≤5	38.99	33.33	38.52	27.97	31.97	30.71	24.79	23.66	31.84
	5–10	16.35	19.33	19.26	23.78	18.85	22.05	20.51	13.98	19.41
	10–20	16.35	18.67	15.56	16.08	17.21	15.75	11.11	18.28	16.16
	20–50	25.79	20.67	22.22	20.98	18.85	20.47	29.06	30.11	23.23
	50–100	5.66	9.33	8.89	13.29	14.75	12.60	14.53	19.35	11.76
	100+	3.14	6.00	1.48	1.40	4.10	6.30	9.40	11.83	5.07
Private loan	≤5	40.88	32.00	38.52	27.27	32.79	28.35	24.79	20.43	31.36
	5–10	13.21	20.67	19.26	24.48	19.67	22.83	22.22	13.98	19.60
	10–20	16.35	18.00	14.81	17.48	16.39	14.96	7.69	15.05	15.30
	20–50	23.90	18.67	19.26	18.88	21.31	18.90	27.35	30.11	21.89
	50–100	5.03	7.33	7.41	10.49	6.56	10.24	12.82	17.20	9.18
	100+	0.63	3.33	0.74	1.40	3.28	4.72	5.13	3.23	2.68

4.2.3 B&L and Savings

It is shown in Fig. 4.6 that throughout the 17-year observation period, there is some relationship between household savings and their B&L behaviour. To be specific, the percentage of households with both savings and B&L by the year end has decreased generally, which has fluctuated since the Ninth Five-Year Plan. Since 1995, such households have accounted for 4–7% of all the households observed, with the lowest level of 4.40% in 1997 and the highest of 6.19% in 2001. The percentage of households with neither savings nor B&L by the year end first increased and then started decreasing. The figure decreased from 32.00% in 1995 to 21.60% in 2002, with a drop of 10.40% over eight years. The ratio of households with savings but no B&L by the year end exhibited a 'U'-shape trend, and the ratio has been on the rise since 1995, increased from 39.20% in 1995 to 51.60% in 2002, with the rise of 12.40% within eight years. Meanwhile, the change in the ratio of households with B&L but no savings has shown an 'M' shape. Since 1995 the change has shown an inverted 'U'-shape trend, with an increase from 23.40% in 1995 to 30.20% in 1999, but a decrease to 21.00% in 2002. This has indicated that there is a certain degree of overlapping between savings and B&L among rural households in Zhejiang, but they are mainly independent from each other. The frequency of the co-occurrence of savings and B&L is getting lower.

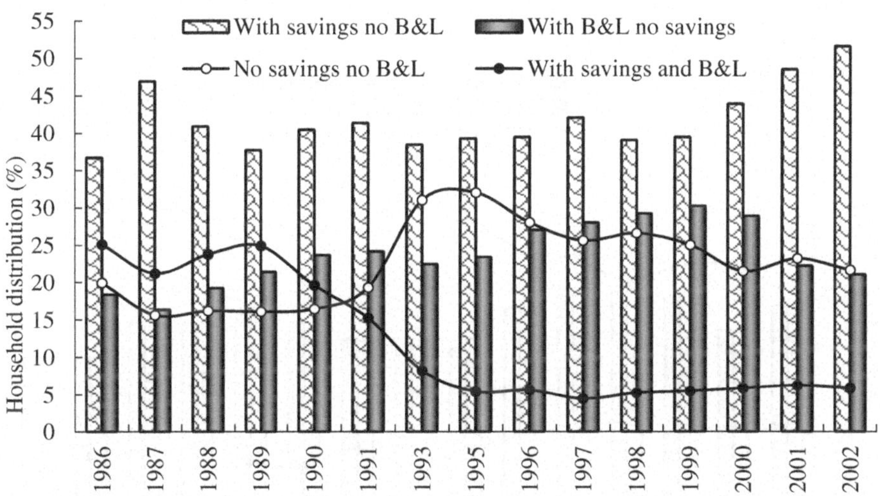

Fig. 4.6 B&L and savings for rural households

4.2.4 Relationships Between Lending and Borrowing

It can be seen from Fig. 4.7 that throughout the 17-year observation period, the proportion of rural households with no lending or borrowing increased significantly from 31.94% in the initial stage of the observation to 61.00% in 2002, an increase of 29.06% over 17 years. From 1987 to 1991 and 1995 to 2002, there were two prolonged periods with stagnated economic development. At the same time, the ratio of rural households with both lending and borrowing presented an obvious declining trend, decreasing from 13.33% at the beginning of the observation period to 4.40% in 2002, with a drop of 8.93% over 17 years. The changing proportion of rural households with only lending showed a down-up-down trend. There has been an obvious decreasing process since 1996, changing from 24.60% in 1996 to 12.20% in 2002, with a decrease of 12.40% over seven years. Meanwhile, the changing trend of household proportion with borrowing only showed an up-and-down process after another up-and-down process. Since the middle and late 1990s, the proportion has also showed a downtrend, decreasing continuously from 28.80% in 1998 to 22.40% in 2002. This result shows that lending and borrowing are two types of behaviours comparatively independent although quite a few rural households have both of them, but the ratio of households with both lending and borrowing behaviour has decreased sharply over time. It has also indicated that with the growth and development of household economy, the frequency of private fund exchange has been obviously reduced.

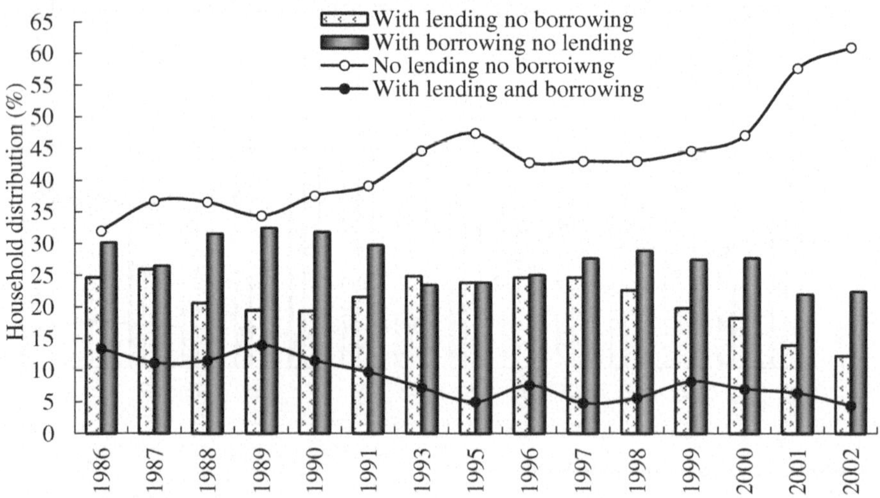

Fig. 4.7 Lending and borrowing of rural households

4.3 Borrowing and Lending for Different Types of Households

The previous studies on rural household behaviour have found that there exists some correlation between rural household type and its economic behaviour, and different types have different behaviours. In order to further illustrate the relationship between household B&L behaviours and corresponding types of households, income level and non-agriculturalisation degree of household operation have been selected in the current study for comparison.

4.3.1 B&L Behaviour of Rural Households at Different Income Levels

4.3.1.1 Comparison of B&L Levels

It can be seen from Table 4.9 that with the income increase of rural households, the levels for both lending and borrowing have presented an increasing trend. Over times, the lending level has presented an inverted 'U'-shape uptrend, while the borrowing level presented a simple uptrend. Taking income into consideration, households with high and low incomes have shown a bigger difference in lending level than in borrowing level. In the 17 years of observation, the lending level of the high-income households could be several times that of the low-income households, with the biggest difference of 17.73 times in 1998 and the smallest of 3.51 times in 2000, with the difference averaged at 10.04 times from 1995 to 2002. In terms of borrowing, the largest gap once appeared in 1993 when the level of the high-income households was 5.02 times that of the low-income households, and the lowest level of the high-income households was only 61.55% of the low-income households. From 1995 to 2002, the borrowing level for high-income households was only 39.28% higher than that of the low-income households. Comparing the borrowing and lending for the high and low-income households, the low-income ones are marked by a low level of lending but high level of borrowing, and the latter could be several times or dozens of times of the former, with the highest level of 22.60 times in 1998, the lowest of 3.78 times in 1993, and the average level being 10.28 times from 1995 to 2002. Meanwhile, the high-income households demonstrate high level of both lending and borrowing, and borrowing is almost equal to lending or slightly higher. Over the 17 years of observation, the highest borrowing level was 2.71 times that of the lending in 2000, and the lowest level was only 78.48% of that for lending in 1998, which averaged 1.43 times from 1995 to 2002.

As for the changes in the growth rate of lending level, with the income increase of rural households, the growth rate presented an inverted 'U' shape. The highest rate appeared for the middle-income households which increased by 21.46 times over the 17 years, while those for the low and high-income households were 13.32 and

Table 4.9 Borrowing and lending for rural households with different incomes

	Year-end lending (yuan/person)					Year-end borrowing (yuan/person)				
	Low income	Lower middle income	Middle income	Upper middle income	High income	Low income	Lower middle income	Middle income	Upper middle income	High income
1986	16.33	40.45	80.58	118.69	217.13	149.32	154.75	134.59	191.20	249.69
1987	28.95	50.29	74.44	108.59	267.63	163.38	178.74	199.29	262.53	217.25
1988	57.55	86.36	85.54	146.70	238.14	248.14	280.77	298.56	432.23	686.01
1989	64.45	75.10	105.37	177.54	322.85	807.47	331.61	480.86	393.15	704.71
1990	56.63	77.53	140.25	165.38	327.19	530.77	440.50	488.67	525.24	813.28
1991	146.15	97.81	156.24	194.46	427.37	747.96	711.47	498.51	569.57	1127.29
1993	105.54	136.72	277.26	662.90	866.80	399.15	497.78	672.83	681.92	2005.29
1995	113.45	338.37	497.25	1108.97	1733.51	1685.96	1030.44	1727.88	1375.10	2340.48
1996	319.80	669.98	988.13	1531.76	3342.27	2029.22	1824.19	1282.38	3532.55	3709.94
1997	406.53	421.43	773.27	1498.98	4371.58	2721.02	1577.53	1375.62	1396.87	5655.74
1998	249.26	480.10	560.36	1707.88	4418.92	5634.12	1217.79	1565.29	3046.20	3467.84
1999	271.06	769.40	680.82	1639.14	3871.58	4922.88	1652.47	2924.38	2213.14	3520.49
2000	593.31	868.79	643.75	1793.73	2081.30	2880.78	1515.68	2104.26	2213.90	5648.73
2001	338.81	762.54	745.20	1949.18	2346.68	3218.00	1543.78	2038.20	2524.73	5344.26
2002	217.47	726.49	1728.95	1118.16	3052.78	2931.72	1643.38	2548.71	3207.95	6413.26
1995–2002	314.23	627.36	822.95	1540.96	3155.38	3229.55	1499.88	1943.42	2427.49	4498.07

14.06 times respectively. There are also differences for specific periods. From 1986 to 1990, with the income increase of rural households, the growth rate of lending level presented a 'U'-shape downtrend, which evolved into an inverted 'U' uptrend in the Eight Five-Year Plan period, before it resumed its 'U'-shape down trend in the Ninth Five-Year Plan period, and finally turned to an inverted 'U' uptrend from 2000 to 2002. Therefore, the growth of lending for rural households has shown an alternate changing trend.

For the changes in the growth rate of borrowing level, with the income increase of rural households, the growth rate presented a "W" trend, the borrowing level increased slowly for lower-middle and upper-middle income households, while it increased rapidly for high, low and middle-income households. High-income households had the fastest growth rate, followed by the low-income and then the middle-income households. There are certain differences for specific time periods. From 1986 to 1995, with the income increase, the growth rate of borrowing level for households presented a 'W' trend, which evolved into a 'U'-shape uptrend in the Ninth Five-Year Plan period, and since the new century on the contrary, it turned into an inverted 'U' uptrend. This has indicated that the borrowing and lending behaviour of rural households, especially the borrowing level, is indeed related to the income level, which has been to some extent the guaranteed or 'assurance' of their expected income. The specific changes in borrowing and lending, however, have been related to the different economic and social backgrounds in different time periods. Meanwhile, the changes in the growth of borrowing and lending are found to be a periodic phenomenon.

4.3.1.2 B&L Occurrence

It can be seen from Table 4.10 that with the increase of rural household income, the occurrence probability of lending for rural household becomes higher, while that for borrowing is the opposite. As time goes on, the occurrence of both borrowing and lending declines (Figs. 4.8 and 4.9).

In term of changes in borrowing occurrence, throughout the 17-year observation, 45.72% of the low-income households have borrowed, and the ratios were 37.91% for the middle-income households and 31.56% for the high-income households, with the difference of 14.16% between the highest and the lowest. In the initial observation period (1986–1990), the average borrowing occurrence rates for the low, middle and high-income households were 47.54, 44.42 and 35.26% respectively, with the difference of 12.27% between the highest and the lowest. In the Eighth Five-Year Plan period, the average rates of the three categories of households became 44.20, 37.69 and 33.78% respectively, which all decreased sharply compared with the initial stage, and the middle-income households had the biggest drop of 6.37%. Meanwhile, the difference between the highest and the lowest level decreased to 10.42%. In the Ninth Five-Year Plan period, with the decrease of borrowing occurrence rates for other categories of households, low-income households had an obvious increased rate, and the rates for low, middle and high-income households were 49.33, 30.33

Table 4.10 B&L occurrence of rural households with different incomes

	Year-end lending (%)					Year-end borrowing (%)				
	Low income	Lower middle income	Middle income	Upper middle income	High income	Low income	Lower middle income	Middle income	Upper middle income	High income
1986	19.91	29.17	43.06	44.44	53.24	45.37	50.93	47.22	38.43	35.19
1987	23.04	29.26	42.36	41.48	48.70	43.04	41.92	40.17	38.86	23.48
1988	20.69	33.33	33.33	39.83	33.19	44.83	49.35	44.16	41.56	34.91
1989	18.91	27.73	37.55	40.34	42.02	54.20	44.12	47.68	41.60	43.70
1990	17.43	27.39	30.99	36.93	41.08	49.79	47.30	42.98	37.34	38.59
1991	17.75	28.57	34.48	36.80	38.53	43.72	44.16	37.50	35.50	35.93
1993	24.00	25.00	35.00	42.00	34.00	32.00	34.00	38.00	20.00	29.00
1995	19.00	30.00	32.00	33.00	30.00	44.00	29.00	25.00	24.00	22.00
1996	26.00	32.00	39.00	27.00	37.00	53.00	35.00	26.00	31.00	18.00
1997	21.00	29.00	34.00	30.00	33.00	46.00	35.00	32.00	23.00	26.00
1998	13.00	35.00	22.00	32.00	39.00	57.00	33.00	28.00	31.00	23.00
1999	17.00	29.00	26.00	34.00	34.00	53.00	40.00	37.00	25.00	23.00
2000	19.00	31.00	23.00	28.00	25.25	43.00	35.00	34.00	29.00	32.32
2001	12.00	20.00	21.00	25.00	23.76	37.00	30.00	24.00	24.00	26.73
2002	6.00	18.00	18.00	24.00	17.00	30.00	27.00	23.00	23.00	31.00
1995–2002	16.63	28.00	26.88	29.13	29.88	45.38	33.00	28.63	26.25	25.25

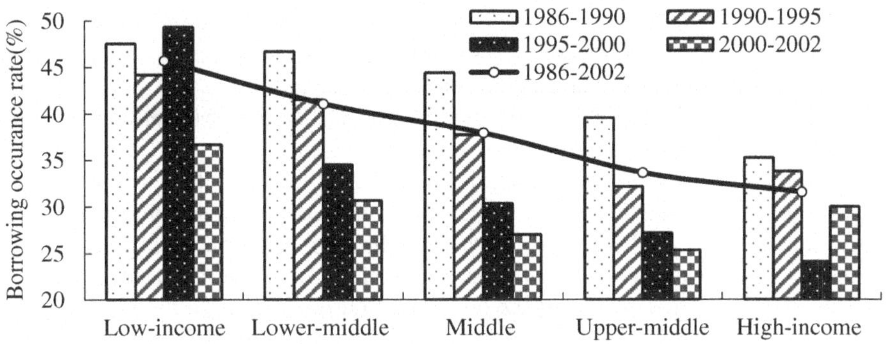

Fig. 4.8 Borrowing occurrence rates for households with different incomes

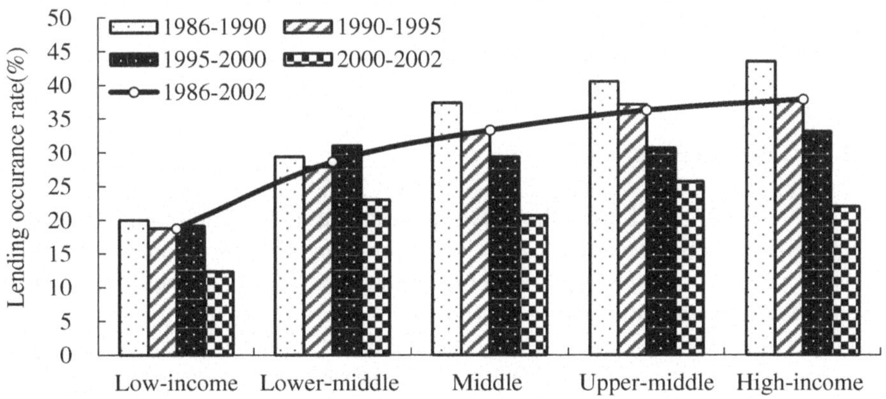

Fig. 4.9 Lending occurrence rates for rural households with different incomes

and 24.04% respectively, with the gap between the highest and the lowest level expanded to 25.29%, which further increased by 14.88% compared with the Eighth Five-Year Plan period. Since the new century, the changes in borrowing occurrence have shown that the rates decreased for low and middle-income households, especially for the low-income households, but the rates increased substantially for the high-income households. From 2000 to 2002, the rates for low, middle and high-income households were 36.67, 27.00 and 30.00% respectively, and the difference between the highest and lowest level decreased to the lowest point of 6.67% since the observation. Taking into consideration of previous analysis, it can be seen that the changes in borrowing occurrence rates for rural households are closely related to the changes in household economy. To be specific, when the economic growth was slow or stagnated, borrowing of rural households would occur more frequently, especially for middle and low-income households with rapid increase of their borrowing occurrence. When the economy entered periods with rapid development, borrowing would occur less frequently among the households, except for high-income households. This result reflects in some ways that the growth rate of farmer economy can be fully reflected from the changes in borrowing occurrence.

In terms of the lending behaviour, throughout the 17-year observation, the average rate for the low-income households was 18.75%, and the rates for the middle and high-income households were 33.28 and 37.81%, with the difference of 19.06% between the highest and the lowest. In the whole observation period, the gap in occurrence rates was at the highest level of 23.51% in the initial stage, which decreased to 18.75% in the Eighth Five-Year Plan period and 13.89% in the Ninth Five-Year Plan, before it touched bottom at 9.67% in the first three years of the new century. Meanwhile, over time, except for the low-income households with an inverted 'U' downtrend in lending, the occurrence rates for middle and high-income households both declined obviously. The most rapid decrease occurred for high-income households, from 43.47% in the initial stage of the observation (1986–1990) to the current 22.00% (2000–2002), with a drop of 21.47%. This has indicated that with the increase of rural household income, rural household lending has been shrinking.

4.3.1.3 Loan Sources

It is seen from Table 4.11 that although the loan sources of rural households with different income levels are mainly from private borrowing, the low-income households mainly depend on the households with higher incomes. Of all the households at five income levels, the ratio of bank loans is the highest for high-income households, and over time, their bank financial support has increased. In 2002, nearly half of their household borrowing was from the bank, while the ratio from the bank was less than 1/4 for low-income households. A typical 'Matthew Effect' is found in the relationship between the banks and rural households, in which it is easier for a household with a better economic condition to obtain bank support, otherwise it is harder to get any bank support. This has aggravated the inequality in rural economic development.

In terms of interest payment ratio of private borrowing, it is obvious that with the income increase of rural households, the payment ratio has shown an inverted 'U' downtrend. Over the eight years since 1995, the private loans with interest payments accounted for 41.61% out of all private loans for low-income households, 43.63% for middle-income households, and 24.12% for high-income households. This has indicated that rural household capability in loan acquisition and the necessity to pay interests are obviously related to household economic status. Low-income households cannot provide necessary loan guarantee due to the weak economic capability. Yet, they are weak in obtaining bank loans and have to resort to private borrowing, despite high interest rates. Accordingly, their interest payment ratio is higher than other categories of households, while the high-income households are the opposite.

Table 4.11 Loan sources and interest payments of rural households with different income levels

	Current-year private borrowing (%)					Current-year interest payment from private borrowing (%)				
	Low income	Lower middle income	Middle income	Upper middle income	High income	Low income	Lower middle income	Middle income	Upper middle income	High income
1993	96.05	93.00	94.06	91.68	89.17	53.17	53.96	41.43	54.04	26.89
1995	82.98	94.56	82.85	81.79	66.35	31.76	32.24	21.89	21.54	13.73
1996	82.62	84.23	74.18	77.99	69.63	43.98	49.65	63.67	39.84	17.92
1997	86.50	92.99	87.88	87.93	70.64	37.09	47.46	71.08	15.81	44.18
1998	95.66	90.67	92.80	82.59	81.87	39.31	60.99	50.71	31.82	35.13
1999	85.76	81.81	84.77	88.08	61.08	45.11	39.94	34.25	22.77	33.74
2000	90.54	82.59	93.44	92.17	71.97	47.25	45.14	70.04	39.82	19.92
2001	81.61	96.15	96.01	82.90	67.10	44.18	23.72	39.13	43.39	17.74
2002	76.86	81.36	70.95	79.13	44.11	44.44	22.37	27.93	20.51	21.08
1995–2002	85.69	87.71	84.81	83.19	65.25	41.61	39.32	43.63	31.03	24.12

4.3.1.4 Loan Purposes

It can be seen from Table 4.12 that with the income increase of rural households, the loan purposes of rural households at different income levels have varied. Compared with other categories of households, the loans for lower-middle income households are mostly used for living, and seldom for production. Over the eight-year observation since 1995, of the loans used for living, the ratio was highest for lower-middle income households to as high as 40.72%, which is followed by 27.68% for low-income households, 26.36% for upper-middle income households, 25.88% for middle-income households, and 25.22% for high-income households. On the contrary, for the loans used for production, the ratio for the high-income households was the highest with the average level of 74.78% over eight years. This is followed by middle-income households with 74.12%, upper-middle income households with 73.64%, low-income households with 72.32%, and lower-middle income households with the lowest level of 59.28%.

Obviously, with the income growth for rural households, of the household loans used for production, the ratio of loans used for agricultural production has been decreasing. Over the eight years since 1995, 77.27% of production loans for low-income households were used in agriculture, while the figure was 13.34% for high-income households. This has indicated that the current income sources of rural high-income households in Zhejiang have little to do with agricultural production. It suggests on the other hand that if the government is trying to provide credit support for agriculture, the key support targets should be the rural households with comparatively low incomes which depend more on agricultural production. This will be further explained in the subsequent analysis.

4.3.2 B&L Behaviours of Rural Households with Different Operation Types

In previous research, I have found out that rural household economic behaviours are closely related to the types of operation in a household (Shi, 1999, 2001). Especially in terms of B&L behaviour, the differences of types of operation are not only in capital demand elasticity, but also in loan level and structure. The operations with high capital demand elasticity would usually have lower borrowing occurrence rate and level, while operations with low capital demand elasticity might have higher occurrence rate and level. To further illustrate, a comparison analysis is carried out concerning households with different operation types.

Table 4.12 Loan purposes of rural households with different incomes

	Current-year loans used for production (%)					Loans used in agriculture/loans for production (%)				
	Low income	Lower middle income	Middle income	Upper middle income	High income	Low income	Lower middle income	Middle income	Upper middle income	High income
1993	72.71	67.04	58.64	63.81	85.25	38.77	40.47	28.43	6.94	2.79
1995	76.80	80.70	88.88	79.28	82.53	71.60	57.18	62.70	35.72	10.57
1996	62.86	69.36	53.96	82.71	77.60	69.98	77.10	38.76	53.22	40.40
1997	72.16	29.55	46.80	55.62	68.12	56.14	40.71	30.74	68.75	5.17
1998	76.24	44.18	56.90	68.70	67.91	88.36	14.32	48.15	25.58	0.00
1999	65.77	73.61	81.03	70.80	70.98	71.32	44.04	34.31	18.42	11.29
2000	63.86	58.38	71.22	75.78	81.88	60.49	50.18	26.04	57.50	24.05
2001	65.13	67.42	94.00	68.99	82.95	87.51	70.92	46.56	11.97	3.88
2002	90.41	43.03	70.43	75.07	63.70	92.01	42.92	1.83	26.26	5.90
1995–2002	72.32	59.28	74.12	73.64	74.78	77.27	52.33	36.75	37.16	13.34

4.3.2.1 Comparison of B&L Levels

It can be seen from Table 4.13 that with the increase in the degree of non-agriculturalisation of household operation, the level of funds lent by rural households generally shows an upward trend. As time goes by, the change in the level of lending for complete agricultural households presents a rising trend, while the capital lending levels of other types of households present an inverted 'U'-shape change (Fig. 4.10). If careful observation is carried out, during the entire 17 years' follow-up observation, the relationship varies between the lending level of households and their non-agricultural degrees in different periods. In the early stage of observation (1986–1990), with the increase of non-agriculturalisation of households, their capital lending showed a trend of an inverted 'U' shape. After the 1990s, the trends evolved from a low rise during the Eight Five-Year Plan period to a steep rise during the Ninth Five-Year Plan period. In the new century (2000–2002), it further evolved into a 'U'-shape trend. During the period of 2000–2002, the per capita lending level was 894.61 yuan for agricultural households, 949.99 yuan for complete agricultural households, 594.04 yuan for agriculture-dominated households, 1143.47 yuan for non-agricultural dominated households and 1382.50 yuan for non-agricultural households. If compared with household income of the same period, the ratios of capital lending to the current-year income became 16.88, 16.38, 11.83, 16.65 and 8.51% for different categories of rural households. Obviously, during the lending process, rural households with different operation types bear different pressures. The pressure was the lowest for non-agricultural households and the highest for agricultural households. Compared with the corresponding ratios of 14.76, 14.17, 20.92, 26.30, and 16.53% during the Ninth Five-Year Plan period, the pressure was slightly increased for agricultural households, but substantially decreased for non-agricultural dominated and non-agricultural households.

Likewise, it can be seen from Table 4.13 that with the increase of non-agriculturalisation of household operation, the borrowing level of rural households generally present an uptrend. As time goes on, the borrowing levels for the most and the least non-agriculturalised households present an obvious uptrend, while those of other categories of households present an inverted 'U' trend (Fig. 4.11). The changes are different in each specific observation stage. Before 1995, with the increase of non-agricultural degree of household operation, the borrowing level of rural households presented an uptrend. After 1995, it evolved into a typical 'U'-shape trend. From 2000 to 2002, per capita borrowing level of the agricultural households was 2549.29 yuan, which was 2742.51 yuan for complete agricultural households, 931.75 yuan for agriculture-dominated households, 1521.38 yuan for non-agricultural dominated households and 4283.17 yuan for the non-agricultural households. Such levels were equivalent to 46.69, 48.74, 18.55, 22.15 and 26.36% of the per capita income of the corresponding categories of rural households. Obviously, during the economic growth process of rural households, the income obtained by agricultural households contained a large proportion of debts. When comparing the debts with the figures of 44.21, 50.86, 41.11, 24.18 and 24.49% in the Ninth Five-Year Plan period, it can be seen that after going through the income increase fluctuations in the middle and

Table 4.13 B&L levels for rural households with different operation types

	Year-end lending level (yuan/person)					Year-end borrowing level (yuan/person)				
	Complete agricultural	Agricultural	Agriculture-dominated	Non-agricultural dominated	Non-agricultural	Complete agricultural	Agricultural	Agriculture-dominated	Non-agricultural dominated	Non-agricultural
1986	67.85	72.63	203.82	153.60	64.94	154.82	147.97	197.02	289.69	222.68
1987	59.53	86.84	185.41	196.43	100.82	147.01	158.42	187.00	429.96	359.13
1988	55.95	92.25	295.30	88.66	140.15	242.21	277.59	376.60	678.66	573.36
1989	82.52	115.55	200.58	255.54	150.23	518.79	447.17	514.78	634.35	1162.71
1990	92.61	116.32	196.74	275.64	217.51	358.10	414.49	528.02	760.68	1343.03
1991	131.22	170.44	339.93	287.51	190.59	396.81	470.37	699.76	790.79	1471.80
1993	161.78	289.39	378.17	518.72	789.53	453.05	492.48	293.65	1177.34	1778.99
1995	420.78	434.76	1023.04	1345.16	1000.73	1272.42	1272.81	1971.73	1495.11	2280.05
1996	622.83	613.91	590.05	2218.09	2753.17	2281.23	2510.33	2431.69	778.95	3256.21
1997	707.64	614.70	876.02	2171.43	2890.36	2701.64	2579.96	1713.75	1171.43	2635.97
1998	880.41	724.19	1042.37	1942.68	2508.45	2823.24	2990.87	1676.27	1442.68	3289.40
1999	1155.66	964.97	1116.24	1793.94	1883.81	2083.16	3105.44	1571.07	2536.87	3210.04
2000	866.11	846.10	828.67	986.73	1556.01	2415.27	2503.45	1376.72	1910.71	3736.43
2001	920.00	895.92	469.78	1504.67	1322.26	2706.19	2474.80	747.03	341.12	4472.61
2002	1068.09	942.58	351.15	1076.27	1282.07	3116.49	2677.29	400.34	1944.92	4600.00
1995–2002	799.21	734.64	808.73	1644.44	1859.44	2380.05	2481.37	1544.54	1512.86	3510.99

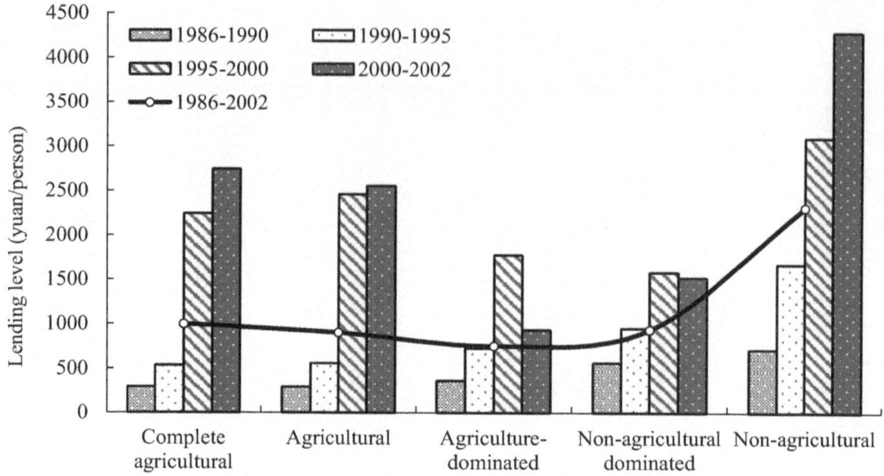

Fig. 4.10 Lending levels of rural households with different operation types

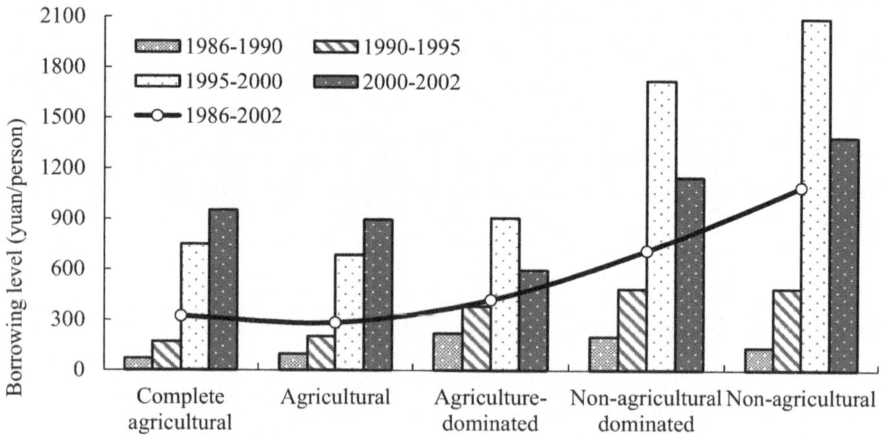

Fig. 4.11 Borrowing levels for rural households with different operation types

late 1990s, except the complete agricultural households, the ratios of debt to income decreased for all other categories of rural households in the new century.

4.3.2.2 Comparison in B&L Occurrence

It can be seen from Table 4.14 that with the increase of the non-agriculturalisation of rural household operation, both the lending and borrowing occurrence rates present an inverted 'U'-shape downtrend (Figs. 4.12 and 4.13). As for the lending occur-

Table 4.14 Changes in B&L occurrence of farmer households with different operation types

	Year-end lending occurrence rate (%)					Year-end borrowing occurrence rate (%)				
	Complete agricultural	Agricultural	Agriculture-dominated	Non-agricultural dominated	Non-agricultural	Complete agricultural	Agricultural	Agriculture-dominated	Non-agricultural dominated	Non-agricultural
1986	28.41	34.14	65.93	51.61	26.32	51.81	47.19	41.48	48.39	36.84
1987	28.65	36.05	52.67	50.00	23.21	37.67	39.46	36.64	50.00	32.14
1988	27.40	30.27	49.09	32.18	26.61	37.29	43.04	56.97	44.83	37.10
1989	29.55	31.85	42.96	47.17	30.36	41.16	47.10	57.75	50.00	43.75
1990	27.20	28.82	41.10	36.07	32.50	36.79	44.52	48.63	43.44	47.50
1991	29.30	30.87	38.61	40.21	27.86	33.24	39.00	42.41	44.33	44.29
1993	23.28	30.80	40.58	30.61	36.23	26.98	30.43	27.54	38.78	31.88
1995	31.18	30.12	36.54	33.33	24.49	23.66	28.57	38.46	31.37	28.57
1996	26.42	27.84	26.92	55.10	39.56	33.96	36.08	48.08	22.45	28.57
1997	22.49	23.08	40.00	47.50	31.36	33.14	35.75	41.43	27.50	24.58
1998	19.63	23.93	39.13	38.46	31.50	34.36	38.89	41.30	28.21	30.71
1999	23.81	24.55	47.06	34.00	23.44	30.61	37.73	43.14	46.00	28.13
2000	21.21	20.44	32.79	34.62	27.27	36.36	37.02	42.62	30.77	34.09
2001	14.08	16.33	25.49	30.77	20.95	30.28	32.65	23.53	11.54	26.35
2002	15.75	14.12	11.11	24.24	18.31	31.50	31.64	19.44	21.21	24.65
1995–2002	22.46	23.18	33.41	37.94	26.42	31.61	34.77	38.19	28.82	28.15

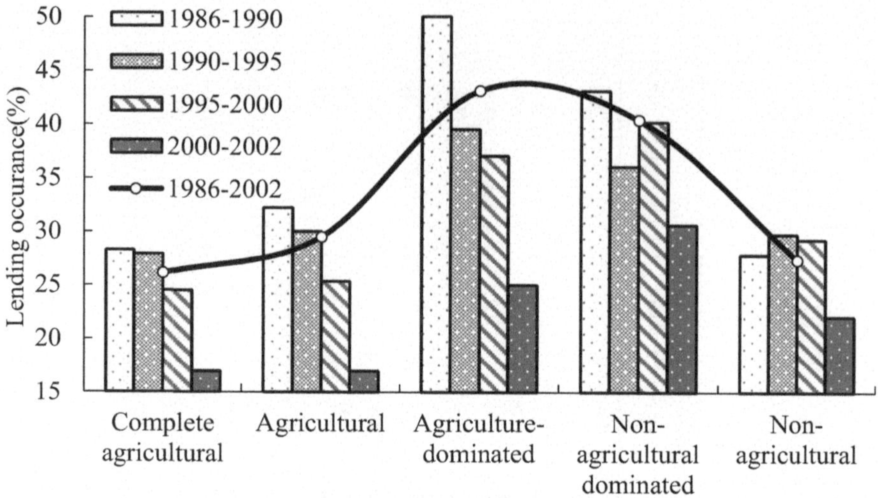

Fig. 4.12 Changes in lending occurrence for rural households with different operation types

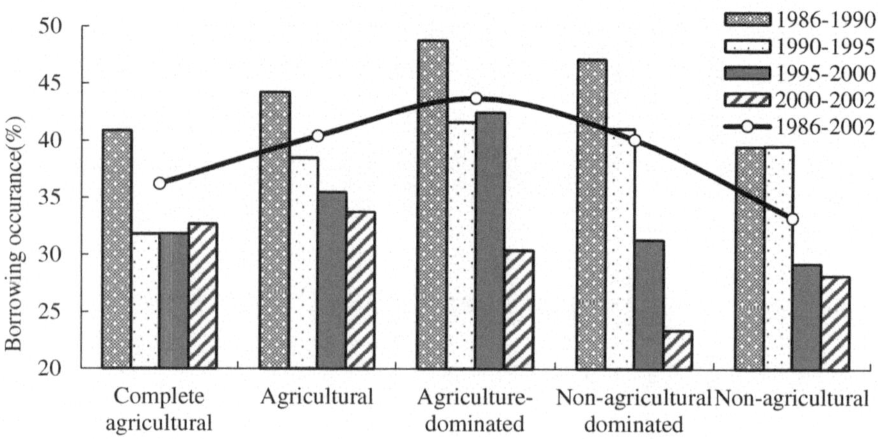

Fig. 4.13 Changes in borrowing occurrence for rural households with different operation types

rence rate, in the initial observation stage before 1995, the highest rate occurred in agriculture-dominated households which later shifted to the non-agricultural dominated households after 1995. As time went on, the rates for agricultural and agriculture-dominated households presented an obvious downtrend, that for the non-agricultural dominated households presented a fluctuating downtrend, and that for the agricultural households presented an inverted 'U'-shape downtrend. Combined with the borrowing level of rural households, it can be seen that the lending for agricultural and agriculture-dominated households is small in quantity but large in scale, while that for non-agricultural and non-agricultural dominated households is large in quantity but small in scale. Household lending is completely in line with the household economic development. The lending capacity of non-agricultural households with high incomes is obviously higher than other categories of households, but its occurrence rate is not high. Why? In my opinion, it might be related to the borrower's credit and the ability to return. There is a folk saying that 'the God of Wealth is surnamed Stingy', meaning it is rather difficult to borrow from the rich. In fact, data from Zhejiang have also proved that to borrow from agriculture-dominated households with a slightly higher income is easier than from non-agricultural households with more income.

In terms of the changes in borrowing, before 2000, the borrowing occurrence rate of rural households presented an inverted 'U'-shape downtrend with the increase of non-agriculturalisation for rural household operation. After 2000, this change evolved into a 'U'-shape. As for the changes in borrowing occurrence over time, there has been a general decreasing trend. When comparing the observations of 17 years, the borrowing occurrence rate of the non-agricultural dominated households decreased most rapidly and obviously, from 47.18% in the initial observation period (1986–1990) to the current 23.42% (2000–2002), with a decrease of 23.75% over 17 years. This is followed by agriculture-dominated households with the level decreasing by 18.41% over 17 years, from 48.82% in the initial observation period to 30.41% currently. Households with the highest and the lowest non-agricultural degree, i.e. agricultural and non-agricultural households have seen slow decreases in borrowing with declines of only 10.46 and 11.32% over the 17 years, of which the decrease for complete agricultural households was the smallest of only 8.20%. The changes in the borrowing occurrence of rural households and the non-agricultural degree of their household operation have reflected to some extent that when the agricultural households are non-agriculturalised, the B&L behaviour would go through a process when B&L has a high occurrence ratio but a small amount. This process is of great importance for the rural households to carry out non-agricultural activities with comparatively low capital demand elasticities. It also provides us the indication that during the process of promoting rural industrialisation, it is necessary and obligatory for the government to provide rural households with necessary capital guarantee in policy. This will become an importance assurance for farmers currently suffering from private loans to develop out of agriculture (Shi & Li, 2003). It is also an important measure for increasing rural income.

4.3.2.3 Comparison of Loan Sources

It is indicated from Table 4.15 that the loan sources of rural households are in some way related to the household operation types. Although the loans for various rural households are mainly from private sources, there exist certain differences. To be specific, the loans for agricultural and non-agricultural households with the highest and lowest non-agricultural degrees have relatively higher proportions of bank support, while agriculture-dominated and non-agricultural dominated households are in the transition process, and obtain funds mainly from private sources. Therefore,

Table 4.15 Changes in loan purpose of rural households with different operation types

	Current-year private borrowing (%)					Current-year private borrowing with interest payment (%)				
	Complete agricultural	Agricultural	Agriculture-dominated	Non-agricultural dominated	Non-agricultural	Complete agricultural	Agricultural	Agriculture-dominated	Non-agricultural dominated	Non-agricultural
1993	89.94	92.66	90.58	95.20	92.43	83.21	74.43	34.72	38.64	7.69
1995	86.70	87.12	67.32	90.16	73.29	22.76	29.79	23.38	18.39	16.08
1996	84.50	83.78	78.61	81.01	71.93	51.36	52.05	27.89	33.67	20.54
1997	95.98	96.51	84.88	100.00	63.48	44.26	46.98	58.34	11.22	31.82
1998	96.55	95.77	91.96	100.00	76.93	36.20	39.81	71.40	99.27	43.72
1999	72.64	79.05	95.66	59.18	84.57	56.77	64.41	55.40	25.37	3.87
2000	94.94	88.79	84.94	87.10	79.77	53.44	49.33	46.28	73.83	36.03
2001	87.13	85.08	88.89	100.00	72.78	32.94	41.32	38.09	13.21	25.48
2002	72.85	72.80	100.00	58.76	63.19	40.43	43.36	21.77	75.44	17.21
1995–2002	86.36	73.39	83.24	83.19	73.39	43.33	23.57	43.45	42.46	23.57

private loans play an extremely important role in the non-agricultural process of rural households. However, we should also recognise that this is based on the payments of high interests. Accordingly, if the government could provide certain credit support to meet the fund demands of rural households in the non-agricultural process through policy-making, it is believed that the non-agriculturalisation of household's economy will be improved greatly, and the rural industrialisation and urbanisation goals set by the government will be realised in the near future.

4.3.2.4 Comparison of Loan Purposes

It can be seen from Table 4.16 that during the process of non-agriculturalisation, different farming households have different loan purposes. Rural households with the highest and lowest non-agricultural degrees will use a relatively large proportion of loans for production, while the agriculture-dominated and non-agricultural dominated households in the transition process will mainly use the loans for living. This result shows that, in the economic non-agriculturalising process of rural households, due to the low demand elasticity of funds, when rural households are using a lot of funds in non-agriculturalisation, they are facing a serious shortage of funds for living, and have to resort to private loans. Such loans might not have high interests, but it is the production loans with very high interest rates that have forced rural households to borrow a lot for living in the transition process of non-agriculturalisation. In order to solve this problem, it is necessary for the government to provide policy support for the capital needs in the transition process of rural households.

In terms of the production loans of the farmer households, the loans used for agricultural production have decreased obviously with the increase of the non-agricultural degree of the household operation. From 1995 to 2002, the proportions of production loans used for agricultural purposes were 90.43% for agricultural households, 53.22% for agriculture-dominated and 19.36% for non-agricultural dominated households, and that for non-agricultural households was at a much lower level of 4.64%. Therefore, if the goal is to support agricultural development, the credit policy should mainly benefit the agricultural households, whereas if the goal is to promote the non-agriculturalisation of rural economy, the policy should mainly support the agriculture-dominated households, because they are in the greatest need of capital.

4.4 Conclusion and Comments

In general, the saving levels of rural households present an uptrend over time. However, it is not the case for bank saving rates, which presented an uptrend in the late 1980s and showed a gradual downtrend after the 1990s. This result has indicated that the increase of saving levels for rural household is obviously based on the continuous increase of income. However, the changes in bank saving rates are strongly related to

Table 4.16 Changes in loan purpose for rural households with different operation types

	Current-year borrowing used for production (%)					Loans for agriculture/loans for production (%)				
	Complete agricultural	Agricultural	Agriculture-dominated	Non-agricultural dominated	Non-agricultural	Complete agricultural	Agricultural	Agriculture-dominated	Non-agricultural dominated	Non-agricultural
1993	31.39	41.89	73.91	80.53	93.03	63.25	69.38	38.24	3.61	1.51
1995	75.14	77.96	77.11	83.80	84.57	90.64	92.49	63.10	0.45	0.16
1996	67.47	68.69	67.79	84.49	75.74	87.84	89.10	86.37	3.75	20.47
1997	54.09	48.73	66.21	46.64	82.11	76.58	77.46	47.46	100.00	2.01
1998	62.61	66.47	41.70	35.98	70.98	86.23	85.04	26.23	20.41	5.75
1999	80.90	65.63	53.51	62.97	89.24	96.51	95.21	5.92	0.00	0.00
2000	79.48	76.88	37.83	59.35	78.73	100.00	92.33	34.57	9.42	15.84
2001	71.01	67.90	69.12	0.00	83.16	95.12	92.93	50.18	–	0.00
2002	73.90	74.01	74.97	45.77	79.97	93.86	93.69	0.00	72.97	0.00
1995–2002	70.01	68.47	61.40	61.39	80.52	91.27	90.43	53.22	19.36	4.64

differences in regions, investment environments, development degrees of financial market and humanistic values.

Over time, the B&L level in cash of rural households has also presented a continuous uptrend. However, the loan occurrence of rural households presents a downward trend. This result indicates that the rural loan level rises continuously, while occurrence is not widespread but more centralised.

As for the saving and B&L behaviours, the lending and borrowing behaviours generally occurred independently. Although borrowing and lending may occur simultaneously in some rural households, the co-occurrence rate has presented an obvious downtrend over time. The increased saving rate and the limitation of B&L occurrence have in some ways reflected the favourable development trend of the current rural income growth in Zhejiang.

Over the years, great changes have taken place in the loan structure of rural households. The loans are mainly private, but those from formal financial institutions are on the rise. The purpose of the loans is mainly for production, and both the interest payment amount and payment rate are very high with small changes. Combined with the previous study, there has appeared the indication that with the commercialised transformation of the financial system, the financial investment focus in rural areas from formal financial organisations has been transferred from the inland to coastal areas. This also provides a new explanation for us as to why the loans of rural households in Shanxi present an inverted 'U' trend. Rural households in Shanxi used to rely on the formal financial sector. With the commercialised transformation of the financial system, more funds have been invested in coastal areas, resulting in the fluctuations or decrease of inland rural economy in the late 1990s.

The changes in income have a lot of influence on the saving behaviours of rural households. As time goes on, although the levels of savings for rural households with different incomes increase by different degrees, the growth in savings for high-income households is obviously faster than that of low-income households, and the difference has been obviously enlarged. This trend is also reflected in saving occurrence rate. Therefore, the high level of savings of rural residents is not driven by the income growth of all residents, but by a small number of high-income households. The difference in income is the cause of the polarised development of rural saving.

References

Ma, H. (1993). *Household economic behaviour in China*. Shanghai: Shanghai People's Press.

Shi, Q. (1999). *Rural household economic development*. Beijing: China Agriculture Press.

Shi, Q. (2001). *Rural household economic activity and behaviour*. Beijing: China Agricultural Press.

Shi, Q., & Chen, K. (2002). Empirical analysis of rural houeshold lending behaviours in underdeveloped regions. *issues in Agricultural Economy, 6*, 66–78.

Shi, Q., & Li, D. (2003). Trial implemtation of reform of tax and fee and its influence on peasants' burden. *Journal of South China Agricultural University (Social Science Edition), 2*(2), 1–11.

Shi, Q., & Zhuo, J. (2003). A positive analysis of saves and borrowings of peasant families. *Contemporary Economic Research, 8,* 52–58.
Shi, Q., Wan, G., & Huang, J. (2004). Saving and borrowing behavior of household in Shanxi and Zhejiang of China. *China Rural Survey, 2,* 26–33.
Zheng, H. (1996). *Empirical analysis on rural society transit in contemporary China.* Beijing: China Renmin University Press.

Chapter 5
Imbalanced Economic Development and Its Origin

Contents

People who have read the book *Economics* by Paul Samuelson will be impressed by the dialogue between F. Scott Fitzgerald and Ernest Hemingway cited at the beginning of the chapter 'Income and Wealth'.[1] There exist differences between the rich and the poor and as said by Fitzgerald, the life of the rich and the poor is different because the rich would earn more money than the poor. Income inequality clearly exists among people, families and their social circles. This is, on the one hand, a phenomenon indicating social progress and economic development and cannot be

[1]F. Scott Fitzgerald: You know, Ernest, the rich are different from us. Ernest Hemingway: Yes, I know. They have more money than we do (Samuelson, 1992).

Q. Shi and Y. Gao, *Sustainable Development of Rural Household Economy*,
https://doi.org/10.1007/978-981-15-2747-0_5

changed by people's will. On the other hand, it is not what we would like to see in social development, and is against the goals of fairness, equity and balanced development in human society that the majority of people have been striving for. Especially in such a country in China where we are working towards communism, income inequality deserves much of our attention and in-depth research, which is crucial to realise the goal of common prosperity.

With the continuous deepening of rural reform and opening-up, great changes have taken place in the basic household units of rural economy, and farmers' economic capability has been improved significantly. However, it is undeniable that with the enhancement of farmers' economic capability, the stratification of rural economy has become more evident and the development imbalance has been intensified. Some rural households have been out of poverty and progressed from just fulfilling basic needs of food and clothing to being well-off and prosperity, while other households are still in the difficult process of escaping poverty and struggling for food and clothing. The imbalanced economic development of rural households has become a critical issue in China's rural economy, which cannot be ignored in the study on rural household economic growth. This chapter focuses on the theme of development imbalance of rural household economy, by analysing the economic development inequality and its evolution based on empirical evidence from the observed rural households in the ten villages of Zhejiang from 1986 to 2002.

5.1 Rural Household Imbalanced Economic Development and Stratification

5.1.1 Per Capita Income and Its Changes

It can be seen from Fig. 5.1 and Table 5.1 that generally, the per capita income of the observed rural households in the ten villages of Zhejiang has been increasing since 1986 when the observation started, and reached 9540.16 yuan (current price) in 2002, increasing by 10.69 times compared with the income of 861.87 yuan in 1986, with an average annual growth rate of 16.21%. After deducting the factors for rise in prices, the real growth was 3.03 times compared with that in 1986, and the average annual growth rate still reached 9.11%.

In terms of the trend of per capita income growth of rural households (Fig. 5.2), since 1986, different stages for rural household income growth can been seen in Zhejiang. Over the 17 years, the economic growth of the observed rural households in the ten villages of Zhejiang in general went through a complete cycle, and has entered a new growth stage. The income level presented an uptrend before 1988, fluctuated from 1988 to 1991, presented an uptrend from 1991 to 1995 for the second time, fluctuated from 1995 to 1998 for the second time, presented a further uptrend from 1998 to 2000 for the third time, and has fluctuated since 2000 for the third time.

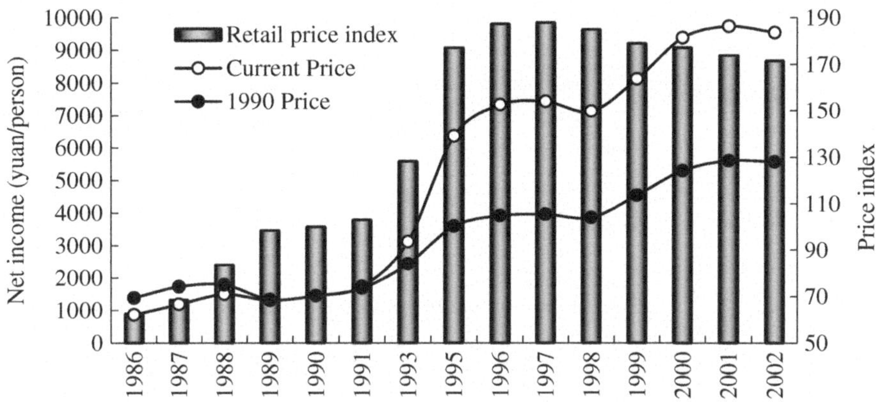

Fig. 5.1 Per capita income in observed households

In the first period, the initial rise was related to the huge price increase of agricultural products nationwide in the late 1980s, and the second rise was related to the non-agriculturalisation transformation of household economic structure. In the late 1990s, the third rise was related to the reform concerning the clarification of rural property rights in Zhejiang. The three fluctuations have all been related to the national macro-economic situations.

With the staged growth of rural household income, the income gap among rural households has enlarged substantially. The kurtosis and skewness of income have both increased obviously compared with the initial observation period, i.e. from 2.01 and 7.17 in 1986 to 6.66 and 65.82 in 2002. The distribution of rural households with a low income presents a sharp rising trend. The income growth imbalances among rural households have been intensified, which has become a key feature of the economic operation of the observed households in Zhejiang.[2] It can also be seen from Table 5.1 that faster income growth is accompanied with higher level of inequality for rural households, otherwise the imbalance level is lower.

5.1.2 *Rural Households Economic Stratification*

It is seen in Fig. 5.3 and Table 5.2 that with the income increase of rural household economy, the rural household economic stratification is very obvious. The proportions of the rural households with incomes higher or lower than a certain level are increasing while that of households with their incomes in the middle is decreasing. The development of stratification of rural households has obviously increased over time.

[2]In fact, such a feature is also applicable to the national rural economic operation (Shi, Ma, & Wu, 2001).

Table 5.1 Per capita income of in observed households and other statistical information

	Household number	Per capita income at constant price in 1990 (yuan)						Per capita income at current price	Retail price index of Zhejiang
		Average	Maximum	Range	Standard deviation	Skewness	Kurtosis		
1986	1082	1379.15	7653.26	7653.26	852.72	2.01	7.17	861.87	62.49
1987	1147	1726.84	14085.18	14085.18	1191.80	3.07	18.90	1181.55	68.43
1988	1158	1782.70	16755.87	16722.96	1479.10	4.26	28.42	1489.50	83.55
1989	1190	1328.20	13937.23	13937.23	990.46	4.16	39.30	1307.28	98.43
1990	1208	1444.33	13996.00	13996.00	949.07	3.20	28.40	1444.33	100.00
1991	1158	1679.79	26617.15	26612.62	1346.83	7.04	107.15	1730.18	103.00
1993	500	2427.24	20832.31	20895.13	2134.20	4.18	25.97	3110.13	128.13
1995	500	3588.49	57614.92	61513.42	4369.17	6.44	61.00	6351.27	176.99
1996	500	3911.00	109654.47	111256.54	6396.23	10.47	155.27	7323.73	187.26
1997	500	3953.33	72340.71	80753.25	5645.46	6.79	65.41	7425.14	187.82
1998	500	3853.59	75291.10	83172.63	6081.26	7.76	79.07	7121.82	184.81
1999	500	4535.13	149062.27	152019.61	9275.04	10.91	148.56	8113.35	178.90
2000	499	5296.76	152463.82	162302.90	10628.78	9.27	108.74	9381.10	177.11
2001	501	5600.82	158298.99	158298.99	11615.34	9.26	105.09	9730.87	173.74
2002	500	5563.10	102821.35	106806.03	7592.91	6.66	65.82	9540.16	171.49

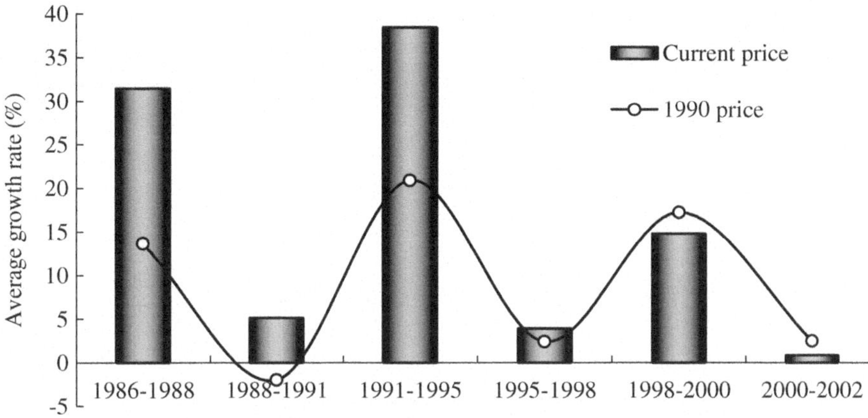

Fig. 5.2 Staged changes in per capita income of the observed rural households

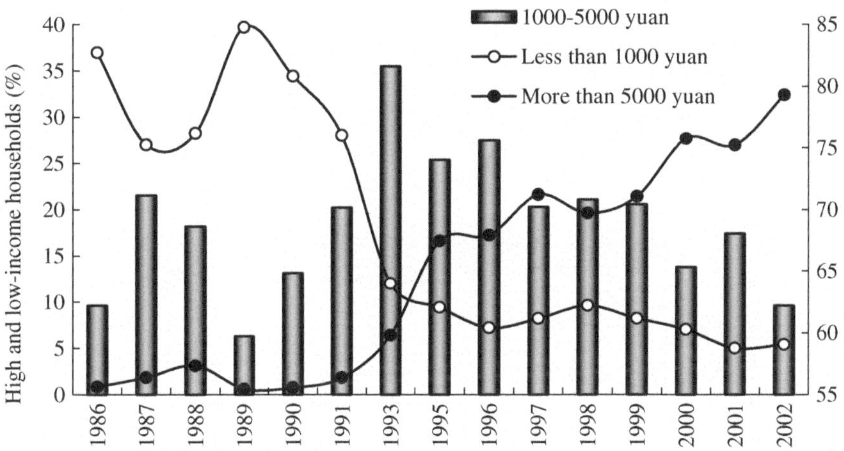

Fig. 5.3 Income stratification of the observed rural households

From the perspective of time periods, the accelerated development of rural economic stratification occurred after the 1990s. Up until 2002, the proportions of high- and low-income households became: 5.40% for rural households with a per capita income of less than 1000 yuan and 32.40% for those with an income higher than 5000 yuan, with a decrease of 29.01% for the former and an increase of 31.66% for the latter compared with 1990, or a decrease of 4.00% for the former and an increase of 15.80% for the latter respectively compared with 1995. Therefore, it is suggested that income inequality is not only reflected in the actual level but also in structure. Based on income categorisation of rural households at the same price level, it is seen that over the 17 years of development, the distribution of the rural households in Zhejiang under observation has clearly shifted upward, and has changed from a

Table 5.2 Income stratification of rural households (constant price in 1990)

	Distribution of rural households at different per capita net income levels (100 yuan)									Less than average
	<0.5	0.5–1	1–2	2–3	3–5	5–10	10–20	20–30	≥30	
1986	7.39	29.57	46.49	12.29	3.42	0.83	–	–	–	61.18
1987	5.41	21.62	46.64	16.30	8.20	1.66	0.17	–	–	64.60
1988	6.83	21.43	46.76	15.90	5.96	2.59	0.52	–	–	67.33
1989	12.36	27.33	44.24	11.69	3.78	0.42	0.17	–	–	58.03
1990	9.12	25.29	45.27	15.01	4.56	0.66	0.08	–	–	56.80
1991	6.31	21.71	45.67	17.73	6.75	1.64	0.17	–	–	62.72
1993	2.60	9.40	39.80	24.60	17.20	4.80	1.40	0.20	–	64.93
1995	2.40	7.00	26.20	26.00	21.80	12.80	2.60	0.60	0.60	68.60
1996	1.80	5.40	28.80	23.00	23.80	11.80	3.60	1.20	0.60	74.00
1997	3.60	4.60	24.40	22.80	23.00	16.20	4.00	0.60	0.80	68.20
1998	4.80	4.80	26.00	17.00	27.80	14.20	4.60	–	0.80	70.80
1999	4.40	3.80	24.40	22.00	24.00	14.60	4.80	0.80	1.20	74.00
2000	2.61	4.41	17.84	21.64	25.85	19.04	5.01	2.40	1.20	75.75
2001	1.80	3.19	17.76	25.15	25.15	18.76	5.39	0.80	2.00	78.24
2002	1.80	3.60	15.40	19.60	27.20	22.00	7.00	2.00	1.40	72.80

low-level distribution before 1991 to a high-level distribution after 1995. Of course, the formation of such a distribution structure is also related to the great reduction in the number of observed rural households in 1993, but the basic trend remains unchanged.

In order to further examine the stratification, analysis is also carried out concerning the correlated distributions of population and income for rural households at different income levels. According to the results (Fig. 5.4 and Appendix Tables 5.17, 5.18, and 5.19), in 1986, rural households with a per capita income of less than 1000 yuan accounted for 36.85% of the observed households, their population was 35.85% of the total, and their income took only 18.11% of the total of the observed households. The corresponding figures for the rural households with a per capita

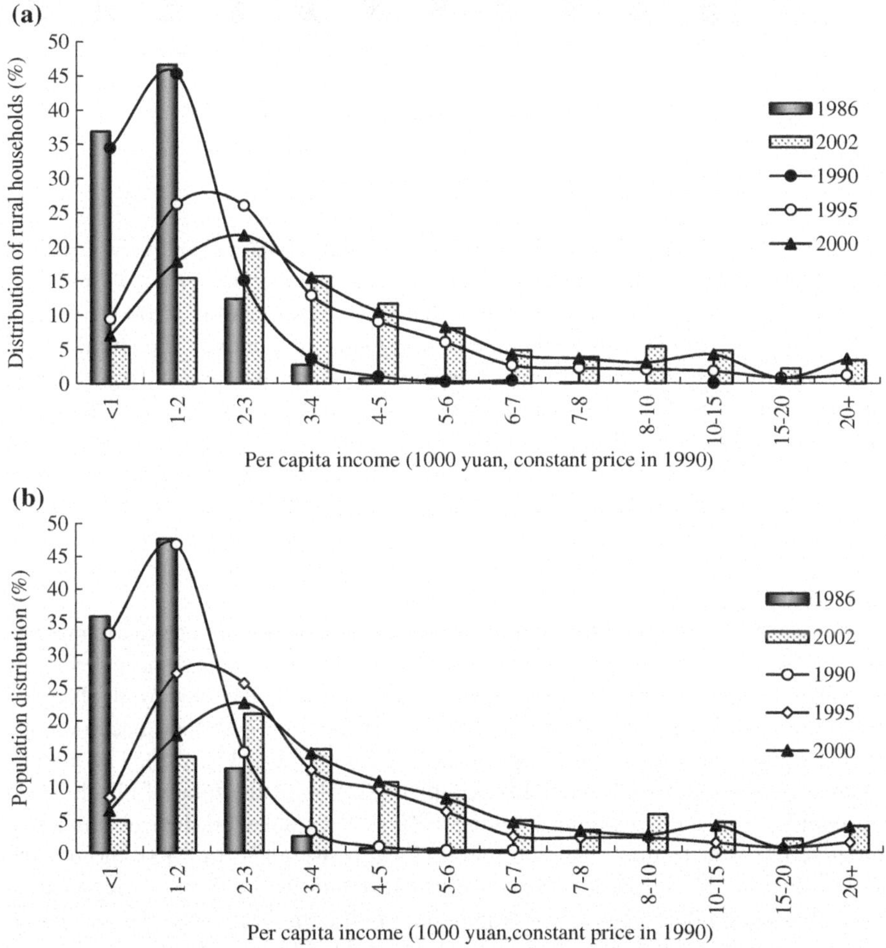

Fig. 5.4 **a** Distribution of rural households at different income levels. **b** Population distribution of rural households at different income levels. **c** Income distribution of rural households

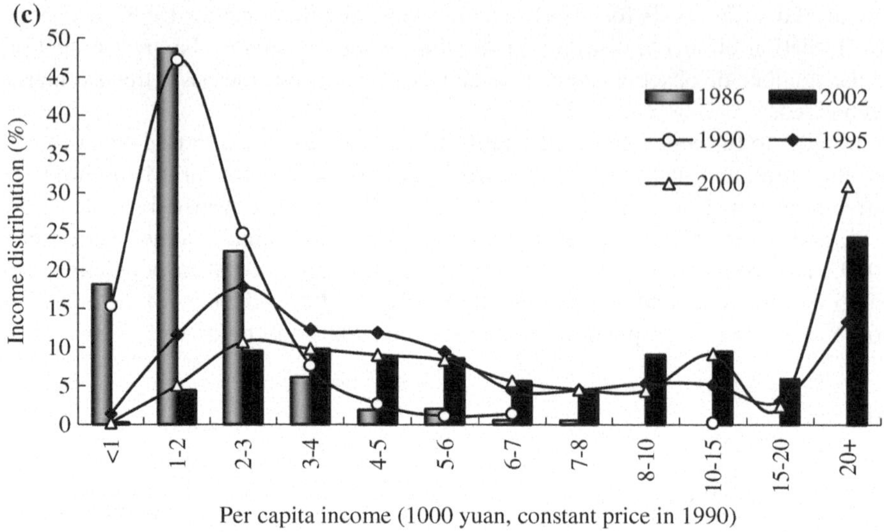

Fig. 5.4 (continued)

income of 5000 yuan and above were 0.83, 0.72 and 3.04% respectively. In 1995, these figures of households, population and income changed to 9.40, 8.42 and 1.36 for rural households with an income less than 1000 yuan, and to 16.00, 16.58 and 45.15% for households with an income of 5000 yuan and above. The stratification further intensified in 2002 in that the corresponding figures of households, population and income became 5.40, 4.92 and 0.25% for households with an income less than 1000 yuan, and became 32.40, 33.15 and 67.51% for households with an income of 5000 yuan and over. It is seen from the evolution trend, although the share of income for low-income households has been small compared with the corresponding population and household numbers, their income level has been increased. However, such an increase seems trivial compared with the economic growth of the high-income households.

After arranging the rural households in sequence based on per capita income and dividing them according to equal numbers into groups, it is found that in 1986, the income of the top 5% households occupied 12.81% of the total owned by all observed households, while their population took 4.64% of the total with their accumulative income equivalent to that of the bottom 29.35% households (Fig. 5.5). The income obtained by the top 10% households occupied 22.97% of the total of all observed households, with their population taking 10% of the total with their accumulated income equivalent to that of the bottom 43.24% households. In 2000, the income ratio of the top 5% households increased to 34.61% to the total, the corresponding population took 5.04% of the total population of all households, and the accumulative income was equivalent to that of the bottom 72.20% households. The income

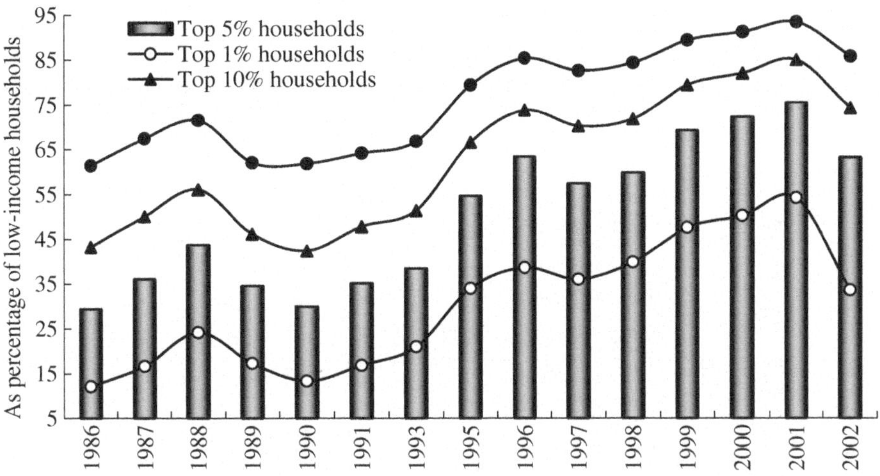

Fig. 5.5 The income ratio of high-income households to that of low-income households

obtained by the top 10% households occupied 44.71% of the total income of all observed households, with their population taking 9.92% of the total and their accumulative income equivalent to that of the bottom 82.00% rural households. In 2002, the polarisation of income distribution was obviously mitigated in that the income obtained by the top 5 and 10% households were equivalent to those of the bottom 63.20 and 74.20% households respectively, decreases of 9.00 and 7.80% compared with the figures in 2000. Again, this result has indicated that the imbalance of economic development among rural households in Zhejiang has generally aggravated. In dividing the income 'cake', the high-income households are obtaining an increasingly larger share, while what is left for low-income households is becoming smaller. Although the situation was alleviated in 2002, this would not have much effect on such a long-term trend. Such mitigation could only be a temporary or short-term phenomenon in the economic growth process, and it can be anticipated that the inequality will further aggravate to some extent.

5.1.3 The Magnitude of Imbalance in Household Economic Development

Generally, two indices can be used for measuring the development inequality of rural household economy, i.e. the Gini coefficient and the Oshima index (the O-index for short, i.e. households are arranged in sequence based on income, and divided into groups of equal numbers, then the index measures the income ratio of top to bottom groups of households). It can be seen from Table 5.3 and Fig. 5.6 that

Table 5.3 Income inequality of rural households at the highest and lowest income levels

	Equally divided by five groups			Equally divided by ten groups			Equally divided by twenty groups			Gini coefficient
	Income (100 yuan/person)		Oshima index	Income (100 yuan/person)		Oshima index	Income (100 yuan/person)		Oshima index	
	Low income households	High income households		Low income households	High income households		Low income households	High income households		
1986	3.38	16.36	4.85	2.58	19.81	7.69	1.71	23.82	13.92	0.3135
1987	4.36	23.63	5.42	3.44	29.46	8.56	2.50	35.70	14.27	0.3513
1988	4.98	31.80	6.39	3.66	41.84	11.42	2.74	55.88	20.37	0.3854
1989	4.06	26.86	6.61	2.64	33.77	12.80	1.72	41.53	24.11	0.3319
1990	5.06	27.30	5.39	3.66	33.21	9.09	2.47	39.79	16.08	0.3108
1991	5.95	34.31	5.77	4.33	43.56	10.07	2.93	54.77	18.69	0.3417
1993	11.12	68.05	6.12	8.42	88.90	10.56	6.12	122.24	19.97	0.3492
1995	16.86	158.71	9.42	10.73	225.34	20.99	5.19	320.86	61.78	0.4420
1996	19.48	202.43	10.39	13.88	302.51	21.80	8.21	425.67	51.87	0.4720
1997	15.36	192.75	12.55	4.66	270.24	57.99	−9.17	388.05	∝	0.4707
1998	11.39	186.82	16.40	−1.21	262.56	∝	−18.14	367.03	∝	0.4875
1999	16.04	229.08	14.28	7.74	342.71	44.28	−3.18	508.07	∝	0.5187
2000	17.53	277.46	15.83	8.82	422.91	47.96	−2.60	644.14	∝	0.5283
2001	22.93	285.64	12.46	16.07	438.74	27.30	11.03	708.29	64.23	0.5353
2002	22.06	255.65	11.59	13.19	366.70	27.80	3.37	504.87	149.60	0.4845

Note "∝" represents that the income of low-income households is negative or zero

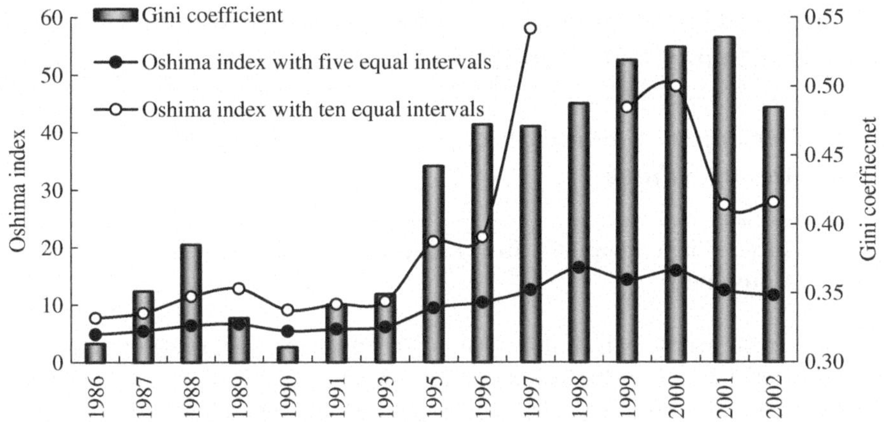

Fig. 5.6 Development imbalance of rural household economy

among the observed rural households in the ten villages of Zhejiang, the imbalance of economic development has been noticeably worsened. According to the changes in Oshima index when the income level is equally divided into five groups, the O-index presented a continuous rising trend since the start of the observation, and was 4.85 in 1986, 5.39 in 1990, 9.42 in 1995, and 16.40 in 1998 (maximum). After that, the situation improved, and the index decreased to 15.83 in 2000 and 11.59 in 2002. Despite a certain level of decline, the income gap between households with the highest and lowest incomes increased by 7 times compared with the level at the beginning of the observation. The Gini coefficient of income also presented a continuous rising trend. At the initial stage of the observation, the Gini coefficient for the rural households was 0.3135, which exceeded the level of 0.4 and increased to 0.4420 in 1995 before further exceeding the critical point of 0.5 to 0.5187 in 1999. After maintaining at this level for three years, the Gini coefficient greatly decreased to 0.4845 in 2002. According to the international standards or the Chinese regulations,[3] since the middle and late 1990s, the income distribution among the observed rural households in the ten villages of Zhejiang had changed from a relatively reasonable state to a serious imbalanced state. After three-year in such a serious imbalanced level, the income distribution resumed the reasonable level in 2002.

[3]According to the international standards, a Gini coefficient is reasonable between 0.2 and 0.5, and is extremely unreasonable above 0.6. According to the Chinese regulations, a Gini coefficient less than 0.2 represents an absolutely balanced distribution, from 0.2 to 0.3 represents a relatively fair distribution, and from 0.3 to 0.5 represents a relatively reasonable distribution (Zheng, 1996: 61).

5.2 Influencing Factors of Rural Household Economic Growth and Development Imbalance

5.2.1 Development Imbalance of Household Economy Among Villages

5.2.1.1 Inter-village Inequality in Per Capita Income of Rural Households

There are many factors which influence the development imbalance of household economy, with the geographic location (of the specific village) as an important factor. Among the ten administrative villages under follow-up observations, there are great income disparities among villages (Table 5.4), and the inequality has been widening over time. In 1986, of the ten villages, six saw their income exceeded the average level, and Xishufu Village had the highest income level of 60.79% above the average. Among the four villages with lower than average income level, Shibanyan Village had the lowest average income at only 62.35% of the average. The income ratio of the highest level to the lowest was 2.58:1. In 1995, there were only four villages with incomes exceeding the average level, with Xushufu Village having the highest income of 124.35% above the average. The number of villages with their income lower than the average level increased to six, and the lowest income in Shibanyan Village was only 47.50% of the average income. The income ratio of the highest level to the lowest increased to 4.72:1. In 2000, the number of villages with an income higher than the average further decreased to three, including Xishufu, Xinmin and Miaoyan, and their incomes were 204.14, 42.35 and 12.44% higher than the average level of 9381.10 yuan. There were seven villages with incomes lower than the average, including Jinhou, Yubei, Yongfeng, Longshang, Bogumen, Hebian and Shibanyan, and their income levels were 22.07, 30.21, 34.97, 39.52, 41.15, 46.69 and 60.52% lower than the average respectively. In 2000, the income ratio of the highest level to the lowest further increased to 7.70:1. Since 2000, the development imbalance of household economy among villages has remained unchanged. However, with the decline of economic income in 2002, the number of villages with an income exceeding the average was back to four, with one village more compared with the three villages below the average income since 2000, including Xishufu, Xinmin, Miaoyan and Yubei, and their income levels were 138.30, 42.53, 20.27 and 15.37% higher than the average of 9540.16 yuan respectively. There were six villages with their incomes lower than the average, including Jinhou, Longshang, Bogumen, Hebian, Yongfeng and Shibanyan, and their incomes were 16.61, 24.23, 28.05, 40.15, 48.17 and 59.08% below the average. The ratio of the highest income to the lowest came back to 5.82:1. Therefore, as time goes on, the economic development of areas with a solid economic foundation and preferable natural condition is obviously better than those with relatively weak economic foundations and poor natural conditions (Fig. 5.7). This also reflects the great influence of location on the economic development, and

Table 5.4 Location and per capita income of observed households (100 yuan/person)

	Longshang	Yongfeng	Yubei	Xishufu	Miaoyan	Xinmin	Jinhou	Bogumen	Hebian	Shibanyan
Location	Mountain	Plain	Plain	Plain	Plain	Plain	Hill	Island	Hill	Hill
1986	11.54	6.59	7.95	13.86	9.14	8.69	9.44	10.15	5.49	5.37
1987	12.00	10.03	9.37	16.77	10.86	10.66	19.31	17.24	6.91	6.14
1988	11.60	13.62	13.04	18.24	14.62	14.22	28.30	16.09	9.10	8.89
1989	14.03	14.59	15.56	16.48	16.80	13.52	10.25	12.54	9.76	9.57
1990	14.43	15.69	15.43	20.74	18.40	14.75	14.03	15.54	9.01	9.13
1991	16.51	16.54	16.25	24.60	21.96	18.16	19.80	21.12	10.80	11.29
1993	31.69	25.77	26.72	53.10	32.68	37.99	36.00	30.97	17.95	17.74
1995	52.48	38.65	41.43	142.49	81.60	81.90	77.66	57.62	32.92	30.17
1996	47.42	36.64	45.81	196.48	96.21	75.00	101.45	56.07	37.74	34.62
1997	50.47	44.20	54.27	182.56	93.01	97.05	82.67	55.51	41.94	34.30
1998	49.90	34.79	54.51	190.40	94.10	84.32	79.06	35.61	45.58	34.55
1999	52.79	37.33	58.84	241.05	94.49	99.66	82.84	41.97	49.13	33.18
2000	56.74	61.00	65.47	285.31	105.48	133.54	73.10	55.21	50.01	37.03
2001	64.65	51.85	67.33	307.23	105.45	136.84	79.41	55.84	54.29	38.57
2002	72.29	49.45	110.06	227.34	114.74	135.98	79.55	68.65	57.10	39.04

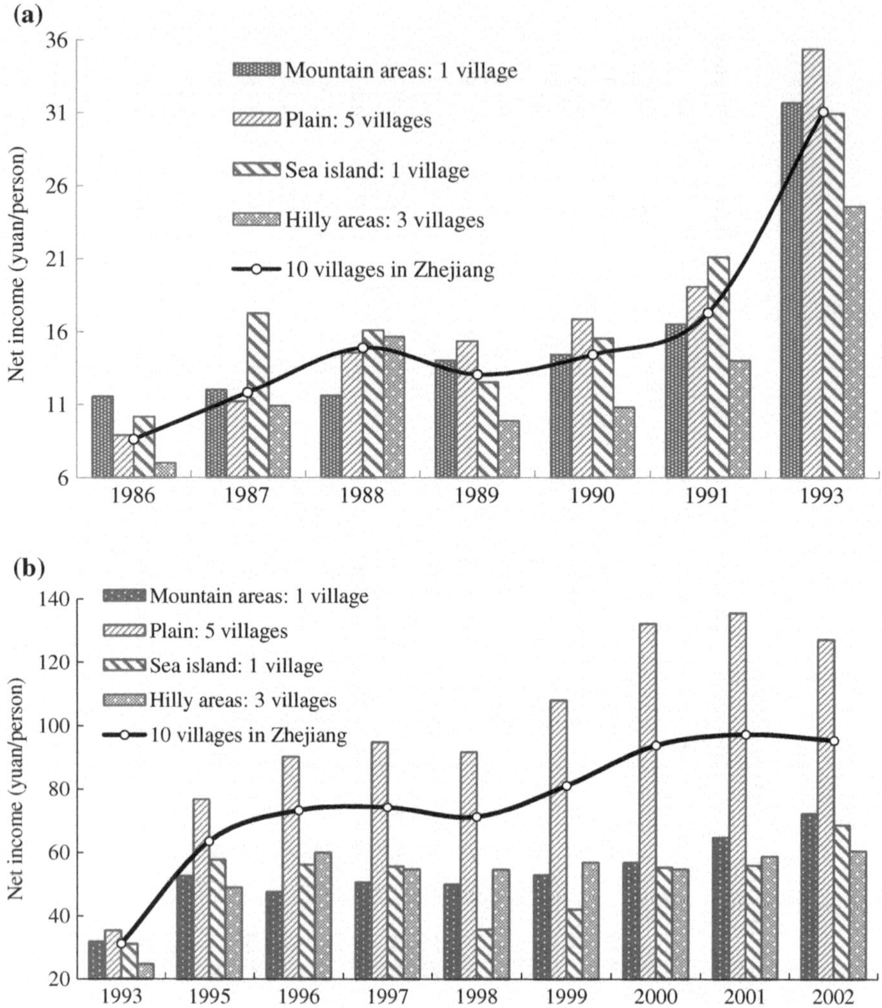

Fig. 5.7 **a** Rural household economic development and geographic location 1986–1993. **b** Rural household economic development and geographic location 1993–2002

location is one of the important factors resulting in the regional imbalanced economic development.

5.2.1.2 Location Distribution of Rural Households at the Highest and the Lowest Income Levels

In terms of the location distribution of rural households (Table 5.5), due to the significant differences in geographic location of the observed villages, the economic

Table 5.5 Location distribution of rural households with the highest and lowest incomes (%)

	Plain: 5 villages			Hill: 3 villages			Island: 1 village			Mountain: 1 village		
	Household number	L	H	Household number	L	H	Household number	L	H	Household number	L	H
1986	538	10.97	19.52	347	40.63	12.97	126	10.32	30.95	71	5.63	39.44
1987	543	10.68	16.57	407	39.56	15.48	125	4.80	50.40	72	6.94	19.44
1988	558	10.93	20.07	394	35.28	18.27	129	11.63	29.46	76	22.37	13.16
1989	578	7.44	29.58	405	39.51	7.41	128	22.66	17.97	78	7.69	17.95
1990	602	9.14	27.74	410	38.78	8.29	115	13.91	24.35	79	13.92	15.19
1991	559	11.45	23.43	406	37.19	13.05	114	7.89	33.33	77	10.39	12.99
1993	250	11.20	22.80	150	40.67	15.33	50	10.00	26.00	50	12.00	14.00
1995	250	16.80	23.60	150	28.00	14.67	50	18.00	22.00	50	14.00	16.00
1996	250	15.20	24.80	150	26.67	15.33	50	18.00	20.00	50	26.00	10.00
1997	250	14.00	25.60	150	26.67	12.00	50	26.00	24.00	50	24.00	12.00
1998	250	15.60	26.40	150	20.67	14.67	50	38.00	10.00	50	22.00	14.00
1999	250	17.20	28.40	150	23.33	13.33	50	26.00	8.00	50	18.00	10.00
2000	250	15.20	30.00	150	27.33	8.67	51	21.57	11.76	48	20.83	10.42
2001	250	16.00	27.60	153	26.14	13.07	50	22.00	10.00	48	18.75	14.58
2002	250	17.20	30.00	150	28.00	9.33	50	12.00	10.00	50	18.00	12.00

Note In the table, L and H refer to the bottom 20% and the top 20% rural households ranked by per capita income. It is the same for the other tables

development modes and development levels vary greatly. For the observed households in the five villages in the plain area of Zhejiang, their distribution in the bottom 20% low-income households are obviously lower, but their distribution in the top 20% high-income households are higher. The three villages in the hilly area of Zhejiang have just the opposite distribution to the plain villages. The fishing village on the sea island and the forestry village in the mountainous area of Zhejiang have similar distributions, i.e. the distribution of low-income households higher than that of high-income households. In summarising the trend, the distribution of plain villages presents a 'double-increase' mode, i.e. the proportions of distributions at both the highest and the lowest income levels have shown uptrends, with the rising speed of high-income household distribution dramatically faster than that of the low-income households. On the contrary, the distribution of the villages in the hilly area presents a 'double-decrease' mode, i.e. the proportions of distributions for rural households at both the highest and lowest income levels present downtrends, especially for the distribution of low-income households, and the distribution of the high-income households has generally decreased in a reciprocating manner. The distributions of the fishing village on the sea island and the forestry village in the mountainous area present 'one increase and one decrease' mode, i.e. the distribution of low-income households presents an uptrend, while that of high-income households presents a downtrend. This result has indicated that, during the rural economic development in Zhejiang, distinct economic stratification and development imbalance have been found mainly in plain areas with a higher degree of non-agriculturalisation and a comparatively developed economy.

5.2.2 Imbalanced Economic Development of Rural Households with Various Education Levels

For a rural household, whether its economy is able to grow and develop rapidly relies on its human capital, and the householder is usually the main labourer of the household. The education level of the householder, as well as the life cycle stage of the household, have great influence on the growth and development of the household economy. According to the data from the observed households in the ten villages (Table 5.6), the changes in per capita net income of rural households are closely related to the educational level of its main labourer (householder), and such a link has become more obvious over time. The incomes of the illiterate and semiliterate households are obviously the lowest, while those of the households with senior high school education or above are the highest. In 1986, the income of households with senior high school education or above was only 6.05% higher than that of the illiterate and semiliterate households, which expanded to 29.24% in 1990, 87.26% in 1995, and several times more around 2000. Specifically, the income of households with senior high school education or above was 130.53% higher than that of the illiterate and semiliterate households in 2000, which expanded to 160.89% in 2001, and declined to

Table 5.6 Income distribution of rural households with different education levels

	Distribution of rural households (%)				Net income (100 yuan/person)				
	Illiterate	Primary school	Junior high	Senior high+	Illiterate	Primary school	Junior high	Senior high+	Total
1986	20.33	50.46	24.21	4.99	8.43	8.34	9.32	8.94	8.62
1987	24.06	48.65	22.76	4.53	12.03	11.67	12.04	11.32	11.82
1988	19.53	50.39	24.98	4.93	16.98	13.96	14.99	16.60	14.89
1989	20.86	47.69	26.07	4.96	11.53	13.27	13.73	13.93	13.07
1990	19.24	48.01	27.45	5.31	12.55	14.42	15.36	16.22	14.44
1991	18.51	46.71	29.07	5.71	13.89	16.74	19.41	20.89	17.30
1993	11.80	53.20	28.80	6.20	25.05	29.77	32.35	46.07	31.10
1995	10.60	52.20	29.80	6.40	47.96	64.01	62.50	89.81	63.51
1996	10.40	51.80	31.80	6.00	52.94	74.67	69.58	109.83	73.24
1997	10.40	50.00	32.80	6.80	63.42	72.83	71.49	109.78	74.25
1998	10.00	51.00	32.40	6.60	51.99	65.77	70.91	133.05	71.22
1999	10.40	47.60	34.40	7.60	49.20	77.02	72.50	176.41	81.13
2000	9.62	47.70	34.87	7.82	54.77	99.51	87.29	126.26	93.81
2001	9.38	47.50	35.53	7.58	51.67	105.91	87.54	134.80	97.31
2002	9.00	46.80	36.60	7.60	67.53	101.56	83.79	140.07	95.40

107.42% in 2002, yet the absolute difference did not shrink, but increased by 105.53 yuan/person in 2002 compared with the level of 7148.77 yuan/person in 2000. In terms of the growth rate, the levels for the illiterate and semiliterate households were also the lowest, and those for the households with senior high school education or above were the highest. Over the 17 years, the annual average growth rate of per capita income was 13.89% for the illiterate and semiliterate households, 16.91% for the households with primary-school education, 14.71% for those with junior high school education, and 18.76% for the households with senior high school education or above. The difference of average income growth rate between the rural households with the highest and the lowest levels was 4.88%.

This result indicated that the household education background has become an important reason for the aggravated development imbalance of rural economy. However, it should also be noted that the illiterate and semiliterate rate has decreased rapidly with the popularisation of basic education in rural areas in the country. For the education structure of the ten villages in Zhejiang, the illiterate and semiliterate rate has decreased by 11.33% over the 17 years. Such a decrease provides solid support in terms of human capital for the rapid economic growth of rural households in Zhejiang.

Among the ten villages, the households with senior high school education or above might not be the only group with their income higher than the average level in the 1980s, yet over time their income growth has been exceptional compared with other groups of households with less education (Fig. 5.8). This result indicated that the basic education in rural areas has played an important role in enhancing the development of rural economy, and the local saying is incorrect that people who make a fortune in Zhejiang are all illiterate. In the new era, the enhancement of human capital reserves in rural households brought about by education has become a key factor for the sustainable growth of rural and household economy. However, we have also seen the reality that less attention is being paid on rural education, and the illiterate and semiliterate rates remain high, which is a very true situation in rural areas of Zhejiang. To some extent, the deep origin for the aggravated development inequality of rural and household economy is not the social and economic status, but the human capital reserve. In fact, in the new century in terms of developing profitable agriculture, and modernising agriculture and the countryside, the primary job of the government should be long-term investment projects such as education and technology, rather than short-term projects with immediate investment returns. It should be noted that the 'nine-year compulsory education' in rural area is of great significance, and its investment is the foundation for maximising the benefits of other investments such as in secondary and tertiary education, as well as in science and technology. It is seen from Fig. 5.8 that although there are income differences within each category of households, households with higher levels of education generally have higher levels of income, while illiterate and semiliterate households mostly have lower incomes. This has indicated that without a good education foundation, chances are few for households to realise high economic growth. Only with the certain level of human capital reserves, can households have better chances to gain high incomes.

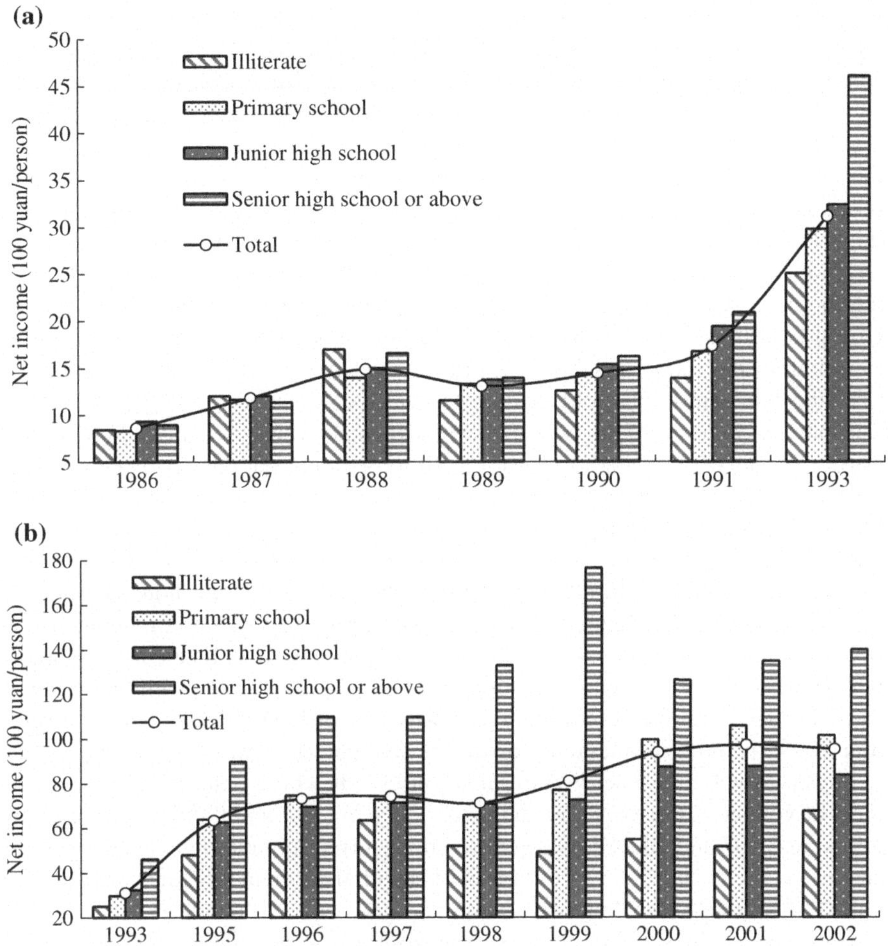

Fig. 5.8 **a** Income of rural households and householder education level 1986–1993. **b** Income of rural households and householder education level 1993–2002

5.2.3 Development Imbalance of Household Economy at Different Life Cycle Stages

5.2.3.1 Development Imbalance of Household Economy at Different Ages

Human life is limited, and so is the life of a household. In this limited life cycle, it is inevitable that economic development must involve both rise and fall. As a special economic organisation, the economic growth and development of a household will be influenced by its life cycle. In the beginning and at the end of the life cycle, the income level must be low, while in the middle stage of the life cycle, the income level is certainly high. In general, an inverted 'U'-shape curve is the best description of the economic cycle of a rural household. The starting stage of a household life cycle is when the householder is about 30 years old, the middle stage is when the householder is between 30 and 50 years old, and the late stage is when the householder is more than 50 years old. Influenced by the periodic law of rural household life cycle, household income generally presents the pattern of a low level in both ends and a high level in the middle, and the income growth peak usually appears when the householder is between 35 and 45 years old. Therefore, the life cycle law of rural households is also an important reason for the imbalanced economic development of rural households, and such a reason will not be impacted by human intention. According to the rural household data in the ten villages in Zhejiang (Table 5.7), the changes in rural household income generally correspond to the life cycle law. The households have the highest per capita income when their householders are between 30 and 40 years old, followed by those with householders between 40 and 50 years old, and then come those whose householders are between 50 and 60 years old. Newly established households and old households have the lowest income. In terms of income growth, between 1995 and 2000, of the observed villages in the ten villages, the annual growth rate was at the highest of 13.52% for households with their main labourers between 30 and 40 years old, followed by households with 40–50-year-old labourers at the annual rate of 9.09%, and those with labourers younger than 30 years old at an annual growth rate of 4.38%. Households with labour aged 50–60 and aged over 60 had the annual growth rates of 1.00 and 3.44% respectively. After 2000, the order of income growth rate changed slightly. From 2000 to 2002, the higher growth rates occurred in rural households whose householders were the oldest or youngest, i.e. above 60 and below 30 years old, and their average growth rates were 21.07 and 10.24%. Slower growth occurred for households at the golden stage of the life cycle, 11.03% for households with their main labourers aged 30–40 and 1.01% for those with their main labourers aged between 40 and 50. Such a result is mainly due to the sharp decline of household operation in 2002. It is seen from Table 5.7 that due to the generational relationship, the income growth is more likely to occur in younger rural households. Influenced by the life cycle law, the income of rural households at the golden stage was once more than twice that of the older households. Although the strong trend was much weakened in 2002, it does not mean their operation capabilities deteriorate at the golden stage, but indicates that such households have a stronger sense of responsibility for supporting the elderly.

It can be seen from Fig. 5.9 and Table 5.8 that the rural households at the middle stage of the life cycle has an obviously higher probability to become better-off than the households at both ends, and this is an inevitable result of the life-cycle law. Such a result has indicated that during the eradication of the development imbalance of rural household economy, the older households influenced by the life cycle should be well protected with social security system, while guidance should be given to the younger households to improve their human capital reserves, which is vital in household economic development. In other words, the government should enhance the investment in rural education, and strengthen the improvement in rural

Table 5.7 Income of rural households at different life cycle stages

	Rural households (%)					Net income (100 yuan/person)				
	≤30	30–40	40–50	50–60	>60	≤30	30–40	40–50	50–60	>60
1995	8.25	33.20	35.61	16.50	6.44	52.69	57.02	65.56	84.90	37.72
1996	6.01	33.47	39.88	15.23	5.41	56.63	64.47	74.74	101.61	47.57
1997	4.80	33.80	39.80	15.60	6.00	92.72	70.13	77.09	78.05	44.90
1998	4.60	31.60	39.60	17.60	6.60	59.06	76.25	67.84	83.81	30.61
1999	5.20	29.40	40.60	17.40	7.40	81.93	99.49	73.67	78.59	32.01
2000	3.41	24.25	37.68	23.85	10.82	65.28	107.50	101.30	89.21	44.66
2001	3.19	22.95	37.13	24.95	11.78	74.60	109.38	100.96	92.39	68.70
2002	3.00	23.20	34.60	26.60	12.60	79.34	85.09	99.26	112.90	65.46

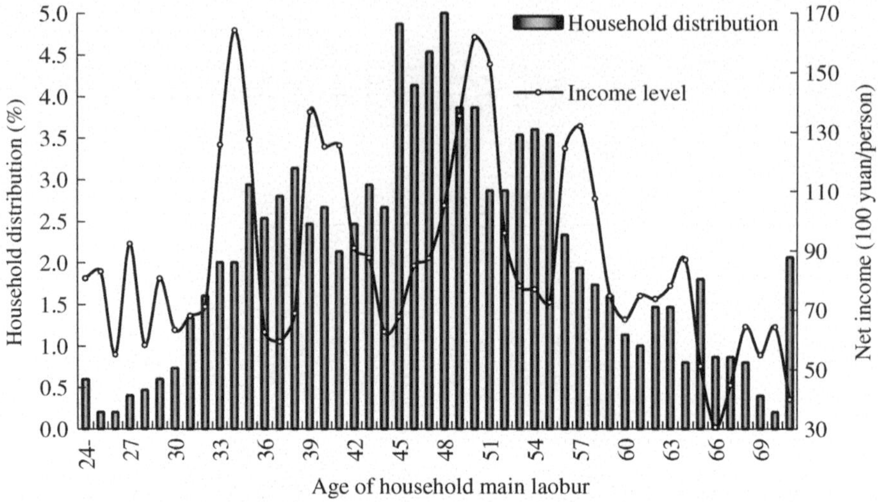

Fig. 5.9 Income and life cycle of rural households in 10 villages of Zhejiang from 2000 to 2002

education management system, so as to accelerate the development of rural and household economy.

5.2.3.2 Economic Development Imbalance of Households with Different Labour Burden

Population is a necessary element of household composition, but the number of members in a household is not necessarily a positive element for its economic growth and development. A person can become a positive element only when his (her) role changes from a consumer to labourer. If the labour burden (i.e. consumer-labourer ratio) in a household is high, the overall economic situation of that household will not be good; but on the contrary, the low labour burden will be beneficial for a household. This is determined by the life cycle law of household development itself. The economic development of the rural households under closely tracked observations in the ten villages of Zhejiang has fully confirmed this conclusion. The higher the household labour burden is, the lower the per capita income will be; otherwise, per capita income will be higher.

It can be seen from Fig. 5.10 that due to the differences in labour burden among rural households, their economic development paths are different. Households with lighter labour burden have a higher development level than those with heavier burden. According to the evolution of the ten villages of Zhejiang over the 17 years, the rural households with the labour burden of less than 1.5 ranked the second place in terms of per capita income among the five groups in 2002, and ranked the third in annual growth rate, which reached 15.47%. The rural households with the labour burden from 1.5 to 2 ranked the first place in both income and its annual growth rate, which

Table 5.8 Income and distribution of households at different life cycle stages

	Distribution of rural households (%)					Net income (100 yuan/person)				
	<1.5*	1.5–2	2–2.5	2.5–3	>3	<1.5	1.5–2	2–2.5	2.5–3	>3
1986	36.04	25.05	23.11	6.93	5.18	9.94	8.50	7.69	7.99	6.67
1987	36.62	24.59	24.41	7.24	3.49	13.56	11.50	11.01	9.91	10.02
1988	36.73	27.31	23.42	5.96	3.03	17.31	14.00	13.35	14.96	10.64
1989	36.42	28.93	23.97	4.29	3.03	15.00	13.93	12.13	8.52	7.77
1990	39.55	28.19	22.47	4.56	2.90	16.51	14.85	12.66	10.19	10.16
1991	40.14	27.94	22.84	4.67	2.42	19.82	17.89	15.11	11.60	11.66
1993	40.00	25.40	26.00	6.20	1.40	35.59	29.61	29.52	21.55	20.23
1995	41.20	24.20	26.20	5.20	2.00	78.36	58.78	52.97	40.53	41.11
1996	41.40	26.60	25.40	4.20	2.00	88.29	71.61	61.15	45.76	31.99
1997	42.20	25.40	24.40	4.60	2.60	83.39	77.06	66.28	45.41	58.49
1998	43.40	26.00	22.80	4.00	2.40	79.76	73.45	63.62	36.00	63.82
1999	44.20	26.60	21.40	4.60	2.00	82.81	84.70	89.52	39.83	55.84
2000	46.45	27.59	18.46	5.27	2.23	108.26	107.21	72.38	42.02	32.05
2001	45.03	29.01	18.66	4.87	2.43	107.25	108.28	85.93	51.41	48.10
2002	45.71	28.57	18.37	4.29	3.06	99.29	108.27	89.68	57.87	57.66

*The number of population burdened by each labourer of the household. Same for the tables and figures below

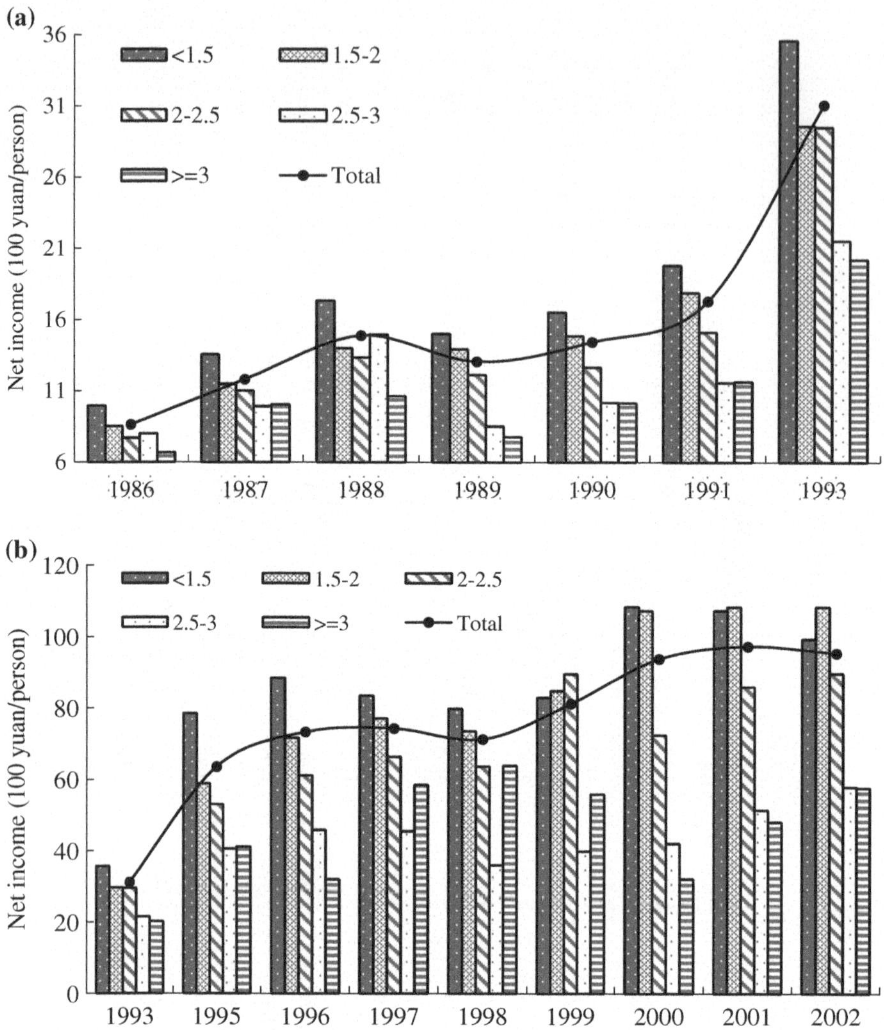

Fig. 5.10 **a** Income level and labour burden of rural households 1986–1993. **b** Income level and labour burden of rural households 1993–2002

reached 17.24%. The households with the labour burden from 2 to 2.5 ranked the third place in income level, and the second in annual growth rate, with the level of 16.59%. For the rural households with the labour burden of 2.5–3 and above, the income levels were obviously the lowest, and the annual growth rates were similar of 13.17 and 14.43%, markedly 3–4% lower than the households with lighter burden.

It is also seen from Table 5.9 that with the increase of the labour burden, the possibility becomes significantly higher for a household to fall into the low-income group. When the labour burden of a household was less than 1.5, the probability of

Table 5.9 Labour burden distribution for rural households with the highest and lowest incomes (%)

	<1.5		1.5–2		2–2.5		2.5–3		≥3	
	L	H	L	H	L	H	L	H	L	H
1986	9.23	30.00	14.02	17.34	26.00	15.20	29.33	10.67	58.33	7.29
1987	8.81	29.05	17.73	15.25	23.57	17.50	26.51	10.84	67.07	8.54
1988	11.76	30.82	13.92	17.09	28.41	11.44	28.99	17.39	53.95	5.26
1989	14.78	27.94	13.70	22.45	18.60	11.93	45.10	5.88	66.23	3.90
1990	12.58	27.88	17.94	22.06	19.93	9.59	40.00	5.45	69.84	6.35
1991	13.39	26.78	15.74	21.60	22.73	12.50	38.89	7.41	74.51	1.96
1993	12.50	29.00	19.69	16.54	24.62	13.08	25.81	9.68	83.33	8.33
1995	14.56	27.67	14.05	15.70	28.24	16.03	19.23	11.54	68.75	0.00
1996	14.98	28.02	18.80	18.80	24.41	11.02	23.81	9.52	66.67	8.33
1997	13.74	25.59	16.54	18.90	27.05	13.93	26.09	13.04	64.71	11.76
1998	14.68	25.69	17.05	19.38	22.81	14.91	15.00	10.00	89.47	0.00
1999	13.57	29.41	20.30	15.79	24.30	11.21	13.04	4.35	87.50	6.25
2000	15.72	23.58	15.44	23.53	14.29	23.08	0.00	7.69	54.55	0.00
2001	16.22	22.52	16.08	25.17	29.35	14.13	16.67	8.33	33.33	0.00
2002	13.84	20.98	21.43	26.43	26.67	14.44	23.81	4.76	26.67	13.33

falling into the low-income group was 15.26% from 2000 to 2002, but the probability of entering the high-income group was 22.37%. When the labour burden increased to above 3, the probability of falling into the low-income group increased to 36.84%, and the probability of entering the high-income group decreased to 5.26%. Over time, the probability for households with low labour burden to fall in the low-income group decreased, but the probability of entering the high-income group increased, and it was the opposite for the households with high labour burden.[4] Therefore, the issue of labour burden has become an important reason for the development imbalance of rural household economy. However, this is an objective reason, because the labour burden issue of a rural household is affected by the periodic law of the household life cycle, and the development of each household will go through this process. Although not all households will be fall into poverty, it is inevitable for the household economy to enter certain slow-growth periods. During the years without birth control, households must have faced a much more serious problem of labour burden than a current situation under birth control. With the further implementation of family planning policy in rural areas, the problem of population burden is alleviated. Along with the improvement of living standards and medical conditions, the problem due to the aging population has aggravated, which has become the core burden of rural households.

5.2.4 Economic Development Imbalance of Rural Households with Different Operation Types

The development imbalance of rural household economy is also closely related to the operation types of the households (Table 5.10 and Fig. 5.11). Rural household income rises with the increase of the non-agricultural degree of the household operation, which has become more evident over time. Since 1995, the average income of non-agricultural households has become the highest among rural households of different operation types, which is also the only category of households with their income exceeding the average level. According to the data from the observations in Zhejiang, over the 17 years, the income level of agricultural households has always been below the average level in the ten villages, and the income gap has been widening. At the beginning of the observation in 1986, per capita income of agricultural household was 95.13% of the average income of the ten villages, which decreased to 83.03% in 1990, further to 61.01% in 2000, and finally to 57.73% in 2002. Meanwhile, the per capita income for non-agricultural households has been above the average level of the ten villages, with the income gap widening over the years. In 1986, the per capita

[4]This result appears to show that the possibility to be well-off is increasing for households with heavy population burden. However, the fact is, after having enforced the family planning policy for more than 20 years, the population size of rural households has been shrinking generally. There have been the increasing numbers of aged households being cared for by the children or the community. This will lead to an opposite result, and can be proved by Table 5.7.

Table 5.10 Income of rural households with different operation types

	Distribution of rural households (%)					Net income (100 yuan/person)				
	Completely agricultural	Agricultural	Agriculture-dominated	Non-agricultural dominated	Non-agricultural	Completely agricultural	Agricultural	Agriculture-dominated	Non-agricultural dominated	Non-agricultural
1986	33.27	61.00	12.48	8.60	10.54	8.20	7.81	8.98	10.21	10.43
1987	32.87	64.08	11.42	7.67	9.76	11.66	10.51	12.17	11.80	18.28
1988	30.60	60.24	14.26	7.52	10.72	13.57	14.12	16.00	12.46	16.14
1989	33.31	62.32	11.94	8.92	9.42	13.48	12.04	11.40	14.86	18.74
1990	32.01	61.28	12.11	10.12	9.95	11.99	13.88	14.83	15.74	15.64
1991	30.71	58.56	13.67	8.39	12.11	14.65	15.66	16.68	18.75	21.18
1993	37.80	55.20	13.80	9.80	13.80	29.57	28.31	27.97	28.70	44.19
1995	37.20	51.80	10.40	10.20	19.60	57.56	54.79	39.77	50.41	95.53
1996	42.40	51.00	10.40	9.80	18.20	53.90	51.38	41.06	69.07	84.69
1997	33.80	44.20	14.00	8.00	23.60	51.52	50.68	41.62	65.69	124.87
1998	32.60	46.80	9.20	7.80	25.40	50.70	52.11	42.94	55.66	115.28
1999	29.40	44.00	10.20	10.00	25.60	49.56	46.40	47.39	61.96	151.36
2000	26.45	36.27	12.22	10.42	26.45	57.23	56.49	41.68	61.24	174.43
2001	28.34	39.12	10.18	5.19	29.54	55.68	52.41	56.83	77.34	164.92
2002	25.40	35.40	7.20	6.60	28.40	55.90	55.08	56.18	73.21	148.85

Note 1. The complete agricultural household is an exception. 2. Categorisation standards: in household operation, the agricultural degree of household operation = agricultural income/total operation income × 0.5 + agricultural expenses/total operation costs × 0.3 + agricultural labour/total operation labour × 0.2. Households with the degree of less than 20% are non-agricultural households, those of 20–50% are non-agricultural dominated households, those of 50–80% are agriculture-dominated households, and those of over 80% are agricultural households including complete agricultural households with the degree of 100%. 3. The percentage of these four categories added up is less than 100% because some households are not engaged in household operation

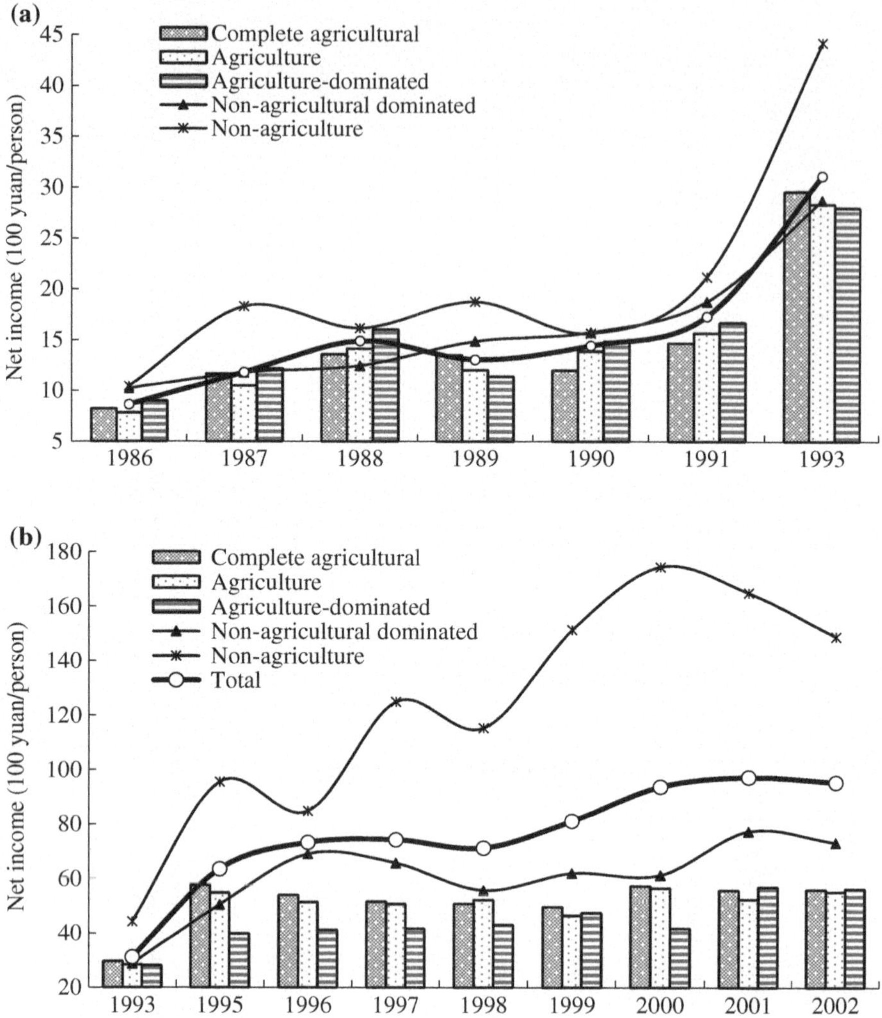

Fig. 5.11 **a** Income and operation types of rural households 1986–1993. **b** Income and operation types of rural households 1993–2002

income of non-agricultural households was only 21.00% higher than the average level, which expanded to 50.42% in 1995 and further to 85.94% in 2000. In 2002, although the gap became smaller, the income level was still 56.02% higher than the average. Therefore, the differences in the non-agricultural degrees of the household operation types have greatly influenced the development of rural household economy. Accordingly, non-agriculturalisation is the inevitable trend for rural household economic development, but a lot of human and material capital reserves are needed to transform agricultural households into non-agricultural households. Since 1995, for households with different operation types, all five categories of households have seen their incomes increase, except the complete agricultural households with a slight decrease. The non-agricultural households had the highest increase with the annual growth rate of 6.54% over eight years, while agricultural households, agriculture-dominated households and non-agricultural dominated households had the growth rates of 0.08, 5.06 and 5.48% respectively. Therefore, it is the income growth of the non-agricultural households that has driven the high-speed growth of household economy at the rate of 8.11% since 1995 in the ten villages in Zhejiang, while the agricultural households contributed a little to the overall income growth even though they are the absolute majority of the rural households.

5.3 Origins of Rural Household Imbalance in Economic Development

In order to further analyse the origins of the development imbalance in household economy, some special considerations have been made concerning the data from the rural households under follow-up observations in the ten villages of Zhejiang, and households with the highest and lowest 20% income groups have been selected for the study in order to find out further answers.

5.3.1 Imbalanced in Occupation of Production Factors: Farmland

With the non-agriculturalisation of rural households, their operation of farmland has been decreasing, but the size, quality and use of the farmland occupied still have great impact on the economic development of rural households. It is seen from Table 5.11 that for the rural households with the highest and lowest levels of income, an imbalance in farmland occupation exists. In terms of the amount of land occupied, the low-income households have occupied more land compared with the high-income households,[5] but the quality and the utilisation degree are apparently lower. The fragmentation degree of cultivated land occupied by high-income households is obviously lower than that of the low-income households, and the land is noticeably used more for orchards or non-grain planting. Even if the land is used for crop farming, its returns are better than the low-income households. In terms of crop planting (Fig. 5.12), high-income and low-income households have shown the same trend that yield per unit is increasing but the net return per unit is decreasing continuously.

[5]This is dissimilar to the situation of rural households nationwide and in north China. This has indicated that the role of farmland quantity in the growth of rural economy in Zhejiang is obviously weakened, and the farmland contracting concept of rural households has changed from traditional quantity expansion to quality improvement (Shi, 2001).

Table 5.11 Imbalances of the quantity, quality, composition and utilisation of the farmland occupied by rural high/low-income households

	Farmland scale (*mu*/household)		Proportion of cultivated land (%)		Cultivated land fragmentation (*mu*/plot)		Multiple cropping index (%)		Crop yield (kg/*mu*)	
	L	H	L	H	L	H	L	H	L	H
1986	5.79	13.40	43.19	22.17	0.42	0.50	224.89	224.90	317.44	353.58
1987	6.29	6.07	44.55	32.47	0.46	0.45	225.42	221.40	317.20	361.51
1988	7.62	4.88	29.72	41.47	0.45	0.54	223.38	225.68	302.21	361.40
1989	4.55	6.46	38.30	38.02	0.44	0.59	225.33	237.12	362.40	375.04
1990	6.67	6.25	30.32	39.47	0.44	0.65	234.25	236.17	325.80	373.62
1991	6.63	6.62	35.09	26.29	0.47	0.54	201.70	229.31	364.36	396.21
1993	7.10	6.07	37.96	22.47	0.49	0.60	193.51	206.75	367.84	376.51
1995	6.98	7.76	35.90	23.88	0.57	0.84	167.09	244.55	376.94	340.83
1996	9.71	4.84	25.21	23.10	0.54	0.80	170.26	233.84	406.43	412.41
1997	7.61	4.67	28.30	18.98	0.58	0.76	174.19	227.06	395.01	407.60
1998	8.14	6.35	26.37	19.22	0.60	0.79	178.19	214.92	414.06	434.09
1999	7.70	5.33	30.72	23.58	0.60	0.84	159.41	181.94	390.68	398.77
2000	7.69	4.91	24.79	27.96	0.55	1.28	141.95	161.69	416.03	383.36
2001	6.45	6.07	27.77	18.70	0.54	0.84	131.12	143.13	429.12	451.20
2002	7.44	5.12	22.97	18.54	0.50	0.80	112.52	127.71	474.47	352.53

Note The farmland here includes: cultivated land, garden plot and woodland

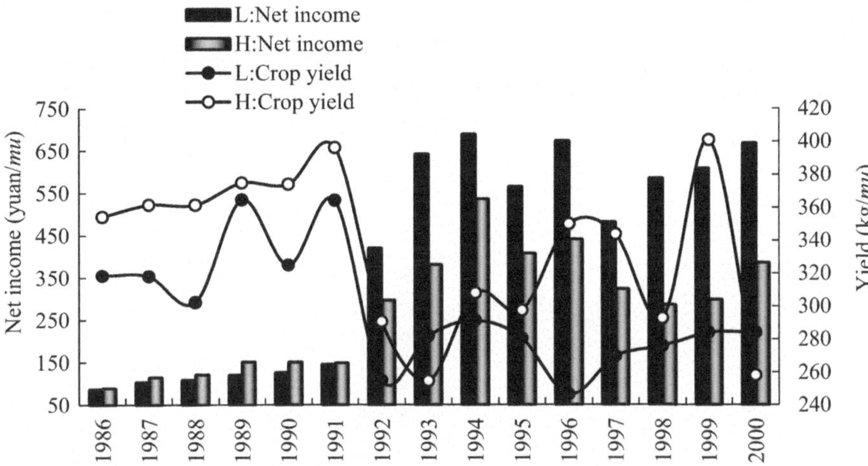

Fig. 5.12 Performance in land use by high-income and low-income households

By comparison, the production level of high-income households is higher, but the net return is lower than the low-income households. However, this trend obviously reversed in the middle and late 1990s, which might be related to the continuous deterioration in efficiency of resource utilisation for agricultural and grain production (Shi, 2000). Despite being in the deteriorating environment, the high-income households have obvious advantages in the structural transformation from yield to profit pursuit. In agricultural production, the non-crop trend for high-income households has become evident. Such effects were certainly also seen in the late 1990s. This result has reflected to some extent that although rural households have paid less attention to farmland operation with the acceleration of non-agriculturalisation, the imbalanced occupation of land, one of the main production factors, has become an important reason for the income inequality among rural households. The differences in quality, utilisation and its utilisation direction of farmland, in particular, have all contributed to the income inequality.

5.3.2 Imbalance in Occupation Production Factors: Human Capital

It can be seen from Table 5.12 and Fig. 5.13, in the development of rural household economy, the quantity and quality of human capital reserves have been very important, especially the quality. With the decrease of rural household size, the number of labourers of each rural household generally declines. Comparatively, the number of labourers in high-income households is obviously higher than the low-income households. In terms of labour quality, the high-income households are much better not only in cultural and technological background, but also in physical condition. In contrast, the labour burden for rural households is just the opposite in that the burden for

Table 5.12 Imbalance in human resource and labour burden of rural high/low-income households

	Household labour (person/household)		Comprehensive school age of labour (year)		Labour technical training rate (%)		Rate of main labour educated at and above junior high level (%)		% of main labour aged 30–50		Labour burden (person/labour)	
	L	H	L	H	L	H	L	H	L	H	L	H
1986	1.96	3.26	5.08	5.37	2.15	6.03	23.04	33.64	–	–	1.91	1.35
1987	1.89	3.02	5.32	5.40	3.27	5.72	22.61	27.39	–	–	1.88	1.37
1988	1.95	3.09	5.46	5.57	4.44	7.77	26.29	30.60	–	–	1.80	1.33
1989	2.06	2.81	4.92	5.80	3.30	10.70	25.21	36.55	–	–	1.86	1.32
1990	1.93	2.84	5.09	5.98	4.72	7.36	25.31	37.76	–	–	1.76	1.29
1991	1.92	2.86	5.10	5.97	3.61	7.86	25.86	39.66	–	–	1.75	1.31
1993	2.31	2.90	5.81	6.19	6.11	8.01	37.00	42.00	63.00	71.00	1.69	1.29
1995	2.20	2.82	5.77	6.36	7.31	12.19	34.00	54.00	58.00	68.00	1.66	1.32
1996	2.41	2.79	5.69	6.39	4.62	11.59	40.00	42.00	67.00	70.00	1.56	1.30
1997	2.21	2.73	5.77	6.53	6.05	14.61	37.00	50.00	64.00	77.00	1.60	1.34
1998	2.23	2.81	5.62	6.48	8.18	12.13	34.00	49.00	61.00	74.00	1.52	1.32
1999	2.32	2.72	5.95	6.74	8.30	12.64	38.00	55.00	58.00	77.00	1.55	1.35
2000	2.25	2.75	5.89	6.50	7.66	13.48	34.00	54.55	44.00	60.00	1.60	1.30
2001	2.11	2.72	5.97	6.64	6.67	12.64	37.00	51.49	51.00	69.31	1.59	1.33
2002	2.12	2.66	6.03	6.74	3.85	12.70	39.00	50.00	51.00	62.00	1.57	1.35

Note 1. Based on the schooling years, illiterate and semiliterate = 1 year of education, primary school = 5.5 years of education, junior high school = 8 years of education, senior high school and above = 10 years of education. 2. "–" indicates that this item was not investigated that year

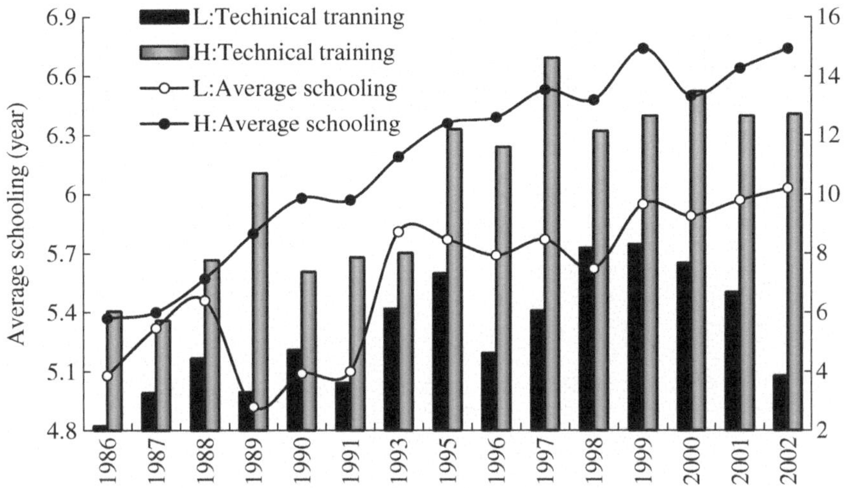

Fig. 5.13 Labour cultural and technological background of high and low-income households

low-income households is obviously heavier than that of high-income households. According to the developing trend, human capital reserves have improved in both the highest and lowest income level households. Yet, the development degree and the inequality between the two are not decreasing, but rather enlarging. Therefore, the difference in human capital among rural households is another important economic reason of the development imbalance of household economy, and this has become the major reason in the non-agriculturalisation of rural household economy. Therefore, the economic development imbalance among rural households will generate and enlarge thereafter.

5.3.3 Imbalance in Occupation of Production Factors: Material Capital

In the growth and development process of rural household economy, material capital is necessary. Material capital, labour capital and land are the three elements for rural household economic growth. As the important economic foundation, material capital has played a vital role in the growth of rural household economy. Generally, with the increase of capital possessed, the household income will increase correspondingly, and the two are obviously positively correlated. The imbalanced economic development is undoubtedly related to the capital occupation of rural households. It can be seen from Table 5.13 and Fig. 5.14 that due to the differences in material capital occupation of rural households, there are obvious disparities in their production and investment capability. High-income households have obvious higher levels of material capital occupation, current-year capital purchasing power and production investment capability than low-income households possess. The high-income households not only utilise their capital and labour for production, but also employ

Table 5.13 Imbalanced occupation of material capital for rural households at the highest and lowest income levels

	Original value of fixed assets (1000 yuan/household)		Proportion of productive fixed assets (%)		Newly-purchased fixed assets for production (100 yuan/household)		Household operating expenses (1000 yuan/household)		Proportion of employment cost in household expenditure (%)		Year-end savings and cash in hand (1000 yuan/household)	
	L	H	L	H	L	H	L	H	L	H	L	H
1986	4.30	13.20	18.58	20.35	1.14	7.25	0.78	3.38	1.69	6.45	0.41	3.15
1987	4.16	14.58	16.91	18.91	0.92	7.95	0.88	5.29	1.57	5.50	0.47	6.04
1988	5.28	22.72	12.47	18.83	0.78	14.89	0.86	7.21	0.81	14.47	0.67	7.85
1989	11.72	20.62	9.60	18.56	1.61	11.57	2.29	6.10	1.17	3.72	2.27	5.81
1990	7.58	21.73	15.74	17.27	1.00	8.32	1.25	3.57	1.45	2.71	1.37	7.05
1991	7.80	26.12	17.48	19.32	4.43	8.63	1.55	5.32	0.96	6.23	1.55	9.10
1993	13.16	47.38	16.11	17.64	7.35	12.77	2.91	11.65	0.13	6.01	1.28	14.73
1995	22.20	108.09	37.42	25.89	49.56	87.90	9.56	18.90	4.44	17.47	1.96	30.17
1996	26.35	135.17	40.20	28.45	54.87	137.10	9.28	24.18	1.60	8.71	3.00	37.40
1997	31.61	161.82	32.26	27.27	5.99	18.68	15.15	45.01	3.13	7.49	3.09	49.40
1998	45.83	164.16	52.74	18.44	11.75	36.17	26.51	43.96	4.06	8.41	3.01	72.02
1999	45.42	185.26	45.21	21.42	7.95	93.91	17.74	40.08	5.57	12.14	3.28	101.85
2000	37.96	209.53	25.84	23.73	3.40	81.06	11.75	67.78	3.98	6.88	4.77	122.58
2001	36.80	246.14	26.44	24.36	45.00	158.50	18.17	93.53	5.07	7.57	3.88	140.03
2002	35.00	291.43	25.06	28.63	13.59	247.98	23.36	89.30	4.82	13.92	7.67	157.48

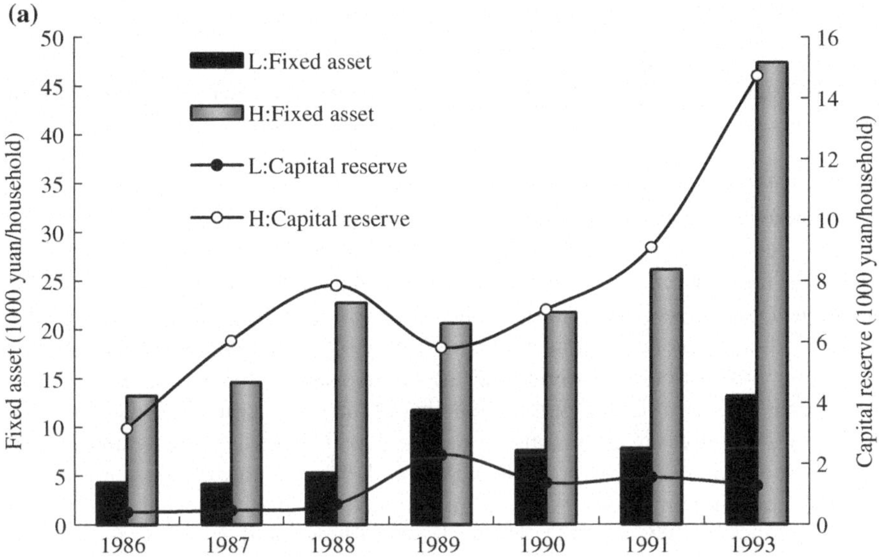

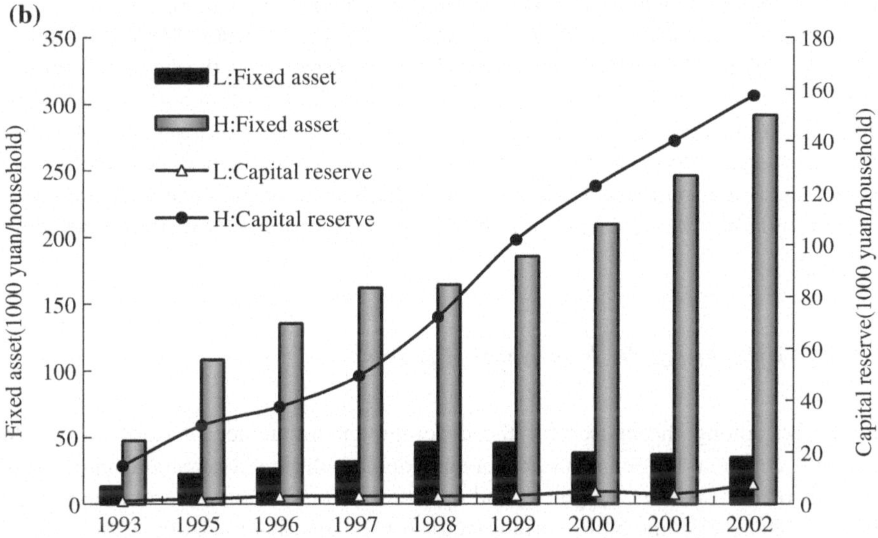

Fig. 5.14 **a** Material capital reserve of rural households with the highest and lowest incomes 1986–1993. **b** Material capital reserve of rural households with the highest and lowest incomes 1993–2002

labour with their own capital, so that the 'surplus value' in their income is obviously higher than that of the low-income households. Therefore, the difference in material capital reserve is also an economic origin for the formation and aggravation of the development imbalance of rural household economy.

5.3.4 Difference in Operation and Management

It can be seen from Table 5.14 that the economic development inequality of rural households is not only reflected in their possession of operation resources, but also in resource use and management. Due to inequality in resource allocation among rural households, the differences in resource use efficiency is obvious. The trends of resource use efficiency in operation for rural households at the highest and the lowest income levels are clearly divergent (Fig. 5.15), indicating the operation management level of the high-income households is better than that of the low-income households. Due to the continuous deterioration of the comparative benefits of agricultural operation, the allocation of economic resources for the high-income households presents an obvious non-agricultural trend, and the non-agricultural degree of their household operation is significantly higher than that of the low-income households. In the marketisation process, high-income households will depend more on market than the low-income households. In terms of the trend, the cash rate of household operation of the high-income households has maintained above 90% since the 1990s, and increased to nearly 95% in 2002. The cash rate of household operation for the low-income households increased from 75% in the early 1990s to about 85% currently. The difference in marketisation degree between the rural households at the highest and lowest income levels has been nearly 10%. This is related to the stagnated or even reversed development of the non-agriculturalisation for the low-income households. This result indicated that in the aggravating process of the development imbalance of household economy, the difference in operation and management among the rural households is a very important factor, which is also one of the most important economic origins for the aggravation in the development imbalance of rural household economy.

5.3.5 Differences in Financial Burden

Obviously, among the causes for the development imbalance of rural household economy, financial burden is an exogenous non-economic reason, and is apparently different from resource occupation and operation management of rural households. However, it has become an important factor for the aggravation of the development imbalance of household economy in some rural areas with relatively underdeveloped economy. It can be seen from Table 5.15 that the tax and fee burdens for rural households have been on the rise over time, and the burdens shouldered by households at the highest and lowest income levels are quite different. The ratio of tax and fee burden to net income for the low-income households has been increasing, especially that of the fee burden, with a sharp increase. However, the situation for the high-income households has been different. It is worth noting that after 2000, a new 'tax for fee' system was put into practice in rural areas and after 2002, it was proposed to abolish the agricultural tax. The agricultural tax has been totally abolished in Zhejiang, a province with relatively developed coastal economy. Therefore, since 2000, the tax and fee burden and its structure for both high and low-income households have

Table 5.14 Difference in the operation efficiency of resources owned by rural households at the highest and lowest income levels

	Employment efficiency (yuan/labour day)		Investment efficiency (yuan/100 yuan)		Cultivated land efficiency (yuan/mu)		Non-agriculturalisation of household operation (%)		Marketisation of household operation (%)		Average cost of employed labour
	L	H	L	H	L	H	L	H	L	H	
1986	−2.32	3.82	−79.78	41.73	−25.31	−5.28	25.61	67.99	63.01	87.26	5.48
1987	−1.64	6.70	−53.36	40.99	−18.40	11.77	21.89	76.71	63.44	92.65	5.71
1988	−2.54	7.40	−73.32	46.50	−44.54	−4.56	16.40	79.39	67.17	93.03	7.23
1989	−2.99	7.78	−25.45	42.97	−32.51	32.63	60.21	67.19	85.70	90.65	7.50
1990	−3.31	7.39	−60.35	67.47	−35.21	17.40	29.57	55.80	73.64	86.64	8.60
1991	−3.03	9.49	−52.22	61.15	−37.29	10.14	26.18	66.38	73.32	91.72	8.48
1993	−10.41	17.42	−127.22	61.07	−193.92	−95.04	22.96	81.53	73.13	93.74	19.05
1995	−11.02	40.84	−36.87	85.67	−99.91	79.60	12.17	78.89	78.80	92.34	25.71
1996	−7.67	58.10	−26.59	63.91	−26.36	151.72	25.44	80.58	75.72	93.94	22.89
1997	−16.37	86.17	−33.21	72.92	−154.57	−34.52	20.33	79.05	87.00	91.85	28.12
1998	−23.99	83.24	−34.22	74.76	−131.92	39.62	8.91	92.46	90.11	92.18	28.29
1999	−18.65	103.86	−36.18	113.12	−248.69	−43.04	9.71	91.56	85.42	93.96	29.17
2000	−17.35	125.12	−41.15	85.37	−266.64	−90.70	24.21	86.11	86.85	94.91	30.64
2001	−14.68	139.78	−22.11	64.27	−265.35	−24.20	19.99	94.14	87.98	98.65	30.90
2002	−12.24	119.98	−18.71	56.47	−149.57	62.51	9.46	91.79	86.05	93.46	22.93

Note Efficiency = (income − expenditure − labour employed × average labour cost) ÷ labour employed (or expenditure or sowing area); non-agricultural degree of household operation = non-agricultural income ÷ total operation income × 0.5 + non-agricultural expenditure ÷ total operation expenditure × 0.3 + non-agricultural labour ÷ total operation labour × 0.2; marketisation degree = proportion of cash income in household operation × 0.6 + proportion of cash expenditure in household operation × 0.4

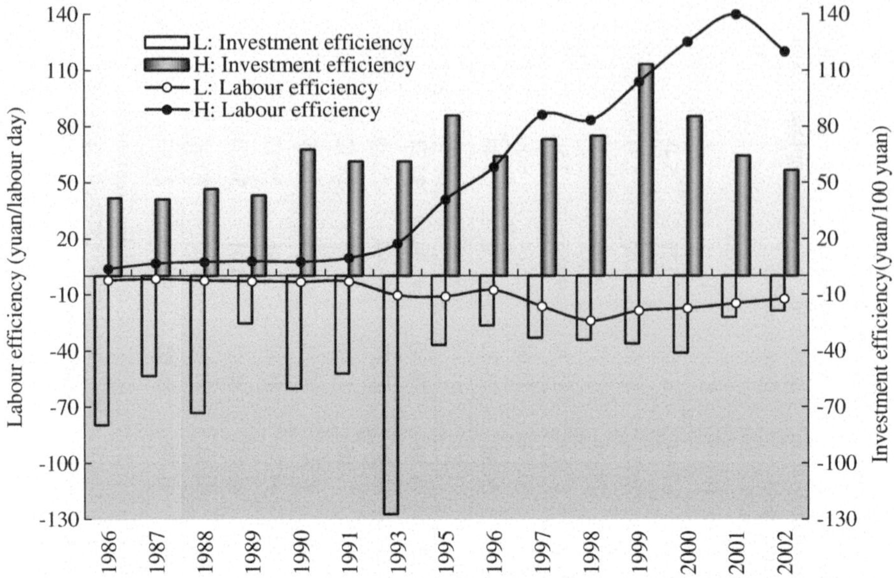

Fig. 5.15 Changes in efficiency of main economic resources owned by rural households at the highest and lowest income levels

changed significantly. In other words, there have been decreases in tax and fee burdens, which are more evident for low-income households, i.e. the decline is sharper than that of the high-income households. In terms of burden structure, the difference remains unchanged that the fee is the main burden for low-income households, and the tax is the major burden for high-income households.

5.3.6 Difference in Social Political Status

In addition to the above factors, the aggravation of economic development imbalance for rural households might also be influenced by the social political status, natural economic geographic location, and the policy environment of the local government. It can be seen from Table 5.16 that the social political status of the rural households at the highest and lowest income levels in Zhejiang has been quite different. High-income households have higher rates in being employed outside, or holding an official (cadre) position within the township, and they have a higher rate of having the CPC (Communist Party of China) members within the households. Obviously, this is also an important sociological cause for the aggravated development imbalance of rural household economy.

Table 5.15 Difference in the financial burdens of rural households at the highest and lowest income levels

	Tax and fee burden (yuan/household)		Tax and fee burden (yuan/person)		Tax and fee burden/net income (%)		Fee burden/net income (%)		Fee/tax and fee burden (%)	
	L	H	L	H	L	H	L	H	L	H
1986	48.76	419.21	13.02	95.36	3.85	5.92	1.23	1.05	31.89	17.78
1987	56.43	377.70	15.81	90.95	3.64	3.84	0.69	0.39	19.08	10.06
1988	47.57	575.53	13.58	139.96	2.73	4.40	1.11	0.41	40.56	9.42
1989	46.90	432.29	12.23	116.29	3.01	4.36	0.94	0.30	31.30	6.77
1990	76.18	371.17	22.40	101.27	4.42	3.71	1.64	0.45	37.06	12.05
1991	78.43	497.48	23.30	132.81	3.91	3.88	1.95	0.72	49.85	18.47
1993	210.35	1031.81	53.94	275.15	4.86	3.99	3.17	0.41	65.27	10.35
1995	359.39	2657.16	98.19	712.38	5.83	4.49	2.39	0.51	40.98	11.44
1996	553.73	1614.50	146.88	445.99	7.54	2.20	2.47	0.34	32.74	15.62
1997	761.76	2986.57	215.19	816.00	14.01	4.23	8.51	0.31	60.76	7.28
1998	428.70	1906.11	126.09	515.16	11.07	2.76	3.46	0.16	31.27	5.89
1999	844.71	3563.95	235.30	973.76	14.67	4.25	8.82	0.28	60.09	6.61
2000	371.88	4683.10	103.59	1309.68	5.91	4.72	3.43	0.18	58.06	3.73
2001	462.50	5967.79	138.06	1646.85	6.02	5.80	2.56	0.19	42.51	3.26
2002	507.31	6558.35	152.80	1821.76	6.93	7.13	4.47	0.10	64.48	1.35

Table 5.16 Difference in the social political status of rural households at the highest and lowest income levels (%)

	Households with members employed outside		Household member(s) as township cadre(s)		Household member(s) as the CPC member(s)	
	L	H	L	H	L	H
1986	3.69	5.07	0.46	6.45	10.14	17.51
1987	4.35	2.61	0.87	6.96	7.39	13.91
1988	3.45	1.29	0.43	6.47	8.19	15.95
1989	2.10	3.78	0.42	4.62	5.88	14.71
1990	2.90	4.56	0.41	4.56	7.47	17.01
1991	2.60	3.90	1.30	5.19	7.79	16.02
1993	0.00	3.00	3.00	9.00	8.00	18.00
1995	0.00	1.00	5.00	11.00	14.00	20.00
1996	1.00	1.00	6.00	10.00	15.00	21.00
1997	1.00	3.00	1.00	9.00	13.00	28.00
1998	3.00	4.00	1.00	11.00	16.00	26.00
1999	2.00	6.00	3.00	12.00	17.00	24.00
2000	2.00	3.03	1.00	13.13	11.00	24.24
2001	1.00	2.97	3.00	9.90	12.00	28.71
2002	0.00	3.00	4.00	11.00	12.00	23.00

5.4 Conclusion and Policy Suggestions

In conclusion, the growth and development process of household economy in Zhejiang has shown the trend of 'aggravated imbalance in income growth'. For a rural area, the higher the average income level is, the more serious the development imbalance will be. Generally, the economic development imbalance is in a basically reasonable range, but its aggravation trend has shown that it is becoming unreasonable, and starting to threaten social stability. For the origins of the imbalance, the life cycle of the rural households is the sociological foundation for the formation of the imbalance. The disparities in occupation of production factors and in operation management are the economic reasons. Some external factors such as the differences in the natural economic geographic location of rural households, inequality in financial burden brought about by macro political environment, and disparities in inter-household social economic status have contributed to the acceleration of the imbalance.

In terms of rural household economic development imbalance, my view point is that imbalance objectively exists and it is the momentum needed for social development. To understand it correctly will be of great practical significance in promoting the rural economic development in China. In order to solve the problem of household economic development imbalance, it is necessary to analyse individual issues specifically, to solve the social problems with the sociological methods, deal with the economic issues with tools in economics, and overcome the political problems with political means. For the income inequality emerged in social development, which has been brought about during the rightful operation and management of rural households, the government has approved and the rural public accepted. However, the government should solve the problem of imbalance caused by political privilege and other improper means, which is unacceptable to the general public. For the inequality caused by objective reasons, the government should not only face the problem but also take various measures to solve it, such as differences in geographic location can be solved by improvement of transportation infrastructure. For households without labour or with the elderly, the government should try to solve by setting up a relief fund for those in poverty. Because these rural households are the important components in absolute poverty, which is an objective social problem existing in development of the rural society, it is necessary and reasonable for the government to take responsibility. Whether or not the poverty problem can be solved or how well it will be solved will be considered as indicators for social progress. To solve the economic imbalance brought about by subjective factors, the major components of inequality, is of great importance for social stability. For example, the imbalance caused by differences in household education should be solved with the common efforts of rural households and the society. Due to the limited funding resources in education for the government, it is acceptable to raise partial funds from farmers in an appropriate manner. However, for the nine-year compulsory education, governments (not villages) should not take it as an excuse to collect fees from farmers. This is because the nine-year compulsory education is related to the overall improvement of the nation's quality, which is of great significance to the state, and the popularisation of compulsory education is an obligatory responsibility of the government, so funds for compulsory education should not be raised from farmers. It is true that the government is able to raise partial funds for farmers' vocational training concerning agricultural modernisation. It is noted that in education and investment, the government shall properly handle the relation between education investment and economic expectation of farmers. If farmers' investment does not match their economic expectations, it will be difficult to generate enthusiasm among farmers for human capital investment, and consequently the government's expectation of partial investment by farmers cannot be achieved. In terms of inequality due to inter-household social and political status, it is caused mainly by objective reasons, and can be generally accepted by villagers. However, some imbalanced problems are not acceptable, i.e. those brought about by cadres' abuse of power, corruption, wrongful occupation of production materials such as land, and robbery of villagers' properties. These have become the major origins of instability in social society, and will threaten the security of the whole society.

Appendix

See Tables 5.17, 5.18, and 5.19.

Table 5.17 Population accumulation by income level at 1990 constant price (%)

Per capita net income (100 yuan)	<5	5–10	10–20	20–30	30–40	40–50	50–60	60–70	70–80	80–100	100–150	150–200	≥200
1986	5.71	30.14	47.61	12.76	2.46	0.60	0.51	0.12	0.09	–	–	–	–
1987	3.49	21.78	47.23	16.89	5.61	3.00	1.07	0.42	0.11	0.27	0.13	–	–
1988	5.35	20.37	48.21	16.17	4.51	1.90	1.13	0.93	0.33	0.44	0.57	0.09	–
1989	12.26	27.82	44.58	11.12	2.68	1.01	0.15	0.09	0.09	–	0.20	–	–
1990	7.39	25.90	46.79	15.19	3.25	0.87	0.29	0.31	–	–	0.02	–	–
1991	4.94	21.19	46.65	18.76	4.94	1.94	0.73	0.21	0.19	0.35	0.02	–	0.07
1993	2.38	9.31	40.95	24.30	11.84	5.48	2.48	0.57	0.52	0.52	1.29	0.21	0.16
1995	1.69	6.73	27.22	25.69	12.50	9.59	6.20	2.44	2.17	2.17	1.43	0.69	1.48
1996	1.33	5.47	30.18	22.58	16.31	7.55	4.94	1.81	2.55	1.70	2.39	1.06	2.13
1997	3.14	4.11	25.69	23.04	12.55	10.65	6.06	3.46	2.60	3.79	2.49	1.14	1.30
1998	3.99	4.54	27.38	18.14	18.20	8.47	5.14	2.40	2.46	4.32	3.01	1.15	0.82
1999	3.78	4.11	23.92	21.40	15.16	9.80	5.86	3.17	2.08	3.89	3.50	0.99	2.35
2000	2.19	4.22	17.81	22.68	15.07	10.79	8.22	4.55	3.23	2.63	4.05	0.71	3.84
2001	1.11	2.93	17.21	26.40	15.11	9.68	7.47	4.65	3.38	3.49	3.49	2.05	3.04
2002	1.84	3.07	14.59	21.02	15.65	10.68	8.72	4.81	3.35	5.76	4.53	2.01	3.97

Table 5.18 Income accumulation by income level at 1990 constant price (%)

Per capita net income (100 yuan)	<5	5–10	10–20	20–30	30–40	40–50	50–60	60–70	70–80	80–100	100–150	150–200	≥200
1986	1.46	16.65	48.57	22.33	6.08	1.87	1.99	0.53	0.51	–	–	–	–
1987	0.77	9.72	39.34	23.71	11.03	7.63	3.32	1.64	0.47	1.33	1.03	–	–
1988	1.12	8.89	39.13	21.88	8.76	4.73	3.42	3.32	1.37	2.29	4.26	0.83	
1989	2.85	15.77	47.44	20.16	6.89	3.35	0.62	0.44	0.51	–	1.97	–	–
1990	1.78	13.54	47.13	24.69	7.60	2.61	1.06	1.37	–	–	0.22	–	–
1991	0.95	9.68	40.41	26.52	10.14	5.14	2.33	0.81	0.81	1.94	0.15	–	1.11
1993	0.37	3.02	25.19	24.14	16.71	9.94	5.65	1.53	1.60	1.92	6.90	1.70	1.33
1995	−0.10	1.46	11.56	17.77	12.28	11.88	9.40	4.42	4.48	5.34	5.16	3.02	13.33
1996	−0.04	1.09	11.76	14.27	14.47	8.54	6.80	3.00	4.88	3.78	7.47	4.54	19.44
1997	−0.70	0.84	9.93	14.10	11.04	12.09	8.26	5.67	4.89	8.59	7.71	4.85	12.74
1998	−1.02	0.87	10.78	11.69	16.11	9.69	7.13	4.13	4.69	9.87	9.10	5.22	11.72
1999	−0.27	0.74	8.19	11.65	11.46	9.66	6.96	4.53	3.39	7.49	9.18	3.62	23.41
2000	−0.41	0.64	5.03	10.67	9.78	9.02	8.34	5.59	4.54	4.41	9.14	2.36	30.91
2001	0.05	0.41	4.85	11.34	9.37	7.76	7.25	5.38	4.50	5.51	7.29	6.18	30.12
2002	−0.20	0.45	4.39	9.52	9.76	8.58	8.56	5.65	4.51	9.06	9.49	5.94	24.29

Table 5.19 Rural household numbers by income level at 1990 constant price (household)

Per capita net income (100 yuan)	<5	5–10	10–20	20–30	30–40	40–50	50–60	60–70	70–80	80–100	100–150	150–200	≥200	Total
1986	80	318	503	133	29	8	7	1	1					1080
1987	62	248	535	187	61	33	11	4	1	3	2			1147
1988	79	248	541	184	47	22	12	10	3	5	5	1		1157
1989	147	327	522	139	33	14	2	2	1		2			1189
1990	110	305	546	181	43	12	3	5			1			1206
1991	73	251	528	205	56	22	9	4	2	4	1		1	1156
1993	13	46	198	125	61	27	12	3	4	3	6	1	1	500
1995	12	35	131	130	64	45	30	13	11	10	9	4	6	500
1996	9	27	144	115	82	37	26	9	14	10	12	6	9	500
1997	18	24	126	114	62	52	31	16	13	18	13	6	7	500
1998	25	25	133	90	88	43	26	14	10	22	14	6	4	500
1999	22	19	120	110	72	50	28	14	11	19	19	5	11	500
2000	13	22	89	108	77	52	41	21	18	15	21	4	18	499
2001	9	16	89	126	75	51	35	23	17	19	15	12	14	501
2002	9	18	77	98	78	58	40	24	19	27	24	11	17	500

References

Samuelson, P. A. (1992). *Economics (12th edition, translated in Chinese)*. Beijing: China Development Press.

Shi, Q. (2000). Resource use efficiency and comparison of its allocation directions in rural household economy. *Chinese Rural Economy, 8,* 58–61.

Shi, Q., Ma, S., & Wu, Z. (2001). On the income increase and the transference of Chinese famers and its causes. *Hebei Academic Journal, 5,* 24–28.

Shi, Q. (2001). *Rural household economic growth and development imbalance: Rural income and labour transfer*. Beijing: China Agriculture Press.

Zheng, H. (1996). *Empirical analysis on rural society transit in contemporary China*. Beijing: China Renmin University Press.

Chapter 6
Household Economic Development and Rural Tax and Fee Burden

Contents

Rural tax and fee burdens are big problems related to national stability and people's lives. Since ancient times, those in power in the past have attached great importance to this issue. Li Shimin, the Emperor in the Tang Dynasty once told his officials that 'water can carry a boat and can also overturn the boat'. He compared himself and his ruling group to the 'boat', and the vast majority of the people under the heavens as the 'water'. What did the stability of a country or regime depend on? It depended on taxes from the people. Therefore, the formulation of the corresponding 'taxation' laws and regulations to collect taxes became a top priority for the development of a country and the stability of the regime. However, in terms of tax collection, how much is collected in the end, and in what way? How to collect it so as to ensure the lasting stability of the regime and enable the people to live in long-term stability with the smooth and orderly development of the economy? It is a matter of great concern

Q. Shi and Y. Gao, *Sustainable Development of Rural Household Economy*,
https://doi.org/10.1007/978-981-15-2747-0_6

to policy makers and academics, and is also collectively referred to as the 'tax and fee burden' issue. This chapter takes households under fixed-track observation in the ten Zhejiang villages as the research objects, taking rural household economic development and the tax and fee burden as the major contents. By comparative analysis of the changes in income and tax and fee burden of the rural households during the period from 1986 to 2002, this chapter aims to explore the development trend of rural tax and fee burden, so as to provide some evidence for decision-making in rural tax and fee reform.

6.1 Tax and Fee Burden and Its Change for Rural Households

6.1.1 Changes in Population Size, Composition and Income

It is seen from Table 6.1 that since the observation, the size of Zhejiang rural households has shown a continuous downward trend. The average household population dropped from 3.99 in 1986 to 3.58 in 2002, with a decline of 10.28%. Although this decline was affected by the adjustment of observation scale and there was a rebound in 1993,[1] the number continued to show a downward trend. With the rapid shrinkage of the household population, dependency ratio in rural households also showed a corresponding downward trend, which decreased from 1.53 at the beginning of the observation to 1.45 in 2002, with a decline of 5.23%. This change in the population size of Zhejiang rural households provides a solid foundation for the rapid growth of their economic income. According to the current price, the net per capita income in the ten villages in Zhejiang Province increased from 862.53 yuan in 1986 to 9540.16 yuan in 2002, by 11.06 times in 17 years, with an average annual growth rate of 16.21%. But this increase is obviously related to the inflation in the early 1990s. As seen from the growth trend, rural households have experienced obvious periodic economic growth. Before the 1990s, when there was no large-scale inflation, the growth rate was substantial. Between 1986 and 1991, the average annual growth rate of per capita income for rural households was 14.92%. During the period of inflation, the growth rate of per capita income of rural households reached the highest, with an average level of 38.42% between 1991 and 1995. During the Ninth Five-Year Plan, stagflation occurred in domestic economy and the economic growth rate slowed down with obvious stagnated income growth for rural households. Between 1995 and 2002, the annual growth rate of rural household per capita income was only 7.02%. Against this background, the tax and fee burden for rural households has also undergone great changes.

[1] Since 1993, the observation scale has been adjusted from 1000 to 500.

Table 6.1 Rural household tax and fee burden and its change

	Population (person/households)	Population Burden (person/labourer)	Tax (yuan/person)	Fee/tax and fee (%)	*Tiliu* and *tongchou**/fee (%)	Net income (yuan/person)	Tax and fee/current-year income (%)	Tax and fee/last-year income (%)
1986	3.99	1.53	38.84	30.37	84.76	862.53	4.50	–
1987	3.92	1.53	43.95	22.17	84.57	1181.55	3.72	5.00
1988	3.91	1.52	46.63	15.01	91.64	1489.50	3.13	3.94
1989	3.83	1.53	42.32	14.42	77.97	1307.28	3.24	2.78
1990	3.73	1.48	47.04	29.55	57.90	1444.33	3.26	3.50
1991	3.69	1.46	65.05	43.67	82.17	1730.18	3.76	4.46
1993	3.87	1.47	99.40	25.08	71.44	3110.13	3.20	–
1995	3.78	1.44	238.31	23.40	59.57	6351.27	3.75	–
1996	3.76	1.44	213.17	24.25	74.06	7323.73	2.91	3.35
1997	3.70	1.45	300.50	20.87	46.30	7425.14	4.05	4.03
1998	3.66	1.44	207.28	18.11	71.78	7121.82	2.91	2.76
1999	3.65	1.44	349.84	24.00	36.16	8113.35	4.31	4.90
2000	3.66	1.43	360.66	15.16	77.15	9381.10	3.84	4.45
2001	3.61	1.45	434.12	11.72	61.95	9730.87	4.46	4.56
2002	3.58	1.45	494.92	11.93	43.52	9540.16	5.19	5.05

Note **Tiliu* and *tongchou* are both fee collection. *Tiliu* is referred to as remained fees collected at the village level, and *tongchou* is referred to as unified planned fees collected at the township level

6.1.2 *Tax and Fee Burden and Its Change*

With the continuous evolution of household size, structure and economic income, the tax and fee burden and its magnitude have also changed accordingly (Table 6.1). From the perspective of burden level, in 1986 when the observation first started, the burden for farmers was 38.84 yuan per head, and increased to 494.92 yuan per person in 2002, an increase of 11.74 times within 17 years, with an average annual growth rate as high as 17.24%. Obviously, the increase of farmers' tax and fee burden was nearly 1% faster than that of their income. Comparing the changing trend of income and burden (Fig. 6.1), before 1995, the income growth rate (24.84%) was slightly faster than the burden growth rate (22.33%). From 1995 to 2000, the income growth rate (8.11%) and the burden growth rate (8.64%) showed an alternate growth process where the burden growth rate was slightly faster than the income growth rate. After 2000, the burden growth rate (17.14%) was significantly faster than that of income (0.84%). Throughout the observation process, the growth of burden was significantly faster than the income growth for two time periods. Especially since 2000, the growth rate of burden has been significantly higher than that of income. This might be one of the reasons for the recent stagnated economic growth for rural households in Zhejiang.

As far as the burden degree is concerned (Table 6.1 and Fig. 6.2), during the whole observation period, the burden degree (burden level/net income of the previous year) fluctuated twice. The first fluctuation occurred from the mid-1980s to the early 1990s, when the burden degree decreased from 5.43% in 1986 to 2.78% in 1989. The

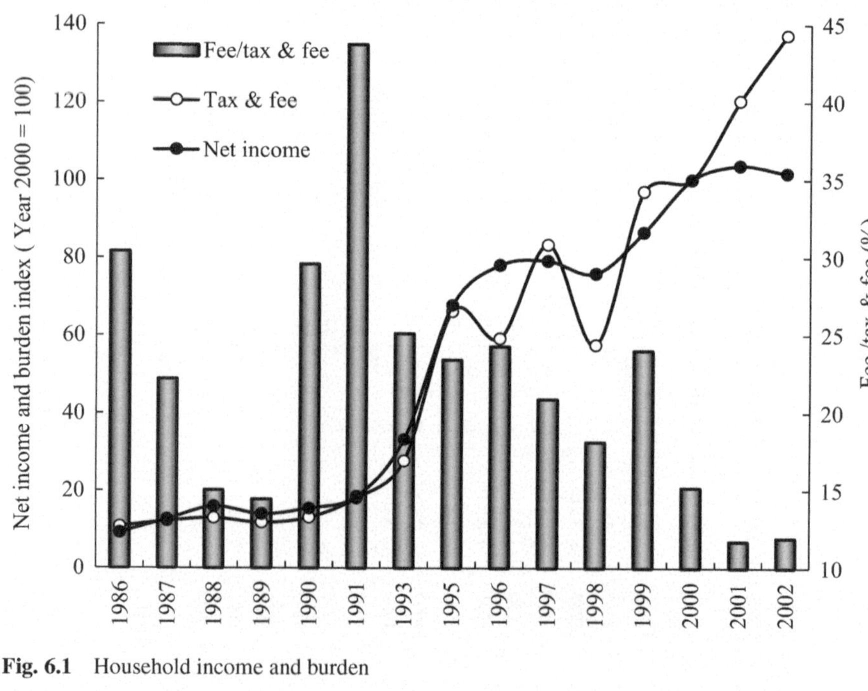

Fig. 6.1 Household income and burden

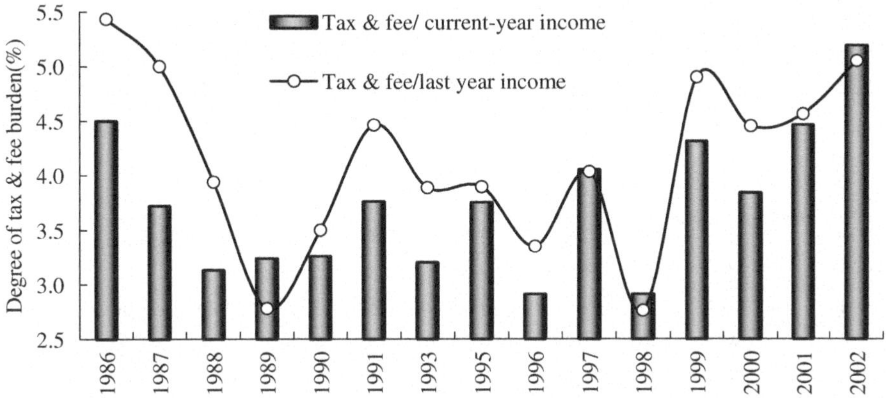

Fig. 6.2 Rural household tax and fee burden and its change. *Note* Data in 1986, 1993 and 1995 come from Zhejiang rural investigation team

situation reversed later when the burden degree reached a high level of 4.46% in 1991, before starting to decline and fluctuate until it rose again to 4.90% in 1999. After that it started to fluctuate again and rose to the top level of 5.05% in 2002. The change in household burden is closely related to the overall development of rural economy in China. At the beginning of the reform and opening up, the rural economy in China developed very fast, but the growth rate slowed down noticeably until 1985. In the following three years, agricultural growth stagnated or declined until it started to rise in the late 1980s, which was accompanied by large-scale inflation. After Deng Xiaoping made a speech in southern China, the development of the whole national economy accelerated, and the era of shortage in agricultural product supply was declared completely over in the mid and late 1990s. In the same period, agricultural policies did not keep up with the pace of rural development, resulting in the overstock of agricultural products, and farmers' income stagnated or even declined for as long as five years. In this process, the burden policy played an extremely disgraceful role. The long-established fee collection in particular, the major part of the rural burden, made farmers feel that the burden had been very high (Shi & Li, 2003; Shi & Zhang, 2003). Of course, we should also notice that in this context, the impact on Zhejiang farmers' economic growth was relatively small and lasted for a relatively short time. One of the main reasons was that the burden structure of Zhejiang farmers was obviously different from that of other provinces and regions in the country. The tax-based burden in Zhejiang has provided intangible support for the rapid development of rural household economy.

It can be seen from Table 6.2 that by 2002, the distribution of tax and fee burden for rural households in the ten villages in Zhejiang showed the following features. The sample households with no burden or with the burden degree of 1% or less accounted for 58.40% of the total. Those with the burden degree between 1 and 5% took 25.20%, and those between 5 and 10% took 8.80%. There were 7.60% of the households with the burden degree over 10%, and 3.60% of them over 20%. Obviously, with a baseline of 5% tax and fee burden in comparison with rural income, the proportion of rural households surpassing this benchmark was only 16.40% in Zhejiang. For

Table 6.2 Distribution of rural household tax and fee burden degrees (%)

	=0	≤1%	1–2	2–3	3–4	4–5	5–10	10–20	>20
1986	21.30	18.06	18.33	12.50	8.52	4.91	7.41	5.09	3.89
1987	22.93	19.53	19.97	12.82	7.24	3.75	7.24	3.57	2.96
1988	28.18	21.61	25.06	10.03	4.58	2.51	3.63	2.42	1.99
1989	27.33	15.90	20.61	16.48	6.22	2.86	4.96	3.28	2.35
1990	22.55	14.43	23.88	13.18	5.80	4.64	9.37	3.57	2.57
1991	23.96	16.78	14.36	9.69	10.03	7.79	10.99	4.07	2.34
1993	17.80	31.80	20.80	8.40	5.20	3.80	8.00	2.00	2.20
1995	10.60	31.40	16.40	9.20	8.00	6.00	9.80	4.60	4.00
1996	12.00	28.60	18.60	9.00	7.20	5.80	10.60	5.60	2.60
1997	11.20	28.80	16.40	9.40	6.20	4.20	13.20	4.80	5.80
1998	15.40	28.40	16.00	9.00	7.00	4.00	10.00	4.80	5.40
1999	13.20	30.80	12.80	8.00	5.00	4.60	14.80	4.80	6.00
2000	18.84	27.66	14.23	9.62	5.21	6.21	11.82	3.81	2.61
2001	20.56	32.93	14.17	6.19	3.99	3.99	11.38	2.79	3.99
2002	23.80	34.60	12.00	6.40	3.80	3.00	8.80	4.00	3.60
2000–02	21.07	31.73	13.47	7.40	4.33	4.40	10.67	3.53	3.40

the 17 years' observation, the distribution of rural household burden degrees showed that the percentage of rural households with the burden degree below 1% increased first before it declined (Fig. 6.3), with an increase of 19.04% compared with the initial observation period, an increase of 16.40% if compared with the 1995 level, or an increase of 11.90% if compared with the 2000 level. Meanwhile the percentage

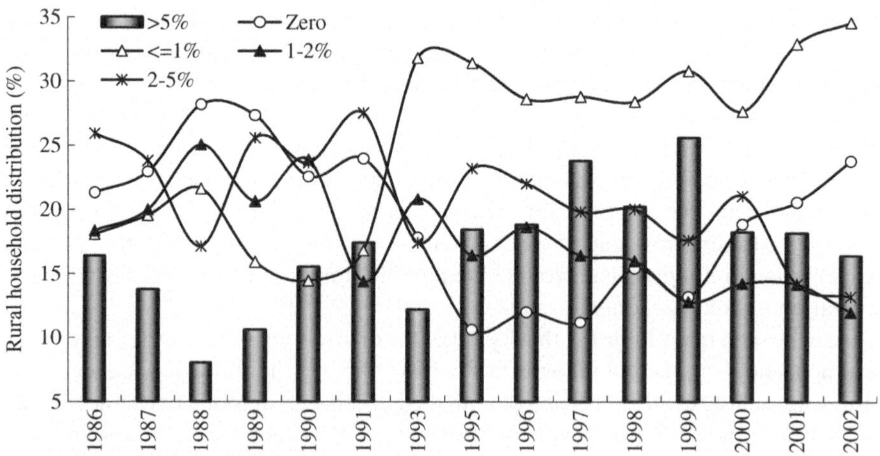

Fig. 6.3 Rural household burden and distribution

of rural households with the burden degree above 2% declined before it rose, and then decreased again. The percentage of rural households with the burden degree of over 5% remained the same as the level in the beginning of the observation, while it decreased by 2% compared with 1995, or by 1.80% if compared with the 2000 level. This result has indicated that in the process of rural economic development in Zhejiang, the problem of farmers' tax and fee burden has been alleviated. Although there are still farmers with their burden degree more than 10%, some of them have special reasons such as poor household operation leading to zero or negative income. For these farmers, any little burden, calculated with the current method, will be a huge amount. Of course, the percentage of such farmers is low, and the highest level was only 3.00% in 1998, and in most years, it was lower than 1%. There were only three years with a percentage more than 1%, i.e. 1997 with 1.40%, and 1998 and 1999 both with 1.80%. Observation data show that although the percentage was not high for rural households with burden degrees over 10%, the figure has been relatively stable, and these households might be the group that needs the most support from the government.

6.1.3 Tax Burden Structure and Its Change

In the development of household economy, the burden of taxes and fees is a very important factor. Its importance lies not only in the burden magnitude, but also in its structure. The way taxes and fees are collected has great influence on the development of rural household economy. The traditional Chinese fee-dominant burden seemed fair but was ineffective. The collection according to number of people or land area has a history of several thousand years, which has been well accepted by the rural public. However, the historic development of Chinese agriculture for thousands of years shows that such a burden pattern could only lead to the cyclical change of social institutions, but was not able to make brilliant achievements. The tax-dominant burden in the modern West seems unfair, but is efficient. It is obviously beneficial to agricultural development and farmers' income when farmers and people of other professions are treated equally and taxed simply according to income. From the entire observation over the 17 years, the burden pattern of Zhejiang rural households was different from that of other rural areas in China (Shi, 2004; Shi & Zhuo, 2003). In Zhejiang, the major burden for farmers was 'tax', and the proportion of taxes in the burden increased from 69.63% at the beginning of the observation to 88.07% in 2002, and increased by nearly 20% in 17 years. In addition, although the share of fees once rose to 43.67% in 1991, the trend of decline has also been persistent. Especially since 2000, the proportion of fees out of total burden has dropped considerably, from 24.00% in 1999 to 15.16% in 2000, and further to 11.93% in 2002. Compared with the national situation, the burden pattern of Zhejiang rural households has developed with the same trend, but the burden magnitude varied greatly (Shi, 2004).[2] As a result, the

[2]According to the observation data for the whole country, of the farmers' burden in 1986, the share of fees took 56.58%. Although it decreased to 31.89% in 2002 after 17 years, the level was still much higher than Zhejiang. In certain provinces, the figure was over 60% (Shi & Zhuo, 2003).

effect was also different in promoting rural household economic development. In the mid and late 1990s (1996–2000) when rural household economic growth stagnated or even declined throughout the country, rural households in the ten villages in Zhejiang were able to get out of the unfavourable situation very soon. It is seen from the burden structure of rural households and its changes in economic growth in Zhejiang, different burden patterns have played different roles in promoting rural economic development (Shi, 2004). Taking Zhejiang's practice into consideration, it is not difficult to find out the 'tax for fee' reform during the Ninth Five-Year Plan period and the phasing out of 'agricultural taxes' during the Tenth Five-Year Plan period initiated by the Chinese government were in line with the general strategy of increasing farmers' income. In 2003, Zhejiang Province, as a coastal developed province, took the lead in implementing the policy of agricultural tax exemption. It is believed that this policy will bring a great impetus to the development of rural areas, agriculture and rural economy in Zhejiang Province.

6.2 Comparison of Tax and Fee Burden and Its Change Among Different Types of Rural Households

6.2.1 Comparison of Tax and Fee Burden Among Households with Different Incomes

From the view point of economic development, the absolute value and relative value of tax and fee burden should both increase with income growth. Only in this way can economic growth be promoted more effectively. However, it is not the case in real economic activities (Shi, 2004; Shi & Zhuo, 2003). In real life, the burden of rural households could be divided into taxes and fees, collected on completely different bases. Tax collection was mostly based on income, taking into account the number of people and land area (agricultural tax); while fee collection was based solely on number of people or land area, without consideration of income level. The former focused on efficiency while the latter on equity. The collection type had direct impacts on the income growth of rural households. Traditionally, the ratio of fee burden was obviously higher than that of taxes. The fee-dominant burden led to fact that, for rural households, the differences in burden magnitude were obviously larger than the differences in the burden level. The trial of 'tax for fee' practice during the Ninth Five-Year period was the tax-based burden. Such collection was clearly beneficial to the economic development of low-income households, and provided some policy adjustments and mitigation to the polarisation of rural economic development (Shi & Li, 2003; Shi & Zhang, 2003). In 2004, the central government decided to phase out agricultural taxes, which would have direct impacts on economic growth for all farmers engaged in agricultural operation.

It can be seen from Table 6.3 that in the tax-dominant province like Zhejiang, farmers' burden obviously increased with their household income. At the beginning of the observation in 1986, the average tax and fee per capita was 98.94 yuan paid by high-income households, 13.09 yuan by low-income households, and the burden

Table 6.3 Rural household tax and fee burden and household income

	Per capita tax and fee (yuan)					Tax and fee/current-year income (%)				
	Low	Lower middle	Middle	Upper middle	High	Low	Lower middle	Middle	Upper middle	High
1986	13.09	16.47	34.82	28.21	98.94	3.88	2.96	4.70	2.86	6.05
1987	15.72	26.87	30.14	51.02	90.58	3.61	3.76	3.13	3.95	3.83
1988	13.58	18.31	22.26	31.78	139.96	2.73	2.11	1.91	2.04	4.40
1989	12.19	19.18	30.54	36.21	116.82	3.00	2.37	2.63	2.35	4.35
1990	22.47	26.09	41.65	43.50	101.44	4.44	2.87	3.19	2.52	3.72
1991	23.42	38.86	60.21	65.46	133.29	3.94	3.62	4.10	3.34	3.88
1993	56.14	48.54	49.22	80.14	269.69	5.05	2.60	1.98	2.32	3.96
1995	98.19	92.62	94.87	197.81	712.38	5.83	2.91	2.12	3.01	4.49
1996	146.88	111.58	105.26	266.84	445.99	7.54	3.32	2.18	3.88	2.20
1997	215.19	141.98	150.71	187.26	816.00	14.01	4.02	3.04	2.41	4.23
1998	126.09	75.68	120.41	197.54	515.16	11.07	2.31	2.38	2.78	2.76
1999	235.30	161.87	148.54	228.27	973.76	14.67	4.69	2.97	3.06	4.25
2000	103.59	113.87	125.64	185.34	1313.39	5.91	2.90	2.21	2.20	4.73
2001	138.06	108.34	92.23	167.04	1646.85	6.02	2.80	1.70	2.03	5.80
2002	152.80	177.75	129.72	180.12	1821.76	6.93	4.17	2.11	1.95	7.13

level of high-income households was 7.56 times that of low-income households. Until 2002, the burdens of the high and low-income households increased to 1821.76 and 152.80 yuan, with the former being 11.92 times that of the latter. It is obvious that with the further 'taxation' of rural burden, there has been polarisation of rural households in terms of burden shouldered. If we look closely, in fact, this kind of polarisation has occurred only since the new century. Before 2000, the burden gap between the high- and low-income households did not enlarge with the passage of time, where only once was it significantly narrowed, from the highest level of 10.31 times in 1988 to 3.04 times in 1996, which became 4.14 times in 1999. However, after the trial of 'tax for fee' in 2000, the burden gap between the high- and low-income households became enlarged so that the disparity once increased to 12.68 times, and then decreased again in the following two years, at 11.93 times in 2001 and further down to 11.92 times in 2002. If only the burden growth rate is considered in the ten villages in Zhejiang, with the income growth of rural households, the burden growth rate exhibited a 'U'-shape trend in that the growth rates for the high and low-income households were faster than those in the middle. From 1986 to 2002, the burden growth rates for high, middle and low-income households were 19.97, 8.57 and 16.60%, respectively. In terms of changing trends, the burden for high-income households was increased continuously, while for middle-income households it showed a fluctuating upward trend, and the low-income households showed an inverted 'U' shape.

In terms of the burden degree, with the increase of household income, the burden degree presented a 'U'-shape trend (Fig. 6.4). Although the trend varied in individual years, it is generally in line with the 'U' shape. In the first five years of observation,

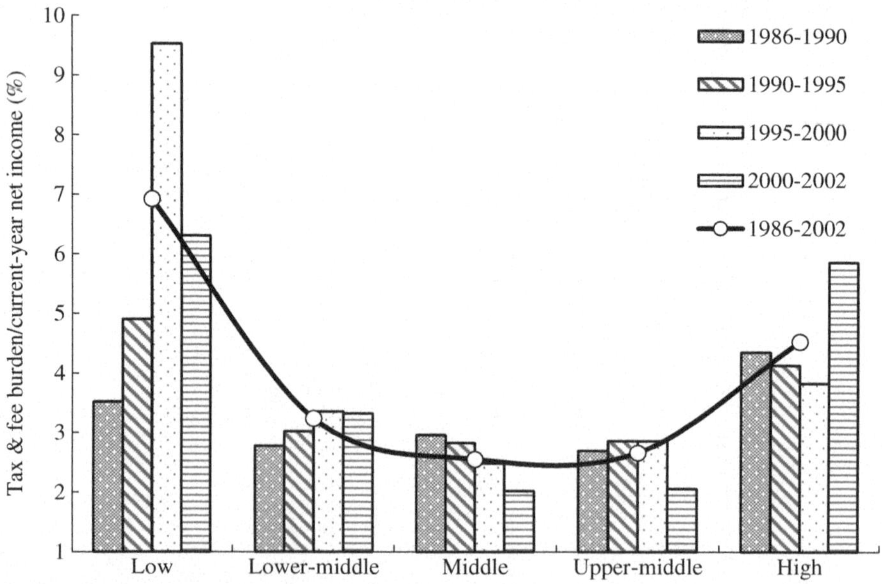

Fig. 6.4 Rural household tax and fee burden and income

i.e. from 1986 to 1990, the average burden degrees of the three types of rural households were 3.52, 2.96 and 4.34% respectively. From 1995 to 2000, they became 9.52, 2.48 and 3.82, and from 2000 to 2002, it further evolved to 6.30, 2.02 and 5.85%. In terms of the evolution of the burden degrees, households of low income, lower-middle income and upper-middle income showed an inverted 'U' shape, while middle-income households showed a downward trend and high-income households showed a 'U'-shape trend. Therefore, in terms of tax and fee burden, the rural households really heavily burdened were those with high and low economic development, especially low-income households. Because of their very low economic development level, a slight burden growth would put their household economy in trouble. Accordingly, when we pay attention to farmers' burden, we need to focus on those rural households with high and low incomes. While trying to make the economy of low-income households grow as fast as possible, we must not forget to give due consideration to the burden of high-income households. Since they are the most important tax source, and only by ensuring their normal profits, can we ensure the tax revenue growth at the same time.

6.2.2 *Tax and Fee Burden for Households of Different Operation Types*

Due to the different household types, there exist differences in ways to bear the economic burdens. Such differences have been mostly determined by Chinese history.[3] According to modern economics, the collection of taxes and fees should be consistent with the economic development. Over-levied taxes and fees will inevitably slow down the economic development and even cause a retrogression. Insufficient taxes and fees will affect the security of the country or region. Moderate tax and fee collection is a necessary strategy for the economic development of a country or region. Only in this way can the society be stable for a long time, the economy be sustainable, and the people live and work in peace and contentment. However, the traditional way of tax collection in China did not take this into account, and the idea of 'equalisation' always played a leading role in the society dominated by agricultural production, although policy makers were also aware of the relationship between 'water and boat', and attached great importance to it at the beginning of each dynasty. With the passage of time, the bureaucratic troops became larger, and the traditional low-level collection based on land area or household members encountered

[3]As we all know, the history of China is also a history that evolved with the change in agricultural civilization. The state's tax collection had been based on land area and population for a long time. This tax collection method seldom considered much regarding income level. Agricultural production is an industry with great natural risks. Frequent natural disasters used to force a large number of farmers to leave their homeland because they could not afford the land rent (including imperial grain). In extreme years, due to insufficient consideration of excessive burden, there were collective tax resistance and even riots among the people periodically. The change of dynasty has provided a good proof.

more difficulties in supporting the whole bureaucratic expenditure. Thus, raising the level of collection became a habitual means to solve this problem. Because of the disproportionate economic development and the increased collection, the excessive growth of burden greatly harmed the development of household economy, especially the interests of farmers living at lower levels, which directly threatened their survival. As a result, social unrest inevitably erupted periodically. Admittedly, such outbreak was also influenced by other factors, such as the social system represented by the private ownership of agricultural land, but the equalisation of collection was an important factor. After the foundation of the new China, the Chinese government noticed the impact of private ownership of agricultural land on national stability, but paid less attention to the impact of tax collection. Therefore, in the vast rural areas, the idea of evenly distributed burden was adopted up until now, and has been quite common. This is generally manifested in the structure of taxes and fees, that is, the proportion of fees was higher, while that of taxes was lower. From the perspective of modern economic development, tax is income-based, and its existence plays a safeguarding role in maintaining social stability and promoting economic development. However, fees are a kind of punitive deprivation in that although its existence is good for maintaining social stability, it is by no means the main source of expenditure for maintaining the overall social stability as a whole. Since income level is seldom considered in fee collection, if the collection standard is too high, it will inevitably lead to the subsistence crisis for some rural households, and in serious cases, it will lead to an economic downturn. In fact, the slowdown of China's rural economy for four to five years in the mid and late 1990s was directly related to this. At the same time, the idea of 'tax for fee' in rural areas was formed against this background.

From Tables 6.4 and 6.5, it can be seen that since 1986, the tax and fee burden of rural households in the ten villages in Zhejiang Province has changed into an inverted 'U'-shape trend, which is mainly manifested in agricultural or agriculture-related households, but not in non-agricultural households. The changes in tax and fee burden has been obviously contrary to the changes in economic growth. When tax and fee burden grew particularly fast, the income growth slowed down significantly, which was most notable in the mid and late 1990s. As far as the relationship between family operation type and the burden is concerned, with the non-agriculturalisation of household operation, the burden level and income level of rural households have basically maintained an upward trend. At the same time, the burden degree has also shown an upward trend (Fig. 6.5). With the increase of non-agricultural degree of rural households, the evolution of their burden structure has showed a change from 'fee' to 'tax' collection. With the continuous reform concerning rural burden and the abolition of agricultural tax in Zhejiang Province, the proportion of fees shouldered by rural households has experienced a decline for a period of time. For three years since 2000, however, the proportion of fee collection has shown an upward trend. In 2002, the proportions of fee burden for agricultural and agriculture-dominated households became 56.03 and 54.07, with increases of 9.55 and 3.74% compared with 1995. The fee collection is still the major burden for rural households engaged in agriculture.

Table 6.4 Rural household tax and fee burden and operation types (I)

	Per capita tax and fee burden (yuan)					Per capita net income (100 yuan)				
	Agriculture	Complete agricultural	Agriculture-dominated	Non-agricultural dominated	Non-agricultural	Agriculture	Complete agricultural	Agriculture-dominated	Non-agricultural dominated	Non-agricultural
1986	28.28	22.71	30.76	107.49	59.30	7.82	8.21	8.98	10.21	10.43
1987	21.19	18.43	38.80	107.32	150.00	10.51	11.66	12.17	11.80	18.28
1988	16.09	16.00	28.16	75.86	216.53	12.54	14.13	12.43	13.92	27.57
1989	21.49	24.51	36.10	74.53	174.15	12.04	13.62	11.40	14.86	18.74
1990	28.89	32.98	49.74	64.92	149.16	13.34	15.24	13.61	15.98	19.00
1991	41.85	52.71	60.27	95.07	176.36	15.36	16.71	15.08	17.69	24.37
1993	51.60	61.26	47.12	51.82	410.30	26.20	26.85	23.68	32.48	41.01
1995	125.40	132.51	233.38	109.33	569.82	43.06	44.78	45.84	68.52	80.58
1996	135.95	127.43	82.33	145.32	515.69	51.38	53.90	41.06	69.07	84.69
1997	183.59	170.16	152.93	129.94	669.95	50.68	51.52	41.62	65.69	124.87
1998	125.03	135.67	111.59	145.91	413.82	43.94	47.92	42.79	66.58	120.25
1999	145.84	137.87	98.67	197.64	845.07	46.40	49.56	47.39	61.96	151.36
2000	154.99	134.65	73.91	166.62	932.74	56.49	57.23	41.68	61.24	174.43
2001	135.27	152.36	191.26	268.62	1063.60	52.41	55.68	56.83	77.34	164.92
2002	126.87	144.96	95.48	123.91	1117.25	55.08	55.90	56.18	73.21	148.85

Table 6.5 Rural household tax and fee burden and operation types (II)

	Fees/taxes & fees (%)					Taxes & fees/current-year net income (%)				
	Agriculture	Complete Agricultural	Agriculture-dominated	Non-agricultural dominated	Non-agricultural	Agriculture	Complete agricultural	Agriculture-dominated	Non-agricultural dominated	Non-agricultural
1986	36.60	21.22	17.99	12.73	10.30	3.62	2.76	3.43	10.53	5.69
1987	34.04	26.05	12.70	12.84	8.83	2.02	1.58	3.19	9.09	8.21
1988	21.77	16.37	20.90	12.17	5.99	1.28	1.13	2.27	5.45	7.86
1989	28.57	24.71	16.23	4.89	1.92	1.79	1.80	3.17	5.02	9.29
1990	42.21	42.46	18.63	6.67	7.79	2.17	2.16	3.65	4.06	7.85
1991	55.20	57.32	25.56	10.27	11.49	2.72	3.16	4.00	5.37	7.24
1993	60.16	66.11	41.75	23.30	5.65	1.97	2.28	1.99	1.60	10.00
1995	46.48	47.44	50.33	33.86	7.28	2.91	2.96	5.09	1.60	7.07
1996	37.08	39.83	39.96	21.94	10.19	2.65	2.36	2.01	2.10	6.09
1997	29.89	35.48	43.15	27.12	14.42	3.62	3.30	3.67	1.98	5.37
1998	34.00	35.57	34.30	25.95	7.51	2.85	2.83	2.61	2.19	3.44
1999	43.97	49.35	76.89	64.32	7.78	3.14	2.78	2.08	3.19	5.58
2000	54.33	54.95	66.31	31.63	3.84	2.74	2.35	1.77	2.72	5.35
2001	55.48	57.30	46.01	11.79	2.82	2.58	2.74	3.37	3.47	6.45
2002	56.03	55.74	54.07	28.51	5.66	2.30	2.59	1.70	1.69	7.51

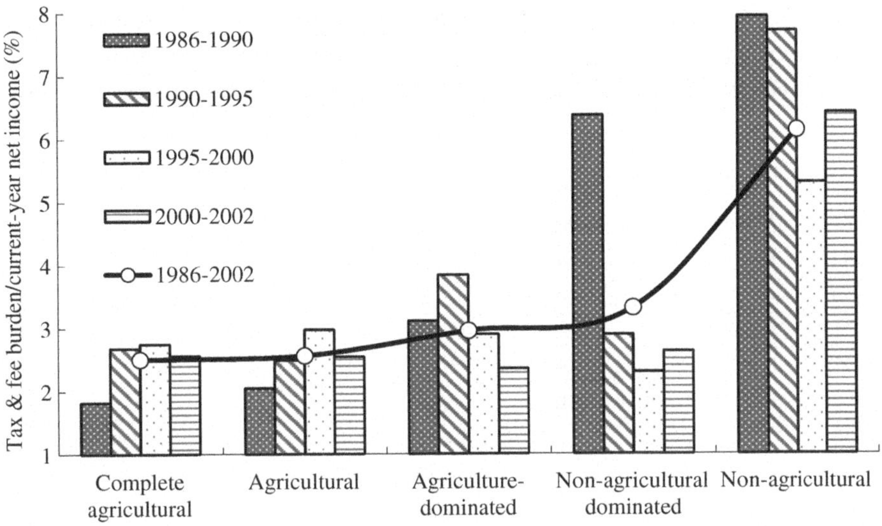

Fig. 6.5 Rural household tax and fee burden and household operation type

Comparing the burden structure and its changes of rural households with different operation types, the burden for agricultural and agriculture-dominated households is mainly from fee collection, which is on the rise, while for non-agricultural households the burden is mainly from taxes. With the passage of time, rural tax and fee burdens in Zhejiang have evolved from fee-dominant to tax-dominant collection, which is consistent with the current tax reform in rural areas. However, as the majority of rural households, agricultural households still have 56.03% burden from fees. Therefore, it is quite difficult to reform the traditional way of collection.

6.2.3 *Tax and Fee Burden for Households with Different Education Levels*

Many studies have found that the economic growth of rural households is directly related to the education level of their main household labourer (Shi, 1999, 2001). Households with relatively high education level for the main labourer have relatively higher incomes, and income is positively correlated with the education level. This is demonstrated in Table 6.6. As Zhejiang is a province with taxes as the major burden for households, farmers' tax collection was closely related to their income level. The relationship between tax burden and the educational level is that, with the improvement of the education level, the level of burden also showed a corresponding upward trend. Generally speaking, families with higher educational levels were also those with higher expenditure on tax payment. As time goes on, the burden disparities among households with good and poor educational levels tend to increase. At the

Table 6.6 Rural household tax and fee burden and household educational background (I)

	Per capita tax and fee (yuan)				Per capita net income (100 yuan)			
	Illiterate	Primary school	Junior high	Senior High+	Illiterate	Primary school	Junior high	Senior High+
1986	29.02	33.01	53.76	67.71	8.45	8.34	9.32	8.94
1987	33.99	39.25	59.98	69.33	12.03	11.67	12.04	11.32
1988	27.71	50.95	51.36	49.40	16.98	13.96	14.99	16.60
1989	26.38	41.90	50.76	65.48	11.47	13.31	13.72	13.74
1990	24.97	47.22	55.34	75.46	12.55	14.42	15.36	16.22
1991	36.24	72.46	61.75	99.79	13.89	16.74	19.41	20.89
1993	66.83	57.24	190.26	89.92	23.91	29.98	32.29	46.39
1995	180.90	209.50	305.29	248.65	47.96	64.01	62.50	89.81
1996	177.77	190.56	236.30	324.62	52.94	74.67	69.58	109.83
1997	109.66	239.81	426.33	345.18	63.42	72.83	71.49	109.78
1998	73.44	181.14	277.55	221.89	51.99	65.77	70.91	133.05
1999	94.34	335.85	369.35	618.38	49.20	77.02	72.50	176.41
2000	59.91	389.64	336.00	585.35	54.77	99.51	87.29	126.26
2001	49.43	496.93	346.90	828.68	51.67	105.91	87.54	134.80
2002	67.34	456.25	482.30	1171.71	67.53	101.56	83.79	140.07

beginning of the observation, the average per capita tax and fee burden for illiterate and semi-illiterate households was 29.02 yuan, for households with primary school education was 33.01 yuan, for those with junior middle school education was 53.76 yuan, and for those with high school education and above was 67.71 yuan, which was 2.33 times of that of the illiterate and semi-illiterate households. By 2002, the burden levels for all types of households had changed to 67.34, 456.25, 482.30 and 1171.71 yuan, with the burden for the households with a high level of education 17.40 times that of those with a low level of education. A detailed observation has shown that the widening of the burden gap for households with different educational levels did not apply to the entire observation period but a phenomenon that appeared only after the middle and late 1990s. Before 1997, the burden of well-educated households remained about twice that of poorly-educated households, and the gap rose to 3.15 times in 1997, 6.55 times in 1999, 9.77 times in 2000, 16.76 times in 2001 and 17.40 times in 2002. This manifestation of different tax and fee burdens for households with different education backgrounds fully reflects the orientation of tax and fee reform in rural areas of Zhejiang Province in pursuit of economic development efficiency.

As for the degree of tax and fee burden (Fig. 6.6 and Table 6.7), with the improvement of the education level of the main household labourer, the burden of rural households presented an inverted 'U'-shape upward change. With the passage of time, the burden showed an inverted 'U'-shape decline for illiterate and semi-illiterate households, an inverted 'U'-shape rise for households with junior high school education,

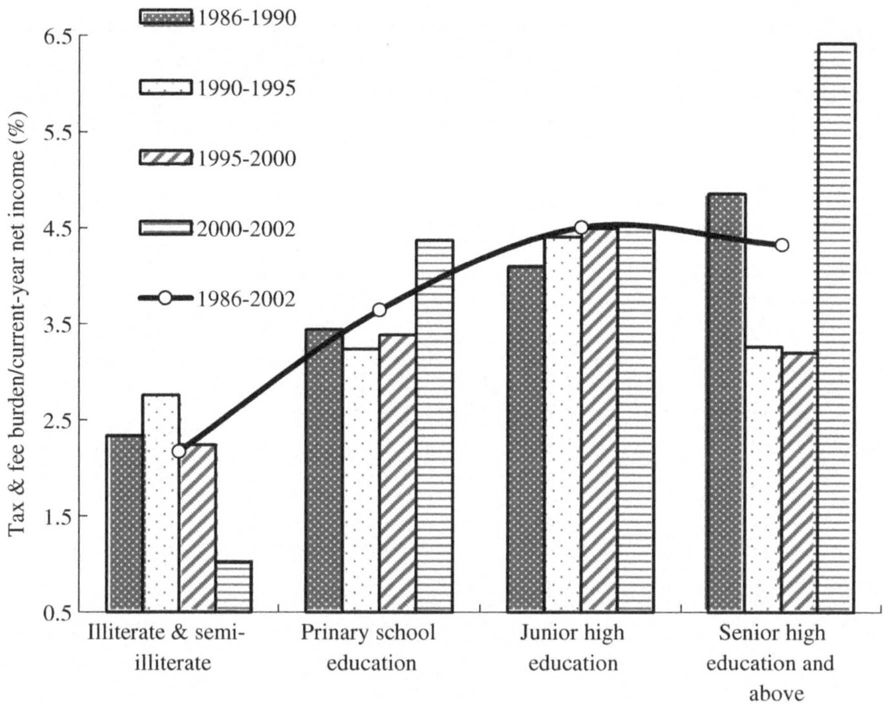

Fig. 6.6 Rural household tax and fee burden and household education level

and a 'U'-shape rise for households with primary school and high school or above education.

As far as the composition of taxes and fees is concerned (Table 6.7), with the improvement of the educational level of the main household labourer, the burden shifted from 'fee' oriented to 'tax' oriented (Fig. 6.7). During the initial five years of observation (1986–1990), fees accounted for 18.53% of the total burden for illiterate and semi-illiterate households, 18.19% for households with primary school education, 17.97% for those with junior high school education, and 13.82% for those with senior high school education and above. For the three years in the 2000s (2000–2002), the ratios of fee burden increased to 63.70% for illiterate and semi-illiterate households, decreased to 11.48% for households with primary school education, declined to 17.78% for households with junior high education, and dropped to 3.12% for those with senior high education and above. In the whole observation period (1986–2002), the ratios of fee burden became 34.34% for illiterate and semi-illiterate households, 18.29% for those with primary school education, 20.01% for those with junior high education and 7.99% for those with senior education and above. The burdens for households with different educational levels have shown different trends. The fee ratio for illiterate and semi-illiterate households has shown an upward trend, especially in the mid-1990s when the fee ratio rose rapidly and once reached 74.46%

Table 6.7 Rural household tax and fee burden and household educational background (II)

	Fee/tax and fee (%)				Tax and fee/current-year net income (%)			
	Illiterate	Primary school	Junior high	Senior High+	Illiterate	Primary school	Junior high	Senior High+
1986	13.80	25.58	26.87	13.46	3.44	3.96	5.77	7.57
1987	11.05	23.83	15.53	10.11	2.83	3.36	4.98	6.12
1988	19.99	10.90	16.55	3.66	1.63	3.65	3.43	2.98
1989	18.42	10.75	11.15	21.45	2.30	3.15	3.70	4.76
1990	35.82	23.21	20.01	16.79	1.99	3.28	3.60	4.65
1991	38.86	27.13	37.44	19.67	2.61	4.33	3.18	4.78
1993	28.07	32.33	21.28	19.54	2.79	1.91	5.89	1.94
1995	21.44	28.00	20.13	13.09	3.77	3.27	4.88	2.77
1996	67.50	24.43	19.10	9.94	3.36	2.55	3.40	2.96
1997	50.74	21.09	20.78	9.07	1.73	3.29	5.96	3.14
1998	58.51	22.31	12.88	8.79	1.41	2.75	3.91	1.67
1999	38.44	22.43	28.17	15.78	1.92	4.36	5.09	3.51
2000	74.46	14.22	18.42	4.93	1.09	3.92	3.85	4.64
2001	70.03	9.35	18.56	3.71	0.96	4.69	3.96	6.15
2002	48.81	11.43	16.80	1.76	1.00	4.49	5.76	8.37

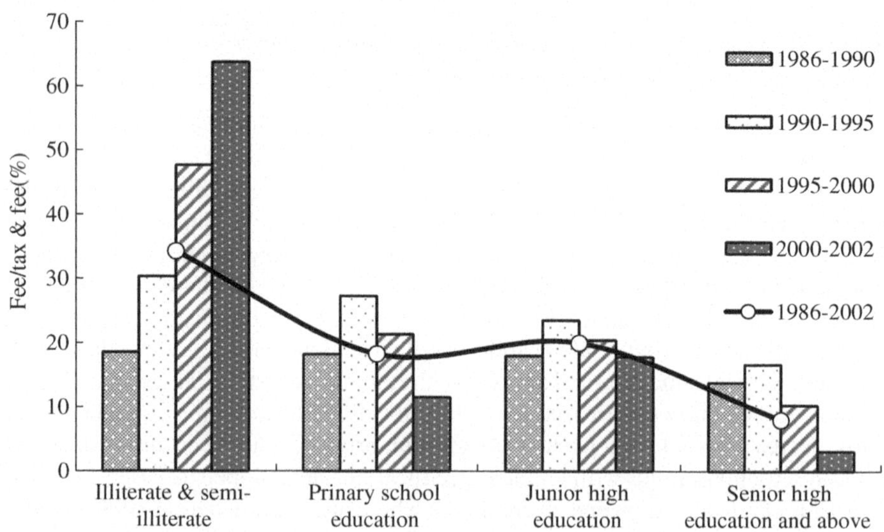

Fig. 6.7 Rural household tax and fee composition and household educational background

in 2000. It declined later, and in 2002 it reduced to 48.81%. The trends for households with junior high school and primary school education were basically the same, both showing an inverted 'U'-shape change, but their proportion of fees was much lower than that of illiterate and semi-illiterate households. In the whole observation period, the highest fee ratio reached 32.33% in 1993 for households with primary school education, 37.44% in 1991 for households with junior high school education, which decreased to 11.43 and 16.80% respectively in 2002. The fee ratio for households with senior high school education and above showed a downward trend, which decreased from the highest level of 21.45% in 1989 to 1.76% in 2002.

6.2.4 Rural Household Tax and Fee Burden in Different Villages

From Table 6.8 and Fig. 6.8, it can be seen that due to the different villages where households live, the tax and fee burdens varied greatly, and over time, the burden differences among villages have changed dramatically. In the whole observation period, comparatively speaking, of the ten observation villages in Zhejiang, Longshang village in Lin'an had the highest burden for rural households, with an average level of 8.85% over 17 years. In the early observation period (before 1995), the burden degree reached 11.85%, and then declined to 8.73% in the Ninth Five-Year Plan

Table 6.8 Tax and fee burden in different villages (%)

	LS	YF	YB	XSF	MY	XM	JH	BGM	HB	SBY
1986	16.77	2.84	3.68	0.91	4.67	3.98	2.45	1.26	7.27	4.49
1987	18.17	1.84	3.41	0.91	5.87	3.89	2.12	0.43	4.87	3.41
1988	7.52	1.42	2.35	0.59	5.92	4.43	2.12	3.73	3.52	1.81
1989	8.02	2.16	4.19	1.39	4.43	4.86	1.48	2.28	2.67	2.00
1990	8.94	1.79	6.44	1.46	3.64	4.12	1.57	0.99	4.24	2.86
1991	11.59	4.65	6.62	2.17	3.11	4.14	1.27	0.72	6.78	2.09
1993	14.23	2.31	3.70	1.00	1.05	2.61	1.81	1.69	3.68	1.97
1995	12.28	3.66	3.14	0.46	4.28	1.59	4.53	9.96	0.84	1.83
1996	8.62	9.31	3.74	0.54	2.75	1.81	3.09	5.23	0.97	1.85
1997	7.61	9.56	4.07	1.90	5.10	1.54	4.43	10.57	1.08	1.71
1998	8.09	4.22	2.87	1.05	3.95	1.51	3.13	7.58	3.38	1.53
1999	7.98	5.50	2.47	2.85	3.53	3.93	4.45	10.93	7.90	2.43
2000	7.80	3.61	1.30	4.44	3.05	2.35	3.52	5.34	4.98	2.27
2001	7.27	12.70	0.99	4.88	3.17	3.52	2.85	3.66	3.15	1.91
2002	3.46	5.48	5.43	8.32	2.13	5.64	1.83	5.85	5.08	1.39
2000–2002	5.97	7.07	3.07	5.66	2.77	3.84	2.70	5.02	4.38	1.85

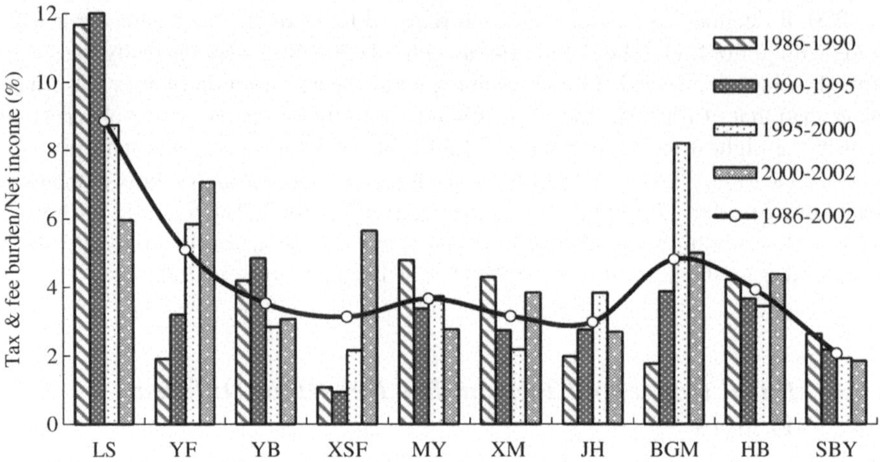

Fig. 6.8 Rural household tax and fee burden and location

period, and further decreased to 5.97% from 2000 to 2002. The next was Yongfeng Village in Huzhou, with an average degree of 5.10% in 17 years. In the early observation period (before 1990), the figure was only 1.91% which rose to 3.19% during the Eighth Five-Year Plan period, and to 5.85% during the Ninth Five-Year Plan period. Between 2000 and 2002, it further increased to 7.07%, making the village the most heavily burdened at present. The third was Bogumen Village in Putuo, with an average degree of 4.83% in 17 years. In the initial five years of the observation, the average degree was 1.77%, which climbed all the way up to the highest level of 8.21% during the Ninth Five-Year Plan period. In the 2000s, the burden decreased, with the average level of 5.02% between 2000 and 2002, ranking the fourth highest among the ten villages. The fourth was the Hebian Village of Lishui, with an average degree of 3.93% in 17 years, which remained comparatively stable during the whole observation period, between 3.4 and 4.3%. The fifth was Miaoyan Village in Yinxian County, with an average burden of 3.67% in 17 years. During the whole observation period, the burden of Miaoyan Village showed a slow downward trend, which dropped to 2.77% between 2000 and 2002. The sixth was Yubei Village in Jiaxing, with an average burden of 3.53% in 17 years, and its change in the whole observation period also showed a slow downward trend, which dropped to 3.07% during the period between 2000 and 2002. The seventh was Xinmin Village in Wenling, with an average burden of 3.16% in 17 years. During the whole observation period, the change of the burden degree showed a trend of a 'U'-shape. From 2000 to 2002, the burden degree rose to 3.84%, which was 1.65% higher than the level of 2.19% during the Ninth Five-Year Plan period. The eighth was Xishufu village in Shaoxing, with an average burden of 3.14% in 17 years. Its change in the whole observation period showed a marked upward trend. Before 1995, the average degree was only 0.99%. During the Ninth Five-Year Plan period, it rose to 2.16%. In the 2000s, it further increased to 5.66%, with an average increase of 3.50% compared with the Ninth

Five-Year Plan period. It made this village one of those with the heaviest burdens among the ten observed villages, ranking the third highest in the ten villages. The ninth was Jinhou Village in Rui'an, with an average burden of 2.98% in 17 years. The trend of change during the whole observation period was identical with that of Bogumen Village, which showed the shape of an inverted 'U', but the magnitude was much lower. Between 2000 and 2002, the average burden was 2.70%, 1.14% lower than that of 3.84% during the Ninth Five-Year Plan period. It was also one of the villages with the lowest burden, ranking the ninth highest. The tenth was Shibanyan village in Jinhua, with an average burden of 2.07% in 17 years. The change during the whole observation period showed a downward trend, from 2.64% at the beginning of the observation to 1.85% at present. This village was also the one with the lowest burden among the ten villages in the whole observation period.

As far as the burden structure was concerned, the differences among villages were very obvious, and the changes over time were substantial (Table 6.9 and Fig. 6.9). In the whole observation period, Shibanyan Village in Jinhua had the highest level of fee burden, reaching 48.50% on average during the 17 years. It showed a continuous upward trend in the whole observation period, with 43.23% in the first five years and 65.73% between 2000 and 2002. It became the village with the highest fee burden in the ten villages under observation. The second was Yubei Village in Jiaxing, with an average of 47.25%. It was 36.30% in the initial five years of the observation. After that, it rose to the highest level of 70.71% in the Ninth Five-Year Plan. After 2000, it declined significantly to 22.75% for the period between 2000 and 2002. The third

Table 6.9 Tax and fee burden composition for rural households in different villages (%)

	LS	YF	YB	XSF	MY	XM	JH	BGM	HB	SBY
1986	10.25	0.25	24.13	26.00	22.31	3.52	23.58	18.87	70.96	67.54
1987	7.08	0.00	22.91	46.39	19.70	3.09	22.50	24.95	52.36	43.67
1988	16.52	0.00	21.37	29.60	27.73	3.04	2.83	0.42	22.34	21.46
1989	12.83	0.00	25.17	58.49	10.63	1.42	0.86	0.00	21.10	24.97
1990	16.59	1.05	55.67	64.35	0.41	0.00	43.13	0.00	21.84	54.34
1991	8.98	40.64	54.29	79.97	0.66	12.23	5.87	32.42	44.08	51.28
1993	11.84	23.88	74.67	62.04	10.86	0.00	0.46	19.22	71.44	47.21
1995	11.34	35.24	66.51	33.18	0.47	10.42	7.19	49.23	45.83	22.68
1996	13.41	18.31	69.59	18.56	0.92	0.68	42.52	28.31	5.74	39.07
1997	13.24	11.84	74.96	1.01	9.52	6.97	43.73	18.36	31.93	37.64
1998	13.79	37.83	71.64	2.92	9.43	0.00	14.18	21.84	9.24	27.20
1999	18.00	49.98	64.09	0.49	8.50	0.00	8.36	45.88	70.04	70.06
2000	11.32	72.46	78.62	0.27	2.18	16.12	9.55	32.84	6.92	71.27
2001	8.89	27.54	82.02	0.28	3.93	6.00	27.05	14.77	6.25	66.94
2002	14.30	58.79	8.03	0.18	8.60	4.91	16.46	67.32	0.00	55.28
2000–2002	11.01	43.51	22.75	0.23	4.53	7.52	17.47	43.67	4.01	65.73

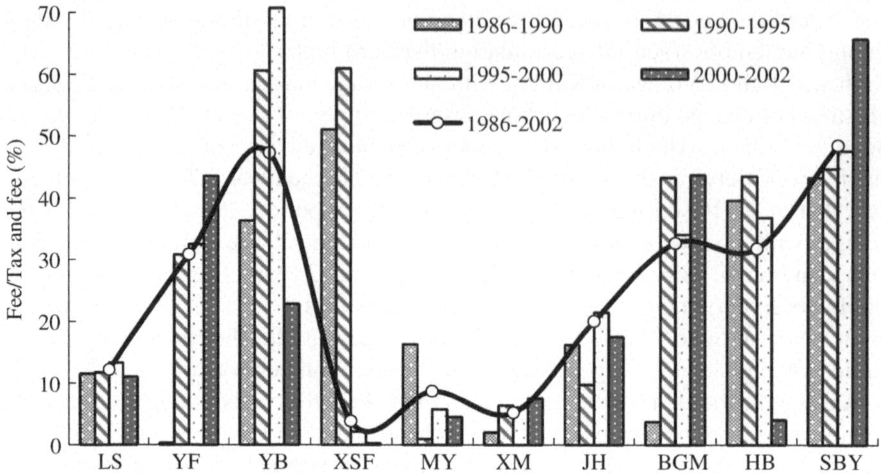

Fig. 6.9 Tax and fee burden composition for rural households in different villages

was Bogumen Village in Putuo, with an average level of 32.68%, which was 3.70% in the initial stage of the observation, but rose to 43.35% in the Eighth Five-Year Plan. During the Ninth Five-Year Plan period, it declined but rose again to the highest level of 43.67% from 2000 to 2002. It is also one of the villages with a high ratio of fee burden, ranked the second among the ten villages at present. The fourth was the Hebian Village of Lishui, with an average of 31.79%. During the whole observation period, it showed a process of rising first and then declining rapidly, from 43.49% in the period of the Eighth Five-Year Plan to 4.01% from 2000 to 2002, making it one of the villages with the heaviest tax burden, ranking the second among the ten villages in Zhejiang. The fifth was Yongfeng Village in Huzhou, with an average level of 30.81%. Its change in the whole observation period showed first a fast and then slow upward trend, rising from 0.30% in the first five years to 30.77% in the Eighth Five-Year Plan period, further to 32.50% in the Ninth Five-Year Plan period and 43.51% in the period between 2000 and 2002. It became one of the villages with a relatively high ratio of fee burden in Zhejiang, ranking the third in the ten villages. The sixth was Jinhou Village in Rui'an, with an average level of 20.02%. Its change showed a fluctuating upward trend, which dropped to 17.47% between 2000 and 2002. The seventh was Longshang Village in Lin'an, with an average level of 12.20%, which remained quite stable, with little change in the past 17 years. The eighth was Miaoyan Village in Yinxian County, with an average of 8.71%. Its change showed a 'U'-shape downward trend, from 16.27% in the first five years of observation to 4.53% at present. This also became one of the villages with the highest ratio of tax burden, ranked the third among the ten villages. The ninth was Xinmin Village in Wenling, with the level averaged 5.19%. Its change showed a slow upward trend, from 2.00% in the first five years of the observation to 7.52% at present. At the same time, Xinmin Village was one of the villages with burden mainly from taxes in the ten villages in Zhejiang during the entire observation period. The tenth was Xishufu village in Shaoxing, with an average level of 3.83%. Its change in the whole observation showed a significant downward trend, from 51.03% in the first five years of the observation to 0.23% at present. It became the village with the highest ratio of tax burden among the ten villages in Zhejiang.

6.2.5 *Tax and Fee Burden for Rural Households of Different Sizes*

I have discussed previously that there are two types of rural household burdens, one being collected based on economic income known as the 'tax' burden and the other collected according to household members or land area, known as the 'fee' burden. From the observation data of the ten villages in Zhejiang Province (Table 6.10 and Fig. 6.10), the relationship between the fee burden and rural household size over the 17 years showed an inverted 'U' shape. With the increase of the household population size, the fee burden showed a trend of initially rising before falling. In comparison, the fee burden for three-member households was the highest. A close observation

Table 6.10 The fee burden of rural households by size (%)

	Fee burden (yuan/person)					Tax and fee/current-year net income (%)				
	≤2	3	4	5	≥6	≤2	3	4	5	≥6
1986	15.26	10.19	9.26	5.88	9.60	3.50	4.72	4.28	4.40	4.94
1987	2.55	13.82	10.23	4.43	5.68	1.37	3.86	3.88	3.91	3.65
1988	4.13	10.48	8.27	2.60	2.85	1.28	3.36	4.14	2.46	2.33
1989	2.47	5.71	5.00	7.20	4.37	2.03	3.40	3.52	2.70	3.54
1990	7.11	10.93	11.37	9.78	12.08	1.60	4.33	3.49	2.63	2.34
1991	8.51	16.81	26.54	17.51	16.68	2.11	3.59	4.87	3.42	2.00
1993	18.27	17.78	40.68	12.88	16.42	2.33	2.09	4.31	3.64	1.43
1995	49.39	80.90	60.97	39.49	30.32	2.95	3.18	4.91	3.32	2.53
1996	59.34	41.51	41.70	65.93	74.13	1.94	2.22	2.84	3.93	3.42
1997	63.75	59.31	43.69	33.69	196.02	3.23	4.23	2.65	4.38	8.48
1998	54.23	37.31	37.74	35.36	29.28	2.03	3.10	3.58	2.11	2.77
1999	43.82	133.81	71.87	70.72	69.37	2.06	4.05	4.41	5.78	3.61
2000	41.32	56.34	62.76	51.77	48.16	1.68	3.29	4.32	4.21	4.77
2001	31.18	47.28	48.15	69.36	47.07	1.16	3.90	3.52	6.70	5.78
2002	37.61	109.66	31.14	51.66	46.17	1.23	5.86	4.90	4.12	9.48
2000–2002	36.68	70.68	47.33	57.74	47.24	1.37	4.31	4.28	5.04	6.28

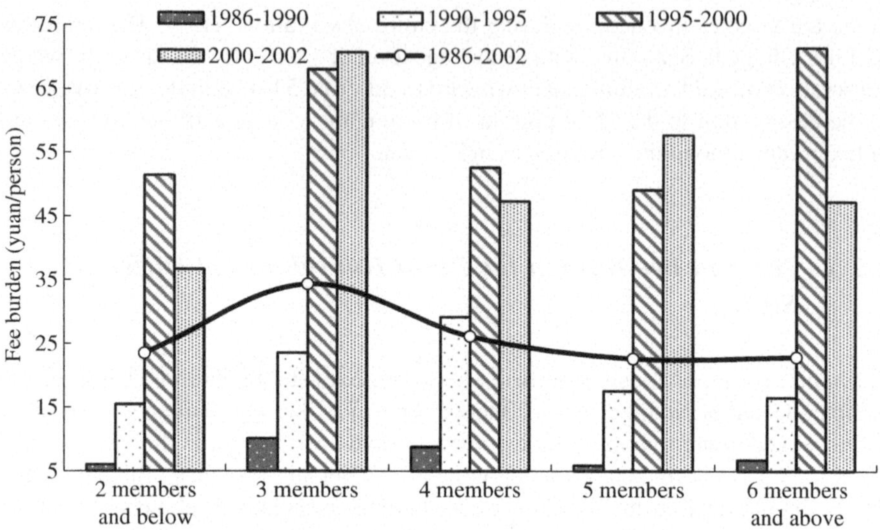

Fig. 6.10 Rural fee burden and household size

shows that the per capita burden difference of households of different sizes is not very obvious. In 17 years, the average level was 23.47 yuan for households with two members or less, 34.33 yuan for households with three members, 26.14 yuan for households with four members, 22.66 yuan for households with five members, and 22.91 yuan for households with six members and above, with the maximum difference of 12 yuan between the highest and the lowest. Even at present (2000–2002), the difference among various types of households is only 24 yuan, with the highest level of 70.68 yuan for households with three members, followed by the level of 57.74 yuan for households with five members, 47.33 yuan for households with four members, 47.24 yuan for households with six members and above, and the lowest level of 36.68 yuan for households with two members and below. This result shows that the fee burden of farmers in Zhejiang Province is indeed charged according to household members. For households with a low income level and a large population size, such collection is certainly a financial burden.

Influenced by the tax-based collection of burden in Zhejiang Province, farmers' burden is positively correlated with their household size (Table 6.10 and Fig. 6.11). In the entire 17-year observation process, except for the burden significantly lower for households with two members and below, the burden differences among the other four categories of households of different sizes are very small, and when the population increases, the household burden is slightly rising. During the 17 years, the average burden degrees were 1.93% for households with two members and below, 3.77% for households with three members, 3.94% for those with four members, 4.06% for those with five members, and 4.42% for those with six members and above, and the gap being 2.5% between the highest and the lowest. The observation data indicate that over time, the burden of households with two members and below showed an

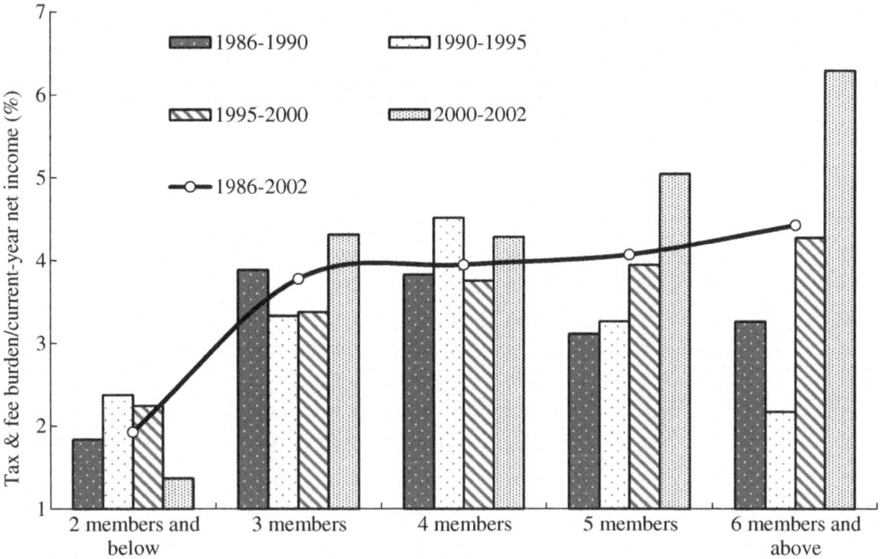

Fig. 6.11 Rural tax and fee burden and household size

inverted 'U'-shape downward trend, a decrease from 1.84% in the initial observation period to the current 1.37%; three-member households showed a 'U'-shape upward trend, an increase from 3.88 to 4.31%; four-member households showed a fluctuating upward trend, an increase from 3.82 to 4.28% at present; five-member households showed an upward trend, which was one of the categories with the highest increase from 3.10 to 5.04%, with an increase of nearly 2%; and households with six members and above showed an upward 'U'-shape trend, with the figure increased from 3.26 to 6.28%, which was also the household category with the heaviest burden.

6.2.6 Tax and Fee Burdens Among Rural Households with Different Social Political Status

It is found in previous studies that social and political status is an important source of inequality in economic development for rural household economy and is a key source of the increasing burden on farmers and of their corresponding complaints (Shi & Gu, 2003; Shi & Zhuo, 2003). Generally, the burden of prestigious rural households is relatively low, whereas that of ordinary households is the opposite, especially in economically underdeveloped areas where the burden is mainly from apportioned fees based on household members and land area. However, the situation was totally different in Zhejiang where the burden was mainly from tax collection. From the

Table 6.11 Rural burdens for households by status

	Tax and fee burden (yuan/person)				Tax and fee/current-year net income (%)			
	Carders	Party members	Carders and Party members	Ordinary	Carders	Party members	Carders and Party members	Ordinary
1986	129.56	73.10	151.36	33.54	11.29	7.43	13.47	3.99
1987	120.55	78.22	153.30	39.25	8.19	5.92	10.25	3.39
1988	17.54	41.68	16.38	47.53	1.03	2.42	0.89	3.25
1989	65.32	56.07	73.39	40.55	4.15	3.66	4.45	3.17
1990	73.90	88.83	83.88	41.47	4.29	5.01	4.59	2.96
1991	111.40	71.71	75.55	62.30	5.57	3.38	3.63	3.71
1993	116.05	105.10	138.79	99.70	3.26	2.51	3.49	3.37
1995	340.74	381.70	401.13	214.50	5.45	4.75	6.27	3.54
1996	286.09	264.57	266.92	200.56	4.62	2.59	4.32	2.95
1997	261.36	516.70	275.23	259.50	2.75	5.82	3.57	3.72
1998	260.69	222.75	288.39	205.14	3.05	2.74	3.66	3.00
1999	808.82	535.81	844.85	308.47	9.63	6.27	12.73	3.91
2000	888.05	460.78	521.73	310.43	5.62	4.08	5.18	3.63
2001	1122.07	472.86	553.14	389.13	5.54	3.98	4.97	4.47
2002	1619.51	709.23	1382.86	426.87	9.97	6.05	9.04	4.75
2000–2002	1176.02	539.64	736.62	375.41	6.77	4.64	6.30	4.29

observation data of the ten villages in Zhejiang Province (Table 6.11), the burden level of prestigious rural households was higher than that of ordinary households in most observation years. In 2000–2002, the average burden of cadre households reached 1176.02 yuan, and that of households with Party members reached 539.64 yuan, 213.26 and 43.74% higher than that of ordinary peasant households, a change by 117.96 and −23.38% compared with the levels of 95.30 and 67.13% in the first five years of observation. This result implies that cadres and Party members were the leading taxpayers in Zhejiang, a region with a relatively high degree of non-agriculturalisation and with the household burden mainly coming from tax collection. Although their income level was much higher than that of ordinary households, with the net per capita incomes of cadre households and Party member households as high as 17,365.37 and 11,618.91 yuan between 2000 and 2002, 98.46 and 32.79% higher than the level of 8749.89 yuan for ordinary households, their leading role in tax payment set up a model for the general public. They have been the real rural leaders to become better off as advocated by the government, in contrast with those in inland China (Shi & Gu, 2003; Shi & Zhuo, 2003).

Similarly, in terms of tax and fee burden (Fig. 6.12), in the ten villages in Zhejiang, the burden of ordinary farmers was the lowest, followed by Party member households and that for cadre households was the highest. During the 17-year observation, the average burden of cadre households was 5.65%, and that of Party member households was 4.41%, while that of ordinary rural households was only 3.68%. Although only

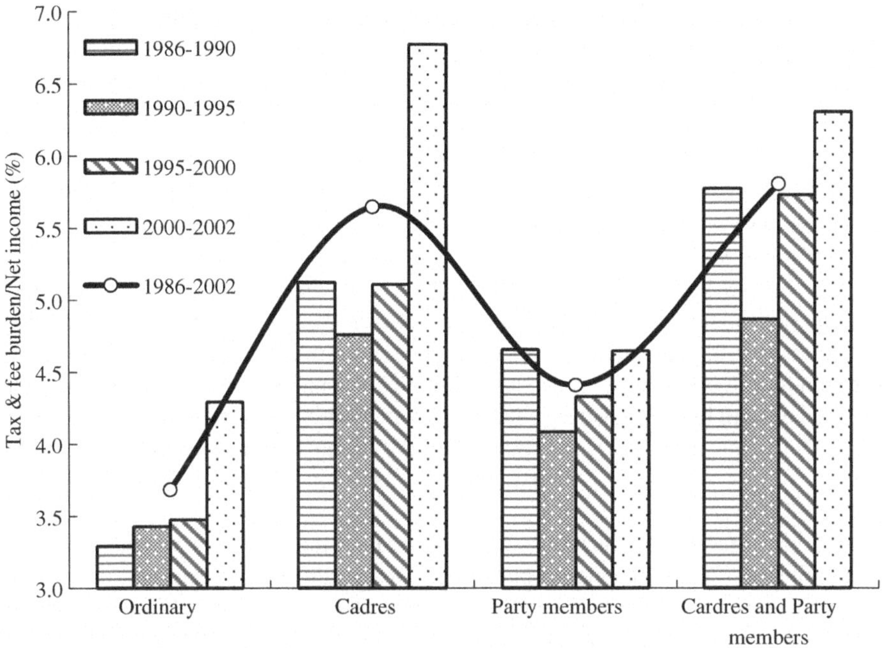

Fig. 6.12 Rural household tax and fee burdens and social status

the burden of ordinary households showed a continuous upward trend over time, with both cadre and Party member households showing a 'U'-shape trend. In 2000 to 2002, the heaviest burdened households were still cadre households with the level of 6.77%, followed by Party member households of 4.64%, and the average level for ordinary households was only 4.29%. This result shows once again that in rural Zhejiang, cadres and Party members took the lead in paying taxes and fees, and played an exemplary role. This also explains the reason as to why rural economy in Zhejiang has risen rapidly since the reform and opening up.

6.3 Origins of Increased Tax and Fee Burdens

The above analysis has helped for a better understanding about the changes in household tax and fee burdens, but to understand the causes of the rising tax and fee burdens, it is necessary to make further analysis concerning how the tax and fee burdens were used. Limited by data availability, analysis is made only concerning the village collective financial revenue and expenditure, as well as the tax composition.

6.3.1 *Village Collective Fiscal Revenue and Expenditure and Farmers' Contribution*

From Table 6.12 and Fig. 6.13, it can be seen that during the 17-year observation, the fiscal income of the ten villages and villages in Zhejiang showed a cyclical trend of falling and rising. It fell from 463,100 yuan in 1986 to 120,900 yuan in 1989, then increased until it reached the peak of 613,900 yuan in 1995, then kept falling and reached a low level of 290,700 yuan in 1999, but started to increase after 2000 to 327,900 yuan in 2002. In the fluctuations of fiscal income at the village level, the direct participation of farmers appeared to improve. Before 1997, the direct contribution of farmers to village finance was relatively low with just over 10% in 1993 and even less than that in other years. After 1997, the direct contribution of farmers to village financial growth began to rise significantly, from 11.44% in 1997 to 21.58% in 1999. In the following three years, although farmers' contribution appeared to declined slightly by less than 1.00%, their contribution remained at the level of 21% from 2000 to 2002.

In terms of farmers' contribution, there were two major types, *tiliu* and *tongchou*. Although there were changes in percentage shares during the observation period, the share of *tiliu* was generally higher than that of *tongchou*. By 2002, their shares were basically the same, each accounting for nearly 50%. As for the expenditure structure of rural households, on average *tiliu* and *tongchou* collected by the village collectives consisted of 60.51% of the total fee burden from 2000 and 2002, with the share of apportionment reaching 20.54%. Since 2000, the fee burden shouldered by Zhejiang farmers has changed significantly, with the obvious decline in the proportions of *tiliu* and *tongchou*, decreasing from 77.15% in 2000 to 43.52% in 2002, whereas the share of apportionment increased from 5.75% in 2000 to 30.13% in 2002. Thus, since 2000, in terms of collective financial growth, there were changes in farmers' contribution with a substantial increase in apportionment, although the overall contribution remained stable.

6.3.2 *Village Collective Fiscal Expenditure and Share Shouldered by Farmers*

Similarly, from Table 6.12 and Fig. 6.13, it can be seen that the changes in village-level financial expenditure was very consistent with that of income. In most of the 17 years of observation, the revenue level was in line with expenditure, and slightly higher. However, in 2001 and 2002, there was a serious deficit in village finance, which reached 151,100 and 112,300 yuan. To some extent, the village financial deficit is an important factor or source of farmers' increased burden. So why was there such a serious 'deficit'? In terms of the changes in financial expenditure composition, the share of farmers directly benefiting from collective services did not increase but declined, dropped from 14.50% in 1998 to 1.54% in 2002, while the share of

Table 6.12 Village fiscal income and its composition

	Income (10,000 yuan/village)	Farmers' contribution (%)	Composition (%)		Expenditure (10,000 yuan/village)	Composition (%)			
			Tiliu	*Tongchou*		Public affairs	Administration	#Cadres' subsidies	Household dividend
1986	46.31	1.25	–	–	51.39	8.36	1.83	1.42	3.01
1987	23.52	4.22	–	–	30.98	6.35	3.59	2.14	4.59
1988	14.96	3.81	–	–	13.51	23.47	7.07	5.41	10.00
1989	12.09	7.74	–	–	10.24	14.95	15.70	8.61	17.80
1990	16.58	7.20	–	–	14.20	15.64	14.03	8.13	13.65
1991	18.08	6.59	–	–	17.44	11.01	11.16	6.11	9.55
1993	26.25	11.10	70.72	14.68	24.70	27.72	14.01	4.73	13.69
1995	61.39	5.31	51.41	30.32	33.83	35.84	22.39	8.27	16.25
1996	52.63	5.77	31.54	39.51	46.33	38.17	16.77	6.93	10.32
1997	54.14	11.44	31.91	30.42	43.41	35.09	29.60	12.77	7.23
1998	36.30	15.57	36.99	22.41	30.65	36.20	29.28	15.65	14.50
1999	29.07	21.58	48.42	32.39	35.71	31.30	33.93	12.48	12.27
2000	31.96	21.82	47.89	49.22	30.82	31.45	33.65	11.16	9.78
2001	32.96	21.34	51.64	48.36	48.07	33.82	24.83	10.62	4.44
2002	32.79	21.17	49.17	49.36	44.04	33.17	24.31	10.80	1.54

Note #as part of the previous category

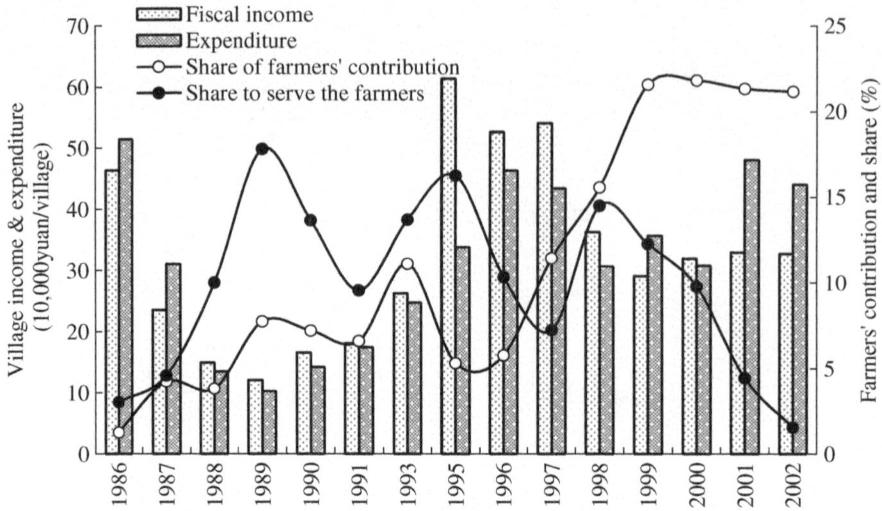

Fig. 6.13 Village income and expenditure in Zhejiang

village administrative expenditure increased significantly. At the beginning of the observation, such share only took up 1.83% of the financial expenditure at the village level. After ten years, it rose to 22.39% in 1995. After another four years, it rose further to 33.65% in 1999. Since then, it declined for three consecutive years, to 24.31% in 2002. Meanwhile, the subsidies for village cadres increased from 1.42% at the beginning of the observation to 15.65% in 1998, and then decreased to 10.80% in 2002. This result reflects to some extent that the expansion of village cadres and the improvement of their subsidies have been an important reason for the deficit in rural financial expenditure, which is also an important source of the farmers' rising fee burden.

6.4 Conclusion and Policy Implications

The multi-level structure of rural tax and fee burdens and their relationship with economic growth have not received sufficient attention. The empirical evidence of the ten villages in Zhejiang Province shows that the structural feature of 'taxes' and 'fees' not only lies in regional differences, but is also closely related to the changes in farmers' income and their status in economic development. Compared with the 'fee'-based structure in the inland China, rural burden in Zhejiang is dominated by 'tax' collection. The effect of the new rural tax-for-fee reform is very obvious in the hinterland, which is manifested in the substantial decrease of fee burden for farmers. However, the same reform has a relatively small impact on Zhejiang due to 'tax' collection. Comparing the changes in farmers' income in the process of economic development, and the tax and fee burden structure, it is found that at a certain income level, farmers' burden in Zhejiang increases with their income growth. For farmers with different income levels, there are also great differences in their household burden structure, with the burden for high-income households mainly from tax collection but that for the low-income households mainly from fee collection. Finally, the impact of social status (reputation) on farmers' tax and fee burden and its structure has also been analysed. The hinterland of China is dominated by fee collection, and the burden of prestigious households is lower than that of ordinary ones, while in Zhejiang province, the situation is the opposite. This result not only shows that Zhejiang has unique ways to deal with the burden of village cadres, but also forces the prestigious households to face the burden and become the leading taxpayers and contributors.

The study also shows that a detailed analysis of the structural characteristics of rural taxes and fees, and the relationships among various influencing factors has a strong empirical value, and provides policy implications for the ongoing rural tax and fee reform. The policy design of tax and fee reform should not only pay attention to the decline of the absolute level of farmers' tax and fee burden, but also highlight its structural adjustment, such as narrowing the differences of tax and fee burden among regions, reducing the burden of low-income farmers, controlling and correcting the negative impacts of social identity on farmers' burden.

References

Shi, Q. (1999). *Rural household economic development*. Beijing: China Agriculture Press.

Shi, Q. (2001). *Rural household economic activity and behaviour*. Beijing: China Agriculture Press.

Shi, Q. (2004). Rural household tax and fee burden and its changing trend. *Research on Development, 4*, 39–44.

Shi, Q., & Gu, H. (2003). Tax and fee burden of rural households and economic growth in China. *China Businees Review, 2*(2), 1–15.

Shi, Q., & Li, D. (2003). Trial implemtation of reform of tax and fee and its influence on peasants' burden. *Journal of South China Agricultural University (Social Science Edition), 2*(2), 1–11.

Shi, Q., & Zhang, G. (2003). Analysis of peasant on burden after reforming of tax and fee in Shanxi. *Issues in Agricultural Economy, 8*, 8–14.

Shi, Q., & Zhuo, J. (2003). *Well-off society and development of farmers, agriculture and the countryside*. Beijing: China Agriculture Press.

Chapter 7
Changes in Rural Expenditure

Contents

In daily economic life, consumers are one of the major decision-making units. Their spending or buying activities are known as consumer behaviour in economics. The changes in consumer behaviour is an important part of economic research. A consumer does not usually refer to just an individual person, but also a family

Q. Shi and Y. Gao, *Sustainable Development of Rural Household Economy*,
https://doi.org/10.1007/978-981-15-2747-0_7

(Mansfield, 1992). Such a family usually exists in the form of a household in the countryside. Since the reform and opening up, as an expanded family in rural areas, a rural household's economic behaviour has changed from the most basic decision-making unit in simple consumption in the collective-farming period to the most fundamental economic decision-making unit in the integration of production and consumption. It is of great practical significance to study the changes in the economic behaviour of this decision-making unit, especially how the changes will initiate the rural consumer market so as to develop appropriate economic policies. This chapter focuses on the consumption of rural households and their members. The research objects are the ten villages under follow-up observation in Zhejiang, and the research time span is from 1986 to 2002.

7.1 Nominal Consumption and Its Changes

To study the consumer behaviour of rural households, the consumption level and its composition are the fundamental of the research. The consumption level can usually be measured in value and quantity. Generally speaking, the consumption level reflected in value is the nominal consumption level, and the level reflected by quantity is the actual consumption level. The determination of the consumption level can be based on nominal levels, such as the Engel coefficient, with the higher value indicating the lower level, and vice versa; it can also be based on actual levels, such as the quantity of food and durable goods consumed, with more consumption indicating the higher level and vice versa. These two types of indicators in the study of consumer behaviour are often complementary. However, due to the high comprehensiveness, nominal consumption is mostly used in some advanced research on consumer behaviour, such as the study of consumption function.

7.1.1 Changes in Nominal Consumption

As can be seen from Table 7.1 and Fig. 7.1, since 1986, the per capita nominal consumption level of rural households in the ten villages in Zhejiang has shown a periodic upward trend. Before 1988, per capita consumption was less than 1000 yuan, which increased to over 1000 yuan and reached 1304.02 yuan in 1988. The level exceeded 2000 yuan, to 2517.03 yuan in 1993, and further exceeded 5000 yuan, to 5303.32 yuan, which fluctuated between 5000 and 6000 yuan in the next years and exceeded 6000 yuan, to 6615.57 yuan in 2002. Such a level has increased by 24.74% compared with 1995, or 10.45% if compared with 2001. By comparing income and expenditure (Fig. 7.1), it can be clearly found that the staged changes in living expenditure for rural households have been directly related to their changes in income. In other words, the income budget has a great influence on consumption growth.

Table 7.1 Rural household per capita expenditure and its structural change (current price)

	Living expenditure	Cash	A. Living items	Food	Clothes	Housing	Fuel	Necessities	B. Service	Savings*	Income
	100 yuan	%	%	%	%	%	%	%	%	100 yuan	100 yuan
1986	7.18	80.04	96.29	46.22	7.88	26.63	3.18	10.72	3.71	3.51	8.62
1987	8.48	83.91	95.97	44.95	7.23	27.06	2.74	12.17	4.03	5.86	11.82
1988	13.04	86.25	95.39	39.16	5.73	33.53	2.16	13.28	4.61	7.68	14.89
1989	12.36	84.40	94.85	45.33	5.91	28.71	2.51	10.92	5.15	8.22	13.07
1990	11.60	82.65	93.66	50.89	7.35	20.43	2.88	10.76	6.34	10.40	14.44
1991	13.74	84.52	93.41	46.12	7.23	24.81	2.56	11.43	6.59	12.02	17.30
1993	25.17	87.49	88.87	41.81	7.67	24.96	2.20	12.23	8.15	15.46	31.10
1995	53.03	90.56	88.16	33.11	6.52	35.67	1.40	11.46	9.61	29.05	63.51
1996	58.65	91.99	86.72	33.61	6.38	34.77	1.36	10.61	10.94	34.13	73.24
1997	58.69	90.14	85.74	35.52	5.42	26.82	1.35	16.62	12.22	44.53	74.25
1998	53.25	84.27	81.65	39.47	6.01	22.10	1.41	12.66	16.62	56.92	71.22
1999	53.04	88.53	80.42	38.31	5.32	22.95	1.46	12.37	17.61	78.49	81.13
2000	57.52	92.55	79.39	34.75	5.37	24.13	1.51	13.63	16.73	94.33	93.81
2001	59.90	88.25	79.26	34.08	5.33	29.63	1.38	8.84	19.16	112.64	97.31
2002	66.16	88.11	76.67	31.56	5.21	27.43	1.24	11.23	20.95	130.58	95.40

Note There was no regular investigation in 1992 and 1994. Same below. *Savings include cash in hand and deposit balance by the year end

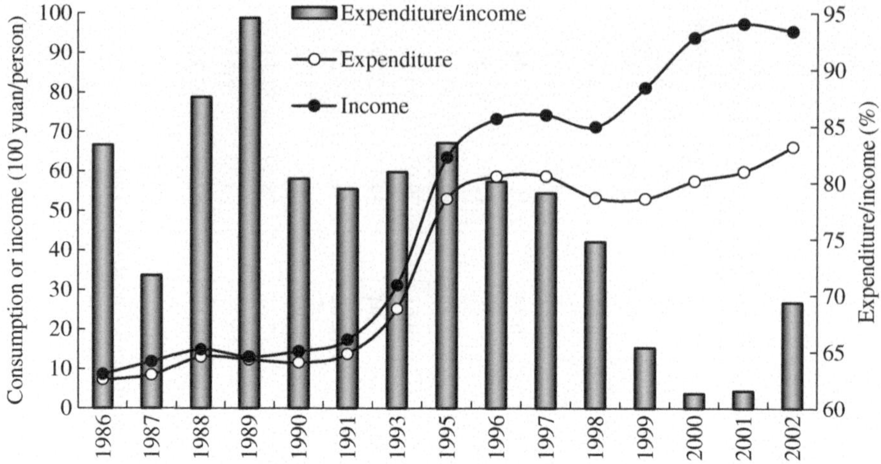

Fig. 7.1 Rural household consumption and its change

The main factors affecting the improvement of rural households' current-year consumption are not only current-year income, but also expected future income, previous-year income (savings) and consumption inertia. During 1986–1988, the annual growth rates of rural per capita net income and savings were 31.43 and 47.92%, and the annual growth rate of per capita living expenditure was 34.76%, with the growth rate of consumption 3.34% faster than that of income, but 13.16% slower than that of savings. From 1988 to 1991, the corresponding annual growth rates became 5.13, 16.10 and 1.76% respectively when consumption growth became slower, which was 3.37% lower than that of income, and 14.35% lower than that of savings. From 1991 to 1996, the annual growth rates of household income, savings and consumption were 33.46, 23.21 and 33.68%. Consumption growth increased again at a faster rate, 0.22 and 10.47% faster than those of income and savings. From the period of 1996–2001, consumption growth fell sharply again, with an annual growth rate reduced to 0.42%, while the growth rates of income and savings changed by 5.85 and 26.97% (Fig. 7.2). It was not until 2002 that this downturn in consumption growth was restored. Compared with 2001, consumption level increased by 15.02% in 2002, while income and savings increased by 1.69 and 38.43% in the same period. This result has also reflected to some extent that in the middle and late 1990s, the stagnated income of the rural households in the ten villages had a long-term impact on consumption growth. However, since the 2000s, with the constant increase of income, rural consumption has entered a new phase of growth.

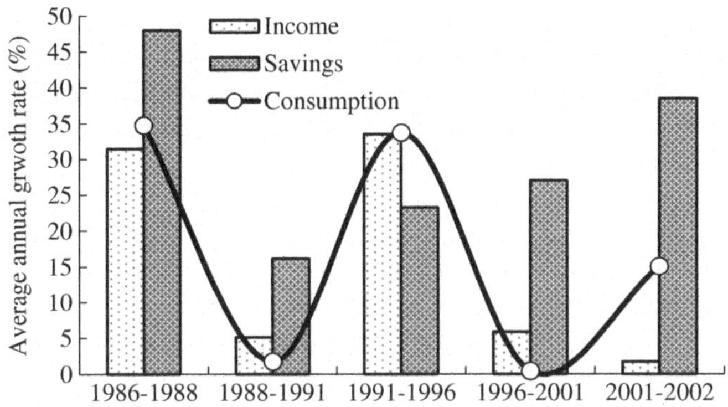

Fig. 7.2 Staged changes in rural household consumption in Zhejiang

7.1.2 Changes in Consumption Structure

From Fig. 7.3 and Table 7.1, it can be seen that the main trend of consumption structure of the rural households in the ten villages in Zhejiang over the past 17 years has been the continuous decline of living necessities out of total consumption, in addition to the rapid increase of service consumption. The cash consumption, or the market dependence to be specific, has shown a fluctuating upward trend. From the perspective of household consumption structure, living goods consumption is the main item. By 2002, household living goods and service consumption accounted for 76.67 and 20.95% of total household expenditure, with the decline and rise of 19.62

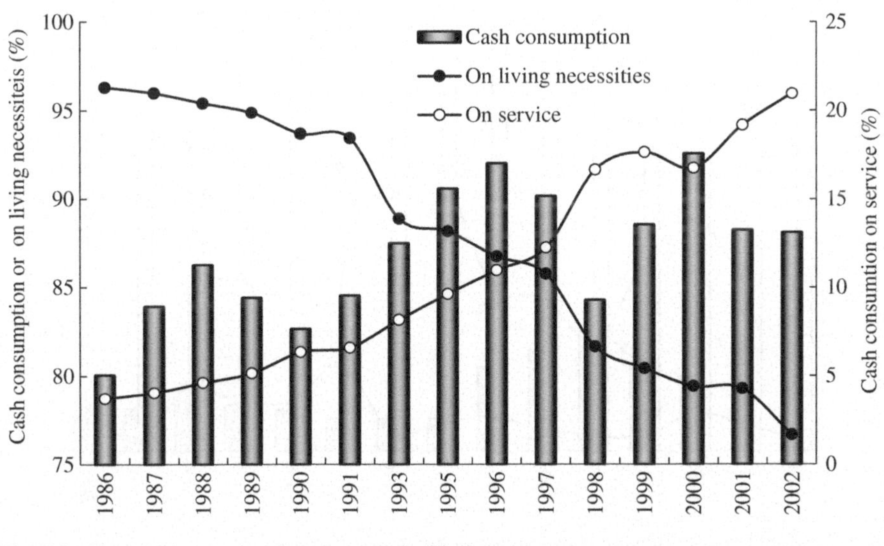

Fig. 7.3 Changes in consumption structure in Zhejiang

and 17.24% compared with the corresponding levels of 96.29 and 3.71% in 1986, or with the decline and rise of 11.49 and 11.34% compared with the levels in 1995, and with the decline and rise of 2.72 and 4.22% when compared with the levels in 2000. It can be seen that the changes in household consumption in the ten villages of Zhejiang have been accelerating. In the course of this rapid change, rural households' cash consumption declined twice, one from 1988 to 1991, and the other from 1996 to 1998. During these two declining periods, the growth of household income was very slow. This result shows that when the change of household consumption structure demonstrates a continuous stable trend, the degree of dependence on the market becomes directly related to the change in income expectation. When income expectation falls, households tend to be more self-sufficient in consumption, while when income expectation rises, the degree of dependence on the market tends to rise also.

From the perspective of consumption structure and consumption changing trend of rural households, food is still the major expenditure item, followed by housing, daily supplies, clothing and fuels. In 2002, food consumption accounted for 41.16%, clothing 6.80%, housing 35.78%, fuels 1.62%, and supplies 14.65% of total consumption. There were changes of −7.68, −1.53, 7.64, −1.74 and 3.32% compared with the numbers in 1986, or 3.61, −0.60, −4.68, 0.03 and 1.65% compared with 1995. When compared with 2000, the changes were −2.61, 0.03, 5.38, −0.28 and −2.52% respectively. It can be seen that the sharp decline in the share of household living necessities was food before 1995 and housing after 1995. It is seen clearly from Fig. 7.4 that in the composition of rural household living consumption, the shares of various types of expenditure items fluctuated with some rising and the others falling.

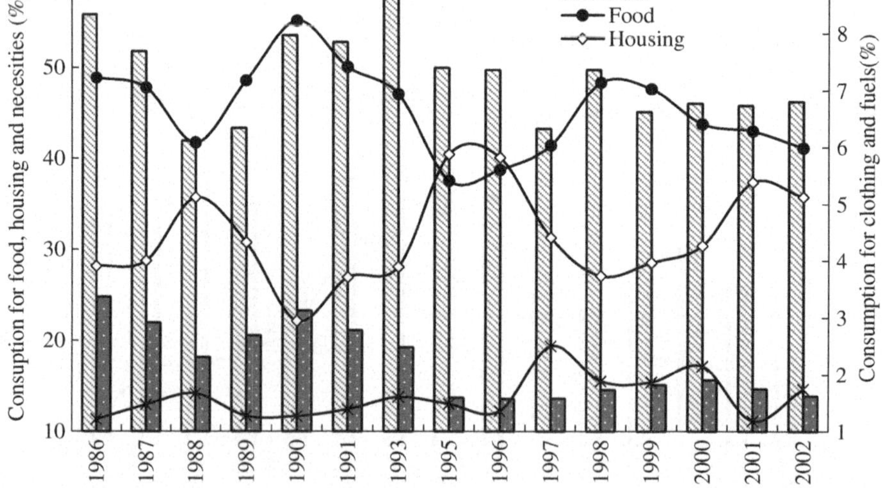

Fig. 7.4 Rural household living consumption in Zhejiang

Of course, when food consumption declines, housing and supplies consumption rise, and the three items have become the foundation of changes in living consumption. Although the shares of clothing and fuel consumption have also changed considerably, they have little impact on the changes of living consumption as a whole. This result shows that the overall living standard of rural households has been significantly improved, and the problem of insufficient food and clothing has been solved. The well-off and affluent consumption represented by housing, entertainment and service expenditures has emerged and started to dominate rural household consumption. In general, Zhejiang rural households' living consumption has been characterised by enjoyment or entertainment consumption.

7.1.3 *Consumption for Major Living Items and the Changing Trend*

7.1.3.1 Food Consumption and Its Composition

It can be seen from Table 7.2 and Fig. 7.5 that, in terms of food consumption, although the proportion of household expenditure on food is declining, the total value consumed has shown a periodic upward trend. In the early stage of the observation in 1986, the per capita food expenditure of the ten villages in Zhejiang was 331.87 yuan, which increased to 2088.08 yuan in 2002, more than two and half times increase

Table 7.2 Per capita living consumption of rural households in Zhejiang (current price)

	Food	#Cash consumption	Staple food	Non-staple food	Eating out	Housing	Necessities	#Durable goods
	yuan	%	%	%	%	yuan	yuan	%
1986	331.87	68.10	31.88	49.54	–	191.17	76.99	63.44
1987	381.35	71.26	28.20	55.44	–	229.60	103.22	73.78
1988	510.59	74.31	24.41	57.71	–	437.23	173.15	77.43
1989	560.14	72.48	26.66	54.92	–	354.80	134.94	71.84
1990	590.49	72.64	23.82	56.58	–	237.08	124.91	66.41
1991	633.78	72.76	22.83	57.24	–	340.98	157.12	71.27
1993	1052.44	74.89	20.96	67.12	11.92	628.21	307.71	69.47
1995	1755.67	76.28	22.55	65.55	10.29	1891.72	607.54	73.44
1996	1971.08	78.91	19.88	67.25	12.79	2039.07	622.22	78.35
1997	2084.66	83.60	15.02	67.30	16.68	1573.99	975.61	82.43
1998	2101.76	82.13	15.51	65.85	18.04	1176.84	673.95	74.89
1999	2031.75	85.28	13.66	65.88	19.55	1217.41	656.25	70.95
2000	1998.91	86.32	12.44	66.72	20.76	1388.02	784.23	65.59
2001	2040.99	88.07	11.57	64.97	23.32	1774.86	529.21	68.29
2002	2088.08	90.15	10.18	64.33	25.49	1814.58	742.87	71.06

Note "–"indicating no investigation was carried out. #indicating as part of the previous category

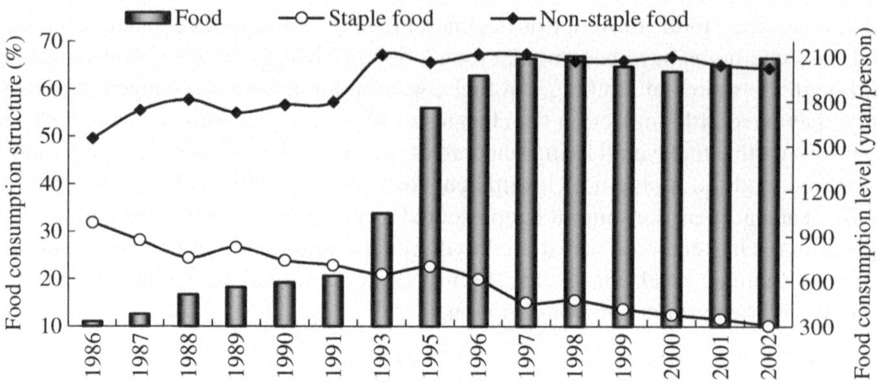

Fig. 7.5 Food consumption structure and its change in Zhejiang

over the 17 years, with an average annual growth rate of 11.43%. The fastest growth occurred during the period from 1991 to 1997, with an annual growth rate of 21.95%, which was 8% higher than the level of 13.81% between 1986 and 1991. By the mid and late 1990s, the growth of food consumption showed a marked slowing trend. From 1997 to 2002, household food consumption stagnated, with an average annual growth rate of only 0.03%. In food consumption, the dominant position of non-staple food has become more secured, and its share increased from 49.54% in 1986 to 64.33% in 2002, an increase of 14.80% in 17 years. On the contrary, staple food consumption showed a sharp downward trend, decreased by 21.69% over 17 years. At the same time, the share of expenditure on eating out also increased significantly, from 11.92% in 1993 to 25.49% in 2002. The share of cash consumption continued to rise, from less than 70% in the initial observation period to 90.15% in 2002. This result shows that with the improvement of consumption, household expenditure has undergone structural changes. One of the changes is that consumption has become more dependent on the market, and commodity consumption has become an important trend for rural households while self-sufficient food consumption is declining. Another change is that consumption is mainly based on non-staple food, and this pattern gradually strengthens. The food consumption of rural households in the ten villages in Zhejiang is substantially different from that in the hinterland.[1] Although the trend is similar, the main and subsidiary food consumption structure is reversed. This fully indicates that rural households in Zhejiang have departed from self-sufficient production and embarked on a way of meeting their living needs by relying on the market.

[1]According to the observation in ten villages in Shanxi, in 1986, household food consumption was 62.50% for staple food and 27.23% for non-staple food, including 41.64% of cash consumption. By 2000, the structure became 51.49% for staple food and 41.30% for non-staple food, with cash consumption taking 61.51% (Shi, Wang, & Shen, 2000). In 2002, staple food accounted for 47.13%, and non-staple food accounted for 42.97% of total consumption, of which cash consumption taking 53.72%.

7.1.3.2 Housing Consumption and Its Change

In terms of housing, per capita housing expenditure showed a fluctuating upward trend (Table 7.2). In 1986, the average level of the ten villages in Zhejiang was 191.17 yuan, which continued to rise to 437.23 in 1988. After that, it declined to 237.08 yuan in 1990, then rose again, reaching a peak level of 2039.07 yuan in 1996, before it declined again until 1998 when it began to rise slowly. After 2000, the growth rate accelerated noticeably, and by 2002, per capita housing consumption rose to 1814.58 yuan, 30.73% higher than in 2000, which was close to the level in the mid-1990s. Obviously, the changing trend was related to the growth of household income. Income growth has directly influenced the investment in construction of new houses for rural households. In the 17 years of observation, the largest per capita newly-added housing area occurred in 1995, reaching 3.65 m^2, and the lowest level was 1.15 m^2 in 1999. In addition to income, the construction cost was also one of the important factors promoting the improvement of housing consumption for rural households (Fig. 7.6). At the beginning of the observation, the cost per square metre was 74.25 yuan, which rose to 124.19 yuan in 1990, an increase of 67.25%. After five years, the cost of rural housing rose to 563.06 yuan, with an increase of 353.38% compared with 1990. Up until 2000, the cost of rural housing climbed to the highest level since the observation, reaching 792.67 yuan/m^2, with an average increase of 40.78% compared with 1995. After 2000, the rising cost was under control and the cost dropped continuously. Until 2002, the rural housing cost dropped to 503.85 yuan/m^2, with a decrease of 36.44% compared with the level in 2000. There might be a few reasons for the decline of housing cost. In my opinion, one important reason is that the implementation of Zhejiang rural housing construction plan since the reform and opening up came to an end. The housing area was nearing

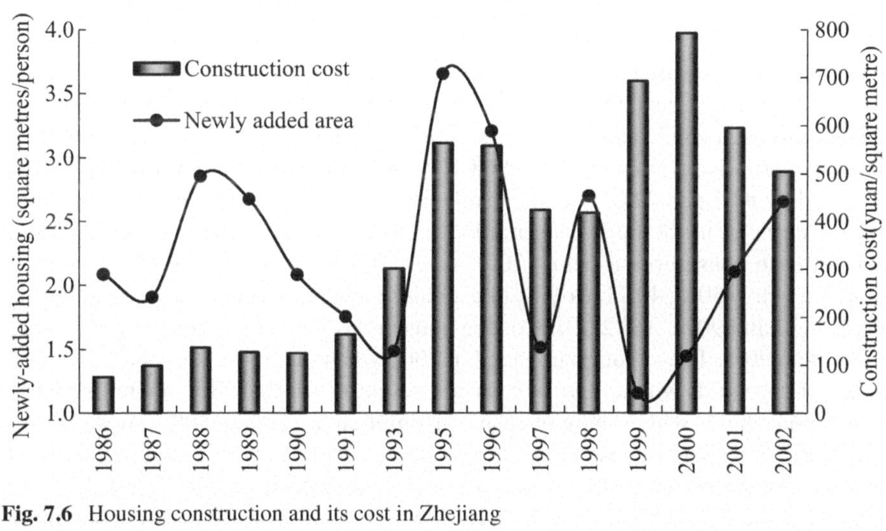

Fig. 7.6 Housing construction and its cost in Zhejiang

the upper limit according to the plan. By 2002, the per capita housing area of the ten villages in Zhejiang reached 47.89 m^2, which was 23.35 m^2 larger than 24.54 m^2 in 1986, with an increase of 95.15%. This result shows that the living standard of farmers has improved significantly. At the same time, it can be seen that housing consumption is affected by many factors and has shown strong volatility.

7.1.3.3 Consumption of Necessities and Its Structural Change

In terms of daily necessities, the trend of per capita consumption was basically in line with the housing consumption, while the consumption value of daily necessities was much lower (Table 7.2). In 2002, the per capita consumption on daily necessities in the ten villages in Zhejiang was 742.87 yuan, with durable goods accounting for 71.06%, increased to 8.65 times and by 7.62% compared with the levels of 76.99 yuan and 63.44% in the beginning of the observation. From the perspective of the whole changing trend, it is seen that durable goods consumption was the majority, but after a period of continuous growth, it started to decline for several consecutive years since 1997, and its share in total consumption decreased from 82.43 to 65.59% in 2000 which is a decrease of 16.84% within those three years. After 2000, this downward trend began to reverse. By 2002, the proportion of durable goods consumption rose back to 71.06%. This result shows that the status of traditional durable goods in the ten villages in Zhejiang started to decline, as the demand for household appliances tends to become saturated, which is then replaced by consumption of new durable goods for ordinary households such as computers and cars.

7.1.4 The Marketisation Process of Consumption Change

Data from the 17 years of follow-up observation have shown that rural household consumption has depended more on market (Table 7.3 and Fig. 7.7). In terms of consumption as a whole and food consumption, the shares of cash consumption fluctuated upward, rising from 80.04 and 68.10% in 1986 to 88.11 and 90.15% in 2002, increased by 8.07 and 22.05% respectively. From the distribution of cash consumption for farmers, in the initial observation period, 32.92% of the households had a share of cash consumption below 70%, where 9.81% of this group had cash consumption below 50%; 40.71% of the households had their share of cash consumption between 70 and 90%; and 27.01% of the households had a cash consumption share higher than 90%. The situation changed in 2002 when the figure dropped to 10.60% for rural households with a share of cash consumption less than 70%, including 6.6% of such households with a share of cash consumption lower than 50%. Those households with their share of cash consumption between 70 and 90% took up 23.80% of the total. Compared with 1986, the above three figures decreased by 21.69, 3.21 and 16.91%, while the percentage of households with their share of cash consumption

Table 7.3 Rural household distribution of cash consumption in Zhejiang (%)

	Cash consumption on living/living consumption (%)					Cash consumption on food/food consumption (%)				
	<50	50–70	70–80	80–90	≥90	<50	50–70	70–80	80–90	≥90
1986	9.81	22.48	19.80	20.91	27.01	22.31	32.59	15.56	12.59	16.94
1987	6.36	26.50	15.69	20.23	31.21	24.06	28.77	13.16	11.60	22.32
1988	2.94	18.93	20.57	24.63	32.93	18.25	30.28	16.52	13.67	21.28
1989	4.63	20.44	20.10	27.42	27.42	16.40	31.96	16.82	17.33	17.49
1990	5.97	23.47	20.07	23.88	26.62	17.83	32.01	16.50	18.49	15.17
1991	4.33	23.70	20.33	23.01	28.63	17.82	32.53	16.70	15.31	17.65
1993	5.00	19.20	18.80	23.20	33.80	18.00	29.20	15.00	16.20	21.60
1995	2.80	15.20	18.00	24.60	39.40	17.00	29.00	14.80	13.20	26.00
1996	2.40	13.00	14.20	22.20	48.20	13.00	31.00	10.80	16.40	28.80
1997	5.61	8.62	13.23	23.45	49.10	8.82	24.85	16.23	17.23	32.87
1998	6.80	8.80	12.80	24.60	47.00	9.80	23.40	16.00	20.00	30.80
1999	6.60	8.00	9.20	24.20	52.00	4.80	21.40	16.80	21.60	35.40
2000	3.81	3.41	8.22	21.64	62.93	5.21	14.43	17.84	22.85	39.68
2001	7.78	4.59	8.78	20.56	58.28	2.79	17.17	13.37	22.55	44.11
2002	6.60	4.00	6.80	17.00	65.60	3.60	10.00	13.20	20.80	52.40

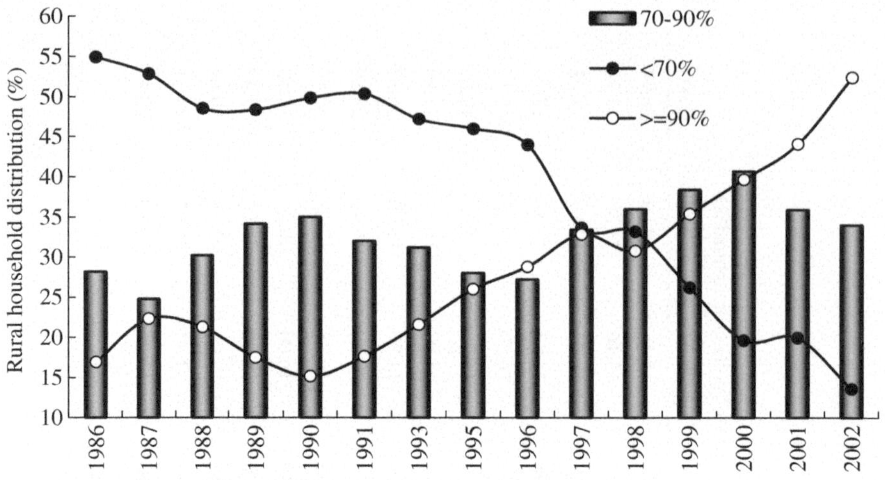

Fig. 7.7 Rural household distribution by cash consumption

higher than 90% rose to 65.60%, an increase of 38.59% compared with the initial observation period.

In terms of cash consumption on food (Table 7.3 and Fig. 7.8), the marketisation trend is more evident. In the mid-1980s, 54.90% of the observed rural household had a share of cash consumption below 70%, including 22.31% of the households below 50%, while 45.09% of the rural households had a share of cash consumption higher than 70%, including 16.94% of the households over 90%. In 2002, the

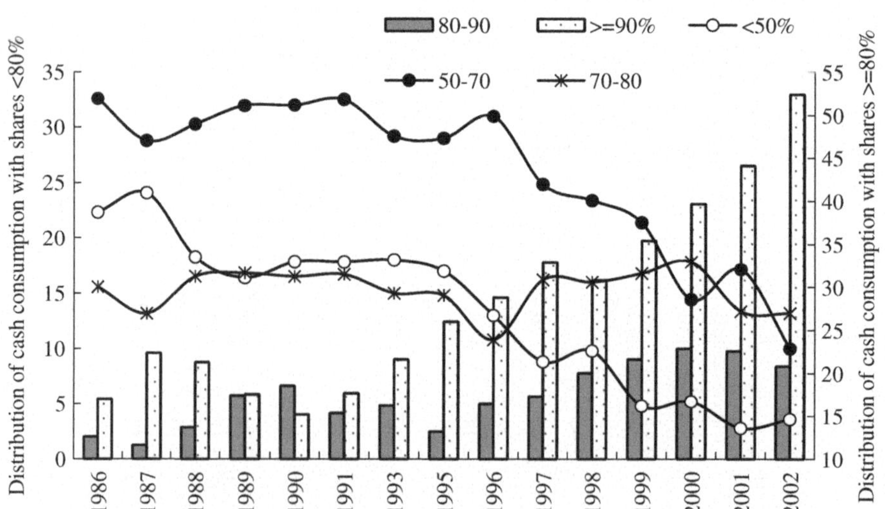

Fig. 7.8 Distribution of cash consumption on food in Zhejiang

structure changed in that the percentage decreased to 13.60% for the rural households with their share of cash consumption below 70%, and the corresponding figure decreased to 3.60% for those with the share less than 50%, with drops of 41.30 and 18.71% respectively compared with the initial observation period. On the contrary, the percentage increased to 86.40% for the rural households with their share of cash consumption higher than 70%, and the corresponding figure increased to 52.40% for those with the share higher than 90%, up 41.30 and 35.46% respectively compared with the initial observation period. This result shows that the living consumption for the rural households in the ten villages in Zhejiang is more influenced by the marketisation process, and the consumption of self-sufficiency has played a less important role in rural life.

7.1.5 Distribution of Households with Different Consumption Levels

Since consumption level is affected by prices in different periods, the consumption quality will be different at the same nominal consumption level. In order to reduce such an impact, the years from 1995 to 2002 are selected to make a comparative analysis as there were smaller changes in price during these years.[2]

In the analysis of consumption and income changes of the ten villages in Zhejiang, it has been mentioned several times that during the years between 1995 and 2002, the changes in rural household income and consumption growth were characterised by stagnated development before a rapid increase, and also by the rapidly widening gap between consumption and income growth. In other words, the stagnated growth of consumption sustained longer than that of income. Due to the double influence of stagnated consumption inertia and income budget, great changes took place in the distribution of rural households at different consumption levels. The percentage of low-consuming rural households decreased rapidly, where the number for middle-level consuming households was on the rise and that for high-consuming households remained roughly stable with a slight decline. From Table 7.4 and Fig. 7.9, it can be seen that the distributions of rural households with per capita living consumption less than 2000 yuan, and between 2000 and 3000 yuan showed significant decreasing trends, with decreases of 5.00 and 7.60% respectively in the past eight years, whereas the distribution of households with per capita living consumption between 6000 and 10,000 yuan showed a significant upward trend, with an increase of 9.00%. The distribution of rural households with per capita living consumption over 10,000 yuan also showed an upward trend, which reached 13.00% in 2002 with an increase of 3.60% compared with that in 1995. These changes indicate that the consumption growth is not completely in line with the income growth. Usually, the response to

[2]During the Ninth Five-Year Plan period, the retail price index of Zhejiang Province changed from 105.8 in 1996 to 100.3 in 1997, 98.4 in 1998, 97.7 in 1999, 99.0 in 2000, 98.1 in 2001 and 98.7 in 2002. Zhejiang Statistical Yearbook 1996–2002.

Table 7.4 Distribution of rural households with different consumption levels in Zhejiang 1995–2002 (%)

(1000 yuan)	1995	1996	1997	1998	1999	2000	2001	2002	1995–02
<2	18.60	12.80	14.43	14.20	14.60	13.63	13.97	13.60	19.89
2–3	29.20	26.60	21.84	23.40	22.80	20.84	24.15	20.60	23.16
3–4	17.40	21.20	21.24	21.00	18.80	23.65	18.76	16.80	18.47
4–5	9.00	12.00	12.63	11.60	14.40	11.62	12.18	12.80	11.02
5–6	7.00	5.00	7.62	6.80	7.80	7.41	6.59	9.40	6.62
6–7	2.80	4.80	4.81	4.20	6.00	5.81	5.39	5.60	4.53
7–8	3.60	2.80	3.21	2.00	4.00	4.01	3.19	4.40	3.09
8–10	2.80	4.80	5.01	7.00	3.00	3.61	3.99	3.80	3.87
10–20	5.60	7.00	5.01	6.00	6.00	6.61	7.19	8.20	5.96
20–50	3.00	2.20	3.41	3.40	2.00	2.00	3.39	3.40	2.60
50+	1.00	0.80	0.80	0.40	0.60	0.80	1.20	1.40	0.80

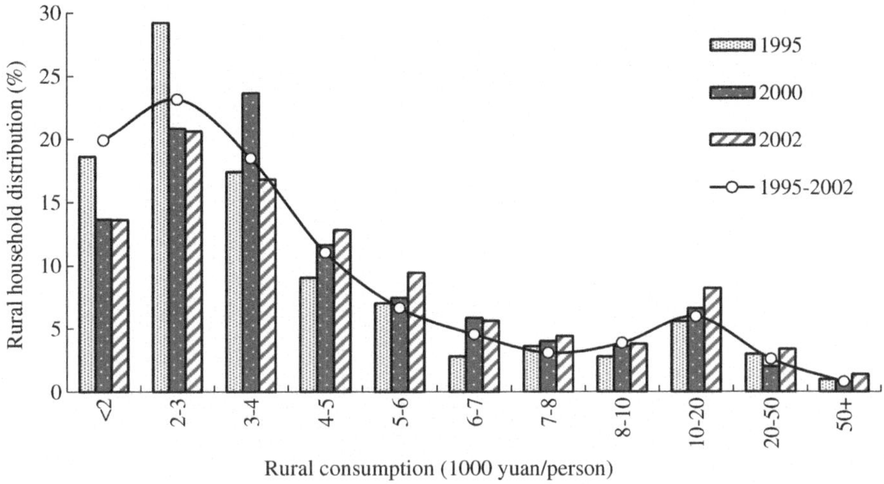

Fig. 7.9 Household distribution by consumption level in Zhejiang

the changes in consumption obviously lags behind the income growth. Only when the income expectation is stable will the consumption of rural household stabilise. Otherwise, once the income growth slows down, there will be a quick response in consumption. However, when income growth speeds up, there is a certain delay in the response of consumption.

7.2 Rural Household Real Consumption and Its Change

In the study of consumption, nominal consumption is certainly important, but real consumption is more essential. To some extent, the changes in real consumption can reflect the true facts of different consumers more clearly.

7.2.1 Household Food Consumption and Its Change

As can be seen from Table 7.5, with the development of society and the changes of the times, rural reform has indeed helped to improve the quality of life significantly for Chinese people. The raw grain consumption has dropped substantially, with rural household per capita consumption decreased from 282.39 kg in the mid-1980s to 176.35 kg in 2002, a decrease of 37.55%. In raw grain consumption, the traditional structure of self-sufficiency production has been greatly changed, and the proportion of grain purchase increased significantly, from 19.44% in 1986 to 39.79% in 2002.

Table 7.5 Rural household per capital food consumption in Zhejiang

	Raw grain	Purchase	Vegetable	Fruit	Edible oil	Meat	Pork	Egg	Fish	Sugar
	kg	%	kg	kg	kg	kg	%	kg	kg	kg
1986	282.39	19.44	94.66	21.71	6.52	18.42	83.92	2.60	11.83	4.46
1987	267.29	19.93	88.93	22.50	6.48	17.19	80.83	2.59	11.40	3.96
1988	270.45	21.21	89.42	21.62	6.34	17.15	80.33	2.86	11.71	3.70
1989	264.57	19.98	88.55	20.22	6.68	17.65	79.67	2.71	12.22	3.68
1990	246.93	17.70	90.28	21.87	7.49	17.16	80.38	2.91	12.93	3.76
1991	252.54	16.17	90.93	27.64	7.59	17.90	79.52	3.42	12.68	3.68
1993	237.56	20.67	96.79	28.77	8.13	20.66	76.72	4.10	13.81	3.66
1995	229.07	25.41	89.02	32.87	9.15	22.61	74.60	4.19	16.91	4.25
1996	230.20	22.13	90.48	36.22	9.78	23.85	68.07	5.15	19.91	3.90
1997	230.21	24.37	92.23	37.39	9.76	23.06	67.15	5.15	19.03	3.66
1998	224.13	25.92	91.37	33.64	9.27	24.52	69.02	5.02	19.51	3.89
1999	219.68	29.42	88.59	32.67	9.61	24.24	70.41	5.33	19.63	3.73
2000	206.01	31.76	85.94	31.31	10.03	25.93	70.01	5.87	19.72	3.71
2001	193.53	34.90	87.95	34.45	9.53	23.21	67.98	5.33	18.58	3.24
2002	176.35	39.79	86.40	33.08	10.25	23.61	66.74	5.61	19.08	3.24

Non-staple food consumption such as meat and eggs increased significantly. Compared with 1986, per capita consumption of fruit, edible oil, meat, egg, as well as fish and shrimp increased by 52.37, 57.21, 28.18, 115.77 and 61.28%, respectively. In meat consumption, the traditional pork-based structure has also undergone a great change. The proportion of pork in meat consumption decreased from 83.92% in 1986 to 66.74% in 2002. The results show that the food consumption structure of rural households in the ten villages in Zhejiang has indeed experienced qualitative changes, so that the quality of life has also been improved significantly.

7.2.2 *Grain Consumption Structure and Its Change*

In order to further analyse the composition of rural household raw grain consumption, the survey data collected by Zhejiang Agricultural Investigation Team are used. By comparing Table 7.5 and Fig. 7.10, it can be seen that in terms of raw grain consumption, there are some differences between the household surveys carried out by Zhejiang Agricultural Investigation Team and those from the fixed observation sites in the ten villages in Zhejiang, but both have shown the same general trend. After the 15 years of development, raw grain consumption of rural households in the whole Zhejiang dropped significantly, showing a decrease of 24.98% over the past 17 years. Compared with the raw grain consumption of rural households in the observation sites, the provincial level of raw grain consumption was high and remains high, with a relatively smaller decline. Why? I believe it is related to the effect of the continuous follow-up observation. The long-term follow-up observation undoubtedly has an impact on the production and consumption of rural households. However, the

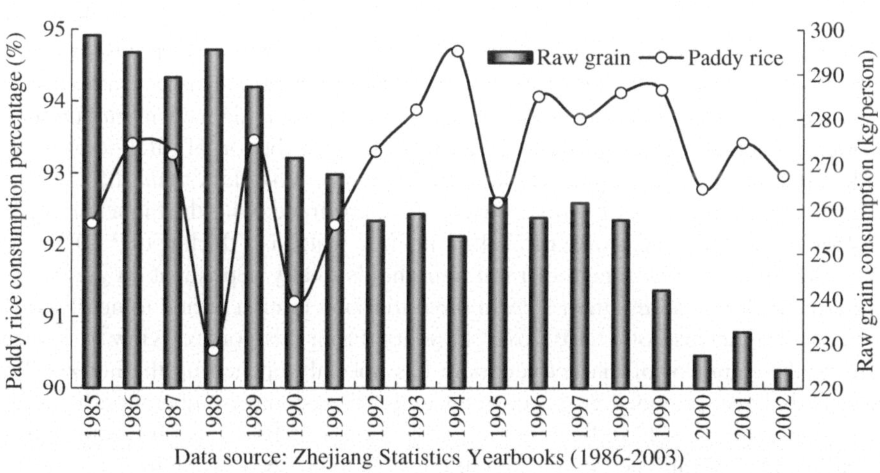

Fig. 7.10 Rural household per capita grain consumption and its composition. *Data source* Zhejiang Statistics Yearbooks (1986–2003)

survey of agricultural investigation team was aimed at the overall situation of the whole province, and the survey samples were changed regularly, which would show smaller impacts on rural households in terms of consumption. In addition, the high level of economic development of farmers in the fixed observation sites is also one of the reasons. As can be seen from Fig. 7.10, rice consumption occupied the absolute dominant position in the raw grain consumption of rural households in Zhejiang, which has remained above 90% for many years. Despite some fluctuations in the 1980s, it has been maintained between 91 and 93%, once reaching 95% after 1994 and then remained at 94% afterwards. This result fully reflects the consumption habits of rural households in southern China, with rice as the main food.

7.2.3 Rural Household Distribution by Raw Grain Purchase Ratio

With the acceleration of the non-agricultural economic development of rural households and the strategic adjustments of rural economic structure, it has become less important for farmland operation in the ten villages in Zhejiang. Meanwhile, rural households engaged in farmland operation have also shifted from grain-based to non-grain production, and there has been an obvious trend of marketisation in household grain consumption. From the follow-up observation of the ten villages (Table 7.6), with the increase of raw grain purchase ratio, the distribution of rural households presents a left skewed 'U'-shape distribution (Fig. 7.11). Over time, for rural households with different purchase ratios, the distribution trends varied (Fig. 7.12). The distribution of rural households without purchase showed a marked downward trend; the distribution of rural households with the purchase ratio less than 10% showed an inverted 'U' shape; the distribution of rural households with the ratio between 10 and 30% showed a fluctuating upward trend; the distribution of rural households with the ratio from 30 to 100% (excluding 100%) showed a fluctuating downward trend, while the distribution of rural households completely dependent on purchase showed a fluctuating upward trend. In terms of the distribution of rural households with different purchase ratios, the households with a ratio less than 10% are the majority, displaying a downward inverted 'U'-shape trend, with the highest level of 57.45% in 1991 and the lowest of 27.40% in 2002 which is a decline of 30.05%. At the same time, the percentage of rural households totally dependent on grain purchase increased from less than 10% in the initial observation period to nearly 40% currently, an increase of 31.15% over 17 years. From this point of view, it is seen that the development of market economy has not only opened up the horizon for farmers, but also provided great convenience for their complete liberation from the traditional mode of self-sufficient grain production. It is based on this premise that the adjustment of rural economic structure is able to proceed smoothly.

Table 7.6 Household distribution by raw grain purchase ratio in 10 Zhejiang villages (%)

	<10%	#=0	10–20	20–30	30–40	40–50	50–80	≥80	#=100
1986	60.95	47.50	3.62	3.06	3.15	3.62	11.32	14.29	7.05
1987	60.35	53.10	3.32	2.88	4.37	3.49	9.17	16.42	10.22
1988	59.05	52.03	3.64	2.42	3.55	3.38	10.39	17.58	11.26
1989	62.05	56.38	2.70	2.11	3.89	3.13	6.93	19.19	9.64
1990	65.01	56.80	3.40	4.23	2.90	2.57	7.96	13.93	7.05
1991	67.50	57.45	4.07	3.29	3.12	1.91	3.47	16.64	8.15
1993	57.52	43.69	5.61	4.41	4.81	2.40	6.61	18.64	13.23
1995	56.20	34.40	6.20	4.20	3.40	2.60	3.40	24.00	23.20
1996	56.20	38.00	5.80	3.60	3.00	1.60	5.20	24.60	15.60
1997	54.31	35.27	5.01	4.41	3.41	2.00	2.61	28.26	19.64
1998	55.20	35.80	5.00	4.40	2.00	1.60	3.40	28.40	21.80
1999	50.40	33.73	5.62	3.41	2.61	2.01	3.41	32.53	25.10
2000	47.48	28.37	6.44	3.62	1.81	2.01	5.03	33.60	29.78
2001	47.11	29.74	4.99	2.40	1.40	0.80	4.59	38.72	32.53
2002	40.00	27.40	4.00	4.20	2.00	1.60	5.40	42.80	38.20

Note #indicating the items being part of the previous category

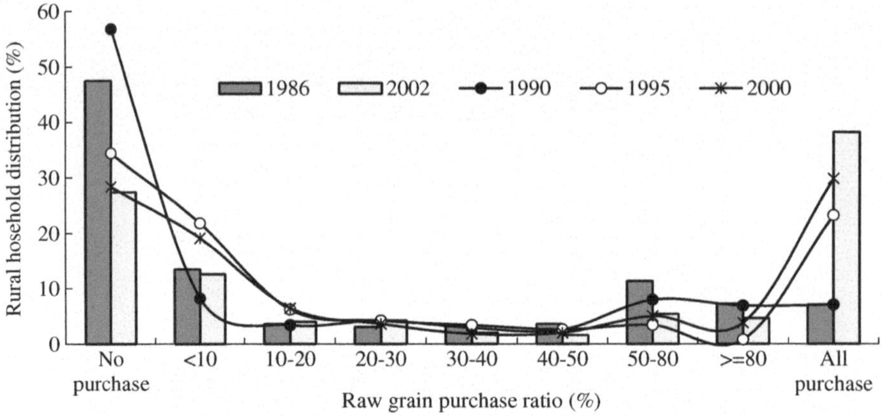

Fig. 7.11 Rural household distribution by grain purchase ratio in 10 villages of Zhejiang (I)

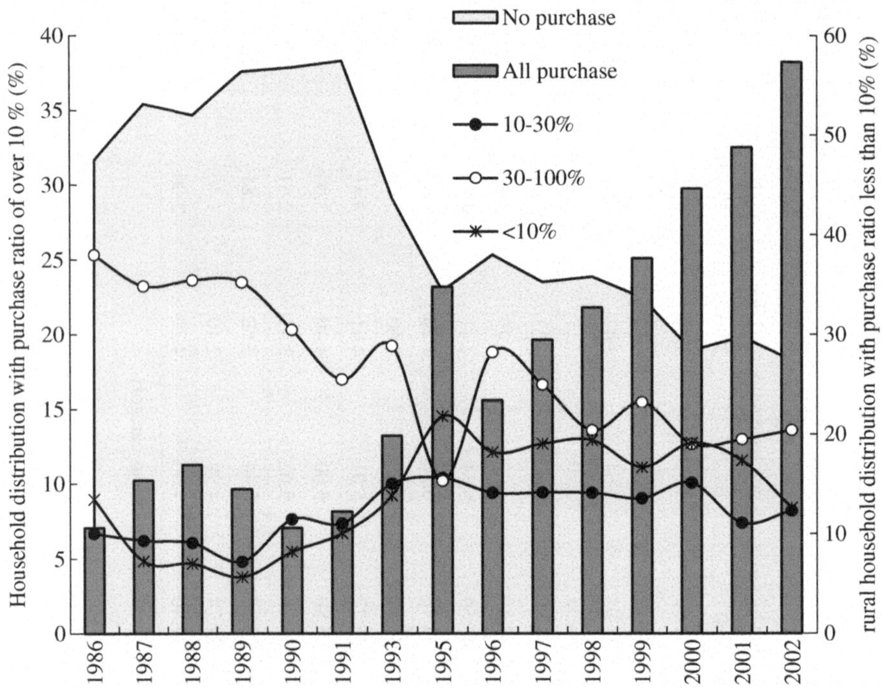

Fig. 7.12 Rural household distribution by grain purchase ratio in 10 villages of Zhejiang (II)

7.3 Rural Household Real Housing Consumption and Its Change

Housing consumption is an important part of household expenditure. Especially after the goal of household consumption has changed from survival to enjoyment, housing has become an increasingly important part of household consumption. To some extent, housing directly affects the level of household consumption. Per capita housing level, together with the housing quality, has become an important indicator of consumption level or household living standard.

7.3.1 Rural Housing and Its Composition Change

The improvement of rural residents' consumption level is not only reflected in food and clothing, but also in living. The results of time series data in Table 7.7 and Fig. 7.13 show that the fever of house construction since the reform and opening up is over for rural residents in Zhejiang. The annual newly-added housing area

Table 7.7 House construction and structure of rural households in Zhejiang

	Construction areas (m^2/person)	#Brick and wood (%)	Steel and concrete (%)	Newly-built housing				
				Households with new construction (%)	Newly-built area (m^2/person)	#Brick and wood	Steel and concreate	Cost (yuan/m^2)
1985	22.07	74.26	9.56	9.04	1.86	64.52	26.88	52.37
1986	23.02	72.24	11.47	9.15	1.82	66.48	24.18	58.99
1987	24.73	68.99	14.31	9.37	2.08	46.15	47.12	82.55
1988	25.98	66.51	17.51	7.13	1.85	42.16	56.76	107.79
1989	27.09	65.89	18.60	6.65	1.66	45.18	51.20	125.91
1990	29.26	66.88	23.31	7.33	2.25	48.89	48.44	118.06
1991	30.77	61.91	26.84	6.00	1.94	37.11	56.70	148.00
1992	31.34	64.71	27.66	4.74	1.57	40.13	57.32	160.00
1993	32.62	63.98	28.63	4.37	1.25	45.60	51.20	202.00
1994	32.77	61.76	30.18	3.04	0.93	31.18	55.91	228.90
1995	34.14	47.83	41.42	5.07	1.78	24.72	72.47	329.83
1996	35.87	44.94	45.53	4.96	1.78	15.73	76.97	331.00
1997	37.30	41.31	49.79	3.67	1.56	19.23	78.85	301.00
1998	38.53	40.57	51.93	3.74	1.58	20.89	72.78	358.00
1999	40.27	40.10	51.20	3.41	1.40	7.14	87.14	332.00
2000	46.42	48.26	46.18	3.48	1.46	20.00	76.85	393.00
2001	47.82	46.24	49.02	1.93	0.98	18.37	75.51	433.00
2002	49.53	42.30	52.59	2.48	1.10	10.91	89.09	493.00

Data source Zhejiang Statistics Yearbooks (1990–2003). #indicating as part of the former category

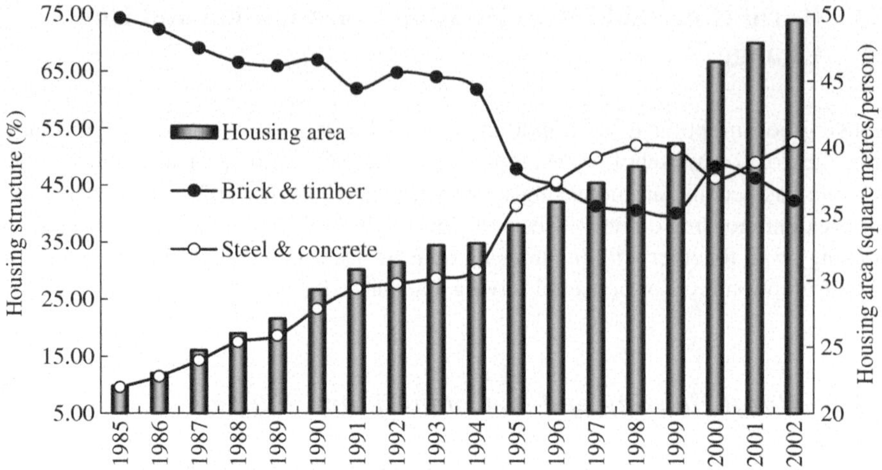

Fig. 7.13 Rural housing scale and structural change in Zhejiang

and the ratio of households with house construction have obviously declined over time. Newly-added construction areas decreased from per capita 2.25 m^2 in 1990 to 1.10 m^2 in 2002, a decline of 51.11%. The ratio of the observed households with house construction also decreased from the peak level of 9.37% in 1987 to 2.48% in 2002, with the drop of 6.89%. However, the unit construction cost increased substantially, from 52.37 yuan/m^2 in 1985 to 493.00 yuan/ m^2 in 2002, an increase as high as 841.38%. As a result of the increase in construction cost, newly constructed housing structure quality has been greatly improved. As a matter of fact, the proportion of brick and wood structure in the newly-built houses of rural households decreased from 66.48% in 1986 to 10.91% in 2002. At the same time, the proportion of steel and concrete structure in house construction increased dramatically, to a high level of 89.09% in 2002. Therefore, to improve the living condition has been the ultimate goal for the construction of rural households.

From the perspective of rural housing, over time the living conditions of rural households in Zhejiang have been greatly improved, which is reflected not only in the increase of per capita housing area, but also in the advancement of housing structure. The per capita housing area increased from 22.07 m^2 in 1985 to 49.53 m^2 in 2002, up 124.42%. Residential buildings have evolved from brick-wood structures to steel-concrete and brick-wood structures, and then to steel-concrete structures. In rural housing, the proportions of brick-wood structures and steel-concrete structures were 74.26 and 9.56% in 1985 and changed to 42.30 and 52.59% respectively, with the share of brick-wood structure decreasing by 31.96%, while that of steel-concrete structure increased by 43.03%. This result fully indicates that after 20 years of reform, rural households in Zhejiang have made significant improvements in their living conditions. However, due to the extensive influencing factors such as the increase of building standards and cost, the tightening control of construction land and the improvement of living areas, the percentage of rural households with newly-built houses decreased dramatically, from 5.07% in 1995 to 2.48% in 2002, and the per capita newly-built housing area also decreased from 1.78 to 1.10 m^2. It can be seen that, since the mid-1990s, both the percentage of rural households with new construction and the housing area have declined. This result reflects that investment or consumption in housing construction has become an issue of individual households in rural areas, and the era for large-scale housing renovation or new construction has been completely over.

7.3.2 *Rural Housing Area*

As seen from Table 7.8 and Fig. 7.14, over time the per capita housing area distribution of the ten villages in Zhejiang has changed. For example, the number of households with small housing area has decreased, and that of households with large housing area has increased, and the mode changed from 10–20 m^2 in the middle 1980s, to 20–30 m^2 in the early 1990s, and further to 50–80 m in the late 1990s, each undergoing a substantial decline in concentration. In the middle and late 1980s, most rural households in the ten villages in Zhejiang had a living area of 10–20 m^2, taking up as high of a percentage as 32.26% of the total observed households in 1986. There were 43.54% of the rural households with the area less than 20 m^2, and only 7.67% of the observed households with the area more than 50 m^2, including only 0.74% of the households with the area more than 100 m^2. By 1990, most rural households had a housing area of 20–30 m^2, accounting for 27.45% of all the households. Rural households with per capita living area less than 10 m^2 took 7.21%. Those with a

Table 7.8 Rural household per capita living area in the ten villages of Zhejiang (%)

	<10 m^2	10–20 m^2	20–30 m^2	30–40 m^2	40–50 m^2	50–80 m^2	80–100 m^2	≥ 100 m^2
1986	11.28	32.26	26.16	15.53	7.12	5.91	1.02	0.74
1987	9.76	29.47	27.46	14.47	8.46	7.93	1.48	0.96
1988	9.33	25.24	28.09	15.64	9.77	9.16	1.64	1.12
1989	8.49	22.62	27.25	18.84	9.17	10.68	1.77	1.18
1990	7.21	20.98	27.45	17.91	9.78	12.94	2.74	1.00
1991	6.66	19.64	27.68	17.82	10.21	13.67	2.94	1.38
1993	4.60	17.20	24.20	20.60	13.40	15.40	2.40	2.20
1995	5.20	14.60	21.20	19.00	13.40	18.20	4.20	4.20
1996	3.60	12.80	19.00	21.20	12.40	22.00	3.60	5.40
1997	2.40	11.40	19.40	18.80	12.40	24.80	5.00	5.80
1998	2.80	11.40	17.60	18.80	12.40	24.00	5.80	7.20
1999	3.60	10.80	17.40	16.60	14.40	23.40	7.40	6.40
2000	3.61	10.22	16.23	16.23	16.23	23.05	6.81	7.62
2001	2.99	10.58	14.97	14.97	16.37	23.55	8.78	7.78
2002	2.80	10.20	13.20	18.80	16.00	22.60	8.20	8.20

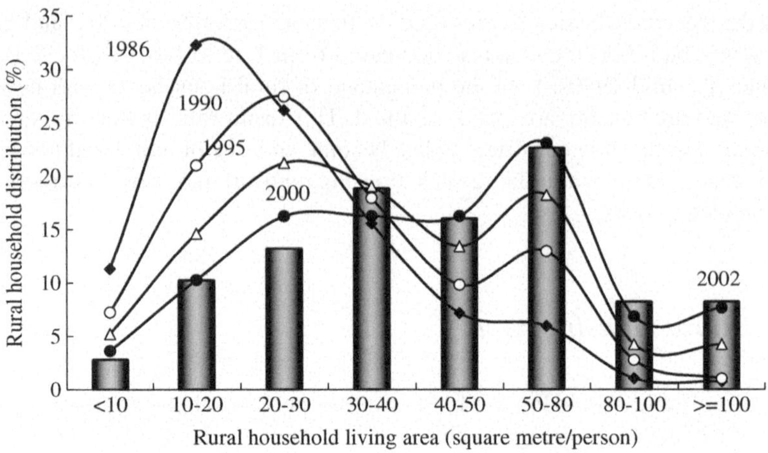

Fig. 7.14 Distribution of rural households by living area in Zhejiang

living area between 10 and 40 m^2 accounted for 66.33%, and those with the area exceeding 50 m^2 accounted for 16.67%. including 1.00% of the households with the area over 100 m^2. By 1995, many rural households still had the per capita living area of 20–30 m^2, but the percentage had decreased to 21.20%. Of all the observed households, 5.20% had a per capita living area of less than 10 m^2, 54.80% had an area between 10 and 40 m^2, 26.60% had an area more than 50 m^2, and 4.20% had an area over 100 m^2. By 2002, the residential area of the highest concentration had risen to 50–80 m^2, involving 22.60% of the rural households. Among the observed households, 2.80% had a per capita living area of less than 10 m^2, 48.00% had an area between 20 and 50 m^2, 39.00% had the area over 50 m^2 including 8.20% with an area over 100 m^2. Therefore, much influenced by the polarised trend of rural household economic development, there is also a polarisation of farmers' housing consumption.

7.4 Rural Household Consumption on Durable Goods

7.4.1 Rural Household Occupation of Durable Goods

The investigation of rural household durable goods consumption needs to be carried out through two aspects, i.e. the quantity owned, which is mainly used to reflect the consumption level of household durable goods, and the penetration, which is used to reflect the market expansion of rural durable goods.

From Table 7.9, it can be seen that after 17 years of development, the household durable goods occupation of the ten villages in Zhejiang has clearly continuously increased. The number of the traditional five items of durable goods possessed, such

Table 7.9 Changes in numbers of durable goods occupied by 100 rural households in Zhejiang

	Bicycle	Sewing machine	TV	Colour TV	Recorder	Washing machine	Electric fun	Fridge	Big furniture
1986	108.41	56.28	31.79	6.38	20.43	4.81	83.18	5.18	534.57
1987	127.20	60.68	41.67	8.63	26.16	7.59	104.71	6.02	585.00
1988	145.60	65.11	55.44	12.35	30.92	14.25	131.17	11.40	644.21
1989	151.68	66.81	60.67	15.55	33.87	18.99	143.95	13.53	684.12
1990	162.91	68.87	66.06	17.47	35.68	19.70	158.28	15.15	693.21
1991	166.15	69.52	71.07	20.21	36.44	20.55	164.85	16.75	722.02
1993	194.20	78.60	93.60	32.80	41.60	26.20	215.20	24.00	766.80
1995	197.00	78.60	104.80	44.40	41.80	33.40	243.80	36.80	746.80
1996	204.60	81.60	112.80	52.60	45.40	36.60	252.60	43.80	758.60
1997	209.60	85.20	122.40	62.20	45.20	40.20	260.00	42.00	804.20
1998	207.40	82.60	131.00	72.00	45.40	42.60	260.60	48.40	782.40
1999	203.40	83.20	135.60	79.20	45.00	41.80	266.40	48.80	783.80
2000	203.01	83.77	143.69	90.18	44.69	44.49	272.55	50.90	804.81
2001	198.40	83.03	151.10	101.20	44.31	44.91	275.65	56.49	789.42
2002	197.60	84.20	159.20	113.00	43.60	46.80	280.40	57.00	787.60

(continued)

Table 7.9 (continued)

	Camera	Motorcycle	Video camera	Telephone	Air conditioner	Microwave	Computer	Car	Camera
1993	2.00	4.60	5.20	3.60	–	–	–	–	1993
1995	5.40	8.60	7.60	11.60	2.80	0.20	0.80	0.60	1995
1996	7.80	11.40	7.80	18.80	4.40	0.20	0.60	0.60	1996
1997	8.20	13.80	10.60	29.20	7.00	1.00	0.20	1.20	1997
1998	9.60	16.80	15.20	38.20	10.40	1.00	0.40	1.20	1998
1999	11.20	20.60	16.20	62.20	9.60	1.60	0.80	1.60	1999
2000	10.22	26.65	18.64	81.76	13.63	2.40	1.80	2.00	2000
2001	10.78	31.74	21.16	98.60	16.77	3.39	3.19	1.60	2001
2002	10.00	34.00	20.60	115.80	21.20	6.00	4.60	2.20	2002

as bicycles, sewing machines, televisions, washing machines, and refrigerators have almost reached 5.44 per household, more than doubled the number of 2.06 in the initial observation period. New durable goods at the same time are penetrating into the consumption of rural households such as air conditioners, computers, cars and so on. This means that the consumption level of durable goods for rural households has been significantly improved. The ownership of large furniture increased from 5.35 pieces per household in 1986 to 7.88 pieces in 2002. The number of bicycles occupied increased from 1.08 in 1986 to 1.98 per household in 2002. The ownership of motorcycles for 100 rural households increased from 0.11[3] in 1985 to 34.00 in 2002 (22.48 for 100 rural households according to sample survey in 1999). The ownership of sewing machines, one of the three traditional items, increased from 56.28 in 100 households in the mid-1980s to 84.20 in 2002. The occupation of TV sets, the new mass media device, increased from 31.79 in the mid-1980s to 159.20 in 2002 for 100 rural households, including 113.00 colour TV sets. Meanwhile, the number of washing machines increased from 4.81 in 1986 to 46.80 in 2002. The ownership of luxury consumer goods, such as refrigerators, cameras and telephones, has also grown from zero to fewer, and to more, which had reached 57.00, 10.00 and 115.80 respectively by 2002 in 100 households in the ten villages in Zhejiang. Owning a car was once only a dream for Chinese people, but by 2002, this dream had become true in some rural areas of China, and 2.20% of the observed households in the ten villages in Zhejiang owned one. The data fully show that the living standards of farmers in the ten villages in Zhejiang have indeed improved significantly.

7.4.2 Penetration of Major Durable Goods for Rural Households

As can be seen from Table 7.10 and Fig. 7.15, in terms of consumption of durable goods, its penetration and occupation have been increasing over the years. In comparison of different goods, the penetration rate of TV sets is the highest of 95.60% with 78.40% for colour TV, which is followed by bicycles at 89.40%, and sewing machines at 76.20%. The top three are followed by telephones, refrigerators, washing machines and motorcycles. The penetration rates for cameras, air conditioners, microwave ovens, computers and cars are relatively low. This has indicated that in the rural consumption of traditional items, the market is nearly saturated with an expansion potential of about only 10%. However, in the consumption of new household appliances, the market capacity can be further developed. For example, the colour TV market still has 20% development potential, while those for washing machines and refrigerators have developed only 40–50% of the potential market, with 50–60% to be further explored. In terms of the market capacity, there is 30%

[3]Data here and below in the brackets are from sample survey by Zhejiang Rural Investigation Team. Data source: Zhejiang Statistics Yearbooks 1986 and 2000.

Table 7.10 Major durable goods penetration for rural households in 10 villages (%)

	Bicycle	Sewing machine	TV	Colour TV	Washing machine	Fridge	Camera	Motor-cycle	Telephone	Air conditioner	Microwave
1986	74.12	53.51	30.50	6.19	4.81	5.18	–	–	–	–	–
1987	79.69	56.67	39.93	8.46	7.59	6.02	–	–	–	–	–
1988	84.53	60.67	51.69	12.01	13.92	9.85	–	–	–	–	–
1989	84.86	62.15	56.85	14.80	17.24	13.20	–	–	–	–	–
1990	86.15	63.93	61.61	16.42	18.99	14.76	–	–	–	–	–
1991	86.25	64.27	66.18	19.03	19.72	15.92	–	–	–	–	–
1993	93.80	73.20	84.20	30.00	25.20	21.60	2.00	4.20	3.20	–	–
1995	92.20	74.00	88.80	40.40	31.20	29.40	5.00	8.00	11.60	2.00	0.20
1996	93.60	76.00	92.20	47.20	35.20	34.40	6.60	10.60	16.80	3.60	0.20
1997	93.20	76.40	92.40	52.80	38.00	37.80	7.40	12.80	24.20	4.80	1.00
1998	91.80	76.00	94.40	58.00	38.80	41.60	8.60	15.20	30.20	7.00	1.00
1999	89.80	76.40	94.40	63.00	38.60	42.60	9.40	19.00	44.60	6.60	1.60
2000	89.38	76.95	94.79	69.14	40.48	44.09	9.02	24.25	58.12	9.82	2.40
2001	88.82	75.65	95.21	74.45	40.52	47.90	9.58	28.34	65.87	12.18	3.39
2002	89.40	76.20	95.60	78.40	42.40	49.00	9.60	30.60	71.60	15.00	5.60

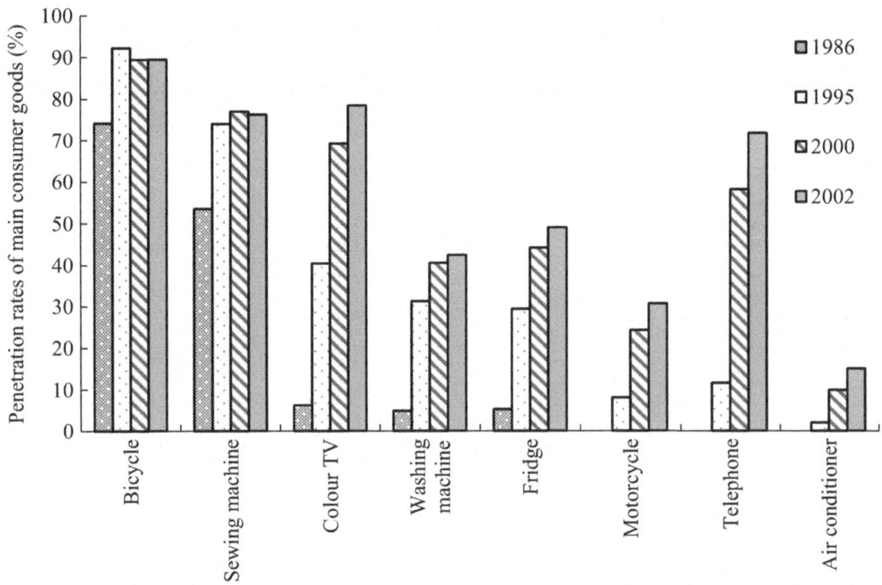

Fig. 7.15 Penetration rates of main consumer goods for rural households in Zhejiang

potential for telephones, 70% for motorcycles, and those for air conditioners, cameras, microwave ovens, computers and cars have just started and the rural market has a huge development potential. Obviously, such an analysis result will provide much inspiration and confidence to developers of living industrial products to explore the rural market. However, it should be noted that rural life is different from that of the city, and farmers' income level has been low with development imbalance. In order to develop rural market for living necessities and durable goods, manufacturers have to do further investigation regarding rural market, so as to develop products suitable for farmers' life and their income level. Only in this way, is it possible to improve rural consumption to realise the comprehensive development of rural market.

7.4.3 Distribution of Bicycle Occupation of Rural Households

Once the possession and penetration of the main durable consumer goods in rural households have been investigated, it is necessary to further analyse the occupation of some of the durable consumer goods. Only bicycles and TV sets are analysed in this chapter. From Table 7.10, it can be seen that as the penetration rate of bicycles is close to one, that is, close to saturation, new alternative goods such as motorcycles and cars have entered rural households, so that bicycle consumption has decreased significantly. There is still purchase of bicycles but it is mostly for replacing the old ones. From Table 7.11 and Fig. 7.16, it can be seen that in the past 15 years, the proportion of rural households without a bicycle in the ten villages in Zhejiang showed a typical 'U' shape, the proportion of one-bicycle households declined dramatically,

Table 7.11 Bicycle occupation distribution in rural households in Zhejiang (%)

	None	1	2	3	5	Over 5
1986	25.88	49.45	17.84	4.99	1.02	0.83
1987	20.31	46.29	23.19	7.32	2.09	0.78
1988	15.47	42.96	27.57	9.94	2.85	1.21
1989	15.14	40.54	29.02	9.92	3.78	1.60
1990	13.85	37.56	30.10	11.44	4.81	2.24
1991	13.75	34.69	33.04	11.59	4.67	2.25
1993	6.20	30.20	36.80	19.40	5.60	1.80
1995	7.80	26.80	36.20	21.20	6.20	1.80
1996	6.40	27.00	34.80	21.40	8.40	2.00
1997	6.80	26.00	33.60	21.20	10.00	2.40
1998	8.20	26.20	32.20	20.80	9.80	2.80
1999	10.20	25.40	30.60	21.60	9.20	3.00
2000	10.62	26.65	28.46	21.04	10.02	3.21
2001	11.18	27.54	28.14	20.96	9.38	2.79
2002	10.60	28.20	29.20	20.60	8.20	3.20

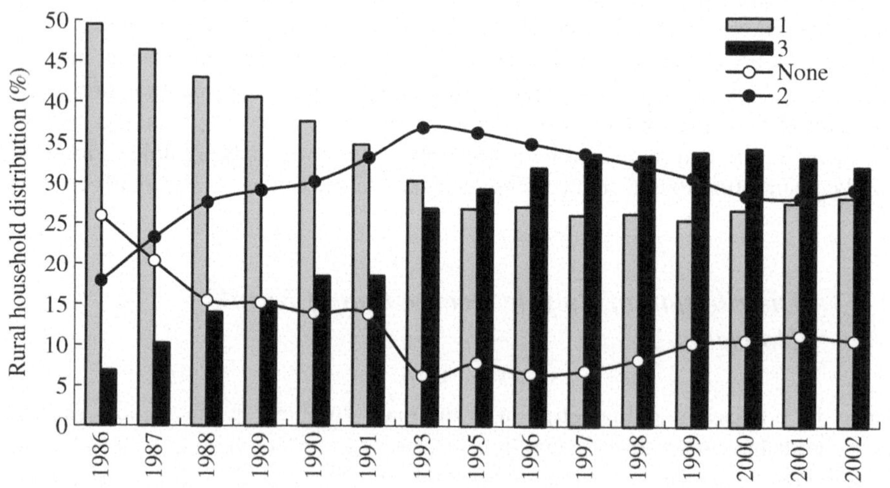

Fig. 7.16 Distribution of bicycle occupation of rural households

that of two-bicycle households displayed an inverted ‘U’ shape and the figure is rising for households with three and more bicycles. Therefore, the expansion of rural bicycle market should focus on bicycle upgrading.

7.4.4 *Occupation Distribution of Colour TVs for Rural Households*

Comparing Tables 7.11 and 7.12, it can be seen that the consumption of bicycles is different from that of televisions. The consumption unit of bicycles has obviously shifted from household to individual. In other words, the ownership of bicycles is nearly saturated for rural households, while the saturation rate of bicycles is only 55.23% for individuals. However, the consumption unit of televisions is the household. In the distribution of TV ownership, 46.40% of the rural households had one TV set, 49.2% of the households had two or more, including 52.80% with one colour TV set, and 25.6% more than one colour TV sets. From the viewpoint of development, the consumption of TV sets has shown the trend that colour TV sets have replaced the black and white ones, and the new ones rapidly replaced the old ones.

Table 7.12 Distribution of household TV ownership in 10 villages of Zhejiang (%)

	TV				Colour TV			
	None	1	2	3+	None	1	2	3+
1986	69.54	29.26	1.11	0.09	93.80	6.11	0.00	0.09
1987	60.07	38.36	1.39	0.17	91.54	8.37	0.00	0.09
1988	48.31	49.01	2.33	0.35	87.99	11.75	0.17	0.09
1989	43.15	53.24	3.36	0.25	85.20	14.13	0.59	0.08
1990	38.39	57.30	4.06	0.25	83.58	15.51	0.75	0.17
1991	33.82	61.33	4.67	0.17	80.97	17.91	1.04	0.09
1993	15.80	76.00	7.00	1.20	70.00	27.80	1.60	0.60
1995	11.20	74.40	13.20	1.20	59.60	37.40	2.40	0.60
1996	7.80	74.60	15.40	2.20	52.80	43.00	3.40	0.80
1997	7.60	68.20	20.20	4.00	47.20	45.80	5.40	1.60
1998	5.60	64.80	24.60	5.00	42.00	47.60	8.60	1.80
1999	5.60	60.40	28.40	5.60	37.00	50.20	10.40	2.40
2000	5.21	55.11	32.46	7.21	30.86	52.91	12.63	3.61
2001	4.79	50.70	35.33	9.18	25.55	53.69	16.37	4.39
2002	4.40	46.40	37.80	11.40	21.60	52.80	18.60	7.00

7.5 Service Consumption and Its Changes in Distribution

7.5.1 Service Consumption and Its Distribution

Considering the impact of price changes on consumption, the period of 1995–2002 is selected for the analysis, as the price changes during the period were relatively small. As can be seen from Table 7.13, over time, the service consumption of rural households in the ten villages in Zhejiang showed a steady upward trend, rising from 509.43 yuan in 1995 to 1385.95 yuan in 2002, with an increase of 172.06% over eight years and an average annual growth rate of 15.37%, which was significantly higher than the living consumption growth rate of 3.21% and the income growth rate of 5.98% during the same period. This result shows that service consumption has become a new growth pole of Zhejiang rural households. From the perspective of the distribution of service consumption for rural households, great changes have taken place over these eight years. In 1995, 19.20% of the households had the per capita service consumption of less than 100 yuan, 52.40% had less than 300 yuan, 73.40% less than 500 yuan and 26.60% higher than 500 yuan. After eight years of changes, in 2002, the percentage of households with per capital consumption of less than 100 yuan dropped to 6.80%, that for less than 300 yuan dropped to 16.40%, and that for less than 500 yuan dropped to 38.60%, a decrease of 34.80% compared with 1995. Meanwhile, the proportion of households whose consumption level exceeded 500 yuan rose to 61.40%, including 39.4% of those households with consumption exceeding 1000 yuan, which was 26.60% higher than the level in 1995. Therefore, the consumption concept of Zhejiang farmers has undergone a dramatic change, from the traditional consumption of pursuing food and clothing to pursuing well-being and prosperity.

7.5.2 Medical Service Consumption and Distribution

In the service consumption of farmers, medical consumption is a major expenditure item due to the need to ensure good health. From eight years' observation (Table 7.14), the total medical expenditure showed an upward trend, from 153.76 yuan per person in 1995 to 405.65 yuan per person in 2002, an increase of 163.82% with an average annual growth of 14.86%. It is also significantly higher than the growth of income and that of living consumption. In terms of the distribution of medical consumption, in 1995, most rural households had a medical consumption below 50 yuan, taking up 58% of the total observed households, including 11% of all rural households who had no medical consumption. There were 42% of the total households with a consumption level of over 50 yuan, including 29.80% with the level of over 100 yuan. After eight years of changes, by 2002, the proportion of households with per capita medical service consumption less than 50 yuan had dropped to 38%, a decrease of 20%. However, the proportion of households without medical consumption increased by

Table 7.13 Distribution of service consumption of rural households in 10 Zhejiang villages (%)

Consumption (100 yuan)	1995	1996	1997	1998	1999	2000	2001	2002	2000–2002
<1	19.20	15.80	11.00	9.20	10.40	8.82	9.38	6.80	8.33
1–2	17.20	17.00	13.20	13.20	11.00	9.22	11.38	9.60	10.07
2–3	16.00	13.80	13.40	10.40	10.60	10.22	7.78	8.60	8.87
3–4	11.20	10.40	11.40	9.40	8.00	8.22	8.78	7.40	8.13
4–5	9.80	8.00	10.40	9.20	9.40	7.21	6.39	6.20	6.60
5–8	11.20	13.80	14.60	18.40	18.00	20.64	17.56	15.40	17.87
8–10	2.60	4.60	6.20	5.00	6.20	9.22	8.18	6.60	8.00
10–20	7.80	10.40	13.20	15.80	15.00	16.43	15.97	20.20	17.53
20+	5.00	6.20	6.60	9.40	11.40	10.02	14.57	19.20	14.60
Consumption (yuan/person)	509.43	641.81	717.18	885.07	934.06	962.18	1147.53	1385.95	893.45

Table 7.14 Distribution of rural household medical service consumption in Zhejiang (%)

Consumption (100 yuan)	1995	1996	1997	1998	1999	2000	2001	2002	2000–2002
=0	11.00	8.20	11.60	8.80	9.80	15.43	19.56	18.00	17.67
<0.5	47.00	43.00	38.40	34.60	28.60	24.45	23.75	20.00	22.73
0.5–1.0	12.20	16.00	17.20	15.20	19.80	16.83	16.97	15.60	16.47
1.0–1.5	7.80	8.20	9.00	11.40	10.60	12.83	9.38	9.00	10.40
1.5–2.0	5.20	4.20	3.40	5.60	6.60	5.21	5.19	6.20	5.53
2.0–3.0	6.60	7.40	7.20	7.60	7.20	7.01	6.39	8.20	7.20
3.0–5.0	2.60	5.40	5.20	5.60	6.80	7.62	7.19	8.20	7.67
5.0–10.0	4.20	4.20	3.60	5.20	5.00	5.01	4.79	6.00	5.27
10+	3.40	3.40	4.40	6.00	5.60	5.61	6.79	8.80	7.07
Consumption (yuan/person)	153.76	184.51	188.77	313.49	281.32	286.28	340.11	405.65	267.88

7%, and the proportion of households with actual medical service consumption less than 50 yuan dropped by 27%. Meanwhile, the proportion of rural households with per capita expenditure exceeding 50 yuan reached 62%, including 46.40% exceeding 100 yuan, up 17.6 percentage points from 1995. The substantial changes in rural household medical consumption have been due to the price increase of medical service on the one hand, and the other due to more attention paid by farmers on their own health.

7.5.3 Education Consumption and Its Distribution

With the deepening of family planning policy in the countryside, the number of children for farmers has significantly decreased (Shi et al., 2000), and their expectation on children to have a bright future increases gradually. In addition, the traditional way of education has become harder to meet the needs of the new era for the quality improvement of the new generation. These have led to changes in farmers' education investment. As a result, educational consumption in rural households began to rise significantly. Data from eight years of observation show that in terms of educational service (tuition and miscellaneous expenses), the farmers' expenditure in Zhejiang has been rising gradually, increased from per capita 192.94 yuan in 1995 to 476.16 yuan in 2002, up 146.79% in eight years, with an average annual growth rate of 13.78% (Table 7.15). From the distribution of educational expenditure, the proportion of farmers without investment in this area increased significantly, from 43.40% in 1995 to 50.80% in 2002, and increased by 7.40% in eight years. However, total investment increased significantly among the farmers with educational investment. In 1995, 12.20% of the households had a per capita investment in education of less than 100 yuan, 39.80% less than 300 yuan and 16.80% more than 300 yuan, of which 9.60% had more than 500 yuan. After eight years, by 2002, the proportion of households with their investment less than 100 yuan had dropped to 2.40%, and that of households with their investment less than 300 yuan had dropped to 18.40%, down 21.40% from the 1995 level. Meanwhile, the proportion of households with investment more than 300 yuan had risen to 30.80%, of which households with investment more than 500 yuan had risen to 21.60%, up 12% from 1995. I believe there are two reasons as to why the expenditure on educational services has risen so much. On the one hand, it is the result of the industrialisation reform of the national higher education. On the other hand, farmers have a better understanding of the role of educational investment in their economic development. Although our survey shows that farmers' perception of investment in education has shifted from active to passive, and the financial burden of education has become heavier in their minds,[4] the severe

---

[4]According to our survey of 1787 farmers in 23 provinces (cities and districts), 19.70% of the farmers think that the burden is 'very heavy', 34.14% think that the burden is 'heavy', 26.64% think that the burden is 'normal', and 19.53% think that the burden is 'comparatively light' or 'light'. This distribution is obviously different in Jiangsu, Hubei and Shanxi provinces where the survey samples are relatively concentrated. The total sample of the three provinces account for 90.82% of the total.

Table 7.15 Distribution of rural household educational consumption in Zhejiang (%)

Constumption (100 yuan)	1995	1996	1997	1998	1999	2000	2001	2002	2000–2002
=0	43.40	44.00	45.00	44.40	47.20	50.10	49.70	50.80	50.20
<0.5	4.40	1.00	1.80	0.80	0.40	0.00	1.00	0.20	0.40
0.5–1.0	7.80	4.80	3.20	4.00	1.60	1.20	1.40	2.20	1.60
1.0–1.5	9.20	6.80	6.60	6.80	5.80	3.01	2.59	4.00	3.20
1.5–2.0	6.20	5.40	4.80	3.80	3.80	3.41	4.99	3.80	4.07
2.0–3.0	12.20	13.40	11.60	9.60	8.00	9.42	8.98	8.20	8.87
3.0–5.0	7.80	11.40	12.60	15.40	13.80	13.43	10.98	9.20	11.20
5.0–10.0	4.80	6.80	8.80	8.00	10.20	11.62	8.58	7.60	9.27
10+	4.20	6.40	5.60	7.20	9.20	7.82	11.78	14.00	11.20
Consumption (yuan/person)	192.94	246.03	262.65	318.74	361.87	345.93	432.65	476.16	328.12

employment situation and the expectation for success have forced helpless farmers to continue spending more on education. As a result, educational expenditure has become a new important item for rural household consumption.

7.6 Rural Consumption Propensity

Consumption propensity is an important index to reflect the relationship between consumption expenditure and disposable income. There are two types of consumption propensity. One is average propensity to consume, which equals to the ratio of expenditure to income, and the other is marginal propensity to consume, referring to the consumption increase with one unit of income increase.

7.6.1 Changes in Average Consumption Propensity

Figure 7.17 shows that since 1990, the consumption propensity of rural households in the ten villages has generally declined, from the highest level of 94.53% in 1989 to 69.34% in 2002, down 25.19%. For rural household consumption propensity, service consumption tends to increase significantly. In 1986, the service consumption propensity was 3.09%, which rose to 12.43% in 1998, and then started to reverse, falling to 10.26% in 2000. It began to rebound in 2001 and reached its highest level of 14.53% since 2002. The trend of durable goods consumption showed a typical 'M' pattern, with two peaks in 1988 and 1997, and the propensities being 9.00 and 10.83% respectively. By 2001, the propensity had fallen to the lowest point of 3.71% since the observation. In 2002, it began to rise, reaching 5.53%. Meanwhile, food consumption and Engel's coefficient showed a significant downward trend, which decreased from 38.47 and 46.19% in 1986 to 21.89 and 31.56% in 2002, respectively, down by 20.96 and 13.76% in 17 years. This shows that the living standards of farmers in the ten villages in Zhejiang have indeed changed greatly. The living standards of farmers have risen from a well-off type in the mid-1980s to a prosperous type at present.[5]

The proportion of 'very heavy' and 'heavy' is as high as 68.82% in Hubei, 63.88% in Shanxi, and 18.60% in Jiangsu. In terms of child raising burden, farmers generally believe that the burden of children's education is the biggest headache. In answering what are the major burdens (multiple choices) in child raising, 79.63% of farmers choose education, 28.82% choose marriage, 13.78% choose daily expenditure, and 12.70% choose employment. Although there are some differences among provinces, the selection order is the same with only differences in magnitude. For example, in the choice of educational burden, the proportion of Shanxi is 74.83%, that of Jiangsu is 78.52%, and that of Hubei is 82.19%.

[5]The Engel coefficient is the ratio of food expenditure to living expenditure. The Engel coefficient proposed by the FAO is the general criterion for determining the stage of life and development. An Engel coefficient of more than 60% indicates poverty, between 50 and 60% indicates food and clothing sufficiency, between 40 and 50% indicates moderate prosperity, and less than 40% indicates prosperity (Yin, 1994: 47).

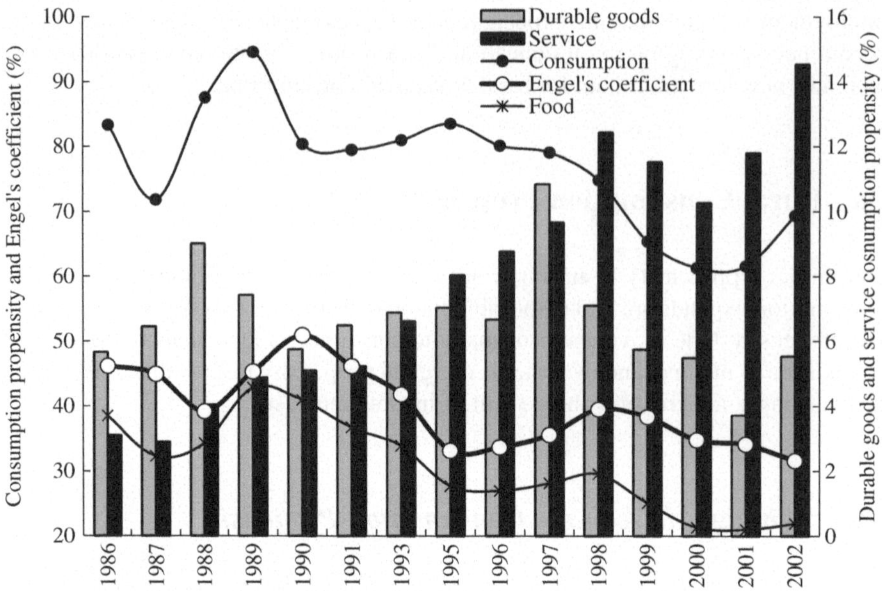

Fig. 7.17 Consumption propensity in Zhejiang

7.6.2 *Distribution of Households with Different Average Consumption Propensities*

From Table 7.16, it can be seen that the distribution of households with the consumption propensity less than 50% has been on the rise, that of households with the propensity between 50 and 80% tends to decrease in a fluctuating manner, that of households with the propensity between 80 and 100% decreases slowly, and that of households with the propensity of 100% and over displays an 'M'-shape decrease. It indicates that in terms of living consumption, the demand for farmers has been declining. However, we should also see that there were 23.05% of rural households whose consumption was obviously overspending. Although the proportion of such rural households in the total was decreasing, the decline was quite small, with only 6.37% in 17 years, and policymakers should attach great importance to this phenomenon. If the spending is based on a high level of savings, then this kind of consumption is mostly welcomed by the government at present. If there is an overdraft due to poverty, it cannot be ignored. According to farmers' consumption psychology, the latter is more likely, which can be confirmed below by the distribution and changes in Engel coefficients of rural households.

Table 7.16 Distribution of rural households by consumption propensity in Zhejiang (%)

	<50%	50–80	80–100	≥100	Including			
					100–120	120–150	150–200	≥200
1986	17.21	35.43	17.95	29.42	10.92	7.68	5.09	5.74
1987	23.71	37.84	16.56	21.88	7.76	5.49	3.84	4.80
1988	17.46	31.46	19.45	31.63	8.21	8.12	5.36	9.94
1989	12.70	32.21	19.93	35.16	11.44	8.33	6.48	8.92
1990	17.50	37.31	18.57	26.62	9.12	6.22	4.56	6.72
1991	19.98	38.67	17.39	23.96	8.39	4.93	4.33	6.31
1993	22.60	39.00	17.80	20.60	6.20	4.40	3.80	6.20
1995	22.80	29.80	18.60	28.80	8.60	5.80	4.60	9.80
1996	21.00	37.00	15.80	26.20	8.40	6.40	3.00	8.40
1997	23.25	33.07	15.23	28.46	8.62	5.41	6.21	8.22
1998	23.40	32.20	15.20	29.20	7.20	4.40	5.80	11.80
1999	23.80	37.00	15.40	23.80	7.00	4.80	4.00	8.00
2000	27.66	35.87	11.82	24.65	8.82	5.61	4.81	5.41
2001	30.00	31.80	14.40	23.80	6.20	7.40	3.80	6.40
2002	31.66	33.87	11.42	23.05	6.61	4.41	4.81	7.21

7.6.3 Distribution of Rural Households with Different Engel Coefficients

From Table 7.17 and Fig. 7.18, it can be seen that in the 17 years of development, the living standard of farmers in the ten villages in Zhejiang has experienced a transformation process from an increase in the standards to a decrease and then an increase again. At present, the living standard of rural households has been greatly improved compared with that in the early 1990s. Specifically, the proportion of prosperous rural households, i.e. those whose Engel coefficient was less than 40%, showed a fluctuating upward trend, the proportion of farmers living at a well-off level and at the level of food and clothing sufficiency showed a slow upward trend, while the proportion of farmers living in poverty showed a decreasing trend. The share of extremely poor households, whose Engel coefficient was 80% or more, declined rapidly in the 1990s after a period of rise. Compared with 1986, the proportion of the extremely poor households decreased by 4.64%, and by 1.60% if compared with 1995. This result indicates once again that after 17 years of development, especially for the most recent ten years of development, the living standard of rural households in the ten villages in Zhejiang has indeed improved greatly, but this improvement also involves the aggravation of polarisation, which is disguised by the average level. It should be noted that nearly 30% of rural households are still living in poverty. This requires policymakers to attach great importance to rural households in poverty when developing rural economy.

Table 7.17 Distribution of rural households with different Engel coefficients (%)

	<30%	30–40	40–50	≥50	Including			
					50–60	60–70	70–80	≥80
1986	11.56	7.12	11.10	70.21	15.82	23.96	21.00	9.44
1987	12.13	6.81	10.12	70.94	19.46	23.73	18.85	8.90
1988	15.92	9.86	12.98	61.25	16.96	21.02	14.45	8.82
1989	10.60	6.98	9.84	72.58	16.90	20.10	22.88	12.70
1990	6.88	6.30	9.70	77.11	17.16	22.89	24.71	12.35
1991	8.82	7.35	8.30	75.52	17.91	24.39	23.53	9.69
1993	9.80	7.00	13.80	69.40	19.80	23.60	19.60	6.40
1995	18.80	9.40	12.20	59.60	18.80	17.20	17.20	6.40
1996	17.80	9.40	16.40	56.40	19.00	16.60	15.00	5.80
1997	15.83	11.82	15.23	57.11	18.84	17.84	13.83	6.61
1998	16.40	9.60	16.60	57.40	19.60	17.00	13.00	7.80
1999	15.40	13.40	14.60	56.60	16.80	19.00	14.20	6.60
2000	17.43	16.43	15.43	50.70	21.24	13.63	11.82	4.01
2001	16.77	16.37	13.77	53.09	18.36	14.37	14.77	5.59
2002	20.40	17.80	17.80	44.00	16.60	12.20	10.40	4.80

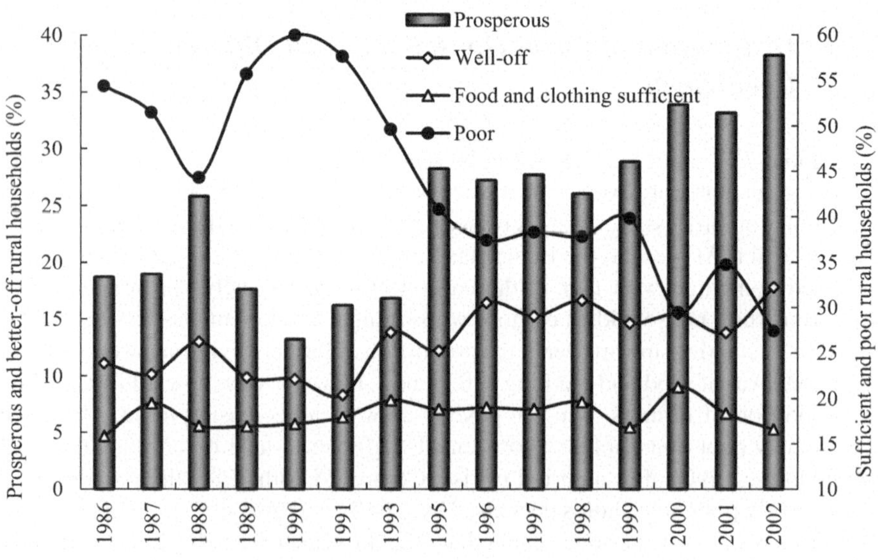

Fig. 7.18 Distribution of rural households by consumption level

7.6.4 *Marginal Propensity to Consume and Income Elasticity of Consumption*

The marginal propensity to consume and the income elasticity of consumption for rural households can be calculated by mathematical regression. From Table 7.18 and Fig. 7.19, it can be seen that since 1986, the marginal propensity to consume of households in the ten villages in Zhejiang has fluctuated. This trend continued to decline in the mid and late 1990s, and did not begin to recover until the beginning of the 2000s. Combining with the previous analysis, it is found that the income growth is closely related to the trend of marginal propensity to consume. When the growth of household income stagnates, the marginal propensity to consume decreases, and when the income rises, the marginal propensity to consume increases. The results show that with the increase of rural household income, farmers' demand for goods and services will increase significantly, and the rural consumer market tends to be prosperous. This can also be proved by the changes in the household income elasticity of consumption. Since the mid-1980s, the income and consumption elasticities of rural households have remained relatively stable. The periods in the late 1980s and the late 1990s were exceptional, when the economic growth of rural households was slow. That is, with the income change around 1%, that of consumption would change about 0.55%, indicating that the income change had an important impact on the consumption growth. Especially after the growth of rural household income

Table 7.18 Marginal propensity to consume and income elasticity of consumption in Zhejiang 1986–2002

	Marginal propensity to consume (b_1) $C = b_0 + b_1 Y$		Income elasticity of consumption (e_1) $LnC = e_0 + e_1 LnY$	
1986	C = 234.982 (7.100) + 0.559Y (17.072)	AR = 0.213 DW = 1.962	LnC = 2.628 (16.774) + 0.566LnY (23.910)	AR = 0.347 DW = 1.846
1987	C = 480.943 (10.861) + 0.326Y (10.400)	AR = 0.322 DW = 1.849	LnC = 2.848 (18.042) + 0.535LnY (23.326)	AR = 0.086 DW = 1.978
1988	C = 704.071 (12.175) + 0.403Y (13.181)	AR = 0.130 DW = 1.988	LnC = 2.955 (17.239) + 0.556LnY (22.921)	AR = 0.313 DW = 1.875
1989	C = 259.041 (4.364) + 0.751Y (20.941)	AR = 0.313 DW = 1.994	LnC = 3.444 (23.208) + 0.493LnY (23.268)	AR = 0.270 DW = 2.005
1990	C = 563.794 (7.814) + 0.436Y (10.481)	AR = 0.083 DW = 1.935	LnC = 3.209 (20.723) + 0.515LnY (23.664)	AR = 0.318 DW = 1.773
1991	C = 30.511 (0.344) + 0.776Y (19.315)	AR = 0.244 DW = 2.014	LnC = 3.530 (22.594) + 0.475LnY (22.063)	AR = 0.297 DW = 2.048
1993	C = 616.69 (2.609) + 0.619Y (10.920)	AR = 0.192 DW = 2.043	LnC = 2.827 (10.175) + 0.601LnY (16.989)	AR = 0.366 DW = 1.892
1995	C = 2141.746 (5.16) + 0.502Y (12.07)	AR = 0.226 DW = 2.197	LnC = 3.019 (9.885) + 0.613LnY (16.985)	AR = 0.367 DW = 1.993
1996	C = −706.051 (−1.784) + 0.900Y (31.928)	AR = 0.672 DW = 1.545	LnC = 3.539 (12.531) + 0.555LnY (16.817)	AR = 0.362 DW = 1.915

(continued)

Table 7.18 (continued)

	Marginal propensity to consume (b_1) $C = b_0 + b_1 Y$		Income elasticity of consumption (e_1) $LnC = e_0 + e_1 LnY$	
1997	C = −210.254 (−0.587) + 0.817Y (29.327)	AR = 0.636 DW = 2.306	LnC = 3.406 (12.038) + 0.571LnY (17.357)	AR = 0.379 DW = 1.849
1998	C = 3488.437 (10.559) + 0.265Y (10.542)	AR = 0.185 DW = 2.002	LnC = 3.953 (14.295) + 0.507LnY (15.72)	AR = 0.337 DW = 1.987
1999	C = 4106.245 (11.189) + 0.149Y (7.577)	AR = 0.103 DW = 1.595	LnC = 3.995 (16.092) + 0.498LnY (17.256)	AR = 0.377 DW = 1.860
2000	C = 3995.838 + 0.188Y (8.228) (8.175)	AR = 0.117 DW = 1.938	LnC = 3.995 (16.634) + 0.496LnY (18.008)	AR = 0.395 DW = 1.815
2001	C = 4276.668 (9.892) + 0.194Y (10.007)	AR = 0.165 DW = 2.037	LnC = 3.446 (12.703) + 0.561LnY (18.006)	AR = 0.393 DW = 1.919
2002	C = 3053.736 (6.095) + 0.379Y (12.141)	AR = 0.227 DW = 2.104	LnC = 3.108 (10.324) + 0.600LnY (17.570)	AR = 0.383 DW = 2.053

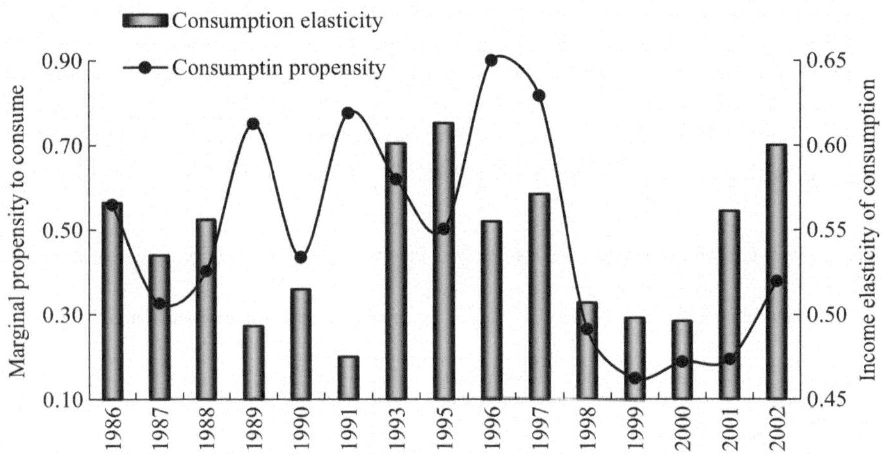

Fig. 7.19 Marginal propensity to consume and income elasticity of consumption

became stagnated, the sensitivity of rural household consumption to the changes in income obviously increased. This result indicates that the key to propel the rural consumer market is to increase rural household income. Only with the increase of farmers' income can the rural consumer market become prosperous.

References

Mansfield, E. (1992). *Microeconomics: Theory and applications (Translated in Chinese)*. Beijing: China Finance Press.

Shi, Q., Wang, A., & Shen, L. (2000). *Research on rural household consumption and purchase power*. Beijing: Shanxi People's Publishing Press.

Yin, S. (1994). *Study on the well-off level*. Xining: Hunan Press.

Chapter 8
Rural Employment Structure and Its Change

Contents

Adam Smith, the founder of economics, considered that the real wealth is the annual produce of the land and labour of the society. Although this statement is based on the traditional agricultural society, it is still very valuable for China in the period of transition. The economic development of a region or a country can be understood by the income level of the local people on the one hand, and by the activity of its labour market on the other. Generally speaking, an area with an active labour market must be a relatively developed area. Especially for a market with labour inflows, it must be the case. Zhejiang is one of the regions with fast economic development since the reform and opening up in China. Its economic development has improved from the average level in the initial stage of reform to currently the upper level. Of course, there are many reasons, and one of them is the active labour market. Drawing on data from the ten Zhejiang villages, this chapter takes as the theme the changes in employment structure of labour force, with the aim to reveal the essence of Zhejiang's economic growth from this aspect.

Q. Shi and Y. Gao, *Sustainable Development of Rural Household Economy*,
https://doi.org/10.1007/978-981-15-2747-0_8

8.1 Labour Force Scale and Quality

8.1.1 Scales of Observed Villages and Their Changes

Generally speaking, when talking about the scale of an observation village, people would first think about the size of the village, while the core issues, namely population, labour force and its constituent households, are the secondary consideration. But as far as the follow-up observation is concerned, the theme is indeed based on the population of a village or a household as the core, focusing on the changes in the number, quality and composition of the population. The changes in the people are the main subject of observation. According to the observation in Zhejiang (Fig. 8.1), since 1986, the number of villages under observation has remained the same at ten, but the number and scale of households, the basic living units, have changed dramatically. The number of households increased from 2607 households at the beginning of observation to 3757 households, and increased by 44.11% in 17 years. Population and labour, the core elements of households, have also undergone tremendous changes, increased by 26.37 and 14.31% in 17 years. Of course, such an increase is not entirely the result of natural changes, as non-natural factors also have a great impact. In 1997, because of the highway construction, there was a transformation of the entire village groups from agricultural to non-agricultural, decreasing the observation scale significantly. In 1999, the agglomeration of villages saw the observation scale expand substantially. These changes, however, have little impact on the size of individual households. Instead, it is the national family planning policy, farmers' adaption to the policy and their corresponding changes in ideology that have made the scale of individual households decline continuously. Affected by

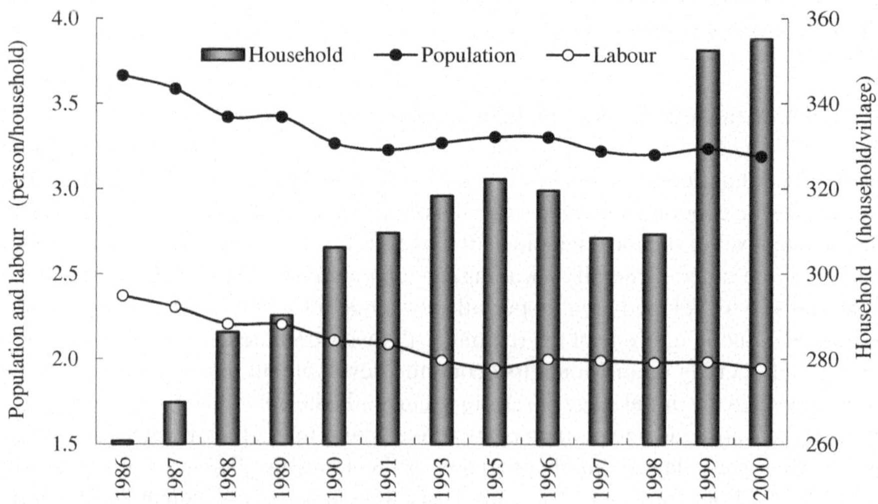

Fig. 8.1 Rural household scale in the ten villages

the size of population, the scale of household labour force has also shown a corresponding downward trend, and the dependency ratio has increased. It had risen from 154% in the beginning of the observation to 171% in 2002, increasing by 10.55% in 17 years. It is this basic change of rural households that has laid a good foundation for the economic development of the ten villages and households under observation in Zhejiang.

8.1.2 Labour Quality and Its Changes

It is seen from Table 8.1 that since the observation, the scale of rural labour in the ten villages in Zhejiang has shown an overall upward trend. However, influenced by the non-agricultural transformation, the scale of labour force was once declined, and due to village agglomeration, the scale was again significantly increased. The labour scale of the original observation villages (before the agglomeration) was maintained

Table 8.1 Labour force scale and composition

	Labour (number /village)	Education (%)				Schooling years	Training (%)	
		Illiterate	Primary school	Junior high	Senior high+		With technical titles	With training
1986	618.40	25.78	70.18		4.04	5.57	–	2.57
1987	621.60	25.82	70.08		4.10	5.57	–	3.08
1988	631.40	28.71	66.31		4.97	5.43	–	3.69
1989	639.40	22.54	72.08		5.38	5.81	–	4.61
1990	645.80	21.54	72.41		6.05	5.89	–	3.86
1991	645.50	21.27	71.99		6.74	5.93	–	3.90
1993	634.10	17.03	39.17	37.25	6.54	5.96	2.43	9.81
1995	625.00	15.78	34.54	43.08	6.61	6.16	2.74	7.57
1996	638.20	14.31	34.52	44.45	6.72	6.27	2.63	7.40
1997	613.70	14.73	33.75	44.79	6.73	6.26	2.38	7.95
1998	611.70	13.52	33.01	46.13	7.34	6.38	5.80	8.78
1999	699.00	10.79	35.85	44.88	8.48	6.52	8.13	9.40
2000	690.40	10.46	36.67	43.55	9.31	6.54	8.27	9.33
2001	716.40	10.06	36.95	42.29	10.69	6.59	7.50	8.29
2002	706.90	9.75	36.54	42.03	11.68	6.64	7.67	17.82

Note In 1997, farmers of a whole village group in an observation villages had their identity changed to non-agricultural because of the land confiscation of the high way construction, which resulted in a sharp drop in the total rural population. In 1999 and 2001, the observation villages were enlarged because of the agglomeration. From 1986 to 1991, the proportion of vocational training was based on data from the observation villages at about 640 people per village, while that of the new observation villages has been maintained at about 710 people per village. With the energetic promotion of the nine-year compulsory education in rural areas, the cultural quality of rural labour force has been improved substantially, with the share of labour with primary and lower education declining rapidly, while that of labour with education at junior high level and above increased significantly. The average time of schooling for rural labour increased significantly, from 5.57 years in 1986 to 6.64 years in 2002, with an increase of 19.17% over 17 years. At the same time, farmers' technical skills have also been improved. The number of labourers receiving technical training in rural areas has been on the rise. By 2002, those with technical training for more than three months had made up 17.82% of the total rural labour, a record high since the observation. It is against this background that the non-agricultural process of Zhejiang's rural economic structure has been greatly promoted. On the one hand, it provides a large number of employment opportunities for migrant workers, and at the same time, it also provides the most basic guarantee for local people to leave Zhejiang. If the 'going out and coming in' usually talked about by the Zhejiang people refers to the high-level talent strategy, then the 'bringing in and getting out' practiced in the grassroots rural areas has started from the very basic flow of labour force. Obviously, this practice of rural grassroots in Zhejiang has played an important role in promoting the steady rise of economic development in the province.

8.1.3 Comparison of Labour Quality Among Villages

Although the overall quality of labour force in the ten villages in Zhejiang has been significantly improved, there have been substantial differences among villages. In terms of the average schooling years of rural labour, the average years for the well-educated villages has reached more than seven years (Bogumen Village and Miaoyan Village), while the poorly-educated villages have only 5.34 years, with a gap of 2.23 years (Table 8.2). In other words, the 'nine-year' education in some villages has been basically completed, while a few villages have only completed primary education. In terms of technical training for rural labour, there are also significant differences among villages. There are three villages with the proportion exceeding 20% for rural labour with vocational training for more than three months, including the highest level of 39.79% in Miaoyan Village, followed by Bogumen Village and Xinmin Village. There are two villages with the level between 10 and 20%, and four villages less than 10%, with the lowest being only 1.37% in Yubei. Although it cannot be proved from the observation that villages with more schooling years or higher proportion of training must have a higher level of income, this has been verified by the rural household economic development in previous studies (Shi, 2000, 2001). Households with more education have higher incomes, and those with training clearly have higher income levels than those without training. Thus, with the development of modern economy and the increasingly fierce competition in the employment market, a certain level of basic cultural education and technical

Table 8.2 Labour scale and composition for villages 2000–2002

	Labour (number)	Education (%)				Schooling years	Training (%)	
		Illiterate	Primary school	Junior high	Senior high+		With technical titles	With training
Longshang	340.33	1.18	61.12	29.19	8.52	6.56	11.75	10.87
Yongfeng	953.00	20.22	55.30	17.49	7.00	5.34	1.26	5.77
Yubei	1243.00	3.89	41.22	46.55	8.34	6.86	7.40	1.37
Xishufu	617.00	11.29	27.44	42.63	18.64	6.90	2.54	2.27
Miaoyan	810.00	1.77	31.56	43.99	22.67	7.54	6.54	39.79
Xinmin	540.33	18.75	51.82	24.00	5.43	5.50	14.62	20.42
Jinhou	1104.67	16.66	23.84	52.75	6.76	6.37	0.54	1.39
Bogumen	808.67	3.87	14.34	71.68	10.10	7.57	23.66	24.73
Hebian	245.33	6.11	37.50	40.76	15.63	6.95	13.45	10.87
Shibanyan	383.33	13.04	42.70	38.26	6.00	6.14	7.30	9.13
10 villages	704.57	10.09	36.72	42.62	10.57	6.59	7.81	11.82

training have become the foundation of rural labour. If we say that the success of Zhejiang's economic development in the past century depended on the traditional and rich business experience, then whether Zhejiang is able to dominate in the economic development in the future will have to depend on the intensive basic cultural education and the extensive vocational training.

8.2 Employment Structure Change

8.2.1 Employment Change in Industrial Structure

With the development of time and the acceleration of the reform and opening up, the dual structure of the labour market has gradually changed, and the employment of rural labour force in Zhejiang has shown a non-agricultural trend (Table 8.3). The proportion of rural labour directly engaged in agriculture has decreased significantly, while that of rural labour engaged in non-agriculture has increased significantly. From 1986 to 2002, the proportion of rural labour engaged in agriculture in the ten villages in Zhejiang decreased by 12.04%, including decreases of 5.92% for planting and 14.69% for breeding, while the proportion of non-agricultural labour increased by 12.04%. With the rise of non-agriculture, the labour proportion in industry did not rise but decreased by 10.09%, and those with rising proportions mainly include transportation, commercial, catering and services as well as other industries, which rose by 2.59, 12.15 and 7.39% respectively. The results show that the employment of rural labour in Zhejiang tends to transition from the first and second industries to the tertiary industry. The rise and development of service-oriented tertiary industry is an

Table 8.3 Labour employment composition (%)

	Agriculture	#Planting	# Husbandry	Non-agriculture	#Industry	#Transportation	#Commercial catering, and service
1986	43.66	24.61	17.58	56.34	42.97	3.61	2.72
1987	39.14	21.12	15.75	60.86	46.51	3.38	3.31
1988	40.69	22.96	15.73	59.31	44.46	3.31	3.85
1989	42.29	26.26	14.45	57.71	42.96	3.75	3.75
1990	41.82	25.72	14.57	58.18	41.41	3.21	6.50
1991	38.71	22.39	14.19	61.29	40.84	4.29	5.96
1993	35.48	22.16	12.22	64.52	33.24	6.34	7.49
1995	28.28	15.33	12.36	71.72	29.81	9.49	8.43
1996	26.84	13.68	11.75	73.16	28.97	6.44	13.84
1997	25.55	15.11	9.24	74.45	27.37	6.37	14.31
1998	27.63	15.74	10.43	72.37	24.26	5.67	17.33
1999	31.39	20.30	10.06	68.61	29.61	5.26	16.62
2000	29.56	19.44	2.58	70.44	31.27	5.88	16.64
2001	32.29	19.51	3.00	67.71	33.14	6.16	13.60
2002	31.62	18.69	2.89	68.38	32.88	6.20	14.87

Note #indicating as part of a former category

important reason for the change of rural employment structure in Zhejiang. Data in Table 8.3 also show that when economic growth was slowed down, there appeared a return of rural labour back to the villages (Shi, 2000, 2001). This result gives us an important indication that although the comparative efficiency of agriculture is low and the benefits to farmers are limited, once there is an economic downturn, agriculture becomes the final guarantee of farmers' employment. For planting, in particular, when the economy is in a downturn, agriculture has become a guarantee for farmers' employment.

8.2.2 *Types of Employment*

In terms of structural changes of employment types, since 1990, the structural changes of rural labour employment types in the ten villages in Zhejiang have shown some features (Table 8.4). The proportion of labour engaged completely in agriculture or mainly in agriculture presented a 'U'-shape trend, and that for farmer workers showed a downward trend. Contrary to these, the proportions of those engaged in direct enterprise operation and management, as well as the employed labour showed an upward trend. At present, in the rural areas of Zhejiang, the employment structure of labour generally includes 1/3 of the labour in agriculture, 1/4 directly in enterprise operation and management (including self-employed individuals), and 1/4 of farmer workers or employed workers.

Table 8.4 Labour employment types (%)

	Agricultural labour	#Complete agricultural labour	Farmer workers*	#Township and village enterprise	TVE managers	Officials	Employed labour*	Others
1993	37.25	23.64	26.08	15.45	19.92	1.58	8.50	6.67
1995	26.04	17.08	26.48	16.39	22.61	1.60	14.05	9.06
1996	22.91	13.85	16.92	8.10	23.43	1.94	23.69	10.53
1997	27.36	16.46	11.10	4.32	25.29	1.91	24.25	9.91
1998	29.25	17.56	11.51	9.71	25.24	1.98	24.02	8.01
1999	33.08	19.51	13.81	7.87	22.98	1.43	22.03	6.68
2000	31.79	18.95	13.67	7.87	25.88	1.58	22.68	4.39
2001	36.36	20.25	8.95	3.11	23.12	1.58	24.92	5.08
2002	35.20	20.14	7.41	0.76	26.81	1.78	22.95	5.86

Note *Farmer workers refer to rural labour engaged in secondary and tertiary industries in rural collective enterprises, state-owned enterprises and institutions throughout the year or for most of the time. Employed workers refer to those employed in partnership, joint stock, private or triple-capital enterprises, individual or partnership businesses, and in other non-state-owned, collective enterprises, or institutions. The same for the next table. #indicating as part of the former category

8.2.3 Comparison of Employment Structure Among Villages

Although there is a non-agricultural trend in the employment of rural labour in the ten villages of Zhejiang (Table 8.3), Table 8.5 has revealed the differences among the ten villages in rural labour employment structure. From 2000 to 2002, there were two villages with the proportion of labour engaged in agriculture exceeding 50%, i.e. Shibanyan Village with the highest level of 78.61%, and Yongfeng Village with the level of 68.63%. Among the villages featured with non-agricultural employment, there were three villages with non-agricultural employment level exceeding 80%, i.e. Jinhou Village with the highest level of 98.61%, Miaoyan Village as the second with 96.79%, and Xishufu Village as the third with 94.27%. The other five villages were in a transitional process. Further analysis shows that planting takes a dominate place in Shibanyan village of Jinhua City, located in the central part of Zhejiang, accounting for 60.52% of the total employment. In Jinhou Village of Ruian City and Miaoyan Village of Ningshao Plain, located on the coast of Zhejiang, industry takes a major place, accounting for 50% of the total employment. In other villages, employment is roughly divided into two industries, or into three industries, or with the coexistence of multiple industries.

Similarly, from Table 8.6, it is seen that the regional differences in labour employment in the ten villages in Zhejiang were not only reflected in the specific industry, but also in the type. The situation was more obvious in the three villages with relatively high levels of non-agriculturalisation where the employment of rural labour was typically polarised. In Jinhou Village of Rui'an in Wenzhou, the polarisation reveals that the labour force was mainly composed of business owners and supplemented by employees, whereas in the two villages of the Ningshao Plain, the situation was the opposite to the two villages in the Wentai area in that employment was mainly composed of farmer workers or employees with fewer bosses. This result indicates that rural employment is obviously influenced by the regional economic development and the differences in culture and tradition. An important reason for the rapid economic development in Wentai is that people are good at doing small businesses. It is also because of this that the bosses in Wentai are small business owners - typical small bosses, as few of them can really grow up to become big business owners (Shi, Jin, Zhao, & Luo, 2004; Shi, Wang, & Qian, 2004).

8.3 Labour Mobility and Idleness

8.3.1 Rural Labour Mobility

Labour is an important element of production in economic development and its relationship with economic growth has been manifested in various aspects. One of these aspects is the flow of labour according to wages, the law of market economy. Generally speaking, the regions with more labour inflows are also relatively developed

Table 8.5 Employment structure of rural labour 2000–2002 (%)

	Agriculture	Planting	Husbandry	Non-agriculture	Industry	Transportation	Commercial and catering
Longshang	30.85	11.66	1.18	0.00	35.26	7.74	18.90
Yongfeng	68.63	36.38	1.57	30.68	24.34	0.77	2.97
Yubei	47.55	41.43	5.15	0.64	32.74	2.47	5.26
Xishufu	5.73	4.97	0.32	0.00	57.86	0.65	34.79
Miaoyan	3.21	2.72	0.49	0.00	41.98	7.24	33.33
Xinmin	21.34	17.58	1.79	1.97	21.53	17.09	26.22
Jinhou	1.39	1.21	0.09	0.00	50.24	14.12	13.91
Bogumen	31.86	0.00	0.00	31.86	3.79	4.78	6.80
Hebian	38.86	24.18	14.67	0.00	49.59	2.04	4.08
Shibanyan	78.61	60.52	16.52	1.04	1.57	2.43	14.35
10 villages	31.17	19.21	2.82	8.13	32.44	6.08	15.02

Table 8.6 Labour employment categories 2000–2002 (%)

	Agricultural labour	#Complete agricultural labour	Farmer workers	#Township and village enterprise	TVE managers	Officials	Employed labour	Others
Longshang	28.50	12.34	7.35	0.00	21.35	32.91	2.06	7.84
Yongfeng	81.74	50.30	2.52	0.59	14.55	0.00	1.15	0.03
Yubei	47.41	24.51	8.64	8.64	19.52	23.33	0.56	0.54
Xishufu	5.24	1.51	24.80	17.50	35.55	32.58	0.92	0.92
Miaoyan	4.81	2.14	39.34	3.25	16.50	36.63	1.73	0.99
Xinmin	23.13	4.81	0.74	0.00	33.44	29.49	1.91	11.29
Jinhou	1.21	0.24	2.78	0.91	45.32	37.02	2.66	11.01
Bogumen	40.73	31.78	3.30	1.69	20.77	18.30	2.47	14.43
Hebian	42.12	17.39	4.35	0.95	32.34	12.91	2.72	5.57
Shibanyan	83.91	55.65	0.78	0.00	11.39	2.61	1.30	0.00
10 villages	34.48	19.79	9.98	3.88	25.25	23.53	1.65	5.11

Note #indicating as part of the former category

regions. From the observation of the ten villages in Zhejiang (Table 8.7), the development of rural economy is more and more closely related to labour inflow, as migrant workers take as high as 27.43% of total rural labour in the villages. Although the percentage has shown an inverted 'U' trend since 1995, changes have been small, within the range of 6%. Obviously, such changes are closely related to the economic development of the villages. When there is rapid economic growth, the scale of migrant labour force increases correspondingly, and vice versa. As far as the employment structure of migrant workers is concerned, changes are obvious. In the early 1990s, joint-stock enterprises were the main employers of migrant workers. The proportion of employment in these enterprises accounted for 2/3 of the total migrant labour. By the end of the 1990s, affected by the development of the tertiary industry and the reform of enterprise ownership, the proportion of migrant employment in enterprises had dropped to 1/2, while the proportion in private enterprises risen to 1/2.

With the increasing labour inflow, the scale of labour outflow also rises correspondingly. The outflow of labour accounts for 17.42% of the total labour force in the villages. Over time, the structure of the labour outflow has also changed correspondingly. To be specific, the labour outflow has increased. By 2002, only 2.71% of the labour flows occurred within the home townships and towns, while 97.29% of the labour went out. Compared with 1993, the change was 26.75%. As far as the current distance of labour flow is concerned, the majority or 53.49% of the labour flow occurred in the home county, and the proportion of migration out of the county is basically the same as that out of the province, each accounting for more than 20%. Compared with 2000, the proportion of migration out of townships but within counties increased most rapidly by 1.38%, those for other categories all decreased. In comparison, the proportion for migration out of the province had the most obvious decrease of 2.15%, and those out of the counties and those out of the country declined by 0.07 and 0.54% respectively. It is worth noting that although there was a decrease for overseas migration in 2002 compared with the levels in 2000 and 2001, there were increases for all those years before 2000, and the year 2001 was also the one with the highest percentage of going abroad since the observation. The high proportion of overseas employment means that the ability of Zhejiang farmers to obtain employment opportunities has been greatly improved, but this improvement is also affected by the international market, and the rising overseas employment fever has decreased recently.

Comparing the inflow and outflow of rural labour in Zhejiang, it is found that the inflow ratio is significantly higher than that of the outflow. Although the net inflow level decreased from 14.11% in 1995 to 10.01% in 2002, the ratio of inflow was still 10% higher than that of the outflow. Thus, the inflow of labour has become an important force to support the development of rural economy in Zhejiang.

Table 8.7 Flow of labour

	Labour inflow (%)	Inflow labour employment (%)			Labour outflow (%)	Out migration distance (%)			
		Collective enterprises	Joint-stock enterprises	Others		Out of township within county	Out of county within province	Out of province domestic	Overseas
1993	26.83	18.05	66.37	15.58	12.90	40.22	16.63	13.20	0.49
1995	28.44	7.99	63.85	28.16	14.33	46.46	26.77	21.37	0.67
1996	26.28	7.16	65.65	27.19	18.52	55.58	17.85	21.49	0.00
1997	31.46	2.85	56.50	40.65	18.58	54.04	24.04	21.40	0.26
1998	31.29	0.42	54.18	45.40	20.94	50.82	24.12	19.20	0.78
1999	25.67	0.39	41.03	58.58	16.45	53.39	23.22	20.70	1.04
2000	27.38	0.00	35.56	64.44	17.45	52.12	21.83	23.07	1.66
2001	22.78	0.12	25.31	74.57	16.14	60.73	15.48	19.38	3.37
2002	27.43	2.64	49.01	48.35	17.42	53.49	21.75	20.92	1.12

8.3.2 Comparison of Labour Flows Among Villages

Influenced by the locations of individual villages, the economic development and the decision-making capability of policy-makers, some villages have become intaking places while others become sending places of rural labour. As for the regional distribution of labour flows (Table 8.8), four of the ten villages in Zhejiang can be regarded as major inflow areas, specifically Hebian Village in Lishui, Xishufu Village in Shaoxing, Miaoyan Village in Yinxian County and Jinhou Village in Ruian, with the ratios of migrant workers to local labour of 151.36, 55.92, 49.22 and 39.53% respectively. Three villages can be regarded as the secondary inflow areas, namely Shibanyan Village in Jinhua, Xinmin Village in Wenling and Yubei Village in Jiaxing, each with the migrant labour ratio around 20%. On the contrary, some villages can be regarded as the sending villages of labour. Of the ten villages, one village has the out migration ratio of over 50%, and it is Longshang Village in Lin'an. There are three villages within the range of 20–30% including Xinmin Village in Wenling, Jinhou Village in Ruian and Bogumen Village in Putuo. There are two villages within the range of 10–20%, i.e. Yongfeng Village in Huzhou and Shibanyan Village in Jinhua. Comparing the inflow and outflow, it can be seen that six villages in the ten villages in Zhejiang are villages with net-inflow (Yubei, Xishufu, Miaoyan, Jinhou, Hebian and Shibanyan), and the other four villages are villages with net outflow.

From the perspective of the labour flow distance, there have been obvious differences among villages. The distance was the longest for Jinhou Village and Xinmin Village of the Wentai area, as villagers' travel distance ranged from local townships and towns, to as far as abroad, and mainly within the provinces, taking 50.24 and 50.29% of total outflows of the two villages. These were followed by Hebian Village in Lishui, Yongfeng Village in Huzhou and Shibanyan Village in Jinhua. The distance for these villages were shorter than the two villages mentioned in Wentai, but there were still 20–30% flows migrating out of the province. Then, there was Miaoyan Village of Yinxian County, in which labour outflows were mostly confined to the home province and city. Labour outflows for the other four villages were mainly concentrated within the home cities and counties. The differences in the observation villages have shown that in the economic development, rural areas in Zhejiang have a wide range of contacts with the outside world. But such a wide range is based on certain locations, as the experiences and tradition of outflows to the specific locations are the foundation of promoting the extensive contacts.

8.3.3 The Idleness of Rural Labour

While analysing the employment of rural labour, the problem of rural unemployment also deserves further research. However, the discussion on this issue has received little attention, either because of people's deliberate avoidance on the topic of unemployment or the difficulty in obtaining information. In the current study, there is a

Table 8.8 Labour flows from 1995 to 2000

	Labour inflow (%)	Inflow labour employment (%)			Labour outflow (%)	Out migration distance (%)			
		Collective enterprise	Joint-stock enterprises	Others		Out of township within county	Out of county within province	Out of province domestic	Overseas
Longshang	0.10	0.00	0.00	100.00	53.48	84.98	13.19	1.10	0.00
Yongfeng	1.43	0.00	0.00	100.00	18.50	54.25	18.34	27.41	0.00
Yubei	10.57	0.00	0.00	100.00	7.75	77.51	10.38	12.11	0.00
Xishufu	55.92	0.00	71.40	28.60	9.02	97.01	2.99	0.00	0.00
Miaoyan	49.22	0.00	0.00	100.00	3.74	39.56	58.24	2.20	0.00
Xinmin	13.39	0.00	97.24	2.76	26.16	24.29	24.53	50.24	0.94
Jinhou	39.53	0.31	41.37	58.32	25.98	23.34	16.61	50.29	9.76
Bogumen	7.42	0.00	0.00	100.00	27.25	83.51	14.52	0.45	1.51
Hebian	151.36	0.45	0.00	99.55	9.51	22.86	47.14	30.00	0.00
Shibanyan	27.46	0.16	27.19	72.65	18.20	56.21	17.40	23.58	2.69
10 villages	28.29	3.02	52.54	44.44	17.66	52.27	22.81	21.18	0.74

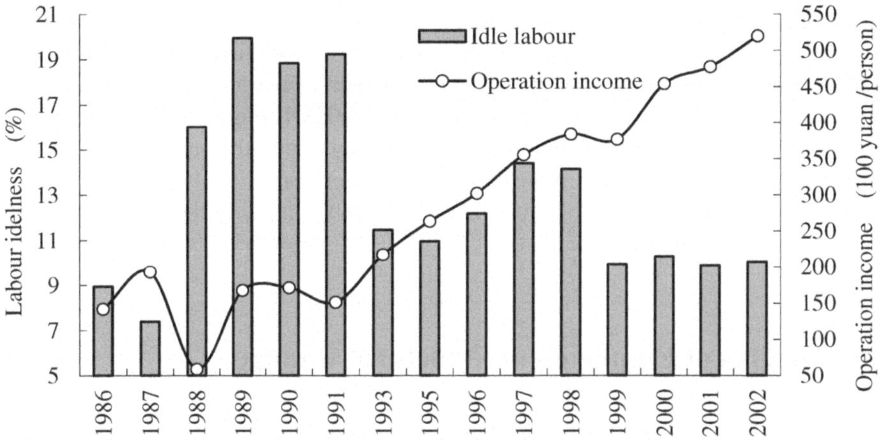

Fig. 8.2 Rural labour idleness and economic growth. *Note* Operation income is based on retail price index of Zhejiang, the price in 2000 = 100

special column in the survey to investigate rural labour idleness.[1] Although the concept of labour idleness is not entirely the same as unemployment, idleness to some extent also means without work. In order to avoid confusion, the concept of labour idleness is used here.

From the observation data (Fig. 8.2), in the mid-1980s, the proportion of idle labour in the ten villages in Zhejiang was about 8.94%. With the passage of time, it rose to 19.24% in the early 1990s, then declined to 10.94% in 1995, and the change in the following five years showed a mild inverted 'U'-shape trend. After 2000, it dropped to about 10% again. Taking into consideration of the economic growth of the ten villages in Zhejiang, it is found that when there is faster economic growth, there is a lower level of labour idleness, but when economic growth is slow, there is a higher level of labour idleness. At the same time, it is found that there is an obvious lag between the labour idleness and the income growth. When the economic income growth stagnates or falls, the labour underemployment increases.

The estimation of labour idleness can be obtained not only from the data in the observation villages, but also from the information concerning rural labour of the observed households and their annual labour input in production and operation. Generally, there are three types of labour use, for household operation, for operation outside the household, and for migration work. Of the three categories, there exists the phenomenon of labour employment for operation both within and outside of household, which must be deducted from the estimation of labour idleness. The estimated results are basically consistent with the observation data from the villages. Since 1995, the labour idleness in the observed households has been on the rise, from 4.79% in 1995 to 9.28% in 1998, and then declined to 2.48% in 1999. After 2000, this

[1]Labour idleness = (total number of labour × 300 − days spent on production of various industries)/300.

indicator rose again, reaching 7.83% in 2000 and 11.25% in 2001. In 2002, the level of labour idleness reached the highest level since the observation, hitting 17.71%. As a result, the average level of idleness during the Ninth Five-Year Plan (1995–2000) increased from 6.25 to 12.21% at present (2000–2002). It might be right to say that rural labour employment was relatively good in Zhejiang in the past century, but the current employment situation is not optimistic. Therefore, to solve the problem of rural employment has become an urgent and important issue in the development of rural economy in Zhejiang.

8.4 Origins of Employment Structural Change

8.4.1 Education Investment Improved the Quality of Rural Labour

Mr. Theodore W. Schultz, the well-known economist and Nobel Laureate in economics, talked about investing in farmers (Schultz, 1986: 132), 'For large population groups, the level and distribution of gifted abilities tend to be the same, but the key acquired abilities are not.' These abilities are precisely the most basic needs for economic development. Investing in farmers is intended to change the level and distribution of such abilities. In fact, in addition to relying on external investment to change their ability to survive and develop, farmers themselves are investing to enhance their own abilities. We generally call it human capital investment which is used to strengthen the ability of self-development.

In existing household surveys, there is seldom data collection concerning human capital investment, but there is one particular item—household cultural expenditure. Although only a few sub-items are included such as tuition and miscellaneous fees, technical training fees as well as entertainment fees, without expenditures on some tangible necessities such as books, stationery and other cultural goods, such household cultural expenditures in the surveys are the major part of human capital investment, and therefore can be used in the current study. As can be seen from Table 8.9, with the increase of household income, the living consumption showed a significant downward trend, and the most obvious decline occurred after 1995. The propensity to consume decreased from 83.5% in 1995 to 61.32% in 2000, before it showed a restorative growth, to 69.32% in 2002. However, the propensity to consume in culture (simply known as expenditure) has not decreased, but instead increased significantly. Expenditures on cultural services in households have been on the rise in both absolute and relative terms. The share of cultural consumption out of household living expenditure has increased from 3.71% in the initial observation period to 10.41% in 2002, increased by 6.70% in 17 years, with a rise of 5.37% since 1995. Cultural consumption has risen by 4.13% over 17 years, or by 3.01% since 1995. With the reform of the national education system, the cultural consumption of rural households was more composed of tuition and miscellaneous fees. The proportion of

Table 8.9 Cultural expenditure and economic growth in observed households

	Net income (yuan/person)	Total expenditure (yuan/person)	Propensity to consume (%)	Cultural expenditure (yuan/person)	#Tuition and miscellaneous fees/cultural expenditure	Cultural expenditure/total expenditure	Cultural expenditure/net income
1986	861.87	717.99	83.31	26.64	–	3.71	3.09
1987	1181.55	848.46	71.81	34.15	–	4.03	2.89
1988	1489.50	1304.02	87.55	60.15	–	4.61	4.04
1989	1307.28	1235.82	94.53	63.66	–	5.15	4.87
1990	1444.33	1160.42	80.34	73.51	–	6.34	5.09
1991	1730.18	1374.15	79.42	90.49	–	6.59	5.23
1993	3110.13	2517.03	80.93	111.90	63.59	4.45	3.60
1995	6351.27	5303.32	83.50	267.48	72.13	5.04	4.21
1996	7323.73	5865.05	80.08	367.44	66.96	6.26	5.02
1997	7425.14	5868.56	79.04	390.69	67.23	6.66	5.26
1998	7121.82	5324.94	74.77	391.64	81.39	7.35	5.50
1999	8113.35	5303.83	65.37	464.13	77.97	8.75	5.72
2000	9381.10	5752.32	61.32	449.97	76.88	7.82	4.80
2001	9730.87	5989.62	61.55	557.35	77.63	9.31	5.73
2002	9540.16	6615.57	69.34	688.74	69.14	10.41	7.22

Note # indiicating as part of the former category

tuition and miscellaneous fees increased from less than 70% before the Ninth Five-Year Plan period to almost 70% in 2002. The rise of cultural consumption, especially tuition and miscellaneous expenses, is on the one hand the result of the reform of the national education system, which has forced farmers to do so. On the other hand, it is also due to farmers' awareness of the role of education in family economic growth. Thus, it can be seen that the improvement of farmers' quality is largely attributed to farmers' understanding and practice of education investment. From the perspective of current economic development, this understanding and practice of farmers have been rewarded accordingly (Shi, 2001).

From Table 8.10, it is seen that households with different education backgrounds have shown differences in their consumption ideology and cultural consumption, and such differences have also changed over time. Whether during the Ninth Five-Year Plan period or since 2000, rural households with relatively high education tend to have a lower propensity to consume, but have a higher tendency in terms of cultural consumption or investment. They not only attach great importance to education investment, but also receive considerable benefits from it. Therefore, since the new century, greatly influenced by farmers with higher level of education, other rural households with relatively low educational level have strengthened their investment in education. Although this strengthening is only manifested in the investment tendency in education, and its intensity is still far from that of better-educated households, the investment growth is considerable compared with that of income. Thus, the return of education investment has made Zhejiang farmers fully aware of the importance of education, so that even if the government's education policy has changed from free to non-free, farmers are still enthusiastic about it. This understanding and practice regarding education by farmers in Zhejiang can be understood as the magic weapon. At the same time, it has laid the foundation for realising the changes in employment structure.

8.4.2 Inter-industry Payment Differences

Once the farmers have realised the significance and role of education investment, their first reaction is to increase investment in their own education. The result of this reaction is that on the one hand, labour quality has been significantly improved as a whole, and on the other hand, it has laid the foundation for rural labour in terms of job selection. In previous studies, we found that farmers' behaviour is economically rational (Shi, 1999: Chap. 4). Their rational behaviour can also be proved in their choice of employment. From Table 8.11 and Fig. 8.3, it can be seen that an important reason for farmers' choice of non-agricultural employment is that the non-agricultural remuneration is significantly higher than that of agriculture. Farmers' employment structure shifts from the secondary industry to the tertiary industry, which is also due to the widening gap in the remuneration of the tertiary industry and the secondary industry. Therefore, the wage gap between industries has been the fundamental reason for the changes in farmers' employment structure. In other agricultural areas, out

Table 8.10 Cultural consumption for households with different education backgrounds

		Net income (yuan/person)	Total expenditure (yuan/person)	Propensity to consume (%)	Cultural expenditure (yuan/person)	#Tuition and miscellaneous fees/cultural expenditure	Cultural expenditure/total expenditure	Cultural expenditure/net income
1995–2000	Illiterate	4827.56	4191.70	86.83	216.70	74.52	5.17	4.49
	Primary	6805.19	4816.81	70.78	325.43	71.31	6.76	4.78
	Junior high	6734.17	5409.07	80.32	391.48	75.22	7.24	5.81
	Senior high+	11536.91	7040.83	61.03	454.50	77.79	6.46	3.94
2000–2002	Illiterate	5788.19	4133.54	71.41	368.21	82.26	8.91	6.36
	Primary	10231.94	6239.81	60.98	506.87	76.54	8.12	4.95
	Junior high	8619.18	5318.18	61.70	576.10	73.32	10.83	6.68
	Senior high+	13359.43	10854.43	81.25	1027.58	65.81	9.47	7.69

Note #indiicating as part of the former category

Table 8.11 Rural household labour price for different operations (yuan/labour day)

	1986	1987	1988	1989	1990	1991	1993	1995	1996	1997	1998	1999	2000	2001	2002
Household operation	5.58	7.41	9.46	9.37	9.76	10.74	18.49	35.25	35.71	45.28	41.89	48.98	60.27	65.00	56.83
1. Agriculture	4.95	6.03	7.24	8.04	8.21	8.49	12.64	25.15	23.61	22.31	18.54	19.12	25.51	20.20	21.61
Planting	4.97	5.78	6.31	7.58	7.80	8.55	12.04	27.09	28.19	22.37	26.71	21.68	22.24	20.86	22.53
Crop	4.83	5.49	6.11	7.40	7.70	8.13	12.38	27.03	26.60	22.21	24.43	19.43	19.82	19.97	20.49
Grain crop	5.04	5.83	6.08	8.04	8.16	8.89	14.60	30.36	30.03	24.38	27.35	20.01	20.78	20.55	18.99
Cash crop	4.08	5.08	6.32	5.98	7.78	7.93	8.18	14.43	18.06	18.22	12.87	13.14	19.22	17.76	28.61
Others	4.24	4.36	6.12	6.08	6.26	5.80	10.01	23.71	21.82	19.14	22.53	20.19	18.71	19.88	19.37
Orchard	6.74	9.34	8.38	9.45	8.62	11.18	9.89	27.39	36.63	23.25	38.55	32.18	32.84	23.69	27.55
Forestry	31.51	35.98	30.89	25.83	20.92	25.47	48.90	58.93	40.03	56.75	41.45	37.86	52.69	45.71	57.14
Husbandry	2.26	3.35	6.91	8.01	6.91	6.45	7.40	14.06	14.12	18.36	13.46	16.95	21.06	21.78	18.85
Fishery	4.33	8.01	8.00	6.07	10.30	8.92	19.54	32.50	23.23	19.95	9.29	15.43	29.43	14.50	17.93
2. Non-agriculture	7.22	10.74	14.09	12.66	13.22	15.15	28.02	46.35	51.52	68.72	66.08	76.20	87.66	101.38	85.92
Industry	6.19	11.59	14.43	11.01	12.48	12.20	27.94	57.29	69.07	54.66	47.33	58.34	63.99	74.82	70.52
Civil engineering	4.14	7.17	8.96	12.02	14.34	17.38	22.18	41.61	49.56	54.91	33.63	48.51	41.52	44.36	47.66
Transportation	10.27	13.31	21.50	21.06	22.09	21.35	26.88	56.86	66.01	56.54	57.51	56.91	75.47	65.27	99.64
Commercial and catering	8.13	11.25	11.50	11.68	13.49	18.05	34.70	42.38	43.37	85.59	83.35	109.55	124.55	146.73	106.52
Others	4.51	6.22	10.86	8.73	8.18	9.27	14.53	25.36	32.11	47.66	41.09	15.44	17.93	25.54	23.30
3. Average labour price	5.48	5.71	7.23	7.50	8.60	8.48	19.05	25.71	22.89	28.12	28.29	29.17	30.64	30.90	22.93

Note Labour price = (total revenue − total expenses)/total labour use

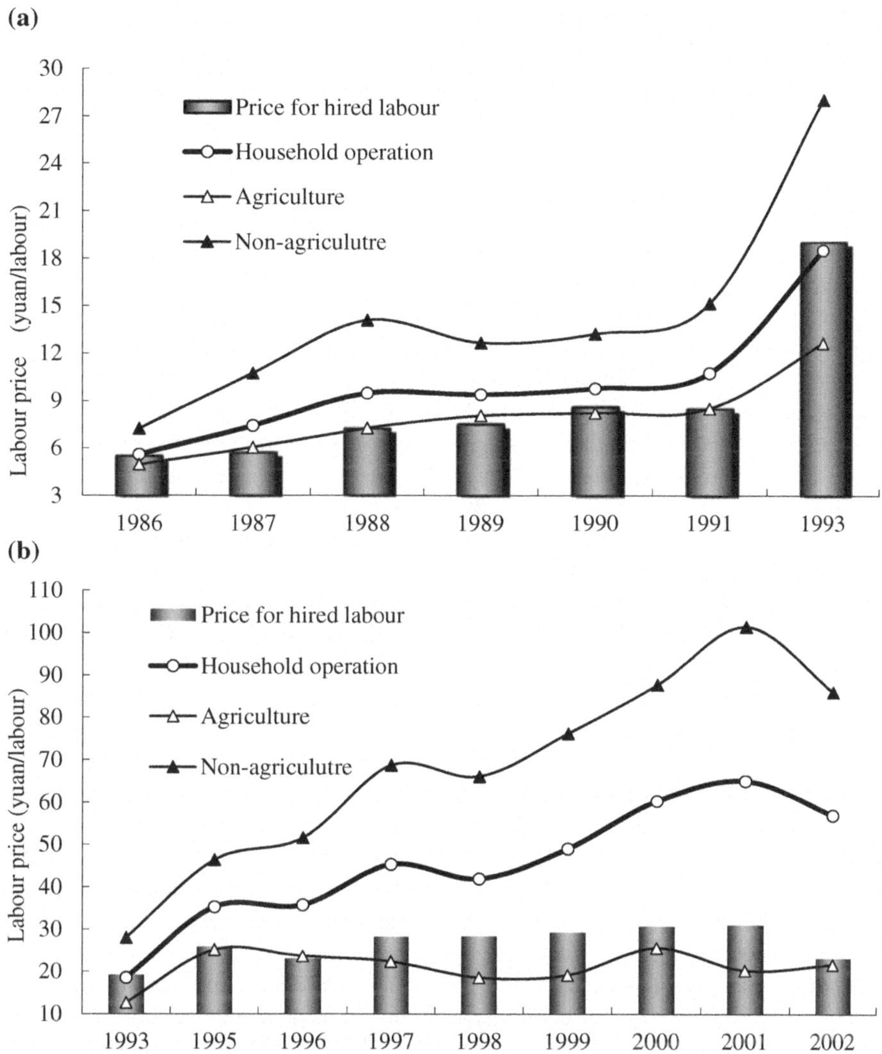

Fig. 8.3 **a** Labour price for different household operations 1986–1993. **b** Labour price for different household operations 1993–2002

migration is very obvious, while in Zhejiang, it is the opposite. Why? This study also finds out that there is a gap between the remuneration of those self-employed and of the employees. When this gap is getting higher, farmers will inevitably choose higher-paid industries or the corresponding type of employment.

8.5 Conclusive Comments

Since the observation, the scale of rural labour force in the ten villages in Zhejiang has been on the rise. With the energetic promotion of the nine-year compulsory education in rural areas, the education level of rural labour has improved substantially. The average number of education years of labour has increased significantly, from 5.57 years in 1986 to 6.64 years in 2002. At the same time, there is also obvious improvement of farmers' technical abilities. It is against this background that the non-agricultural process of Zhejiang's rural economic structure has been greatly promoted. This not only provides a large number of employment opportunities for migrant workers, but also provides the most basic guarantee for local people to leave Zhejiang. If the 'going out and inviting in' often talked about by Zhejiang people is a high-level talent strategy, then in the most grassroots rural areas, rural people have been engaged in 'bringing in and going out' starting from the most basic labour flows. This behavioural change at the grassroots level in Zhejiang has played an inestimable role in promoting the steady rise of its rural economy.

With the development of time and the acceleration of the reform and opening up, the situation of the dual division of the labour market has been gradually broken through, and the employment structure of rural labour in Zhejiang shows a non-agricultural trend. The observation data show that the employment of rural labour in Zhejiang tends to transition from the first and second industries to the tertiary industry. The rise of service-oriented tertiary industry is an important reason for the change in rural employment structure in Zhejiang. At the same time, there is also a phenomenon, that is, the share of labour in agriculture is rebounding when economic growth is slow. This shows that although the comparative efficiency of agriculture is low and the benefits to farmers are limited, during the economic downturn, agriculture becomes the last guarantee for farmers' employment. In particular, planting is still the best guarantee for farmers' employment when the economy is in a downturn. At present, in the rural areas of Zhejiang, the employment is generally composed of 1/3 of labour in agriculture, 1/4 directly engaged in enterprise operation and management (including individual businesses), and 1/3 farmer workers or employed labour.

The development of rural economy becomes more and more closely related to the labour inflows. The proportion of migrant labour to the total labour in the villages has reached 27.43%. When the economy is rising rapidly, the scale of labour in-migration increases correspondingly. Otherwise, if the economy slows down, the scale decreases. In the early 1990s, joint-stock enterprises were the main places of employment for these migrant workers. By the end of 1990s, affected by the development of the tertiary industry and the institutional reform of enterprise ownership, they were attracted to other enterprises such as private enterprises.

At the same time, the scale of labour outflow increased accordingly, accounting for 17.42% of the total labour force in the villages. Over time, the distribution structure of these labour outflows has also undergone changes accordingly. A specific example is that rural labour has travelled to further places. By 2002, only 2.71% of the labour flows occurred within the local townships and towns, while 97.29% have flown out.

Among them, the proportion of out-of-county flows was basically the same as that of out-of-province flows, each accounting for more than 20%.

Comparing the inflow and outflow of rural labour in Zhejiang, it is found that the level of inflow is significantly higher than that of outflow. It can be seen that labour inflow is an important force to sustain the development of rural economy in Zhejiang.

Rural labour idleness is closely related to the economic operation of villages. When the economic income increases faster, the rural labour idleness is lower, or otherwise with economic income decreases, it is higher. Besides, there is an obvious lag between idleness and economic income growth. When economic income growth stagnates or falls, it will be followed by the underemployment of labour. Since 1995, the labour idleness has been on the rise, from 4.79% in 1995 to 17.71% in 2002.

Farmers are increasingly aware of the significance and the role of education, which is demonstrated in the continuous increase of their educational investment for their own sake and the overall improvement of the quality of workers. The change in educational ideology is also the basis of the change in farmers' employment structure. The fundamental reason for the change in farmers' employment structure lies in the existence of wage gaps among different industries in different regions.

References

Schultz, T. W. (1986). *Transforming traditional agriculture (Translated in Chinese)*. Business Press.

Shi, J., Jin, X., Zhao, W., & Luo, W. (2004). *Institutional change and economic development: Study of the Wenzhou pattern*. Hangzhou: Zhejiang University Press.

Shi, J., Wang, W., & Qian, T. (2004). *Private economy and institutional innovation: Study of the Taizhou phenomenon*. Hangzhou: Zhejiang University Press.

Shi, Q. (1999). *Rural household economic development*. Beijing: China Agriculture Press.

Shi, Q. (2000). A comparative study on the unbalanced economic development of rural households and its origin in Shanxi and Zhejiang: Evidence from follow-up observations from 1986 to 1999. *China Economic Studies, 6*, 24–31.

Shi, Q. (2001). *Rural household economic activity and behaviour*. Beijing: China Agricultural Press.

Chapter 9
Structural Change of Village Economy and Finance

Contents

The rural household economic development is not only a matter within an individual household, but also related to national policies, village collective leadership and the geographical environment (Shi, 1999). Therefore, after analysing the evolution of the economic structure and behaviour of rural households, it is necessary to carry out research on the evolution or change in the economic structure of the villages where the rural households are located. Taking the ten villages in Zhejiang as the objects of analysis based on the comprehensive survey data at the village level from 1986 to 2002, this chapter focuses on the analysis of the changes in village economic structure.

Q. Shi and Y. Gao, *Sustainable Development of Rural Household Economy*,
https://doi.org/10.1007/978-981-15-2747-0_9

9.1 Land Scale and Land Use

9.1.1 Land Scale and Its Structure

Generally speaking, in a relatively stable natural village, the total land area under the jurisdiction is also relatively stable. There are three major reasons for the change in village land area and these include the adjustment of administrative village boundaries, the land expropriation within the village and the natural changes, such as the change in river boundaries. For the ten villages in Zhejiang, since the observation, the changes in average land scale have generally shown a 'U'-shape trend, with decline as the basic feature, mainly due to non-agricultural land acquisition. Through the analysis of the whole observation process, it can be seen that the reduction of the total land area of the ten villages in Zhejiang mainly occurred in the early 1990s. In the first five years of the observation from 1986 to 1991, the average size of observation villages decreased slightly by 1.12 hectares in 1991, or 0.62% compared with 1986. In the second five years, the Eighth Five-Year Plan period, the land area decreased dramatically. In 1995, the land area decreased by 22.89 hectares, a decrease of 12.71% compared with 1990, with an average annual decrease of 4.58 hectares and an annual decrease rate of 2.68%. In the third five years, the Ninth Five-Year Plan period, the scale and speed of land area reduction slowed down, but the decline rate was still higher than that of the first five-year observation. Compared with 1995, it decreased by 2.83 hectares in 1998, with an average annual decrease rate of 0.60%. Influenced by the village agglomeration in 1999 (Yubei Village), the average size of the observation villages increased sharply. Compared with 1998, the average size increased by 16.29% in 1999, but the sudden increase was only temporary, and the trend of land scale reduction was unchanged. In 2000, the average land scale of the observation villages decreased by 0.62 hectares, or 0.35%, compared with that of 1999. Due to another round of village agglomeration (Yongfeng Village) in 2001, the average size of the villages increased greatly, but decreased again by 2002. Compared with 2001, the average land area of the observation villages decreased by 0.95 hectares, with a reduction of 0.51%.

In terms of land composition, woodland is the main type of land used by the ten villages in Zhejiang, accounting for 40.35% of the total land, followed by arable land, accounting for 28.30%, water surface and garden land each accounting for about 10%. In terms of changes in land use, the share of arable land has been decreasing constantly since the observation, while woodland and garden land have shown an upward trend. The water surface has been increasing slightly. The area of mudflats and other land use has showed significant downward trends.

9.1.2 Arable Land Change and Structure

From the above analysis, it is seen that since the observation, the land area of the ten villages in Zhejiang has been declining, but what is the reason? In order to answer this question, this study takes arable land change as an example to explore the changes in the ten villages in Zhejiang.

As can be seen from Table 9.2, the decrease of farmland has been observed throughout the years, while the farmland increase has been occasional. Since 1993, compared with the arable land at the beginning of the observation, the highest annual decrease of arable land in the observation villages reached 6.65% in 1995, and the lowest of 0.31% in 1999, with an average decrease of 2.98% from 1995 to 2002. There are various reasons for the reduction of cultivated land, such as land acquisition for national infrastructure, collective infrastructure, housing land for farmers, returning farmland to forests and grasslands, and natural disasters. For the ten villages in Zhejiang, the main reason is the land acquisition by the state infrastructure. Land expropriation due to state infrastructure has become one of the main reasons for the reduction of cultivated land and even land area in Zhejiang. During the period 1995–2002, the land requisitioned by state infrastructure accounted for 44.81% of the total reduction of cultivated land, followed by collective infrastructure, accounting for 36.06%, and the land used by rural households for house construction accounted for only 4.54% of the reduction of cultivated land in rural areas. This result indicates that the process of farmland conversion has been influenced by the state or government actions. Currently there are quite a few legal provisions concerning the use of agricultural land, especially the non-agricultural use of cultivated land, strictly prohibiting or controlling the non-agricultural use of cultivated land. At the beginning of the reform, on the basis of the amendment of the *Constitution*, the State modified or re-promulgated many decrees successively, such as the *Land Management Law*, the *Agriculture Law*, the *Forest Law*, the *Fisheries Law*, the *Regulations on the Protection of Basic Farmland and the Rural Land Contract Law* (Ding, 2000). However, the management of land conversion is only manifested in rural residential or collective land, while the issue of land conversion involving government planning has never been included in the management.[1] In many areas, especially in economically developed areas, non-agricultural land rent has become the main source of fiscal revenue. Yet, as the owner of rural land—rural collective organizations, the benefits in this process are quite limited, so in a previous study on the ownership of rural land, 70%

[1] Both the *Land Management Law* and the *Regulations on the Protection of Basic Farmland* clearly stipulate that 'if the cultivated land is occupied by non-agricultural construction after approval, the occupying unit shall be responsible for reclaiming the cultivated land equal to the quantity and quality of the land occupied. If it is unable to claim or the cultivated land is not up to the standard, the occupying unit shall be responsible to pay fees in accordance with the relevant provisions, and the special funds shall be used for reclaiming new cultivated land'. But in the actual implementation, how many departments have seriously considered this? If they considered and paid the fees, how much was used to compensate the cultivated land? In the whole process of non-agriculturalisation, the real beneficiaries are the local governments, while the loss is born by the collectives, the real land owners, and to be specific, the local farmers.

Table 9.1 Land use structure (%)

	Total area (ha/village)	Arable land	#Household operation	Woodland	Garden land	Water surface	#Household operation	Mudflats and others
1986	181.27	24.48	94.64	42.80	7.41	11.95	14.93	13.36
1987	180.37	24.20	92.82	42.81	7.62	12.07	15.03	13.29
1988	180.17	23.79	93.56	42.63	7.94	12.20	16.01	13.44
1989	180.17	23.93	99.37	42.37	8.20	12.08	19.75	13.41
1990	180.15	23.79	99.13	42.53	8.27	12.09	19.32	13.33
1991	180.05	23.59	99.29	42.54	8.12	12.09	20.64	13.66
1993	171.24	22.97	99.90	44.95	8.27	11.27	10.85	12.55
1995	157.26	22.30	97.70	48.84	8.60	12.26	26.18	8.00
1996	156.25	21.96	97.65	49.17	8.34	12.34	29.91	8.19
1997	155.65	21.75	97.85	48.64	8.92	12.39	29.91	8.31
1998	154.43	21.31	97.79	48.76	8.82	12.48	29.91	8.63
1999	179.58	28.45	98.51	42.06	9.81	12.02	26.72	7.66
2000	178.96	28.48	98.33	42.21	9.87	12.06	26.72	7.38
2001	188.26	28.73	98.39	40.14	10.62	13.55	37.15	6.96
2002	187.31	28.30	98.35	40.35	10.86	13.60	37.12	6.89

Note #being part of the former category

of the farmers believed that land is 'state-owned' (Shi & Chen, 2002). This result is contrary to the *Constitution* and other important laws and regulations. The origin of the error does not lie in the farmers themselves, but in the real performance of government actions in the countryside.

The main users of cultivated land, the major type of land use in agriculture, are rural households (Table 9.1). During the whole observation process, the share of cultivated land contracted by rural households have shown an inverted 'U'-shape. Its formation is mainly related to the acceleration of the economic non-agriculturalisation in rural Zhejiang and the deterioration of the comparative efficiency of agricultural operation (Shi, 2000b; Shi & Huang, 2001; Shi & Zhang, 2000). Meanwhile, it is also related to the phenomenon of rural land transfer due to the above reasons (Shi & Jia, 2002, 2003). The issue of farmland transfer has been specifically discussed in the previous chapters based on the household level, and here I will make a supplementary analysis on the village level. It is seen from Table 9.2, from 1995 to 2002, an average of 10.80% of the cultivate land in the observation villages have been transferred including 4.92% transferred in and 5.88% transferred out. Land transferred in is obviously higher than transferred out. This result implies that the operation of cultivated land in the observation villages has shown a centralised trend, which can also be proved by the frequency changes in land transfer. From 1995 to 2002, 6.25% of rural households had land transferred out, only 4.76% had land transferred in, and the former was 1.49% higher than the latter.

Table 9.2 Cultivated land change and its composition (%)

	Increased/total in the beginning of the year	Decreased/total in the beginning of the year	Decrease due to construction			Transferred land/total			Transferring households/total	
			State	Collective	Household	Total	Out	In	In	Out
1993	0.00	3.15	13.02	44.79	16.67	6.35	–	–	14.42	8.14
1995	0.00	6.65	62.29	26.29	11.43	9.05	4.35	4.70	3.07	2.61
1996	0.80	3.07	26.58	60.76	12.66	14.24	7.07	7.17	5.85	5.23
1997	0.00	0.97	20.41	48.98	14.29	10.75	4.83	5.93	4.87	4.51
1998	0.81	3.67	85.08	9.39	1.66	9.28	3.71	5.57	3.59	3.98
1999	0.00	0.31	0.00	37.50	0.00	12.98	5.47	7.52	10.30	5.99
2000	0.50	2.05	47.13	46.50	0.00	10.58	5.25	5.34	8.96	5.27
2001	0.00	5.58	16.11	49.67	0.00	9.87	4.18	5.69	5.92	4.97
2002	0.00	2.14	70.59	11.76	0.00	9.76	4.62	5.14	6.63	5.19
1995–2002	0.23	2.98	44.81	36.06	4.54	10.80	4.92	5.88	6.25	4.76

9.1.3 Arable Land Use, Structure and Production

As far as the cultivated land use is concerned (Table 9.3), influenced by the decrease of total cultivated land and the changes in planting structure, the average planting area of the observation villages shows a downward trend. The total sown area of crops decreased from over 100 hectares at the beginning of the observation to less than 80 hectares before the agglomeration of the villages, and the decline was very obvious. As an important indicator to measure the utilisation of cultivated land, the multiple cropping index, fluctuated in the observation, and remained between 210 and 250% before 2000. Since 2000,this fluctuation encountered the impact of structural adjustment policies, and declined significantly. The multiple cropping index decreased from over 210 to 191.74% in 2002. In just two years, this decline is considered quite substantial.

At the same time, the changes in planting structure also shows the trend to reduce grain production and increase the production of non-grain crops. The share of grain sowing area decreased from 79.23% in 1995 to 52.19% in 2002. In contrast, the share of the sowing area for other crops increased from 12.82 to 35.44%. In the current grain crop cultivation, the structure of the ten villages in Zhejiang is relatively simple with paddy rice standing out, taking over 80% of the total. Influenced by the continuous reduction of the total cultivated land, the task of ensuring the supply of agricultural

Table 9.3 Cultivated land use, structure and crop production

	Sown area (ha/village)	Planting structure (%)				Yield (kg/hm^2)		Multiple cropping index (%)
		Grain	#Paddy rice	Cash crop	Others	Grain	Paddy rice	
1986	105.06	73.72	–	8.37	17.91	4077.67	–	236.76
1987	102.21	74.09	–	7.92	17.98	4080.68	–	234.15
1988	101.63	75.12	–	8.15	16.72	3967.46	–	237.08
1989	103.69	73.49	–	8.32	18.19	4072.85	–	240.46
1990	108.85	71.71	–	9.69	18.60	4025.85	–	254.00
1991	101.09	72.32	–	9.57	18.11	4319.07	–	238.04
1993	85.18	77.51	85.42	5.69	16.80	5577.10	6084.05	216.60
1995	76.11	79.23	88.41	7.94	12.82	6122.72	6469.30	217.03
1996	80.23	76.22	87.59	0.00	23.78	6441.19	6797.14	233.87
1997	77.43	76.67	88.32	7.09	16.23	6267.83	6547.36	228.76
1998	77.25	72.05	77.05	6.26	21.70	6342.84	7691.23	234.74
1999	125.01	67.66	81.66	10.92	21.42	5848.18	6236.61	244.66
2000	110.07	60.34	84.02	8.17	31.49	6330.05	6415.77	215.96
2001	100.51	53.29	91.39	11.34	35.37	7113.75	7481.21	185.84
2002	101.65	52.19	78.51	12.37	35.44	6375.66	7104.35	191.74
1995–2002	93.53	66.03	84.53	9.21	24.76	6319.85	6782.91	216.70

Note #being part of the former category

products depends entirely on the continuous improvement of yield. With the help of the steady improvement of agricultural comprehensive science and technology, the total supply of agricultural products has not been greatly affected. In fact, the situation has been much improved and in the middle and late 1990s, and there was no shortage of agricultural products anymore which had long restricted the development of China's economy in the past. Taking grain as an example and analysing the period between 1986 to 1998 before the village agglomeration, during the 13 years of follow-up observation in the ten villages in Zhejiang, the total cultivated land decreased by 25.84%, the grain sowing area decreased by 28.15%, and the total grain production decreased by only 17.60%. Obviously, the improvement of yield per unit played an important role in this change. The grain yield substantially increased from 4.08 tons per hectare in 1986 when the observation started to 6.38 tons in 2002. In fact, during the eight years from 1995 to 2002, the average grain yield in the observation villages reached 6.32 tons per hectare, with 6.78 tons per hectare for paddy rice. The corresponding coefficients of variation were 8.55 and 6.84%. Except for 1999 when the yield was less than six tons per hectare, the yield in other years all exceeded six tons per hectare, which reached a record high of 7.11 tons per hectare in 2001. It is under the guarantee of the steady rise of the grain yield in Zhejiang and even the whole country that the state implemented a comprehensive liberalization policy for grain production in coastal provinces such as Zhejiang in the late 1990s.[2] This policy will undoubtedly play a role in promoting rural economic development in coastal Zhejiang, especially in promoting rural industrialisation and rural urbanisation.

9.2 Asset Scale and Composition

9.2.1 Productive Fixed Asset Scale and Composition

As human society transitions from the traditional agricultural economy to the era of modern agriculture, industry and knowledge economy, the dependence of economic development on assets or capital occupation becomes more evident. This is because the amount of assets or capital possessed is an indicator of productivity. In other words, an investigation of the level of assets or capital occupied in a region can reveal its productivity level. Data from the 17-year follow-up observation (Table 9.4) show that the asset level of the ten villages in Zhejiang has increased substantially.

---

[2]According to data from the fixed observation sites in rural areas throughout the country, since 1986, the grain yield per unit area has been in a fluctuating upward process. In 1986, the grain yield was 3745.16 kg/ha, in 1990 it was 4448.56 kg/ha, in 1995 it was 4432.33 kg/ha, in 2000 it was 4325.59 kg/ha, and in 2002 it rose to 4802.79 kg/ha. From 1995 to 2002, the average yield was 4525.55 kg/ha, 3862.13 kg/ha for wheat, 5934.17 kg/ha for paddy rice, 5466.39 kg/ha for corn and 1983.94 kg/ha for soybean. In these eight years, the coefficient of variation of grain yield per unit area was 3.10%, including 3.53% for wheat, 2.59% for paddy rice, 5.52% for corn, and 3.22% for soybean. The coefficient of variation of grain yield per unit area was decreased over half the level of 7.05% at the beginning of the observation (1986–1991).

Table 9.4 Productive fixed asset scale and composition by ownership

	Fixed assets (10,000 yuan)	Ownership of fixed assets (%)				
		Collectives	#Contracted by rural households	Rural households	Joint-stock enterprises	Other
1986	113.73	69.76	0.92	26.39	3.86	
1987	166.69	73.38	4.72	21.25	5.37	
1988	188.59	68.53	1.33	27.27	4.19	
1989	193.18	67.36	1.31	29.16	3.48	
1990	231.50	71.67	1.09	27.13	1.20	
1991	303.85	72.49	0.79	26.16	1.35	
1993	449.69	21.82	1.76	15.23	59.38	3.57
1995	798.29	9.28	4.35	25.28	54.93	10.51
1996	1126.09	5.79	4.94	26.97	59.12	8.11
1997	1688.12	4.17	2.58	15.20	75.50	5.13
1998	1735.79	11.81	0.84	14.36	68.30	5.53
1999	1702.00	4.76	0.39	18.85	61.17	15.22
2000	1693.05	3.73	0.51	17.91	70.13	8.23
2001	1755.39	5.42	0.86	20.44	64.57	9.57
2002	1921.19	5.28	0.81	20.34	61.50	12.88

Note #being part of the former category

The average occupation of productive fixed assets rose from 1,137,300 yuan at the beginning of the observation to 19,219,000 yuan in 2002, with an average growth rate as high as 19.32%, much higher than the economic growth rate of 17.22% at the village level. Thus, the accumulation of assets is the most solid foundation for the sustainable growth of village-level economy. From the perspective of the changes in asset ownership, the accumulation of assets in the ten villages in Zhejiang in the past 17 years can be divided into three stages: the rapid growth stage from 1986 to 1990 with a growth rate of 19.22%, the accelerated growth stage from 1990 to 1996 with a growth rate of 23.11%, and the slow growth stage from 1996 to 2002 with a growth rate of 10.34%. As far as the composition of asset ownership is concerned, the main owners in the ten villages in Zhejiang in 2002 were the restructured joint-stock enterprises, accounting for 61.50% of all village-level assets, followed by rural households, taking 20.34%, and the share of other ownerships was 18.16%. From the perspective of changes in asset ownership, affected by the restructuring of enterprises, village collectives as the main owners of assets have been replaced by joint-stock enterprises, with the share of ownership showing a general trend of increase, while the share owned by rural household has displayed a 'U'-shape trend.

Table 9.5 Productive fixed assets composition by category (%)

	Large animals for labour, reproduction and products	Large iron and wood tools	Agricultural machinery	Industrial machinery	Transport machinery	Productive housing	Others
1993	0.35	0.84	7.74	60.53	4.96	23.00	2.57
1995	0.50	0.43	9.78	61.97	7.61	17.90	1.80
1996	0.51	0.35	10.43	65.77	7.72	14.18	1.03
1997	0.36	0.25	6.28	79.74	5.25	7.56	0.56
1998	0.43	0.24	4.50	81.76	4.87	7.67	0.53
1999	0.62	0.39	5.22	75.22	6.06	11.87	0.62
2000	0.50	0.41	4.96	76.21	5.42	11.03	1.48
2001	0.45	0.40	5.98	72.25	7.73	11.53	1.66
2002	0.34	0.37	5.73	70.25	8.58	13.22	1.51

9.2.2 Categories of Productive Fixed Assets

As for the categories of the assets (Table 9.5), the major asset in the ten villages in Zhejiang is industrial machinery, accounting for 70.25% of the total, followed by production houses, accounting for 13.22%, machinery for agriculture, forestry, animal husbandry and fishery, and transportation machinery, accounting for 5.73 and 8.58% respectively. As far as the changes, the shares of both industrial and agricultural assets showed an inverted 'U'-shape, while the share of productive houses showed a 'U'-shape trend. This result shows that Zhejiang has performed prominently in the process of promoting rural industrialisation. If it is correct to say that China is in the transitional period from agricultural to industrial economy, then rural Zhejiang has completed this transition, with its specific transition from industrial economy to knowledge economy.

9.2.3 Regional Differences in Productive Fixed Asset Scale and Composition

In data analysis, generally, the most common method for analysts is to average the data, and to find out its inherent law of changes through averaging. This is because sociologists are faced with thousands of samples and types, it is impossible and unnecessary to analyse them one by one. Rather, they average the characteristics of samples according to the law of big data. As for the current study, although there are only ten sample villages, few share the similarities. It might be right to say that the ten villages in Zhejiang represent ten different types of rural areas (Table 9.6). Only in terms of the rural asset level, the difference is obvious, with the high level

Table 9.6 Productive fixed asset ownership and category in Zhejiang (average of 2000–2002)

Village	Assets (10,000 yuan)	Ownership (%)				Category (%)			
		Collective	Rural household	Joint-stock	Private	Agriculture	Industry	Transport	Housing
LS	218.85	7.62	92.38	0.00	0.00	0.00	26.14	34.76	31.69
YF	511.55	11.26	71.41	0.00	17.33	14.60	36.69	16.90	21.87
YB	1321.50	10.97	30.04	0.00	58.99	7.44	25.16	3.32	58.31
XSF	8827.43	0.17	0.13	99.70	0.00	0.04	99.65	0.12	0.16
MY	1604.36	26.65	39.48	0.00	33.87	0.99	37.99	21.24	39.01
XM	2987.00	0.60	21.41	75.27	0.14	0.68	77.77	18.06	0.20
JH	947.73	7.60	3.57	65.95	12.84	0.16	53.57	16.35	26.66
BGM	854.63	4.82	95.18	0.00	0.00	90.96	3.12	2.53	1.92
HB	557.67	12.41	62.54	0.00	20.32	0.59	33.16	3.59	46.90
SBY	68.03	6.03	93.97	0.00	0.00	2.35	1.40	20.58	22.15

reaching more than 80 million yuan, while the low level with less than one million yuan. There are also differences in asset attributes and ownership structure. In terms of attribute, of the ten villages, four had the assets over 10 million yuan, including two villages (Xishufu and Xinmin) with the assets mainly owned by joint-stock enterprises, one village (Yubei) with the assets mainly owned by private enterprises, and one village (Miaoyan) with its assets mainly owned by rural households. Of the other villages with the assets less than 10 million yuan, except Jinhou with most assets owned by joint-stock enterprises, all the other five villages (Bogumen, Shibanyan, Longshang, Yongfeng and Hebian) had assets mainly owned by rural households. In terms of asset composition, the ten villages in Zhejiang can be roughly divided into four categories, i.e. villages with industrial assets (Xishufu, Xinmin, Jinhou and Yongfeng), the village with agricultural assets (Bogumen), specifically marine fishing industry, villages with productive housing assets (Yubei, Hebian, Miaoyan and Longshang), and the village with husbandry assets (Shibanyan).

9.3 Level and Composition of Operation Income and Expenditure

9.3.1 Operation Income and Its Composition

Table 9.7 indicates that with the increase of assets or capital accumulation at the village level, village operation income has been on the rise, from 4,786,700 million yuan at the beginning of the observation to 60,786,100 yuan in 2002, with an average annual growth rate of 17.22%. In terms of income structure, there were three main components as from operation incomes of private enterprises, from rural households and from joint-stock enterprises, which took similar shares of the total. As far as the trend is concerned, the traditional village-level main source of income from rural collective operation has given way to joint-stock enterprises or private enterprises under the influence of enterprise restructuring. The income share from private enterprises rose rapidly, from 17.27% in 1995 to 37.65% in 2002. On the contrary, the share from joint-stock enterprises declined significantly, from 40.77% in 1995 to 26.88% in 2002. The share from household operation in village-level operation income was generally on the rise, but in the past five years, it has shown a significant decline. Compared with 1998, the share from household operation decreased by 5.68% in 2002.

In terms of income source (Table 9.8), the major source in the ten villages in Zhejiang is evidently industry, accounting for 76.63% of the total, followed by the commercial, catering and service, the main body of the tertiary industry, with a share of 7.74%. The share from agricultural production has been quite small, and the total share of agriculture, forestry, animal husbandry and fishery is only 7.78%. In

Table 9.7 Operation income and its composition

	Total income from operation (10,000 yuan)	Income composition (%)					
		Collective operation	Household operation	Partnership operation	Joint-stock operation	Private operation	Others
1986	478.67	68.28	17.94	12.45	–	1.33	–
1987	722.99	62.77	16.52	20.45	–	0.26	–
1988	693.60	64.48	23.36	3.53	–	8.63	–
1989	924.39	75.40	18.25	4.68	–	1.66	–
1990	967.28	70.41	21.10	2.73	–	5.76	–
1991	878.93	64.00	26.23	3.62	–	6.15	–
1993	1543.79	19.39	14.17	2.83	58.80	1.98	2.84
1995	2803.41	2.60	31.38	1.85	40.77	17.27	6.13
1996	3367.68	2.42	30.19	2.75	36.78	19.86	8.00
1997	3741.51	2.13	28.35	1.60	33.22	27.15	7.54
1998	3960.51	0.36	33.76	2.33	26.97	30.63	5.94
1999	4340.42	0.40	31.49	2.23	24.81	33.56	7.52
2000	5141.57	0.47	29.87	1.74	28.08	34.66	5.18
2001	5727.11	0.10	27.66	1.49	27.51	37.67	5.57
2002	6078.61	0.08	28.08	1.41	26.88	37.65	5.90

Table 9.8 Composition of operation income (%)

	Planting	Forestry	Husbandry	Fishery	Industry	Transportation	Commercial, catering and service	Others
1986	4.93	1.06	1.75	4,51	82.39	2.40	2.32	0.64
1987	3.52	0.63	1.63	5.54	85.26	1.29	1.80	0.34
1988	3.89	0.52	2.82	6.49	80.02	1.91	3.11	1.24
1989	3.54	0.43	2.42	4.33	84.32	1.52	1.53	1.92
1990	3.56	0.33	2.31	5.42	83.76	1.45	1.70	1.48
1991	4.48	0.52	2.74	6.27	80.37	1.99	2.09	1.54
1993	3.34	0.42	1.99	4.77	83.72	1.76	2.65	1.36
1995	3.14	0.25	2.04	3.84	79.56	3.16	3.58	4.43
1996	2.90	0.17	1.81	3.72	81.00	2.61	4.83	2.95
1997	2.52	0.22	1.40	4.09	80.69	2.52	4.71	3.84
1998	2.39	0.16	1.46	4.61	80.35	2.27	5.10	3.66
1999	2.88	0.13	2.52	3.51	74.96	2.71	9.44	3.86
2000	2.55	0.13	2.23	3.89	77.99	2.79	8.30	2.13
2001	2.32	0.11	2.47	3.90	76.52	2.94	7.04	4.69
2002	2.13	0.12	2.00	3.53	76.63	3.05	7.74	4.81

terms of the trend, the share from agriculture has been declining steadily since the observation, and has dropped from 12.25% at the beginning of the observation to 7.78% at present. The share from industry has also shown a downward trend, with a decline of 5.76% over 17 years. Income share rose mainly in the tertiary industry, by 5.42% over the period. The results show that the rural economic structure in Zhejiang has been changing from the first and the second industries to the tertiary industry.

9.3.2 Operation Expenditure and Composition

From Table 9.9, it is seen that behind the improvement of operation income in rural Zhejiang, there is not only strong accumulation of assets and capital reserves as the guarantee, but also a considerable amount of expenditure. As far as village-level operation expenditure is concerned, with the continuation of the observation, the expenditure has shown a rising trend, with the amount rising from 3,630,300 yuan in the initial observation period to 45,883,200 yuan in 2002, with an average

Table 9.9 Operation expenditure and composition

	Total operation expenditure (10,000 yuan)	Composition (%)					
		Collective operation	Household operation	Partnership operation	Joint-stock operation	Private operation	Others
1986	363.03	72.27	12.08	14.33	–	1.32	–
1987	553.12	64.68	11.46	23.66	–	0.21	–
1988	581.41	75.69	13.15	9.34	–	1.83	–
1989	774.18	80.00	13.10	5.19	–	1.71	–
1990	787.21	75.21	15.24	2.99	–	6.56	–
1991	707.80	68.99	21.26	2.98	–	6.76	–
1993	1263.19	21.20	9.04	2.96	65.76	0.58	0.45
1995	2174.58	2.84	25.58	2.07	48.34	19.80	1.36
1996	2549.16	2.60	28.36	3.01	41.41	20.83	3.79
1997	2970.65	2.57	25.72	1.58	37.34	29.38	3.39
1998	3106.96	0.12	32.25	2.34	29.16	32.44	3.69
1999	3428.32	0.13	29.34	2.71	28.30	34.91	4.62
2000	3979.56	0.07	29.28	1.75	28.76	37.38	2.76
2001	4395.31	0.08	27.15	1.51	27.49	41.71	2.05
2002	4588.32	0.08	26.40	1.46	26.18	41.64	4.25

annual increase rate of 17.18%. This result implies that behind the high-speed growth of village-level operation income in Zhejiang is the high-speed increase of village-level expenditure. The expenditure was composed of three major parts, namely, the operation expenditures of private enterprises, of rural households and of joint-stock enterprises, each taking one third of the total expenditure. The trend of changes in expenditure is completely consistent with that of income. This has indicated that regardless of the type of enterprises or business entities, there is not much difference in their productivity, and they are basically at the same level. They all belong to the type of high output sustained by high input, without much difference in operation efficiency.

In terms of the expenditure composition, the major component is industry, taking about 80% of the total expenditure, followed by the primary industry and the tertiary industry (Table 9.10). As far as the trend is concerned, the share of expenditure in primary industry is rising slightly, that in the secondary industry is declining, and that in the tertiary industry is rising. Comparing income and expenditure among different industries, it is found out that industry as the main body of the secondary industry is a typical high-input industry, and its share of expenditure is 2.36% higher than that of the income on average. As far as changes in expenditure are concerned, the transformation path of rural industrial structure in Zhejiang is also from the secondary to the tertiary.

Table 9.10 Operation expenditure by industry (%)

	Planting	Forestry	Husbandry	Fishery	Industry	Transportation	Commercial, catering and service	Others
1986	1.49	0.13	1.47	3.06	89.97	1.64	1.99	0.26
1987	1.28	0.05	1.18	3.92	91.29	0.90	1.02	0.36
1988	1.38	0.04	1.62	6.06	86.83	0.95	2.29	0.84
1989	1.30	0.03	1.26	3.97	90.29	0.75	0.88	1.53
1990	1.38	0.02	1.43	4.04	90.65	0.95	1.09	0.45
1991	2.06	0.07	1.83	4.55	88.24	1.24	1.11	0.90
1993	1.61	0.05	1.72	3.28	89.84	1.00	1.34	1.14
1995	1.68	0.04	1.64	3.34	85.26	1.86	2.11	4.08
1996	2.04	0.03	1.69	3.82	86.50	1.79	2.96	1.17
1997	1.79	0.04	1.20	3.48	85.65	1.37	3.23	3.23
1998	1.70	0.04	1.15	4.32	84.38	1.69	3.86	2.86
1999	2.06	0.03	2.20	3.43	81.02	1.61	6.37	3.28
2000	1.81	0.10	1.91	3.79	83.93	1.40	6.39	0.67
2001	1.64	0.03	2.09	3.50	79.65	2.14	7.02	3.91
2002	1.65	0.04	1.73	3.12	78.99	1.97	7.84	4.65

9.3.3 Operation Income and Its Structure

To examine the economic development of a region, it is necessary to examine not only its total income, but also its net income. This is because the net income directly reflects the operational efficiency of a region or a village. From Table 9.11, it can be seen that the net operation income of the ten villages in Zhejiang has been on the rise since the observation, but in the process of this rise, there were two evident major slowdowns. The first occurred in the middle to late 1980s, lasting five years from 1987 to 1991, and the second occurred in the middle to late 1990s, lasting four years from 1996 to 1999. In terms of net income composition, there were three main components including household operation, joint-stock enterprise operation and private enterprise operation. The share of household operation was the highest at 33.26%, while the other two categories taking up 29.04 and 25.37% respectively. Of the net income, the highest proportion came from industry, accounting for 69.35%, followed by agriculture and tertiary industry, accounting for 11.58 and 7.43%. In terms of the trend, the share from household operation showed an inverted 'U'-shape trend. Affected by the restructuring of enterprises, the share from collective enterprise operation has declined, while the share taken by stock enterprises has shown a 'U'-shape trend and that of private enterprises has been on the rise. The shares from agriculture and industry have been declining, while that of tertiary industry has been rising. Comparing the changes in income, expenditure and net income composition, it is found that the share of household operation in net income is significantly higher than its share in income and expenditure, and the shares of the first and third industries in net income are also higher than those in income and expenditure. Why? Is it true that household operation is better than other operations in terms of efficiency, and is it true that agriculture and tertiary industry are better than industry? In my opinion, the answer is not simply 'yes' or 'no'. Instead, it is necessary to carry out detailed analysis on the calculation of income and expenditure structure. Taking into consideration of my previous research, one important reason is that there are many omissions in the calculation of labour cost in household operation, so the calculated results are quite different, and the reason why agriculture is better than industry precisely lies in this (Shi, 1999). However, it is undeniable that the efficiency of household operation in Zhejiang is indeed good. In the comparative study of Jiangsu, Zhejiang and Shanghai (Shi, 2001; Shi & Jia, 2003) the authors find that the preference of Zhejiang farmers for household operation is significantly higher than in Jiangsu and Shanghai. On the one hand, it shows that household operation is a better pattern in Zhejiang. On the other hand, it also shows that household operation is consistent with the operational concept of Zhejiang people.

Table 9.11 Operation net income and its structure

	Village average net income (10,000 yuan)	Composition by attribute (%)				Composition by industry (%)			Per capita net income (yuan)
		Collective enterprise operation	Household operation	Joint-stock enterprise operation	Private enterprise operation	Agriculture	Industry	Commercial, catering and service	
1986	115.64	55.76	36.33	–	–	31.40	58.61	3.35	1210.36
1987	169.87	56.55	33.02	–	–	27.20	65.63	4.35	1756.83
1988	112.20	6.37	76.29	–	–	37.77	44.71	7.35	1145.92
1989	150.21	51.70	44.84	–	–	32.19	53.54	4.86	1513.45
1990	180.06	49.43	46.70	–	–	32.35	53.64	4.36	1801.70
1991	171.13	43.36	46.75	–	–	36.80	47.81	6.11	1713.72
1993	280.60	11.26	37.24	27.47	8.25	27.80	56.19	8.53	2697.60
1995	628.83	1.74	51.42	14.60	8.52	18.17	59.85	8.69	5910.61
1996	818.52	1.85	35.90	22.36	16.84	11.77	63.87	10.68	7764.37
1997	770.86	0.44	38.49	17.35	18.53	14.81	61.59	10.44	7768.40
1998	853.55	1.21	39.28	19.03	24.06	13.69	65.70	9.64	8633.05
1999	912.10	1.41	39.58	11.68	28.49	13.99	52.17	20.99	8000.86
2000	1162.01	1.86	31.91	25.75	25.33	12.84	57.66	14.84	10265.11
2001	1331.80	0.18	29.34	27.56	24.32	13.88	66.18	7.11	10893.16
2002	1490.28	0.11	33.26	29.04	25.37	11.58	69.35	7.43	12343.93

Note Net income = total income – total expenditure

9.3.4 Tax Payment and Its Structure

To investigate the economic development of a village, in addition to studying its income directly, it is also necessary to examine its capability in tax payment. From Table 9.12, it can be seen that the tax payment of the ten villages in Zhejiang has been on the rise since the observation. The tax paid increased from 376,900 yuan in the initial observation to 3,152,800 yuan in 2002, with the per capita level increased from 394.54 yuan to 2611.43 yuan, an increase of 5.62 times, with an average annual increase of 12.53%. This rate is significantly lower than the per capita growth of net income (15.62%). This result indicates that in the development of rural economy, Zhejiang adopts a policy of light taxation or enriching the people. When Zhejiang takes the lead in economic development in the whole country, people from many places came to Zhejiang to seek the basis of Zhejiang's experience or spirit, and obtained many results. But according to my understanding, the basic experience or spirit is the implementation of the policy of light taxation. It is precisely this policy that has enabled Zhejiang's economy to develop at the forefront of the country in a short period of just more than a decade.

In terms of the proportion of taxes directly paid by villages, the majority was value added tax, followed by sales tax and corporate income tax, accounting for 54.21, 26.59 and 17.16% of the total tax, respectively. The proportion of agricultural tax, as well as agricultural and forestry specialty tax was quite small, taking up only 1.57%. In terms of changes, since 1995, influenced by the fluctuations of economic growth, the share of value added tax has shown a 'U'-shape trend, while the shares

Table 9.12 Tax payment and its composition

	Total taxation (10,000 yuan)	Tax revenue composition (%)					Taxation (yuan/person)
		Agricultural tax	Agricultural and forestry specialty tax	Value added tax	Sales tax	Corporate income tax	
1986	37.69	–	–	–	–	–	394.54
1987	37.76	–	–	–	–	–	390.52
1988	14.29	–	–	–	–	–	145.90
1989	43.31	–	–	–	–	–	436.40
1990	44.07	–	–	–	–	–	440.98
1991	35.84	–	–	–	–	–	358.94
1993	62.61	2.15	0.73	91.37 (Industrial & commercial taxes)			637.55
1995	101.76	3.28	1.32	61.99	5.68	11.28	962.75
1996	181.18	1.70	0.42	58.01	19.12	20.69	1706.79
1997	156.31	2.61	1.23	45.07	22.17	25.32	1482.98
1998	203.54	2.18	0.72	40.95	28.87	25.95	2051.41
1999	230.35	1.74	0.81	49.31	25.60	11.08	2011.28
2000	231.94	1.43	1.09	46.57	37.48	13.06	2048.93
2001	253.95	1.09	0.95	43.77	37.85	15.78	2077.16
2002	315.28	1.13	0.44	54.21	26.59	17.16	2611.43

of sales tax and corporate income tax have both shown an inverted 'U'-shape trend, and the share of agricultural tax has shown a downward trend.

As far as the composition of tax revenue is concerned (Table 9.13), since the Ninth Five-Year Plan, the tax revenue in rural areas of Zhejiang has been mainly from private enterprises. In 2002, 74.71% of the total tax was paid by private enterprises, followed by households, accounting for 16.46%, and joint-stock enterprises at 8.63%. In terms of change, the tax from private enterprises showed an obvious upward trend, while the share from rural households and joint-stock enterprises showed an inverted 'U'-shape trend. This result indicates that with the clarification of enterprise ownership institution, the tax structure in rural areas of Zhejiang has also changed significantly. Private enterprises with very clear property rights have assumed the main role of tax payment in rural areas. But at the same time, it is undeniable that the private economy has not been perceived in an objective way. Justification of this statement is that the proportion of tax paid by private enterprises out of their net income (tax burden degree) is the highest among all kinds of organizations (Fig. 9.1). From 1995 to 2002, it averaged 48.07%, much higher than the average level of 21.01%, followed by collective enterprises with 24.70%, and joint-stock enterprises with 18.28%, and the fourth came from rural households with 15.15%. In terms of the changing process, the tax payment of private enterprises also declined once, from 59.34% in 1995 to 35.63% in 1997, and then increased to 48.02% in 1999. In the following two years, the tax paid by private enterprises stagnated or declined before rose again in 2002, reaching a historical record of 62.31%.

9.3.5 Tax Payment and Regional Distribution

As can be seen from Appendix Table 9.19, the tax payment of the ten villages in Zhejiang has shown a downward trend since the observation, decreased from 32.60% in the initial observation period to 21.01% in 2002. However, in the whole observation process, there were two significant increases, and both occurred in the economic downturn. This result shows that the tax payment is directly related to the economic income of the villages. When the economic situation is good, the tax burden will be lighter; otherwise, the taxation is heavier. Specifically, the situation of each observation village is completely different. Due to the differences in inter-village industrial structure, there have been obvious differences in the economic development and changes (Fig. 9.2), as well as the tax payment among villages. The highest burden was found in Miaoyan Village of Yinxian County, followed by Yubei Village of Jiaxing, Xinmin Village of Wenling and Yongfeng Village of Huzhou, Longshang Village of Lin'an, Jinhou Village of Rui'an, Hebian Village of Lishui, Bogumen Village of Putuo, Xishufu Village of Shaoxing, and Shibanyan Village of Jinhua with the lowest tax burden. Obviously, the villages with high tax payment are also those with a high level of economic development in Zhejiang, while the villages with low tax payment are the ones with a relatively low level of economic income. This tax collection basically conforms to the principle of tax payment in the development of modern economy, which is good for improving the efficiency of economic development (Shi, 2001; Shi & Wang, 2000).

Table 9.13 Sources of tax revenue

	Collective	#Collective enterprises	Rural households	#Individual businessmen	Joint-stock enterprises	Partnership enterprises	Private enterprises	Others
1993	21.57	21.16	8.71	6.06	64.79	0.45	0.40	4.09
1995	8.73	7.14	26.18	22.69	31.27	0.92	31.26	1.64
1996	3.19	1.96	26.13	23.10	34.97	0.78	34.58	0.34
1997	1.99	1.75	25.04	20.21	35.57	0.19	32.57	4.64
1998	0.20	0.04	33.75	29.24	26.99	0.19	36.12	2.76
1999	0.16	0.00	26.43	2.27	13.34	0.12	54.17	5.78
2000	0.11	0.00	28.29	3.63	13.81	0.05	57.69	0.04
2001	0.10	0.00	29.23	3.63	11.42	0.05	59.14	0.06
2002	0.08	0.00	16.46	3.31	8.63	0.06	74.71	0.05
1995–2002	1.16	0.81	25.95	11.31	19.39	0.22	51.56	1.72

Note #indicating as part of the former category

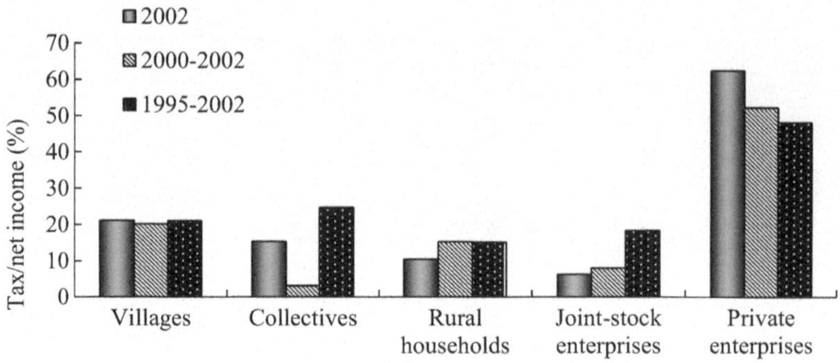

Fig. 9.1 Tax payment by different sources 1995–2002

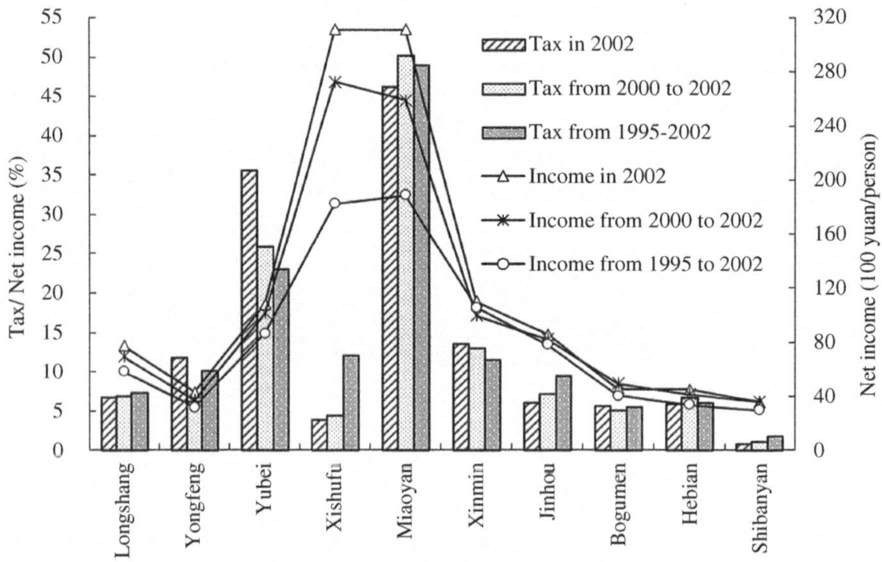

Fig. 9.2 Tax burden and income of individual villages 1995–2002

9.4 Village Revenue and Expenditure, and the Composition

9.4.1 Village Revenue and Its Composition

In addition to investigating the overall inter-village economic situation, it is also important to investigate the revenue and expenditure of the self-governing organizations at the village level. It is seen from Table 9.14 that, since the observation, the annual revenue of the ten villages in Zhejiang has shown a fluctuating trend, which basically coincides with the changes of the whole inter-village economy. When

Table 9.14 Village revenue and its sources

	Revenue (10,000 yuan)	Sources (%)							
		Collectives	Households	#*Tiliu*	#*Tongchou*	Joint-stock enterprises	Private enterprises	Transfer income	Others
1986	46.31	95.21	1.25	–	–	2.03		1.51	
1987	23.52	86.62	4.22	–	–	3.99		5.17	
1988	14.96	55.59	3.81	–	–	20.53		2007	
1989	12.09	31.95	7.74	–	–	39.33		2098	
1990	16.58	57.98	7.20	–	–	17.49		1734	
1991	18.08	52.05	6.59	–	–	16.04		2531	
1993	26.25	37.62	11.10	7.85	1.63	14.93	0.80	3.04	32.51
1995	61.39	14.48	5.31	2.73	1.61	5.01	0.00	2.07	73.13
1996	52.63	8.14	5.77	1.82	2.28	9.70	5.18	0.77	70.44
1997	54.14	7.83	11.44	3.65	3.48	0.00	4.42	6.80	69.51
1998	36.30	15.90	15.57	5.76	3.49	26.14	10.28	2.13	29.98
1999	29.07	7.01	21.58	10.45	6.99	14.36	21.40	3.06	32.59
2000	31.96	4.85	21.82	10.45	10.74	16.97	19.85	2.99	33.53
2001	32.96	12.79	21.34	11.02	10.32	16.03	27.60	4.77	17.47
2002	32.79	3.05	21.17	10.41	10.45	13.14	24.20	5.59	32.85

Note #indicating as part of a previous category

the inter-village economic growth is relatively fast, the revenue at the village level increases correspondingly, or otherwise, it decreases. In the 17 years of observation, the highest annual revenue at the village level reached 613,900 yuan in 1995, and the lowest was only 120,900 yuan in 1989, with large fluctuations. After the Ninth Five-Year Plan, the revenue of the villages began to enter a new downward process. By 1999, the revenue of the villages had dropped to the lowest level within five years, averaging only 290,700 yuan per village, a decrease of 52.65% compared with the level in 1995. Since the 2000s, the village-level revenue has improved, but its growth has still been stagnated. In 2002, the village-level revenue averaged 327,900 yuan, increased by 2.60% compared with 2000, and decreased by 0.52% if compared with 2001.

In terms of revenue composition, rural households, joint-stock enterprises and private enterprises are the main contributors in the ten villages in Zhejiang. Their contributions to the village-level revenue are 21.17, 13.14 and 24.20%, respectively. In terms of the changes in revenue, influenced by the restructuring of enterprises, the main source of village revenue in the early stage was from collective economy. By the mid-1990s, it had been completely abdicated and replaced by joint-stock enterprises, private enterprises and rural households. Simply looking at the changes in the contribution of rural household economy to village finance, it is found out that before the restructuring, the contribution of rural households to village finance was relatively small, and remained within 10% until 1996. After 1997, the contribution of rural households to village finance increased year by year, from 5.77% in 1996 to 21.17% in 2002, which nearly doubled in six years. In the contribution of rural households, *tiliu* used to be the majority, which was followed by *tongchou*, until around 2000 when *tiliu* and *tongchou* were roughly the same, and sometimes *tongchou* was even higher than *tiliu*. Therefore, in Zhejiang, there has been more financial dependence on rural households for the daily operation of village collectives. Similarly, the rise of private enterprises also plays an important role in the operation of village-level affairs, with the share of contribution increasing from less than 5% before 1997 to 24.20% at present.

Influenced by the village economic structure and development, the level and structure of collective revenue among villages are also very different (Table 9.15). In terms of the average village revenue of the three years from 2000 to 2002, Miaoyan Village of Yinxian County had the highest level in the ten villages in Zhejiang, reaching 1,322,400 yuan, while Shibanyan Village of Jinhua had the lowest level with only 12,500 yuan. There was a substantial difference between the revenue of the lowest village and that of the village with the highest revenue. As far as the revenue sources are concerned, in the ten villages, the main sources in four villages of Shibanyan, Longshang, Yubei and Yongfeng were rural households, while for Hebian and Bogumen, the main sources were collective operations, in Xishufu and Jinhou, the main sources were joint-stock enterprises, in Miaoyan, the revenue was mainly from private enterprises and in Xinmin village, the revenue was mainly from other sources.

Table 9.15 Revenue and its sources for villages (average 2000–2002)

	Revenue (10,000 yuan)	Composition (%)							
		Collectives	Rural households	#*Tiliu*	#*Tongchou*	Joint-stock enterprises	Private enterprises	Transfer	Other
LS	4.45	0.00	59.93	49.14	10.79	0.00	0.00	29.36	10.71
YF	36.66	0.00	37.83	15.09	22.73	0.00	20.19	0.00	41.98
YB	51.67	14.39	59.81	27.67	32.14	0.00	0.00	0.00	25.81
XSF	35.76	0.00	1.53	1.53	0.00	97.87	0.00	0.00	0.61
MY	132.24	0.00	7.36	7.36	0.00	5.05	50.95	3.35	33.30
XM	15.95	16.97	22.61	0.00	22.61	0.00	0.00	0.00	60.43
JH	21.44	0.82	8.86	1.09	7.77	39.04	10.57	9.33	31.37
BGM	14.77	40.67	23.79	0.00	23.79	0.00	0.00	31.14	4.40
HB	11.49	54.21	18.51	9.81	0.00	0.00	7.54	18.86	0.87
SBY	1.25	0.00	77.33	77.33	0.00	0.00	0.00	2.67	20.00
All	32.57	6.92	21.44	10.63	10.50	15.37	23.92	4.46	27.88

Note #indicating as part of a previous category

Because of certain reasons, of the ten villages, three were highly dependent on the transfer funds from the upper-level government, with the highest level of 29.36% and the lowest of 18.86% out of the total village-level revenue. Among the four villages with rural households as the main financial contributors, the ways of payments were different, with two villages mainly depending on *tiliu* and the other two mainly on *tongchou*.

9.4.2 Village Financial Expenditure and Structure

Similarly, from Table 9.16, we can see that since the observation, the annual expenditure in the ten villages in Zhejiang has shown a fluctuating trend, which is completely consistent with the change in revenue. In the 17 years of observation, the annual expenditure of village finance reached the highest level of 513,900 yuan in 1986 and the lowest level of only 102,400 yuan in 1989. Since the Ninth Five-Year Plan, the whole village financial expenditure entered a new round of decrease. By 1998, the financial expenditure dropped to the lowest level in five years, averaging 306,500 yuan per village. It was 9.40% lower than the level in 1995 and 33.84% lower than that in 1996 when the level was the highest in the Ninth Five-Year Plan period. Since 2000, the financial expenditure at the village level has started to expand again. By 2002, the average financial expenditure of the observation villages reached 440,400 yuan. Although this expenditure decreased by 8.38% compared with 480,070 yuan in 2001, it increased by 42.89% compared with 308,200 yuan in 2000.

As far as the structure of financial expenditure is concerned, public welfare and administrative expenditure are the main items in the finance of the ten villages in Zhejiang. In 2002, their shares accounted for 33.17 and 24.31% of the total financial expenditure. These were followed by expenditures for collective expansion of reproduction, and expenditures supported by collections of *tongchou* for hiring labour and other management issues. As far as the change in expenditure composition is concerned, the share of expenditure directly used for collective enterprises showed a 'U'-shape trend, while the share of expenditure for rural household production tended to decline. Meanwhile, the share of expenditure for public welfare undertakings, administration and overall planning has displayed an inverted 'U'-shape. Compared with the initial observation period, the share of expenditure for public welfare and administration increased most significantly. In particular, administrative expenditure increased significantly, from 1.83% at the beginning of observation to 24.31% in 2002, an increase of 23.48% in 17 years. In this process, the increase of subsidies for village cadres was an important reason for increasing administrative expenditure. The share of cadres' subsidies rose from 1.42% at the beginning of

Table 9.16 Village financial expenditure and its structure

	Finance expenditure (10,000 yuan/village)	Village expenditure structure (%)							
		Collectives	Rural households	Tax collection	#*Tongchou*	Public affairs	Admin management	#Cadre subsidies	Others
1986	51.39	12.30	3.01	0.14	–	8.36	1.83	1.42	74.75
1987	30.98	21.54	4.59	0.48	–	6.35	3.59	2.14	64.13
1988	13.51	9.99	10.00	1.89	–	23.47	7.07	5.41	50.08
1989	10.24	29.87	17.80	1.03	–	14.95	15.70	8.61	23.80
1990	14.20	16.86	13.65	1.82	–	15.64	14.03	8.13	40.72
1991	17.44	42.05	9.55	0.43	–	11.01	11.16	6.11	27.34
1993	24.70	28.95	13.69	3.22	2.33	27.72	14.01	4.73	12.41
1995	33.83	15.38	16.25	6.00	6.00	35.84	22.39	8.27	4.14
1996	46.33	7.72	10.32	5.17	5.17	38.17	16.77	6.93	21.85
1997	43.41	0.16	7.23	17.99	6.03	35.09	29.60	12.77	9.93
1998	30.65	0.83	14.50	8.17	8.13	36.20	29.28	15.65	11.03
1999	35.71	0.44	12.27	10.59	9.89	31.30	33.93	12.48	11.47
2000	30.82	0.00	9.78	12.43	12.43	31.45	33.65	11.16	12.68
2001	48.07	21.22	4.44	9.08	8.87	33.82	24.83	10.62	6.61
2002	44.04	25.71	1.54	7.82	7.82	33.17	24.31	10.80	7.45

Note #indicating as part of the previous category. Cadres' subsidies included wage and subsidies

the observation to 10.80% in 2002. In 17 years, an increase by 9.38%, or by 2.53% since 1995. Of course, it is necessary to note that administrative expenditure has obviously declined after 2000, and the share of expenditure in 2002 dropped by 9.34% compared with the level in 2000. This shows that, in terms of village financial expenditure, the government's village financial restructure was effective.

Similarly, influenced by the level and structure of the village economy, there are large inter-village differences in collective finance expenditure and composition (Table 9.17). In terms of the three-year average between 2000 and 2002, Miaoyan Village of Yinxian County had the highest level of financial expenditure, reaching 1,887,400 yuan, while Shibanyan Village of Jinhua had the lowest level, with only 11,800 million yuan. The financial expenditure of the lowest village was also much lower than that of the highest village. As far as the structure of financial expenditure is concerned, three of the ten villages had public welfare expenditure as the major expenditure, all with the shares of more than 35%. Four villages had tax collection and administrations as their main expenditure items, including one village with one third of the expenditure for tax collection, one third for public welfare undertakings and one third for administrations, another village with the main expenditure for serving collective and public welfare undertakings, and the third village with the major expenditure on other issues, as well as on public affairs and administrative management. In terms of serving rural households, three villages had a share of expenditure of over 10%, with the highest level at 16.95% and the lowest at 10.07%. In terms of administrative expenditure, six villages had their cadre subsides taking up over 10%, with 26.46% as the highest and 13.61% as the lowest level.

Comparing the changes in revenue and expenditure at village level (Fig. 9.3), it is found that in the whole observation process, financial expenditure at village level basically followed the principle of 'living within one's means'. In the 17-year observation of the villages, there were only five 'deficit' years, namely 1986, 1987, 1999, 2001 and 2002. The highest deficit was 151,000 yuan in 2001 and the lowest was 50,800 yuan in 1986.

From 2000 to 2002, in terms of revenue and expenditure, the villages were unable to make ends meet, with an average deficit of 84,100 yuan. To be specific, five villages showed deficits in financial expenditure. The highest was in Miaoyan Village in Yinxian County, with an average deficit of 565,000 yuan, followed by Jinhou Village in Rui'an, with a deficit of 226,700 yuan, Xinmin Village in Wenling with 159,000 yuan, as well as Yongfeng Village in Huzhou and Longshang Village in Lin'an, with the deficits of 11,300 yuan and 3900 yuan respectively. Five villages were able to make ends meet or with some outstanding balance, including Yubei Village in Jiaxing, with the balance of 87,200 yuan, Xishufu Village in Shaoxing, with 21,200 yuan, Bogumen Village in Putuo, with 8900 yuan, Hebian Village in Lishui, wtih 7000 yuan, Shibanyan Village in Jinhua, with 700 yuan (Fig. 9.4).

Table 9.17 Village expenditure and its structure (average level from 2000 to 2002)

	Expenditure (10,000 yuan)	Expenditure (%)							
		Collectives	Rural households	Tax collection	#*Tongchou*	Public affairs	Administrative management	#Cadre subsidies	Others
LS	4.84	0.00	0.90	31.36	31.36	30.46	32.74	15.85	4.55
YF	27.94	0.00	0.60	43.40	43.40	0.18	43.35	26.46	12.47
YB	52.80	0.00	16.05	32.41	32.10	13.60	37.92	9.05	0.03
XSF	33.64	0.00	10.70	5.95	5.43	41.09	34.39	20.81	7.88
MY	188.74	38.01	0.49	0.47	0.47	34.54	18.38	6.55	8.12
XM	31.85	0.00	5.14	11.32	11.32	59.73	7.11	4.60	16.70
JH	44.11	0.00	9.56	0.68	0.68	41.25	43.87	13.97	4.64
BGM	13.88	0.00	0.00	0.00	0.00	32.44	31.72	13.61	35.85
HB	10.79	0.00	1.55	9.27	9.27	51.95	32.60	18.70	4.64
SBY	1.18	0.00	16.95	20.62	20.62	12.99	46.61	42.37	2.82
All	40.98	17.51	4.74	9.47	9.39	32.99	26.86	10.82	8.43

Note #being part of the previous category

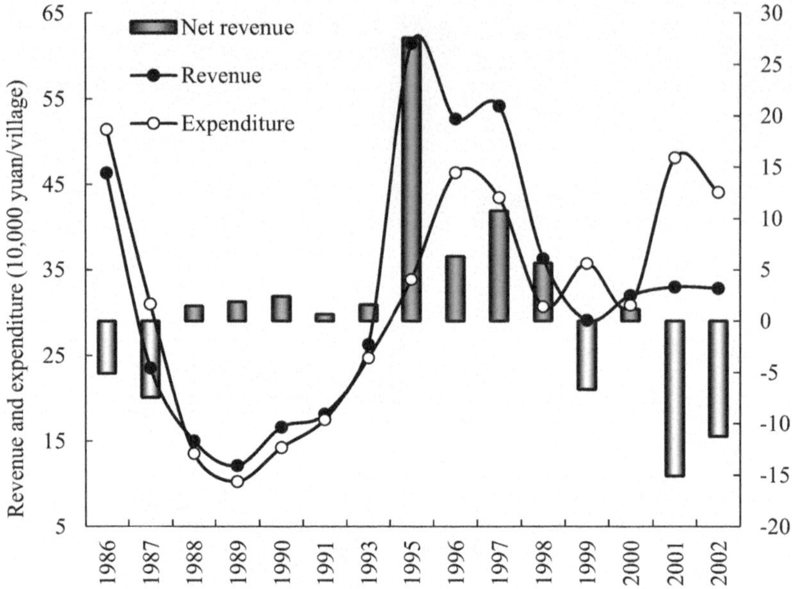

Fig. 9.3 Village revenue and expenditure

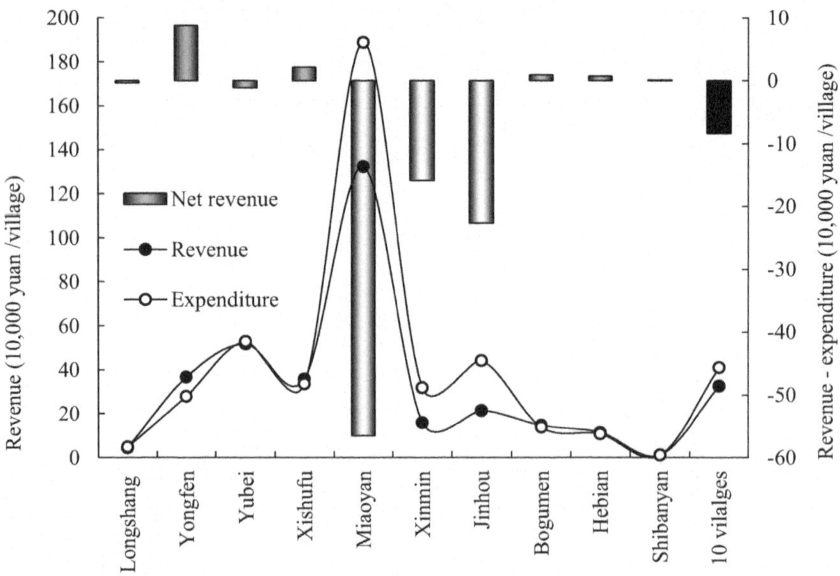

Fig. 9.4 Revenue and expenditure for individual villages 2000–2002

9.4.3 Village Financial Capital Exchange

Based on the analysis of the financial revenue and expenditure at the village level, it is necessary to examine the capital exchange in village finance. From Table 9.18, it can be seen that the bank savings owned by village collectives in Zhejiang once showed an upward trend after the 1990s. It was not until 1997 when the economic growth stagnated (Shi, 2000a) that the trend had a considerable reversal. The bank savings owned by village collectives decreased from the highest of 319,800 yuan in 1997 to 105,900 yuan in 2002, with a decrease of 66.88%. Of course, this reversal was not entirely affected by the stagnation of economic growth, but also by the expansion of investment channels. The fact proves that since the Ninth Five-Year Plan, the foreign investment in the villages under observation has been on the rise substantially and continuously. It increased from 142,300 yuan in 1995 to 517,000 yuan in 2000, an increase of 2.63 times. This process has converged by 2000, with village-level foreign investment of 322,200 yuan in 2002, a decrease of 37.68% compared with 2000. Careful observation of the changing process of foreign investment shows that there were indeed signs of economic growth stagnation, reflected in the yearly decrease in marginal investment growth.

Influenced by the fluctuations of rural economic growth in the mid and late 1990s, the once-declining scale of village-level borrowing increased again in the late 1990s from 37,900 yuan in 1995 to 90,000 yuan in 2002. As far as the loan sources are concerned, there was an alternation of inter-annual composition, with the high level of bank loans in one year and the high non-bank loans in another. After 2000, borrowing obviously relied on bank loans, and the alternation which lasted for many years between the private sector and banks phased out. Compared with borrowing, since the Ninth Five-Year Plan, lending in the observation villages has been obviously higher, which has been in an alternate form in that the level was high one year, and low in the next. Generally speaking, the changes in lending showed an inverted 'U'-shape. The highest level was in 1998, reaching 325,500 yuan, and the lowest was 68,800 yuan in 2002. As far as the situation of pending payments and receivables are concerned, the pending payments showed an upward trend, and there was a rapid increase especially after 2000, while the receivables showed a fluctuating upward trend. Compared the pending payments and the receivables, the latter was significantly higher than the former, with the difference once over 100,000 yuan, but dropped to about 10,000 yuan in 2000, before it increased to 50,000 yuan in 2001, but reversed in 2002, with pending payments higher than receivables by nearly 50,000 yuan. Among the receivables, the transactions between rural households and village collectives did not dominate, with the highest level of rural household involvement of 51.28% in 1995, and the lowest level of 5.64% in 1997. The average level was 16.01% in the Ninth Five-Year Plan period, and the three-year average was 11.24% from 2000 to 2002. This result shows that the relationship between rural households and village collectives is not very close in the capital exchange at the village level.

As far as the inter-village comparison is concerned (Appendix Table 9.20), the difference in capital exchange was also very obvious. First, the bank savings of

Table 9.18 Village level capital exchange

	1993	1995	1996	1997	1998	1999	2000	2001	2002
Bank savings	7.43	20.88	30.78	31.98	25.95	20.01	9.93	9.43	10.59
Cash in stock	3.39	0.99	2.96	3.71	2.65	1.16	0.81	0.52	0.66
External investment	0.06	14.23	37.11	42.58	46.88	50.84	51.70	42.90	32.22
Borrowing	25.90	3.79	4.31	5.55	9.21	2.94	7.16	6.18	9.00
#Bank (%)	17.96	86.80	23.18	5.41	62.45	8.84	61.45	71.20	72.19
Private (%)	7.88	0.00	0.70	9.75	13.77	13.61	4.89	4.85	18.26
Others (%)	74.17	13.20	70.33	84.84	23.78	77.55	33.66	23.95	9.55
Lending	3.19	14.40	7.97	13.19	32.55	7.23	12.86	9.43	6.88
Pending payment	1.26	0.52	3.20	4.68	1.88	3.63	4.54	21.23	20.79
Receivable	3.34	0.23	13.46	10.92	15.58	6.54	5.67	26.52	16.21
#Rural households (%)	17.68	51.28	17.09	5.64	12.03	32.77	23.51	6.95	13.98

Note #indicating as part of the previous category

village collectives varied, with the highest up to 465,800 yuan, and the lowest being nil, including six villages exceeding 10,000 yuan and four villages exceeding 100,000 yuan. Second, external investment was limited to only two villages, of which Miaoyan Village had an amount as high as 419,400 yuan. Although there were seven villages with borrowings, only two villages had an amount of more than 100,000 yuan, i.e. Bobumen and Xishufu, with the loans for Xishufu all from the bank, while the bank loans of Bogumen took only 1/8 of the total. Similarly, there were two villages out of the ten with lending capital, namely, Bogumen and Xinmin. Six villages in total had pending payments and receivables, with only Miaoyan and Jinhou exceeding an amount of 100,000 yuan. In terms of receivables, four villages had rural households highly involved, namely Longshang Village in Lin'an, Yubei Village in Jiaxing, Bogumen Village in Putuo and Shibanyan Village in Jinhua.

9.5 Conclusive Comments

During the whole observation period, the farmland resources of the ten villages in Zhejiang were in a process of decreasing, which was largely a state intention or government action. Unsurprisingly, in the survey of farmland ownership, nearly 70% of the farmers answered that 'rural land belongs to the state'. The reason that farmers' understanding of land ownership is contrary to the *Constitution*, the *Land Law of the People's Republic of China* and the *Agricultural Law of the People's Republic of China* is a concrete manifestation of government control over agricultural land.

The planting structure of the ten villages in Zhejiang is marked by reduction of grain production and expansion of cash crops. In grain cultivation, the structure is relatively single, dominated by paddy rice cropping. With the steady improvement of the comprehensive agricultural science and technology, the impact of decreased land is limited on the total supply of agricultural produce. Taking the period between 1986 and 1998 as an example, before the merging of villages, in 13 years the total cultivated land decreased by 25.84%, the scale of grain sowing area decreased by 28.15%, and the total grain production decreased by only 17.60%. Meanwhile, the grain yield per hectare increased steadily from 4.08 tons in 1986 to 6.38 tons in 2002. It is under the guarantee of the steady rise of the yield that Zhejiang and other coastal provinces have the opportunity to fully open up their grain production policies.

Behind the improvement of the village-level operation income, there are not only strong asset accumulation and capital reserves as guarantee, but also considerable expenditures as supplement. The operation income of the ten villages in Zhejiang mainly consists of three parts, i.e. the operation income from private enterprises, that from rural households and that from joint-stock enterprises, and the shares of the three are basically the same. Heavily influenced by the restructuring of enterprises, the traditional main village economic source, i.e. rural collective operation, has been replaced by joint-stock enterprises or private enterprises. The share of household contribution to the total village operation income is generally on the rise, but in the past five years it has been declining significantly. Village operation income sources have been changed from the second to the tertiary industry.

The annual change in village finance shows a fluctuating trend, which basically coincides with the changes in the whole inter-village economy. When the inter-village economic growth is relatively fast, the revenue at the village level increases correspondingly, and otherwise, a slow economic growth leads to decrease in revenue. There are also three main sources of village-level revenue, namely, rural households, joint-stock enterprises and private enterprises. Their contributions to village-level revenue are 21.17, 13.14 and 24.20%, respectively. In terms of the contribution from rural households, it remained within 10% before 1996. After 1997, the contribution of rural households increased annually, to 21.17% in 2002. It can be seen that there has been increasing dependence on rural households of village collective public affairs in Zhejiang. Similarly, the rise of private enterprises also plays an important role in the operation of village affairs.

Similarly, the annual expenditure change of the ten villages in Zhejiang shows a fluctuating trend, which is completely consistent with the changes in revenue. Public affairs and administrative expenditures are the main items of village finance expenditures at present, with the shares accounting for 33.17 and 24.31% of the total. Compared to the initial observation period, the shares of expenditure for public welfare and administration increased substantially. In particular, the increase in administrative expenditure has been particularly significant.

Comparing the changes in financial revenue and expenditure at the village level, it is found that in the whole observation process, the financial expenditure at village level basically followed the principle of 'living within one's means'. In the 17-year observation, there were not many 'deficit' years with only five years. The highest deficit was 151,100 yuan in 2001 and the lowest was 50,800 yuan in 1986.

Appendix

See Tables 9.19 and 9.20.

Table 9.19 Tax burdens in 10 villages in Zhejiang (%)

	10 villages	Longshang Lin'an	Yongfeng Huzhou	Yubei Jiaxing	Xishufu Shaoxing	Miaoyan Yin County	Xinmin Wenling	Jinhou Ruian	Bogumen Putuo	Hebian Lishui	Shibanyan Jinhua
1986	32.60	16.47	4.74	9.26	62.73	16.56	20.98	12.08	11.00	2.86	1.94
1987	22.23	15.82	4.47	2.69	49.25	9.66	14.90	3.22	13.10	3.06	3.47
1988	12.73	6.97	3.63	13.78	8.48	16.55	19.81	16.08	42.75	3.78	2.27
1989	28.83	9.13	2.63	7.85	56.99	13.50	10.34	9.22	8.10	2.57	3.23
1990	24.48	10.25	5.31	7.90	53.11	8.54	8.83	2.63	11.61	3.68	1.80
1991	20.95	12.02	7.51	9.51	49.54	22.31	5.59	6.67	7.65	4.53	1.34
1993	22.31	12.24	2.17	12.38	55.70	23.27	10.78	21.89	9.79	0.73	1.15
1995	16.18	10.27	8.35	15.53	13.89	45.85	8.31	11.46	5.87	8.94	2.91
1996	22.13	7.29	23.30	16.81	23.62	44.57	5.31	10.68	10.00	6.69	2.70
1997	20.28	6.62	23.22	11.89	24.95	48.57	12.24	12.65	4.19	3.75	2.51
1998	23.85	6.75	8.10	17.27	24.99	46.27	17.43	10.12	5.22	4.76	2.14
1999	25.26	6.51	18.58	23.69	18.90	51.29	10.58	10.04	6.62	4.58	1.13
2000	19.96	6.94	1.65	21.20	5.38	52.29	10.31	9.45	4.74	6.47	1.18
2001	19.07	6.80	1.27	20.18	4.02	53.08	14.99	5.98	4.63	7.85	1.12
2002	21.16	6.67	11.75	35.47	3.75	46.25	13.48	5.93	5.58	5.81	0.83
1995–02	21.01	7.22	10.06	22.93	12.03	48.89	11.48	9.42	5.48	6.01	1.66

Note Tax burden = total tax/(total village operation income − total village operation expenditure)

Table 9.20 Village capital exchange (average 2000–2002)

	10 villages	Longshang Lin'an	Yongfeng Huzhou	Yubei Jiaxing	Xishufu Shaoxing	Miaoyan Yin County	Xinmin Wenling	Jinhou Ruian	Bogumen Putuo	Hebian Lishui	Shibanyan Jinhua
Bank savings (10,000 yuan)	9.98	0.47	0.00	13.69	0.70	46.58	19.64	10.61	2.74	5.17	0.23
#Cooperative funds (%)	0.00	0.00	–	0.00	0.00	0.00	0.00	0.00	0.00	0.00	0.00
Cash in stock (10,000 yuan)	0.66	0.23	0.70	0.22	0.46	0.78	0.19	3.16	0.41	0.40	0.07
External investment (10,000 yuan)	42.27	0.00	0.00	0.00	0.00	419.40	3.33	0.00	0.00	0.00	0.00
Borrowing (10,000 yuan)	7.45	0.50	2.63	0.00	40.00	0.00	0.00	8.33	22.01	1.00	0.00
#Bank (%)	68.47	0.00	0.00	–	100.00	–	–	100.00	12.11	0.00	–
#Private (%)	10.27	0.00	0.00	–	0.00	–	–	0.00	34.74	0.00	–
#Others (%)	21.26	100.00	100.00	–	0.00	–	–	0.00	53.15	100.00	–
Lending (10,000 yuan)	9.72	0.00	0.00	0.00	0.00	0.00	23.83	0.00	73.41	0.00	0.00

(continued)

Table 9.20 (continued)

	10 villages	Longshang Lin'an	Yongfeng Huzhou	Yubei Jiaxing	Xishufu Shaoxing	Miaoyan Yin County	Xinmin Wenling	Jinhou Ruian	Bogumen Putuo	Hebian Lishui	Shibanyan Jinhua
Outstanding payment (10,000 yuan)	15.52	2.30	0.00	0.00	0.00	44.94	0.00	107.21	0.72	0.00	0.03
Receivables (10,000 yuan)	16.14	2.94	0.00	11.39	0.00	83.25	0.00	59.97	3.78	0.00	0.03
#Household exchange (%)	11.24	100.00	–	100.00	–	0.00	–	0.00	100.00	–	100.00

Note #indicating as part of a previous category

References

Ding, G. (2000). *Rural legalities*. Beijing: China Agriculture Press.
Shi, Q. (1999). *Rural household economic development*. Beijing: China Agriculture Press.
Shi, Q. (2000a). A comparative study on the unbalanced economic development of rural households and its origin in Shanxi and Zhejiang: Evidence from follow-up observations from 1986 to 1999. *China Economic Studies, 6,* 24–31.
Shi, Q. (2000b). Resource use efficiency and comparison of its allocation directions in rural household economy. *Chinese Rural Economy, 8,* 58–61.
Shi, Q. (2001). Compasirion study on rural tax and fee tracking investigation in Zhejiang. *Zhejiang Academic Journal, 6,* 171–175.
Shi, Q., & Chen, K. (2002). A surey analysis of peasant' s law diathesis and consciousness at present. *China Rural Survey, 2,* 67–75.
Shi, Q., & Huang, Z. (2001). Transit of rural household economic structure and its origin. *Management World, 4,* 112–119.
Shi, Q., & Jia, S. (2002). A comparison between the farmland factor trend and its origin. *Management World, 1,* 71–77.
Shi, Q., & Jia, S. (2003). Rural houeshold land transfer and its origin: Evidence from three coastal provinces of Jiangsu, Shandong and Zhejiang. *Economic Issues in China, 5,* 41–54.
Shi, Q., & Wang, Y. (2000). Comparative study on rural household tax and fee burden in Shanxi and Zhejiang. *Journal of Agricultural Economic Research, 4,* 45–58.
Shi, Q., & Zhang, H. (2000). The process of non-agriculturalization of rural household operation. *On Economic Problems, 4,* 45–48.

Chapter 10
Community Outlook and Spiritual Civilisation

Contents

Generally speaking, people know more about rural economic activities from follow-up observation and analysis, but less about rural social change. In fact, observation on rural social change is also an important part of this study. Although the theme of the rural follow-up observations is to observe the economic activities of various organisations in rural areas, it also gives full attention to the social changes of the households under observation. Especially after six continuous years of follow-up observation, the National Observation Office organised domestic experts to assess the observation indicators twice. On the basis of maintaining the original observation characteristics, a large number of social indicators were added. This improvement has laid a solid foundation for broadening the range of observation. This chapter takes observation villages as the analysis unit, focusing on the social changes of these villages.

Q. Shi and Y. Gao, *Sustainable Development of Rural Household Economy*,
https://doi.org/10.1007/978-981-15-2747-0_10

Table 10.1 Basic information and changes in observation villages

	Natural location	Economic location		Well-off village designated by county government or above		Economic development level within counties	
		Agricultural industry	Economic location	1995	2002	1993	2002
LS	Mountain	Bamboo		Well-off	Well-off	Upper-middle	Middle
YF*	Plain	Aquaculture		Well-off	Well-off	Middle	Lower-middle
YB*	Plain	Cropping	Suburban	–	–	Middle	Middle
XSF	Plain	Cropping		Well-off	Well-off	Upper-middle	Upper-middle
MY	Plain	Cropping	Suburban	Well-off	Well-off	Middle	Upper-middle
XM	Plain	Cropping		Well-off	Well-off	Upper-middle	Middle
JH	Plain	Cropping		–	Well-off	Upper-middle	Middle
BGM	Hill	Fishing		–	Well-off	Lower-middle	Middle
HB	Hill	Cropping		–	Well-off	Middle	Middle
SBY	Hill	Cropping		–	–	Middle	Middle

Note * Yongfeng (YF) Village used to be a cropping area before 1993, but has been developed as an aquacultural area. Yubei (YB) Village is where the town government is located

10.1 The Basic Features of the Observation Villages

Table 10.1 shows the natural locations of the ten villages in Zhejiang, including six plain villages, three hilly villages and one mountain village. In terms of agricultural industry, seven villages mainly practice crop planting, one does marine fishing, one does freshwater aquaculture and one focuses on bamboo planting. As for their economic locations, there are two suburban villages (including one located in the township seat), and eight non-suburban villages. In 2002, eight villages were named well-off villages or above by the county governments, with the number much higher than the number of five in 1995. With regard to the economic development of the counties and districts where the villages were located in 2002, there were seven middle-income villages, one lower-middle income village and two upper-middle income villages. Compared with 1993, two villages improved its economic level, four villages maintained its level and four villages decreased economically. Generally speaking, the social and economic development of the observation villages are above the average level of rural areas in Zhejiang.

10.2 Population in the Observation Villages

As can be seen from Fig. 10.1, since 1986, the population change of the observation villages in Zhejiang has shown an upward trend. However, the population decreased in the mid and late 1990s due to the transformation of villagers from agricultural to

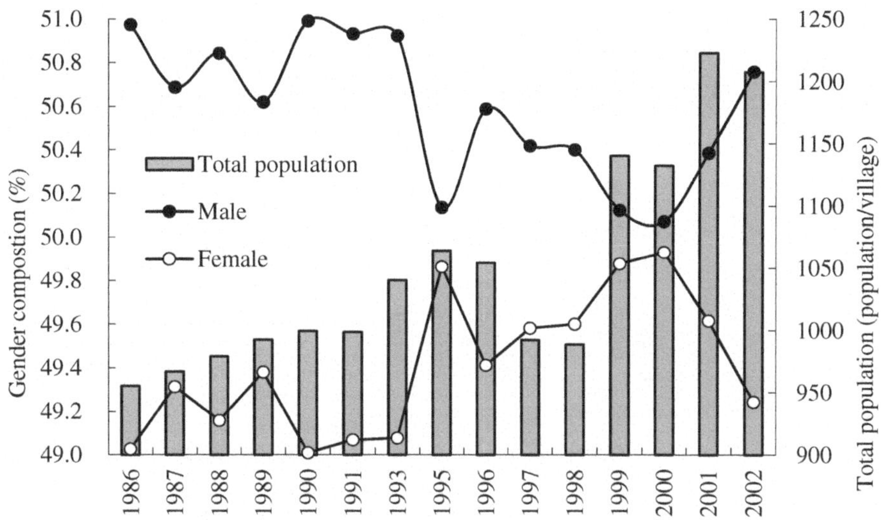

Fig. 10.1 Population and gender changes in observation villages

non-agricultural, and then influenced by the village agglomeration, there appeared a new and significant increase in population in the late 1990s. By the end of 2002, the permanent population of the observation villages reached 12,073, averaged at 1207.3 for each village. Compared with the initial observation, the population size increased by 26.37%. As far as the gender composition of the population in the observation villages, the male to female ratio has been high, up to the level of 100:96.11 in 1990, but over the course of the observation period, the ratio showed a downward trend, while the female to male ratio showed the opposite. By 2000, the gender ratio between males and females had evolved to 100:99.72, and the gender ratio tended to be more balanced. After 2000, the situation deteriorated again, and the male population increased dramatically. By 2002, the gender ratio changed to 100:97.01.

From the perspective of population growth (Table 10.2), the changes in population in the observation villages since 1995 have generally shown a fluctuating downward trend, with the average annual population increase of 18.59, the highest at 25.80 in 1995, and the lowest at 14.40 in 2002. The main body of population growth came from in registry of immigration, with the highest level of 60.51% in 1998 and the lowest of 52.08% in 2002. However, the new-born population also contributed a lot to the expansion of population in the observation villages. Among the new-born population, the rate of first birth averaged 77.07% in eight years, which was over 70% for most of the years except in 1999, and reached the highest level of 85.48% in 2001. This result means that the villagers in the observation villages in Zhejiang have a good understanding of the national policy of family planning and the policy was well implemented. But there is also an unhealthy phenomenon, that is, the gender ratio of the new-borns has been seriously unbalanced, and the proportion of males is significantly higher than that of females. In the eight years

Table 10.2 Population change in observation villages (population/village, %)

	1993	1995	1996	1997	1998	1999	2000	2001	2002
Year-end permanent	1040.2	1063.9	1054.2	992.3	988.7	1140.0	1132.0	1222.6	1207.3
Male	50.92	50.14	50.59	50.42	50.40	50.12	50.07	50.38	50.76
Female	49.08	49.86	49.41	49.58	49.60	49.88	49.93	49.62	49.24
Newly-added in the year	23.80	25.80	21.40	17.70	15.70	18.60	20.30	14.80	14.40
New-borns	59.24	47.29	43.93	46.89	39.49	42.47	45.32	41.89	47.92
Male	–	49.18	55.32	55.42	50.00	59.49	51.09	51.61	55.07
First birth	79.43	77.87	73.40	80.72	80.65	67.09	73.91	85.48	81.16
In registry	40.76	52.71	56.07	53.11	60.51	57.53	54.68	58.11	52.08
Decreased within the year	13.90	18.90	28.70	79.40	19.20	23.90	28.10	24.70	29.90
Death	47.48	30.16	27.18	8.19	30.73	26.36	30.60	34.01	29.77
Out registry	52.52	69.84	72.82	91.81	69.27	73.64	69.40	65.99	70.23
Non-agriculturalised	19.18	48.48	23.44	90.67	27.07	38.64	49.23	51.53	64.76
Year-end temporary	–	171.40	140.30	150.60	168.90	160.20	226.90	285.50	297.20
Temporary/permanent	–	16.11	13.31	15.18	17.08	14.05	20.04	23.35	24.62

since 1995, the male-to-female ratio averaged 100:87.82, with the most unbalanced ratio of 100:68.09 in 1999, which became 100:81.58 in 2002. The gender ratio was relatively balanced in 1995 and 1998, and slightly balanced in 2000 and 2001. In fact, this phenomenon is not specific to the ten villages in Zhejiang, but applicable to the whole country.[1] Therefore, such a phenomenon of new-borns needs to be taken seriously in decision-making.

Regarding the changes in population decline, since 1995, the decrease of population in villages has shown an inverted 'U'-shape trend, with the largest decrease of 79.40 by number in 1997 and the lowest of 18.90 in 1995. The main reason of population decline has been out registry, with the highest proportion reaching 91.81% in 1997 and the lowest of 65.99% in 2001. Except specific years when the main reason for out registry was the population change from agriculture to non-agriculture, in most years the proportion of non-agricultural change out of total out registry was less than 50%. However, after 2000, the proportion was more than 50%, which further reached 64.76% in 2002. Thus, it can be seen that the transformation from agriculture to non-agriculture has become an important reason for the decrease of the permanent population in the observation villages.

Comparing the changes of population, it is found that the net population growth of the observation villages has been negative since 1995. The largest decrease was 61.70 by number in 1997, and the smallest was 3.50 in 1998. Of course, this negative value is not the result of natural population growth. However,the slowdown of natural population growth, especially the negative growth after 2000, has played an important role in the population change of the observation villages. In 1995, the average net population increase in the observation villages was 6.50 per village, and the number decreased by 0.60 in 2000. In 2001 and 2002, the natural population growth in the observation villages was negative, and the average annual net population decrease was 2.1 for each village. This result indicates that the natural growth of rural population in Zhejiang has entered a negative growth era after the implementation of the family planning policy for more than 20 years.

Because of the beneficial strategy of 'introducing in and going out' in rural Zhejiang, the number of temporary residents in the observation villages has been considerable, reaching the highest level of 297.2 per village in 2002, equivalent to 24.62% of the permanent residents. As far as the changes in the size and proportion of the temporary population, there has been an upward trend in general.

As a whole, during the eight years from 1995 to 2002, the total net population growth of the ten villages in Zhejiang was −1041, with an average annual growth of −13.01 for each village, of which natural population growth was 1.03 per village. However, according to the specific situation of individual villages (Fig. 10.2), there were eight villages out of the ten with a negative net population growth, with the

[1]According to a report by Xu Bin on the *30 million Bachelor Battle*, some experts believe that among the 16.04 million people born nationwide in 2002, there were 1.5 million more boys than girls. Accordingly, in 20 years, there would be 30 million more males than females. It is also reported that in 1982, the ratio of men to women at birth was 108.5:100; in 1990 it rose to 113.3:100; and in 2000 it rose further to 116.9:100. Southern Weekend, September 23, 2004, B12.

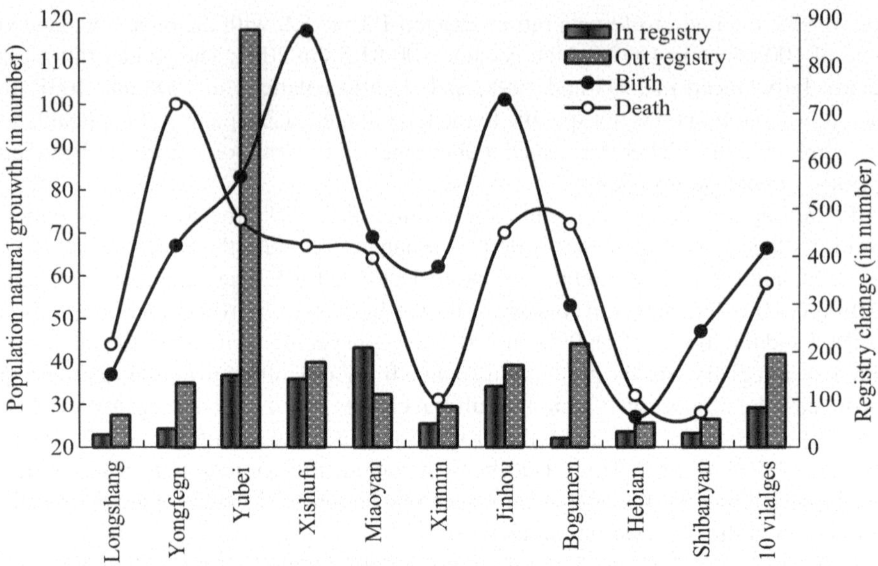

Fig. 10.2 Population growths and changes in the observation villages 1995–2002

largest negative value of 714 in Yubei Village of Jiaxing, and the smallest negative number of five in Xinmin Village in Wenling. The population growths of the other two villages were positive, with the highest number of 104 in Miaoyan Village in Yinxian County, and the lowest of 15 in Xishufu Village in Shaoxing. In terms of natural population growth, among the ten villages, four villages had negative values, with largest being −33 in Yongfeng Village of Huzhou, and the smallest of −5 in Hebian Vilalge of Lishui. Six villages had positive net population growths, with the highest of 50 in Xishufu Vilalge of Shaoxing and the lowest of 5 in Miaoyan Village of Yinxian.

In terms of population mobility, the inter-village differences in size and magnitude of temporary residents also obvious, and the differences varied greatly with time during the observation period (Appendix Table 10.17). In 1995, only one village out of the ten had a temporary population of more than half of its permanent population (Table 10.3), and three villages ranged from 15 to 25%. By 2002, two of the ten villages had a temporary population of more than 80% of its population, two villages ranged from 40 to 50%, and the other six villages were within 5%, including the highest of 3.69%. It should be noted that in Hebian Village of Lishui, due to the replacement of village cadres, a capable young man took up the post of village secretary.[2] In the late 1990s, he selected the non-agricultural industry of wood processing, and through the introduction of talents and recruitment of employees, the

[2]Unfortunately, such a young and promising village cadre died in a car accident. I feel deeply regret at the loss of such a village cadre, but also hope that the villagers of Hebian will continue to realise his established vision—to be well-off, prosperous, and affluent.

Table 10.3 Ratio change in temporary population in the observation villages (%)

	1995	1996	1997	1998	1999	2000	2001	2002
Longshang	1.22	0.88	1.98	1.63	0.36	0.36	1.48	1.49
Yongfeng	0.26	0.27	0.00	0.09	0.28	1.03	0.98	1.10
Yubei	3.58	0.00	0.00	0.00	0.00	0.00	0.00	0.00
Xishufu	62.69	66.15	78.75	78.19	47.13	46.40	44.46	45.32
Miaoyan	20.88	14.69	19.51	30.56	10.34	75.22	76.44	81.40
Xinmin	15.96	18.11	2.12	1.78	1.54	8.52	8.33	3.69
Jinhou	24.44	11.34	11.77	13.39	11.87	29.14	31.03	44.54
Bogumen	0.00	0.15	0.37	1.73	2.46	3.62	2.96	3.75
Hebian	0.00	0.00	0.00	0.42	0.00	135.65	126.47	89.74
Shibanyan	0.87	0.17	0.17	0.17	0.34	0.35	0.36	0.36

original quiet Hebian Village became active. Since 2000, the temporary population has expanded sharply, once exceeding the size of the permanent population of the village. The decision of the village cadre not only made the village economy develop rapidly, but also brought a new atmosphere to the whole village appearance.

10.3 Households in the Observation Villages

As can be seen from Fig. 10.3, over time, the overall household number of the observation area has shown an upward trend, but this trend was affected by the non-agricultural transformation and the village agglomeration in the middle and

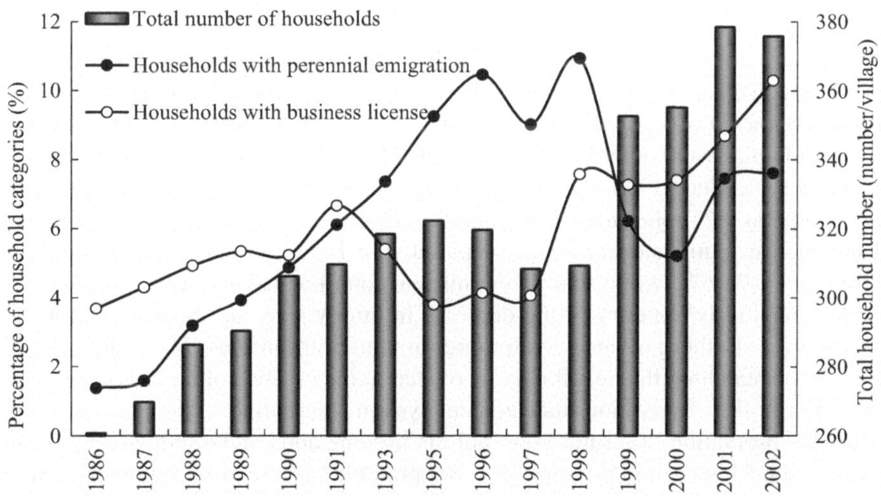

Fig. 10.3 Households in the observation villages and the composition

late 1990s, so that the household number showed a substantial declining and rising process. By 2002, the average number of rural households in the observation villages in Zhejiang reached 375.70 per village, up 44.11% from 260.70 at the beginning of the observation, and up 21.86% from the level of 308.30 in 1997 after a sharp fall, which were much faster than the population growth rates of 26.37 and 21.67% for the same periods. This result shows that, over time, farmers' concept has changed so the reduction of rural household size became the important feature of the societal change in the observation villages.

As far as the occupational composition of the households is concerned (Table 10.4), since 1995, there have been few changes in household occupational types in Zhejiang. The proportions of agricultural households and agricultural-dominated households have both remained at about 20%, and their changes also showed a trend of a 'U'-shape, while the proportion of non-agricultural dominated households has shown a downward trend and that of the complete non-agricultural households, on the contrary, showed a trend of an inverted 'U'-shape. The proportions of other types of rural households have shown an upward trend. Of the rural households, after a long period of sustained rise, the number of households who migrated out to do business showed a significant downward trend by the end of the 1990s, and it did not recover until 2002. On the contrary, the proportion of households with business licenses increased for six years, then declined and stagnated for nearly seven years. It did not rise again until 1998 when a new round of growth started. These results indicate that during the course of observation, in the process of non-agriculturalisation, there was once a difficult period for farmers to apply for licences. Meanwhile, there was a sharp increase for rural households to migrate out to do business. Does this mean that the regulation of business licenses is related to the increase of rural household migration? Although a definite conclusion cannot be made at present, it is almost certain from the general analysis that for farmers in urgent need to engage in non-agricultural business, it is very important to obtain a license. If the license cannot be obtained locally, it might be a good way to migrate to other places and get it.

In terms of the rural household types (Table 10.5), those in the observation villages are mainly nuclear families, followed by stem families. By 2002, nuclear families accounted for 71.60% of the total sample, stem families accounted for 21.60%, extended families and other families accounted for only 6.80%. As far as the change in family type, since 1995, the changes of the observed households have been linearised in that the proportion of the stem families has steadily increased, while that of the nuclear families decreased. Compared with 1995, the share of stem families increased by 3.16%, while that of the nuclear families decreased by 2.40%. This result is obviously contrary to the decrease in family size, and is also contrary to the situation of other provinces with more rural nuclear families (Shi, 1999). Why? In my understanding, this result may be related to the practice of household supplementation in the observation management system. According to the general logic, the fixed observation of a rural household is lifelong and can be removed by death or migration. However, in principle, it is not possible to increase the number of rural households in observation. The increase of households can only be possible by the

Table 10.4 Households and occupation structure in the observation villages (%)

	1993	1995	1996	1997	1998	1999	2000	2001	2002
Year-end households(number)	318.3	322.2	319.5	308.3	309.2	352.5	355.1	378.4	375.7
1. Complete agricultural	27.87	25.42	13.46	17.45	18.11	21.42	21.63	21.86	21.93
Of which: planting	3.30	4.13	4.51	2.53	3.23	4.20	4.22	4.39	4.39
2. Agricultural dominated	17.66	16.17	23.76	16.90	17.14	20.48	20.11	22.57	22.44
3. Non-agricultural dominated	33.90	33.40	26.29	28.25	25.10	22.95	22.84	21.96	21.16
4. Complete non-agricultural	17.31	20.14	27.92	28.80	29.72	25.67	25.57	26.14	28.00
5. Others	3.27	4.87	8.58	8.60	9.93	9.48	9.86	7.48	6.47
Perennial operation in other places	7.35	9.25	10.45	9.02	10.93	6.21	5.21	7.45	8.69
With business license	5.40	3.79	4.13	4.05	7.57	7.26	7.41	7.61	10.30
Population	3.27	3.30	3.30	3.22	3.20	3.23	3.19	3.23	3.21

Table 10.5 Changes in household types in the observation villages

	1993	1995	1996	1997	1998	1999	2000	2001	2002
Nuclear	74.60	74.00	73.40	73.80	73.20	72.80	72.34	73.25	71.60
Stem	19.00	18.00	20.20	20.20	20.80	21.20	21.84	20.36	21.60
Extended	1.00	0.60	0.80	1.00	1.40	1.40	1.20	1.80	1.80
Incomplete	5.40	5.40	3.60	3.20	3.80	4.40	4.41	4.39	4.80
Others	0.00	2.00	2.00	1.80	0.80	0.20	0.20	0.20	0.20

natural division of the original households. In the actual implementation process, however, the understanding of people in different regions is not unified, and attention is only paid to the relative stability of the observation scale, rather than the fixity of individual households. Therefore, the substitution occurred among the same types of households. Of course, the inconsistent understanding is also related to the constraints of the funds and human resources for collecting the observation data.

In fact, influenced by regional cultural differences, villages are composed of different types of rural households. Take the ten Zhejiang villages as an example (Appendix Table 10.18). There were only eight villages out of ten with the nuclear families as the absolute main component. For the other two villages, one was mainly composed of nuclear families (Yubei Village of Jiaxing), but also had a high ratio of stem families; the other was mainly composed of stem families (Yongfeng Village of Huzhou), with the ratio of nuclear families taking the second place. In terms of the changes, in the three villages of north Zhejiang, and Xishufu Village in the Ningshao Plain, there has been obvious linearisation of rural households, and the ratio of stem families has been high, whereas in Xinmin Village of Wentai and Hebian Village of Lishui in Southeast Zhejiang, there has also been the trend of linearisation, but the ratio of stem families has been relatively low. Few changes have taken place in other villages, with nuclear families as the majority.

10.4 Enterprises in the Observation Villages

With regard to the number of enterprises (Table 10.6), since the 1990s, the change in the observation villages in Zhejiang has shown a ‘U’-shape trend. By 2002, the average number of enterprises in observation villages reached 16.40, an increase of 23.31% compared with 14.70 in 1995, and an increase of 78.26% compared with the lowest level of 9.20 in 1998. As for the types of the enterprises, private enterprises were the majority in the observation villages, accounting for 67.07% of all, followed by joint-stock enterprises, accounting for 6.71%. Over the years, great changes have taken place in terms of enterprise structure. In the early 1990s, collective enterprises took up a large proportion. However, with the acceleration of reform and opening up and the reform of enterprise ownership system, village collective enterprises were gradually replaced by joint-stock enterprises and private enterprises, which developed into the situation today. In terms of enterprise development in the observation villages, there has been an obvious process of privatisation, and the share of private enterprises of all enterprises has increased from 1/3 in 1993 to over 2/3 today. It can be seen that the growth of village economy in Zhejiang is closely related to the privatisation of enterprises.

In terms of the enterprise distribution, there is a great imbalance among villages (Table 10.7). The number of enterprises in some villages was on the rise, but was declining in other villages, and there were still some villages without any enterprises. By 2002, three of the ten villages in Zhejiang had no enterprises including Longshang Village, Miaoyan Village and Shibanyan Village. Of the seven villages with enterprises, four villages had a large number of enterprises, i.e. 86 in Yubei Village, 39 in Hebian Village, 18 in Jinhou Village and ten in Yongfeng Village. The remaining

Table 10.6 Enterprises and the structural changes (%)

	1993	1995	1996	1997	1998	1999	2000	2001	2002
Year-end enterprises(number)	13.20	14.70	13.30	12.20	9.20	15.00	13.70	13.00	16.40
1. Collective enterprises	18.94	6.12	5.26	4.92	2.17	1.33	1.46	1.54	1.22
Contract	8.33	3.40	2.26	1.64	1.09	0.67	0.73	0.77	0.61
Partnership	1.52	2.04	3.01	2.46	1.09	0.67	0.73	0.77	0.61
2. Joint-stock enterprises	10.61	10.88	12.78	13.93	20.65	10.67	10.22	7.69	6.71
3. Partnership enterprises	6.06	6.80	6.77	6.56	7.61	2.67	2.19	2.31	2.44
4. Private enterprises	33.33	65.31	74.44	72.95	65.22	82.67	82.48	84.62	67.07
5. Others	31.06	10.88	0.75	1.64	4.35	2.67	3.65	3.85	22.56

Table 10.7 Enterprise distribution in observation villages

	Longshang Lin'an	Yongfeng Huzhou	Yubei Jiaxing	Xishufu Shaoxing	Miaoyan Yinxian	Xinmin Wenling	Jinhou Rui'an	Bogumen Putuo	Lishui Hebian	Shibanyan Jinhua
1993	38	1	8	2	13	5	59	3	2	1
1995	0	5	21	2	26	5	79	3	6	0
1996	0	5	24	2	22	5	52	3	20	0
1997	0	5	21	2	26	4	38	2	24	0
1998	0	5	21	2	14	4	40	1	5	0
1999	0	6	83	1	14	3	37	1	5	0
2000	0	6	85	2	0	4	33	1	6	0
2001	0	10	84	4	0	4	21	1	6	0
2002	0	10	86	4	0	6	18	1	39	0

three villages of Xinmin, Xishufu and Bogumen had six, four, and one respectively. From the change of distribution, it is seen that the stability of enterprise numbers in the observation villages has been extremely low, and the internannual change is very high. Obviously, this change is unfavourable to the development of village economy.

10.5 Villagers' Beliefs in the Observation Villages

Religious belief is one's free choice, and is also supported by the Chinese government. However, in terms of religious beliefs (Table 10.8), the number of rural believers in Zhejiang is not large and relatively stable. By 2002, the average number of people with religious beliefs in the observation villages was 122.10 per village, accounting for 10.11% of the total population. Among those with religious beliefs, the proportion of people who really often participated in religious activities was not high, with only 15.07%, and the data showed a significant downward trend during the observation period, decreasing from 20.67% in 1993 to 5.60% in 2002. As far as the composition of beliefs is concerned, it is relatively simple in Zhejiang. The majority was traditional Chinese Buddhism, making up 74.84%, followed by Catholicism with 18.35% and other religious beliefs made up 6.72%. As for the changes in composition, since the Ninth Five-Year Plan, especially at the end of the century, the proportion of people who believe in Buddhism has declined significantly, decreased by 6% by 2002 compared with 1995. The proportion of people who believe in Catholicism has shown an upward trend, with an increase of nearly 5% in eight years. This result indicates that the beliefs of farmers in Zhejiang have been changing from traditional Chinese Buddhism to Catholicism, although Buddhism still maintains a dominant position.

As far as the distribution of the religious beliefs (Table 10.9), there are significant differences among villages. Of the ten villages, there are two with the high frequencies of beliefs, both located on the Ningshao Plain. They are Xishufu Village in Shaoxing with the largest number of believers, reaching 431.10 in eight years on average, accounting for 42.02% of the total population, and Miaoyan Village in Yinxian, with 231.00 religious villagers, accounting for 22.78% of the total population. More than 80% of these believers were Buddhists, and the rest were Catholics. The religion concentration in other villages was relatively low, with the highest of 8.83% in Bogumen Village and the lowest of 0.90% Yongfeng Village. As far as the participation in religious activities is concerned, the two villages with the largest numbers of religious villagers had the least frequencies in religious activities, while the villages with relatively fewer religious people had the most frequent participations in religious activities. This result implies that having religious beliefs is not directly related to regular participation in religious activities.

Table 10.8 Religious beliefs and the changes in the observation villages (%)

	1993	1995	1996	1997	1998	1999	2000	2001	2002
Believers (number)	115.60	129.10	125.30	112.60	124.40	122.20	122.00	122.00	122.10
As % of total population	11.11	12.13	11.89	11.35	12.58	10.72	10.78	9.98	10.11
Frequent participation	20.67	20.99	12.69	12.97	12.38	13.58	14.10	16.07	15.07
Catholicism	25.78	13.40	14.05	15.63	14.07	18.66	19.18	18.28	18.35
Buddhism	71.54	79.78	79.17	77.80	79.74	74.30	73.77	73.77	74.84
Other	2.68	6.82	6.78	6.57	6.19	7.04	7.05	7.95	6.72

Table 10.9 1995–2002 Distribution of religious beliefs in the observation villages

	Believers (number)	Religion composition (%)				Believers/total villagers (%)
		Participation Frequency	Catholicism	Buddhism	Others	
Longshang	26.30	100.00	18.25	75.67	6.08	5.92
Yongfeng	9.60	89.58	12.50	60.42	27.08	0.90
Yubei	11.10	81.08	0.00	29.73	70.27	0.92
Xishufu	431.10	7.45	18.28	81.72	0.00	42.02
Miaoyan	231.00	0.00	13.90	86.10	0.00	22.78
Xinmin	50.90	47.94	57.37	42.63	0.00	7.53
Jinhou	92.50	11.89	0.00	53.30	46.70	6.27
Bogumen	92.90	8.93	0.00	89.34	10.66	8.83
Hebian	15.30	90.85	23.53	60.78	15.69	4.02
Shibanyan	19.00	58.95	58.95	41.05	0.00	4.14
Ten villages	122.60	14.52	15.80	77.46	6.74	11.41

10.6 Social Security in the Observation Villages

Social security is an important concept that reflects the spiritual outlook of the people in a village or region. Although there are many indicators for the investigation of social security, three are the most important. One is the incidence of 'civil disputes' reflecting the harmonious living conditions of the people, another is the incidence of 'violations of public security regulations' reflecting people's compliance with the government's public security regulations, and the third is the incidence of 'criminal cases' reflecting the occurrence of malignant social events. In the observation villages (Table 10.10), since the 1990s, the social security development has shown a 'U'-shape trend. The changes in the occurrence frequency of civil disputes, violations of public security regulations and criminal cases are very consistent. Obviously, while the social order of the observation villages has been improving generally, since 2000, there have also been signs of deterioration. Civil disputes increased from the lowest level of 2.20 cases per village in 1998 to 3.70 cases per village in 2002, up by 68.18%. At the same time, violations of public security regulations and criminal cases increased more rapidly, and criminal cases in particular reached the highest level since the observation. The changes in these indicators of comprehensive social security indicate that the current public security situation has been the worst in ten villages in Zhejiang since the observation. It might be right to say that in the late 1990s, Zhejiang has made remarkable achievements in economic development, which cannot be separated from the good social atmosphere and stable social order. Therefore, in the new century, if Zhejiang expects to go up to a higher level, it is important to pay attention to rural social security.

Table 10.10 Social security in the observation villages

	Civil disputes	Violations of public security regulations	Criminal cases	Frequency per 10,000 people		
				Civil disputes	Violations of public security regulations	Criminal cases
1993	4.20	3.70	2.70	40.38	35.57	25.96
1995	4.10	0.70	0.50	38.54	6.58	4.70
1996	4.50	1.60	0.50	42.69	15.18	4.74
1997	2.40	0.50	0.20	24.19	5.04	2.02
1998	2.20	0.20	0.20	22.25	2.02	2.02
1999	2.90	0.10	0.30	25.44	0.88	2.63
2000	2.50	0.80	0.00	22.08	7.07	0.00
2001	3.20	1.50	1.90	26.17	12.27	15.54
2002	3.70	1.30	3.30	30.65	10.77	27.33

In comparing the social security situation among these villages (Table 10.11), it is found that there are some clear differences. The social security situation in some particular villages was quite good without any criminal cases for eight years from 1995 to 2002, and the incidence of violations of social security conditions was zero. But the situations in other villages were not the same. In terms of the average number of civil disputes per 10,000 people from 1995 to 2002, the highest reached 83.28 in Longshang Village and the lowest was only 4.40 in Xinmin Village. Among them,

Table 10.11 Social security in the observation villages 1995–2002

	Civil disputes	Violations of public security regulations	Criminal cases	Frequency per 10,000 people		
				Civil disputes	Violations of public security regulations	Criminal cases
Longshang	3.70	0.40	0.20	83.28	9.00	4.50
Yongfeng	1.40	0.30	0.00	13.13	2.81	0.00
Yubei	5.00	0.20	2.30	41.46	1.66	19.07
Xishufu	1.60	0.50	0.10	15.59	4.87	0.97
Miaoyan	3.60	0.30	0.20	35.50	2.96	1.97
Xinmin	0.30	0.00	0.00	4.44	0.00	0.00
Jinhou	4.10	3.50	3.20	27.78	23.71	21.68
Bogumen	4.10	0.90	0.40	38.96	8.55	3.80
Hebian	0.40	0.30	0.30	10.50	7.88	7.88
Shibanyan	1.30	0.30	0.20	28.32	6.53	4.36
10 villages	2.55	0.67	0.69	28.97	7.61	7.84

there were three villages with the number between 30 and 50, i.e. Yubei Village, Bogumen Village and Miaoyan Village, two villages between 20 and 30, i.e. Jinhou Village and Shibanyan Village, and three villages between 10 and 20, including Xishufu Village, Yongfeng Village and Hebian Village. As for the criminal cases, the average number per 10,000 people between 1995 and 2002 in Jinhou Village was 21.68, followed by Yubei Village with 19.07, and Hebian Village with 7.88, and the lowest were Yongfeng Village and Xinmin Village with zero. The number in the other five villages was less than five.

10.7 Social Assistance in the Observation Villages

Social assistance is also an important aspect reflecting the spiritual outlook of people in a village or region. From the observation of the villages in Zhejiang (Table 10.12), since the 1990s, the progress of social assistance has not been satisfactory in that the protection rate for the five-guarantee households has been declining and the assistance rate for poor households is unsatisfactory. The only achievement is that the number has increased for recipients of preferential care. Accordingly, the rate of preferential care in the observation villages has also increased significantly, reaching 100% after 1998, but there have been obvious signs of 'coercion' in this increase.

In terms of inter-village comparison, seven out of the ten observation villages have done well in social assistance, namely, Longshang Village, Yubei Village, Xishufu Village, Miaoyan Village, Xinmin Village, Jinhou Village and Shibanyan Village. From 1995 to 2002, all the five-guarantee households and those with preferential care were cared for or assisted, while the situation in the other three villages was different. The assistance rate of Yongfeng Village for the five-guarantee households was 73.33%, and the figure was only 50% in Hebian Village. In Yongfeng Village, the rate of preferential care for eligible households was 100% but in Bogumen and Hebian, the rates were only 85.71 and 76.27%. It can be seen that the assistance work in the observation villages is generally affected by the 'poor' performance of the specific villages, and the vast majority of villages should be said to have done quite well.

10.8 Culture, Living and Others in the Observation Villages

From Table 10.13, it can be seen that the changes of cultural life in the observation villages in Zhejiang are quite obvious, which can be seen in the following three aspects.

First, there has been a marked improvement in external concerns and interactions. Television, one of the means for external concern, has been widely used in the observation villages; the subscription volume of newspapers and magazines has increased year by year, reaching 39.69 per 100 households in 2002, 39.90% higher than the

Table 10.12 Social assistance in the observation villages (%)

	1993	1995	1996	1997	1998	1999	2000	2001	2002
Eligible for five-guarantee (people)	1.80	1.60	1.30	1.20	0.90	1.40	1.40	1.80	1.20
Assistance rate	100.00	100.00	92.31	100.00	100.00	85.71	85.71	77.78	100.00
As % of village population	0.17	0.15	0.11	0.12	0.09	0.11	0.11	0.11	0.10
Eligible for preferential care (people)	1.70	3.20	3.00	3.00	2.80	4.70	3.60	5.00	4.20
Assistance rate	94.12	78.13	76.67	93.33	100.00	100.00	100.00	100.00	100.00
As % of village population	0.15	0.23	0.22	0.28	0.28	0.41	0.32	0.41	0.35
Poor households (household)	2.40	2.70	3.20	4.10	3.20	3.50	3.50	4.70	4.40
With assistance (people)	2.40	4.00	2.40	11.80	2.20	3.80	3.40	5.30	4.40
As % of total households	0.23	0.38	0.23	1.19	0.22	0.33	0.30	0.43	0.36

Table 10.13 Cultural and life changes in the observation villages

	1993	1995	1996	1997	1998	1999	2000	2001	2002
Movies	16.20	3.90	4.40	4.70	5.60	2.60	2.10	1.90	1.60
Operas	6.00	2.90	3.80	4.20	4.00	9.10	6.70	4.70	6.10
Newspapers	109.90	91.40	87.40	88.50	96.60	122.20	119.50	130.40	149.10
TV owning rate	75.81	86.47	88.86	82.16	89.84	90.04	94.42	97.12	96.78
Still and concrete housing	46.69	51.06	55.99	60.10	61.77	62.13	51.84	55.63	60.18
Brick and wood housing	51.56	47.98	44.01	39.83	38.23	37.87	48.16	44.29	39.87
Safety water	19.10	24.18	18.97	27.05	47.51	53.76	56.32	58.35	58.96
Tap water	70.34	68.19	69.45	75.90	74.97	71.69	70.99	76.43	76.50
With electricity	99.94	100.00	100.00	90.37	94.60	100.00	100.00	100.00	100.00
Telephone penetration rate	6.47	14.74	17.84	20.11	24.58	32.28	53.08	56.90	68.80
Babies	14.30	10.40	9.20	8.10	7.50	8.10	9.90	6.00	6.20
Baby death rate	2.80	1.92	0.00	4.94	1.33	1.23	0.00	0.00	0.00
Children number at 7–13	116.10	127.20	124.40	119.80	111.00	129.10	116.60	147.00	143.70
#In school	97.59	97.33	99.76	77.96	99.10	99.69	99.91	100.00	100.00

Note #being part of the previous category

level of 28.37 in 1995; and the use of telephones, the third means of concerns, has reached a record high, with 68.80 telephones per 100 households in 2002, more than doubled compared with the level of 14.74 in 1995.

Second, the quality of life has been significantly improved, including the significant improvement of the housing quality, the safety and convenience of domestic water and noticeable improvement in medical assurance.

Third, the educational conditions have clearly improved, with the school attendance rate for children aged 7–13 reaching 100%.

Of course, there are some differences among villages in terms of the changes (Appendix Tables 10.19, 10.20 and 10.21), particularly obvious in some specific indicators. For example, the telephone penetration rate has reached 100% in Xishufu Village, but only 28.14% in Shibanyan Village. This result gives us an important indication that social change is not synchronous change, but to a large extent asynchronous, and the inequality is quite high. Differentiated change is the major way of social change.

10.9 The Quality of Collective Leadership

Generally speaking, the change in community appearance and spiritual civilisation of a village comes from the joint efforts of villagers, but it is also necessary to build up a good village collective leadership team. It is under the organisation and command of the leadership that the ability of villagers can be fully developed and the appearance of villages can be greatly improved. The benign changes in the appearance of the ten villages in Zhejiang can be considered to have been achieved with the continuous improvement of the overall quality of village cadres. Therefore, after analysing the above eight aspects of all villages, it is necessary to introduce the quality changes of village collective leaders.

First, it is the change in the scale and cadre-to-villager ratio of the village collective leadership. In previous studies, it is found out that a strong and improving leadership is the key to achieving sustained and staged growth of village economy (Shi, 2001). Generally, this leadership group needs a certain number of members, and the number varied in different periods and villages. For the ten observation villages in Zhejiang, the scale of village-level leadership has generally presented an inverted 'N'-shape (Fig. 10.4 and Table 10.14). During the period from 1988 to 1997 when village economy was developing comparatively rapidly, there appeared an associated phenomenon in that there was the expansion of village leadership with an increase of cadre-villager ratio. The number of collective leaders per village rose from 4.10 in 1988 to 7.00 in 1997, and the ratio of cadres to villagers per 1000 people rose from 4.19 to 7.05, with an increase of more than 70% in 10 years. Although the expansion of village leadership did not cause strong repercussions in rural Zhejiang, this phenomenon directly led to the increasing burden of farmers in economically underdeveloped areas (Shi & Gu, 2003). Therefore, by the mid-1990s, how to reduce the size of leadership at the village and township level became an issue of great concern

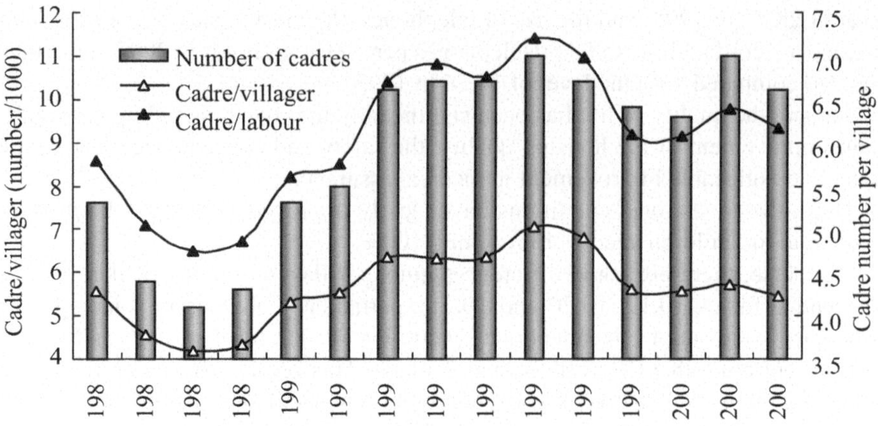

Fig. 10.4 Village collective leadership scale and cadre-villager ratio

to policy makers. Until the end of the 1990s, the central government implemented a policy called 'withdrawing townships to merge as towns'. This policy was also reflected in the ten villages in Zhejiang where in the middle and late 1990s, the cadre-villager ratio decreased significantly. By 2002, the average number of village collective cadres was reduced to 6.60, with the highest being 11 in Hebian Village of Lishui and the lowest being three in Jinhou Village of Rui'an. The ratio of cadres to villagers had also dropped to 5.47 per 1000 people. Although it had not been the lowest since the observation, it had been the lowest since 1995. Such a change is obviously beneficial to alleviating the tense situation of administrative expenditure at the village level.

In terms of inter-village comparison, there are great differences in the number of cadres and the cadre-villager ratio in different observed villages (Table 10.14 and Fig. 10.5). In the observation villages in Zhejiang, the scale of village leadership has indeed increased considerably compared with the level at the beginning of observation, but this increase has converged significantly since 2000, and the cadre-villager ratio has also been significantly reduced. Compared with the period of the Ninth Five-Year Plan, the cadre-villager ratio has dropped by 6.6% and the ratio of cadres to rural labour has dropped by 8.5% in the three years since 2000. For individual villages, the cadre-villager ratio in five villages has been significantly reduced, namely Yongfeng, Yubei, Xishufu, Miaoyan and Jinhou. The ratio has increased for the other five villages, namely Longshang, Xinmin, Bogumen, Hebian and Shibanyan. The most typical case is Hebian Village with the ratio rising to 21.16 per 1000 people, 8.34 per thousand higher than the 12.82 per thousand at the beginning of the observation, which showed an increase of 65.05%. The village also has the largest cadre team in the ten observation villages. Of course, the expansion of cadres in this village has its own special reasons. The number of the migrant population in this village has exceeded that of the permanent residents. It needs a capable cadre force to carry out effective management. However, such a large cadre team is obviously

Table 10.14 Village collective leadership scale and cadre-villager ratio (number/1000)

	1986–1991 (average)			1995–2000 (average)			2000–2002 (average)		
	Cadres	Cadre/general public	Cadre/rural labour	Cadres	Cadre/general public	Cadre/rural labour	Cadres	Cadre/general public	Cadre/rural labour
Longshang	3.00	5.00	7.75	7.17	12.78	19.46	7.00	12.84	20.57
Yongfeng	6.33	5.77	7.92	7.17	6.49	11.71	8.33	4.90	8.74
Yubei	4.17	4.29	6.31	5.33	4.04	7.12	6.00	2.87	4.83
Xishufu	6.67	6.52	10.20	6.00	4.68	7.65	5.00	3.88	8.10
Miaoyan	4.50	3.98	6.03	10.00	7.90	12.11	8.00	6.30	9.88
Xinmin	4.00	4.75	7.42	5.67	6.69	10.35	6.33	7.53	11.72
Jinhou	4.83	2.85	4.45	4.00	2.17	3.68	3.67	1.98	3.32
Bogumen	4.00	2.81	4.82	6.33	4.72	7.49	6.00	4.81	7.42
Hebian	6.17	12.82	21.89	9.33	19.55	38.57	10.00	21.16	40.76
Shibanyan	4.50	8.09	12.72	5.33	9.23	13.28	6.00	10.64	15.65
10 villages	4.82	4.91	7.60	6.63	6.25	10.26	6.63	5.59	9.41

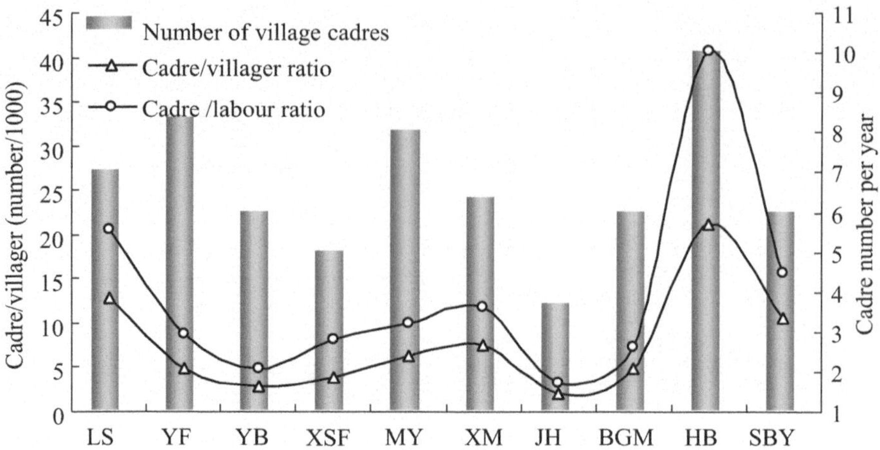

Fig. 10.5 Village collective leadership scale and cadre-villager ratio (average 2000–2002)

inconsistent with the economic development of this village. It should be noted that an additional cadre will certainly increase the burden of many farmers. A good village collective leadership team is fundamental for the economic growth and development of a village, but the key lies in how the team commands or organises, rather than how to expand. Therefore, a village leadership team with a limited number of cadres may be the most fundamental element in the development of village economy. Looking at the ten villages in Zhejiang, the leadership teams of villages with good economic development are not the largest, but with only five to eight cadres. If this number is exceeded, it might be considered as overstaffed.

Secondly, it is worth looking into the quality of village collective leaders. From Table 10.15, it is seen that in addition to the expanding scale, the construction of village-level leadership team in the ten villages in Zhejiang has shown good progress, i.e. the continuous improvement of the overall quality of the cadre team. Both the education level and structure of the cadre team have been significantly improved. The average education for cadres has basically reached the level of junior high school completion. But in the aspect of age, the improvement was not obvious. Although village cadres were not that old, with ages between 46 to 60, there have appeared more cadres in such an age range. What is the implication? From my point of view, it means that after a certain level of development in village economy, there seems to appear an experience-based management in the ideology of village collective cadres, and conservative development thought will occupy a dominant position in the leadership group. This result provides proof in explaining the phenomenon that the rural economy continued to stagnate or decline in the mid and late 1990s. In fact, this phenomenon also explains why the employment ratio of rural migrant workers in Zhejiang has been declining and the proportion of out migrants has been rising since the mid and late 1990s. One important reason is that in the process of economic development, the spirits of innovation and risk-taking of leading groups have been

Table 10.15 Village leadership age and education structure

	Cadre number per village	Education			Education (in years)	Age			
		Primary or below	Junior high	Senior high or above		<35	36–45	46–60	>61
1993	6.60	36.36	45.45	18.18	7.32	21.21	40.91	34.85	3.03
1995	6.70	38.80	40.30	20.90	7.38	14.93	50.75	32.84	1.49
1996	6.70	32.84	44.78	22.39	7.63	17.91	47.76	34.33	0.00
1997	7.00	30.00	47.14	22.86	7.71	20.00	44.29	34.29	1.43
1998	6.70	29.85	50.75	19.40	7.64	17.91	34.33	47.76	0.00
1999	6.40	20.31	54.69	25.00	7.99	17.19	34.38	46.88	1.56
2000	6.30	17.46	57.14	25.40	8.07	17.46	33.33	47.62	1.59
2001	7.00	18.57	58.57	22.86	7.99	12.86	40.00	45.71	1.43
2002	6.60	13.64	57.58	28.79	8.23	16.67	39.39	43.94	0.00

being replaced by conservative and non-progressive ideas. Therefore, the 'aging' of village cadres will become a major obstacle to the development of rural economy in Zhejiang and even the whole country in the future. In the short term, this obstacle will not bring much harm to the rural economic development of Zhejiang. If the time period is slightly longer, the most obvious harm will inevitably appear, that is, the growth rate of economic income will decline.

However, in terms of education level among village cadres, the differences are very obvious (Table 10.16). While the basic cultural and educational qualities of cadres in the ten villages in Zhejiang have been on the rise as a whole, there were also declines in three villages, namely Yongfeng Village, Xishufu Village and Jinhou Village. By 2002, the longest average education time for village cadres appeared in Hebian Village, reaching 9.45 years, which was followed by Yubei Village with 9.00 years. The number of years for the four villages of Longshang, Xishufu, Miaoyan, Jinhou was between 8 and 9 years, and for three villages of Yongfeng, Xinmin and Yuanmen was between 7 and 8 years. The shortest average education time was in Shibanyan Village, which was only 6.75 years. The difference of nearly three years indicates that the overall education of cadres in some villages reached or approached the level of senior high school, while for other villages the level still remained at junior high school. What is interesting is that in the villages where cadres' education level is relatively low, the economic income is comparatively low.[3] With the rise and fall of the village cadres' education, the level of village economic development has fluctuated accordingly. I will take Yongfeng, Xishufu and Hebian villages as examples. In Yongfeng, in the mid-1990s and the 2000s, there were twice large declines of the village cadres' education, and the village operation income fell twice. Such a fall occurred after the change of village cadres, when the average per capita operation income of the whole village also fell from 5958.07 yuan in 1993 to 5897.38 yuan in 1995. It rose to 20,307.08 yuan in 1998 and fell again to 7783.93 yuan in 1999. In the following years, it rose again to 16,909.55 yuan in 2002. In Xishufu Village, the per capita average operation income reached 70,265.63 yuan in 1997, which dropped to 55,150.35 yuan in 1998 after the change of village cadres, and further decreased to 49,819.32 yuan in 1999. Only after 2000 did the village economy improve, rising to 72,869.30 yuan in 2000 and to 88,253.29 yuan in 2002. In Hebian Village, with the continuous improvement of the village cadres' education, the village-level economy has shown an obvious upward trend year by year. In 1993, the per capita operation income of the village was 1933.88 yuan, which rose to 3666.80 yuan in 1995, 5981.05 yuan in 1997, 6205.45 yuan in 1999, 15,232.07 yuan in 2000, and further to 15,623.11 yuan in 2001, while decreasing for the first time to 14,186.97 yuan in 2002.

[3]Of the ten village of Zhejiang, Shibanyan Village of Jinhua, has ranked the lowest in both household income and village collective income, which has been discussed in Chap. 9.

Table 10.16 Education time of village cadres (in years)

	1993	1995	1996	1997	1998	1999	2000	2001	2002
Longshang	6.75	7.21	7.57	7.57	8.21	7.86	7.88	7.88	8.40
Yongfeng	7.38	6.44	6.44	6.44	6.44	7.58	8.00	7.55	7.44
Yubei	7.90	7.50	7.50	7.50	7.50	8.67	8.67	8.67	9.00
Xishufu	9.43	9.43	9.43	9.43	8.40	8.40	8.40	8.40	8.40
Miaoyan	7.92	8.61	8.63	8.83	8.91	8.50	8.50	8.50	8.75
Xinmin	6.63	6.79	6.40	6.40	6.40	7.00	7.00	7.00	7.50
Jinhou	7.88	7.88	8.38	8.38	8.38	8.38	9.50	9.50	8.67
Bogumen	7.06	7.06	7.17	7.17	7.17	7.17	7.17	7.17	7.58
Hebian	6.21	6.21	7.31	7.68	7.68	9.00	8.89	8.80	9.45
Shibanyan	6.50	6.50	6.50	6.50	6.50	6.75	6.75	6.75	6.75
10 villages	7.32	7.38	7.63	7.71	7.64	7.99	8.07	7.99	8.23

10.10 Concussion and Comments

In summary, after 17 years of development, the community outlook of the ten villages in Zhejiang has improved significantly, which is reflected in the following aspects. First, the national family planning policy has been effectively implemented so there appears a negative growth in population in the observed villages. Although such a negative growth is not the result of natural growth, it played an important role in alleviating pressure from natural population growth. Second, under the guidance of the strategy of 'introducing in and going out', the number of temporary migrants in the observation villages has significantly expanded. Although this phenomenon does not exist in all the observed villages, in villages with increasing migrants, their economic growth is obvious. Third, the number of enterprises has increased significantly. Despite some minor twists and turns in the process of enterprise restructuring, the situation reversed quickly. A system with clarified ownership has helped private enterprises develop rapidly. To some extent, the continuous expansion of the number of enterprises is an important reason for the rapid expansion of migrants. Fourth, the quality of village cadres has been significantly improved, which is the fundamental reason for the sustained rise of the whole village economy. However, there are also some phenomena that deserve further attention, such as the problem of social security in the villages. In the past century, the economy of the observation villages was able to develop well, with an important reason being that the social security in villages was improving. Since 2000, the once strong social security environment has now shown signs of deterioration, and the current situation has been the worst since the observation started. Therefore, it is important to pay attention to the social security of the villages for the development of rural economy.

Appendix

See Tables 10.17, 10.18, 10.19, 10.20 and 10.21.

Table 10.17 Population and its change in the observation villages 1995–2002

		Longshang Lin'an	Yongfeng Huzhou	Yubei Jiaxing	Xishufu Shaoxing	Miaoyan Yinxian	Xinmin Wenling	Jinhou Rui'an	Bogumen Putuo	Hebian Lishui	Shibanyan Jinhua	10 villages
Year-end permanent residents	In number	555.38	1332.50	1507.63	1282.50	1267.75	845.00	1845.00	1315.50	476.13	573.88	1100.13
Including: Male	%	51.86	51.89	50.61	51.48	47.95	50.16	50.70	49.55	48.25	50.34	50.36
Female	%	48.14	48.11	49.39	48.52	52.05	49.84	49.30	50.45	51.75	49.66	49.64
Newly-added population	In number	7.88	13.13	29.25	32.50	34.75	13.88	28.63	9.00	7.38	9.50	18.59
Including: Birth	%	58.73	63.81	35.47	45.00	24.82	55.86	44.10	73.61	45.76	61.84	44.59
Male	%	56.76	46.27	56.63	45.30	46.38	64.52	57.43	47.17	55.56	65.96	53.24
First child	%	67.57	62.69	74.70	63.25	98.55	83.87	78.22	98.11	70.37	80.85	77.07
In registry	%	41.27	36.19	64.53	55.00	75.18	44.14	55.90	26.39	54.24	38.16	55.41
Reduced population	In number	13.88	29.38	118.50	30.63	21.75	14.50	30.25	36.13	10.25	10.75	31.60
Including: Death	%	39.64	42.55	7.70	27.35	36.78	26.72	28.93	24.91	39.02	32.56	22.98
Out registry	%	60.36	57.45	92.30	72.65	63.22	73.28	71.07	75.09	60.98	67.44	77.02
Non-agricultualised	%	43.28	49.63	93.49	29.21	0.91	40.00	30.81	45.16	36.00	41.38	61.33
Net population growth	In number	−6.00	−16.25	−89.25	1.88	13.00	−0.63	−1.63	−27.13	−2.88	−1.25	−13.01
Including:natural growth	In number	−0.88	−4.13	1.25	6.25	0.63	3.88	3.88	−2.38	−0.63	2.38	1.03
Year-end temporary population	In number	6.50	7.88	5.25	676.63	522.13	63.50	410.13	23.88	208.38	2.00	192.63
As % of permanent population	%	1.17	0.59	0.35	52.76	41.19	7.51	22.23	1.81	43.76	0.35	17.51

Table 10.18 Household type and its change in the observation villages

		Longshang Lin'an	Yongfeng Huzhou	Yubei Jiaxing	Xishufu Shaoxing	Miaoyan Yinxian	Xinmin Wenling	Jinhou Rui'an	Bogumen Putuo	Hebian Lishui	Shibanyan Jinhua	10 villages
Nuclear family (%)	1993	76.00	34.00	50.00	78.00	78.00	88.00	84.00	96.00	72.00	90.00	74.60
	1995	64.00	36.00	52.00	64.00	82.00	94.00	88.00	94.00	76.00	90.00	74.00
	1996	62.00	38.00	50.00	64.00	98.00	92.00	84.00	90.00	66.00	90.00	73.40
	1997	52.00	38.00	56.00	70.00	98.00	86.00	86.00	86.00	76.00	90.00	73.80
	1998	52.00	38.00	54.00	60.00	92.00	84.00	92.00	88.00	80.00	92.00	73.20
	1999	54.00	38.00	52.00	60.00	96.00	86.00	88.00	88.00	76.00	90.00	72.80
	2000	62.50	42.00	50.00	58.00	96.00	82.00	86.00	90.20	66.00	90.00	72.34
	2001	60.42	44.00	48.00	58.00	96.00	84.00	86.00	96.00	66.00	92.45	73.25
	2002	56.00	36.00	50.00	56.00	96.00	84.00	86.00	96.00	68.00	88.00	71.60
Stem family (%)	1993	16.00	66.00	34.00	12.00	2.00	10.00	16.00	4.00	24.00	6.00	19.00
	1995	22.00	54.00	36.00	14.00	2.00	6.00	12.00	6.00	20.00	8.00	18.00
	1996	24.00	58.00	38.00	18.00	2.00	8.00	12.00	6.00	28.00	8.00	20.20
	1997	32.00	60.00	34.00	16.00	2.00	14.00	10.00	4.00	22.00	8.00	20.20
	1998	36.00	58.00	36.00	30.00	2.00	12.00	6.00	4.00	18.00	6.00	20.80
	1999	34.00	56.00	38.00	30.00	2.00	14.00	6.00	4.00	22.00	6.00	21.20
	2000	29.17	50.00	40.00	34.00	2.00	18.00	6.00	3.92	28.00	8.00	21.84
	2001	29.17	48.00	40.00	32.00	2.00	16.00	6.00	0.00	26.00	5.66	20.36
	2002	30.00	56.00	40.00	34.00	2.00	16.00	6.00	0.00	24.00	8.00	21.60

Table 10.19 Cultural and life change in the observation villages in 1995

		Longshang Lin'an	Yongfeng Huzhou	Yubei Jiaxing	Xishufu Shaoxing	Miaoyan Yinxian	Xinmin Wenling	Jinhou Rui'an	Bogumen Putuo	Hebian Lishui	Shibanyan Jinhua	10 villages
Movie	Number/village	3.00	0.00	0.00	0.00	26.00	0.00	0.00	5.00	4.00	1.00	3.90
Opera	Number/village	3.00	0.00	0.00	6.00	0.00	0.00	20.00	0.00	0.00	0.00	2.90
Newspaper/magazine	Issue/village	114.00	28.00	109.00	215.00	108.00	20.00	180.00	52.00	72.00	16.00	91.40
TV occupation	%	87.74	97.54	89.75	98.55	94.96	96.14	97.35	63.81	70.35	57.51	86.47
Steel and concrete housing	%	0.00	96.49	0.00	88.41	34.88	73.68	38.50	77.99	29.07	17.10	51.06
Brick and wood housing	%	105.81	3.51	100.00	11.59	65.12	26.32	50.44	23.88	70.93	82.90	47.98
Safe drinking water	%	100.00	0.00	0.00	0.00	0.00	0.00	100.00	0.00	100.00	0.00	24.18
Drinkable tap water	%	87.10	0.00	44.17	99.13	100.00	100.00	100.00	0.00	100.00	88.08	68.19
With electricity	%	100.00	100.00	100.00	100.00	100.00	100.00	100.00	100.00	100.00	100.00	100.00
Telephone	%	7.10	5.61	11.31	35.94	17.05	3.86	37.61	1.68	7.56	0.52	14.74
Babies below one year	Number/village	3.00	0.00	12.00	24.00	13.00	10.00	14.00	12.00	3.00	13.00	10.40
Birth and baby death rate	%	0.00	–	0.00	0.00	0.00	10.00	7.14	0.00	0.00	0.00	1.92
Children at 7–13	Number/village	53.00	160.00	105.00	162.00	129.00	120.00	263.00	157.00	55.00	68.00	127.20
#In school	%	100.00	80.63	100.00	100.00	100.00	100.00	99.62	100.00	100.00	97.06	97.33

Note #being part of the previous category

Table 10.20 Cultural and life change in the observation villages in 2002

		Longshang Lin'an	Yongfeng Huzhou	Yubei Jiaxing	Xishufu Shaoxing	Miaoyan Yinxian	Xinmin Wenling	Jinhou Rui'an	Bogumen Putuo	Hebian Lishui	Shibanyan Jinhua	10 villages
Movie	Number/village	0.00	0.00	0.00	0.00	16.00	0.00	0.00	0.00	0.00	0.00	1.60
Opera	Number/village	0.00	3.00	0.00	16.00	28.00	0.00	4.00	0.00	10.00	0.00	6.10
Newspaper/magazine	Subscription/village	41.00	65.00	240.00	32.00	627.00	65.00	180.00	35.00	200.00	6.00	149.10
TV occupation	%	95.03	100.00	89.32	100.00	100.00	91.78	99.12	89.71	98.77	95.85	96.78
Steel and concrete housing	%	10.56	100.00	0.00	95.92	47.80	100.00	60.93	87.65	40.74	31.09	60.18
Brick and wood housing	%	90.68	0.00	100.00	3.21	52.20	0.00	39.07	12.35	61.11	68.91	39.87
Safe drinking water	%	100.00	100.00	0.00	100.00	100.00	0.00	100.00	0.00	100.00	0.00	58.96
Drinkable tap water	%	100.00	100.00	27.05	100.00	100.00	100.00	100.00	0.00	100.00	100.00	76.50
With electricity	%	100.00	100.00	100.00	100.00	100.00	100.00	100.00	100.00	100.00	100.00	101.06
Telephone	%	39.13	28.14	77.80	100.00	83.17	74.34	97.79	49.79	95.68	31.09	68.80
Babies below one year	Number/village	1.00	9.00	7.00	9.00	6.00	5.00	9.00	9.00	3.00	4.00	6.20
Birth and baby death rate	%	0.00	0.00	0.00	0.00	0.00	0.00	0.00	0.00	0.00	0.00	0.00
Children at 7–13	Number/village	53.00	548.00	133.00	65.00	57.00	121.00	278.00	79.00	33.00	70.00	143.70
#In school	%	100.00	100.00	100.00	100.00	100.00	100.00	100.00	100.00	100.00	100.00	100.00

Note #being part of the previous category

Table 10.21 Cultural and life change in the observation villages 1995–2002

		Longshang Lin'an	Yongfeng Huzhou	Yubei Jiaxing	Xishufu Shaoxing	Miaoyan Yinxian	Xinmin Wenling	Jinhou Rui'an	Bogumen Putuo	Hebian Lishui	Shibanyan Jinhua	10 villages
Movie	Number/village	0.50	0.00	0.25	6.00	23.75	0.00	0.00	0.88	2.00	0.13	3.35
Opera	Number/village	0.75	0.38	4.38	9.13	15.63	0.25	13.75	0.00	7.63	0.00	5.19
Newspaper/magazine	Issue/village	61.00	34.13	179.13	70.13	325.88	55.63	193.75	46.25	131.63	8.88	110.64
TV occupation	%	90.56	100.00	78.28	100.00	100.00	91.87	93.31	77.81	88.91	78.81	91.05
Steel and concrete housing	%	6.35	98.84	0.00	95.76	44.89	88.88	54.56	82.24	35.76	24.84	57.31
Brick and wood housing	%	94.44	1.09	100.00	4.13	55.06	11.12	44.03	18.01	64.54	75.16	42.56
Safe drinking water	%	100.00	64.33	0.00	69.01	50.83	12.87	100.00	5.54	62.37	0.00	44.13
Drinkable tap water	%	98.17	70.53	31.32	100.00	99.95	100.00	100.00	0.00	87.56	95.39	73.09
With electricity	%	100.00	100.00	95.02	100.00	99.95	100.00	100.00	92.83	100.00	100.00	99.04
Telephone	%	18.97	17.58	38.80	79.20	40.19	33.79	56.50	17.86	45.28	9.67	37.44
Babies below one year	Number/village	4.00	7.25	10.13	12.88	8.13	8.00	14.00	6.88	3.50	7.00	8.18
Birth and baby death rate	%	0.00	0.00	0.00	0.97	0.00	3.13	2.68	3.64	0.00	0.00	1.22
Children at 7–13	Number/village	59.88	280.75	109.50	109.00	92.50	122.63	269.75	121.75	41.00	66.75	127.35
#In school	%	97.08	98.62	100.00	100.00	100.00	100.00	87.67	100.00	100.00	99.06	96.90

Note #being part of the previous category

References

Shi, Q. (1999). *Rural household economic development*. Beijing: China Agriculture Press.
Shi, Q. (2001). *Rural household economic activity and behaviour*. Beijing: China Agricultural Press.
Shi, Q., & Gu, H. (2003). Tax and fee burden of rural households and economic growth in China. *China Businees Review, 2*(2), 1–15.

Afterword

This book should have been finished two years ago, but has been delayed until today, and I have an indescribable sense of feeling, a mixture of loss and joy. Because of my temperament, things that happen around me usually have two totally different impacts on my research, where one supports the development of my career, while the other makes me bewildered, unable to find a way out.

Five years ago, I went to Zhejiang University with a dream, and embarked on my postdoctoral research. In the following two years, I successfully completed my established goals. To be specific, I was successful in the application of two projects supported by the National Natural Science Foundation of China, one supported by the Social Science Foundation of Zhejiang, two supported by the Soft Science Project Foundation of Shanxi, and one supported by the Postdoctoral Foundation of China. Meanwhile, I published three monographs, and over 30 research articles on rural household behaviour in the core journals of agricultural economics and management, such as *Management World*, *Chinese Rural Economy*, and *Issues in Agricultural Economy*. In addition, I also won three research awards, i.e. the second prize of Shanxi Science & Technology Progress, the first prize of Zhejiang Excellence Youth Achievement, the third prize for National Excellent Postdoctoral Paper Award. I could achieve this because, on the one hand, I have a supportive environment at Zhejiang University, and on the other hand, it is the result of the smooth and successful completion of every piece of work. It is all these that still provide me with the nostalgia and memories of Zhejiang University today, including the open-minded university leadership, my magnanimous collaborating professor, sincere colleagues, as well as amiable and lovely students. The two years of paradise life has also become the happiest and the most fulfilling period in my life with the greatest sense of achievement.

However, on completing my postdoctoral research, when I was considering whether to stay in Hangzhou, an accident made me determine to leave for good. In 2001, after a research project was completed which was hosted by myself and supported by the Zhejiang Provincial Social Science Foundation (N95E33), I applied for further research funding with the same title, ‘a follow-up study on the changes of rural household economic behaviour’. At a meeting to decide the key projects,

Q. Shi and Y. Gao, *Sustainable Development of Rural Household Economy*,
https://doi.org/10.1007/978-981-15-2747-0

one of the panel members said, 'He is leaving Zhejiang University soon.', and my application was thus rejected. I was angry and depressed when I heard of the reason for the rejection, and for a long time had been unable to get out of depression. Why? What was the purpose of the application review? Was it not to find the most suitable applications to work out the most appropriate solutions to the problems that the government, academia and the general public were most concerned about? Was it related to the status of the applicants? I believed whether I was a Zhejiang resident or not had nothing to do with whether I could complete the project. However, this was the precise reason that brought a lot of trouble to my application. In fact, in the final stage of the application review, I was still holding a work permit of Zhejiang University and my household registration was also in Hangzhou. Should the rejection be based on something that would happen in the future? As a postdoctoral fellow of Zhejiang University, 'a daughter of her own', in deciding where to go in the future, I had followed the principle of 'waiting for the in-laws at home'. Due to the waiting, I did miss quite a few good opportunities. While I was about to abandon the principle, what happened in the application review of Zhejiang Social Science Foundation changed my view completely. Meanwhile, it also greatly postponed the publication of my dream research on Zhejiang rural households, and a monography which was supposed to be finished years earlier had been postponed for three years. For the three years after I left Hangzhou, I had lost my motive once I thought of the unfinished manuscript. I was not clear on why to do this and I was totally discouraged to write. Only until the beginning of this year, did I make up my mind to finish it.

Fortunately, I started to get out of the bad mood this spring, and I combined the writing with my current project funded by the National Natural Science Foundation and the National Social Science Foundation. In fact, thanks to the support of the two funds, I got to acquire more materials for my research, which helped to achieve a more in-depth study. Although much time was spent on it, there was an obvious academic improvement in return. Therefore, the book was able to be published as one of the results supported by the funds. Of course, Zhejiang rural households are the most important study objects in the design of the funded research I have undertaken. It is significant to carry out relevant research for their own sake. In addition, as one of the provinces with rapid rural economic development since the reform and opening up, its successful experience and the spirit of Zhejiang people's efforts are exactly what other regions are deliberately seeking and exploring. The book is based on 'transition' as a theme, and it is believed that the information about rural households and the countryside in Zhejiang will benefit those domestic decision-makers devoted to economic development concerning China's '*sannong* issues'. Meanwhile, it will also provide important indications for scholars in their research regarding the '*sannong* issues'.

As I often say, 'one hero needs three helpers', the smooth completion of the book would have never been achieved without help. During the process, I got full support and encouragement from a lot of leaders, experts, scholars, friends, colleagues and students. Without their support and encouragement, there would certainly be a lot more difficulties. Therefore, I would like to show here my sincere gratitude to them.

It is worth mentioning the following people. Mr. Yikang Gu, Director of Agricultural Office of Zhejiang Province, not only made research contribution to the project, but also wrote a foreword for the book. Director Feng Shao and Director Jianxin Li of Zhejiang Agricultural Office are both my good friends and they contributed a lot to the research financially and spiritually. As leaders of the top management organization of the observation system in the National Rural Fixed Observation Office, Director Bingsheng Ke, Director Ruijie Guan, Director Changbao Zhao, Director Liqun Cao, Director Zhigang Wu and Director Liying Zhu from the Agricultural Research Centre, Ministry of Agriculture, are the best collaborators and supporters for my sustained research and academic career. The National Natural Science Foundation and the National Social Science Foundation have provided financial support for my research. The leaders from the Antai School of Economics and Management of Shanghai Jiao Tong University have provided me with great support and financial help in terms of working and living. They include the following professors: Fanghua Wang, Jianhua Ji, Fangyu Fei, Haiying Gu and Leng Yu. Some PhD and master students have offered their most sincere support, including Zhiquan Fang, Deyun Zhao, Jun Huang, Yun Chen, Mingwang Cheng, Yuehua Zhang, Wei Wang, Shouli Hou, Shengnan Jiang, Longzhen Zhen, and Ying Zhang. I would give my special thanks to two of them, Deyu Zhao, and Yun Chen for their proofreading of the manuscript, and their efforts have helped to reduce the errors. Of course, the love from my dear family cannot be forgotten in the writing of the monograph. It was their orderly work that made me able to devote all my time to the research work. On the publication of the manuscript, I would like to express my sincere gratitude to all of them for their support and funding towards the writing and publication of the book.

At the same time, I would also like to give special thanks to the following people. Prof. Wencong Lu from Zhejiang University and his student Aiqin Xi for they spent much of their time and money on the data collection in Zhejiang. Mr. Weifeng Jiang from the Agricultural Committee of Zhejiang had to work on weekends and accompanied me to visit the rural households in the ten Zhejiang villages, and he also provided great support with data collection and compilation. Three Associate Professors, Jianwei Zhuo, Dechang Chen and Xiaowei Zhou, have offered me a cosy working environment with their family-like care as senior members and colleagues in the agricultural economics group of Shanghai Jiao Tong University. In addition, there were the undergraduate students in Class 701 of 2002. As their class teacher, the respect for teachers was certainly important, but I was more pleased to see their unity and fraternity, working together for the glory of the entire class, which became the biggest drive in my writing.

In addition, the staff in the fixed observation sites in the ten villages of Zhejiang, village leaders, and all the observed rural households have contributed a lot in the long-term and tedious information collection. They also deserve my heartfelt gratitude as it is their selfless efforts that have made it possible today for the observation of the development in the ten Zhejiang Villages.

Due to the anonymous registration of farmers in the observation villages, as well as the careful recording, compilation and management of the departments at the national, provincial and county levels, their endeavour concerning the information about the changes of rural households, the micro cells of the Chinese society, are able to be presented to the readers through the effort of the author.

The publication of this book originally was planned to be supported by a special publishing fund through application from the National Natural Science Foundation. However, on completing the application, I was informed that the publication fund was cancelled in 2005, which almost made the publication temporarily suspended. Yet, as the saying goes, there is no end in the world. Through the joint efforts of my friends and myself, the Antai College of Management of Shanghai Jiao Tong University, together with the Agricultural Modernisation and Rural Development Research Centre of Zhejiang University, agreed to provide generous help and support. Here, I would like to express my sincere gratitude to the leaders of the two organisations.

Qinghua Shi
Haodifang, Minhang Districut of Shanghai
November 28, 2004

The manufacturer's authorised representative in the EU is Springer Nature Customer Service Centre GmbH, Europaplatz 3, 69115 Heidelberg, Germany. If you have any concerns regarding our products, please contact ProductSafety@springernature.com

Printed and bound by CPI Group (UK) Ltd, Croydon, CR0 4YY
30/09/2026
02225556-0012